Friends in High Places

Also by Douglas Frantz

TEACHERS: Talking Out of School (*with Catherine Collins*)

A FULL SERVICE BANK (*with James Ring Adams*)

FROM THE GROUND UP

SELLING OUT (*with Catherine Collins*)

LEVINE & CO.

Friends in High Places

The Rise and Fall of Clark Clifford

Douglas Frantz and David McKean

LITTLE, BROWN AND COMPANY

BOSTON   NEW YORK   TORONTO   LONDON

First Edition

Library of Congress Cataloging-in-Publication Data

Frantz, Douglas.
    Friends in high places : the rise and fall of Clark Clifford /
Douglas Frantz and David McKean.—1st ed.
       p.   cm.
    Includes bibliographical references (p.) and index.
    ISBN 0-316-29162-5
     1. Clifford, Clark M., 1906–   . 2. Statesmen—United States—
Biography. 3. Lawyers—United States—Biography. I. McKean,
David. II. Title.
E840.8.C55F73 1995
973.9′092—dc20
   [B]   95-2361

10 9 8 7 6 5 4 3 2 1

MV-NY

*Published simultaneously in Canada
by Little, Brown & Company (Canada) Limited*

Printed in the United States of America

For Catherine and Kathleen
and our children

Contents

Acknowledgments

This book is based largely on the recollections of the men and women who have known Clark Clifford over the past half century and on records from five presidential libraries, the National Archives, and numerous public agencies. In addition, we learned a great deal about Mr. Clifford and his place in history from thousands of books and articles in magazines, newspapers, and scholarly journals. We have tried to go beyond the public record to examine what was done behind the scenes. Many of Mr. Clifford's former law partners spoke with us at length concerning the inner workings and rivalries of the law firm; some of them allowed us to use their names, others did not. In every instance, we have tried to talk to all sides involved in any episode or case.

This is an unauthorized biography. However, near the conclusion of our research, Mr. Clifford finally agreed to sit with us and answer any and all of the questions that we wished to put to him. In all, we had more than fifty hours of taped conversations with Mr. Clifford. His assistance and candor were invaluable in helping us understand his life and times. In addition, he provided us with access to some of his private papers and helped arrange interviews with his family members. The conclusions and judgments, however, are our own. We are solely responsible for their fairness and accuracy. Mr. Clifford will no doubt disagree with some of them.

While we learned a great deal more about Mr. Clifford's personal life than has been published previously, we have written a political biography. We have described events in his personal life in instances where they parallel or reflect on critical events in his public career. However, the primary focus of this book is to place Mr. Clifford as a political figure in the context of his times.

We are grateful to the more than one hundred people who shared their time and insights with us. We could not have completed the book without their thoughtful assistance. We offer special thanks to the following people who were extremely generous: Jonathan Alter, Donald

Barlett, Marty Baron, Dennis Bilger, Chris Carey, Catherine Collins, Rowland Evans, Alan Henrikson, Todd Kosmerick, Sam McIlwain, Kathleen Kaye-McKean, James C. Olson, Mary Ellen Pauli, and James Steele. We are also grateful to the Truman Presidential Library for a research grant. We are lucky to have Dominick Abel as our agent, and at Little, Brown and Company, we thank Janice Pomerance and our editor, Fredrica Friedman.

Friends in
High Places

1

Friend of the Court

AT PRECISELY TEN O'CLOCK on the morning of November 17, 1959, the purple velvet draperies behind the long mahogany bench parted and a clerk banged his gavel as he proclaimed, "The honorable, the chief justice and the associate justices of the Supreme Court of the United States." Everyone in the high-ceilinged room rose as nine men stepped through the openings in the draperies and took their places behind the large black chairs that sat on a marble platform about a foot above the courtroom floor.

The justices stood silently as the clerk called out, "Oyez. Oyez. Oyez. All persons having business before the honorable, the Supreme Court of the United States of America are invited to draw near and give their attention, for the court is now sitting. God save the United States and this honorable court. Please be seated."

As Justice William O. Douglas eased into his big swivel chair to the left of Chief Justice Earl Warren, he could glance across the bench at the attorneys in front of him and see one of his closest friends shuffling papers into a neat stack as he prepared to argue his case. For more than a decade, Douglas had been friends with Clark Clifford. They seemed a likely pair, handsome, intelligent liberals who enjoyed wielding power and living well.

Clark McAdams Clifford could have come from central casting. Tall and square-shouldered, a month shy of his fifty-third birthday that November morning, he possessed the features of a matinee idol. His wavy golden hair was turning silver at the temples, framing his classically handsome face. His brown eyes sparkled with intelligence. In college, he had trained as an actor, and his voice was a Stradivarius, deep, melodious, and soothing. When he spoke, it was with such resonance and authority that the simplest statements conveyed an aura of Olympian wisdom.

Clifford, the only son of a quiet St. Louis railroad auditor and an ambitious theatrical mother, was confident and relaxed as he stood before the black-robed justices of the Supreme Court. Although he appeared infrequently before the court, there was no reason for him to be nervous. He was a lawyer of unprecedented influence, an important Washington insider, an adviser to presidents and senators, counselor to tycoons, privy to the secrets of some of America's most powerful people. The men who sat behind the mahogany bench with Douglas listening attentively to his carefully prepared pleadings on behalf of the Phillips Petroleum Company that day were part of Clifford's circle, to one degree or another. Several were regular guests at Clifford's famous New Year's Day party, members of the same exclusive Washington clubs. Just a few months earlier, Clifford had taken Chief Justice Warren and Justices Tom Clark and Douglas and their wives to the Washington appearance of the renowned Bolshoi Ballet.

But Justice Douglas, who would join the others in deciding the fate of the tax case involving Clifford's most important client, was more than simply a member of the lawyer's circle of friends. The surface aspect of their relationship was known among Washington insiders. Clifford and Justice Douglas were sometimes seen having lunch together. Clifford had occasionally invited the justice to play poker with President Harry S. Truman when Clifford's duties at the White House had included organizing the president's card games. Twice, he had tried to persuade Douglas to leave the bench and join Truman's administration.

Years later, Clifford would describe Douglas as "my closest friend" throughout the fifties. So frequently was the justice a guest at his home over the years that Clifford's middle daughter, Joyce, referred to him fondly as "Uncle Bill." The two men often socialized at night. When Douglas got into trouble with one or another of his four wives, Clifford would be there to help him. He tried to reconcile Douglas with his second wife after the justice had fallen for a woman less than half his age. When Douglas threatened to sue one of his former wives over a traffic accident, Clifford persuaded him that it would be undignified for a member of the Supreme Court. Unbeknownst to Douglas, Clifford was covering up for a mistake by a lawyer in his firm who had been handling the accident case for Douglas and had missed the filing deadline for the lawsuit.

What no one else in the courtroom knew that day, and what remained buried within Clifford's law firm and the justice's own letters, was the ethical twilight in which their relationship existed. Theirs was a friendship rooted not only in personal affection but in the highly unusual financial ties between a lawyer and a sitting justice of the United States Supreme Court, who had occasion to decide high-stakes cases involving the lawyer and his corporate clients.

At the time he argued the Phillips case and for years after when he was involved with other legal matters that reached the very pinnacle of the American judicial system, Clifford had power of attorney from Douglas, one of the court's most influential members. Indeed, Clifford's law office quietly managed many of the justice's legal affairs, from drawing up his will to paying his bills when he spent the court's summer recess in his home state of Washington.

"Summer after summer, when he would go away, Justice Douglas gave us the authority to sign checks for him," said Sam McIlwain, the lawyer who handled administrative matters for the Clifford firm. "His secretary would prepare bills and send them down, and I'd sign the checks."

In addition, and more extraordinary in the relationship between a judge and a lawyer who argued cases before him, Clifford personally provided financial help to Douglas. The justice's frequent marital problems and lifestyle often left him so broke that he could not meet the mortgage for his house on Third Street, not far from the majestic court where he tirelessly promoted the causes of human dignity and civil liberties. In those times of crisis, he often turned to Clifford. For instance, when he was chronically missing mortgage payments in the early fifties, it was Clifford who personally loaned Douglas several thousand dollars so he could refinance the mortgage.

"Your advance is deeply appreciated and I cannot put into words my full gratitude," Douglas wrote to Clifford in late 1954. "You are a prince."

Three years later, Douglas was trying to finish paying off a loan from one of his many creditors. He again wrote to Clifford and appealed for help. "I hate to talk personal matters on the telephone because I am sure it is tapped," the justice wrote. "Hence this note." The letter went on to mention that one of the lawyers at Clifford's firm kept a file for Douglas on his home loan and regularly negotiated payments for the justice. Douglas referred mysteriously to "nervous money" that he owed a creditor.

The financial relationship lasted as long as Douglas was on the bench.

Years later, for instance, at another desperate financial juncture for the justice, Clifford used his influence at a bank where he served as a member of the board of directors to ensure that the strapped Douglas would be granted a much-needed loan.

Neither man apparently found anything untoward in their close relationship. For his part, Douglas never saw the need to disqualify himself and step aside when a matter involving his close friend and financial benefactor came before the court. To the contrary, Douglas openly praised Clifford's performances before the court. And he even appeared to go out of his way to help Clifford. One Washington lawyer, who was involved in a case before the Supreme Court with Clifford on behalf of billionaire Howard Hughes, recalled later that Douglas had seemed to take an unusual interest in the matter. The case was decided in favor of the reclusive tycoon, with the help of Douglas's vote.

One cannot, of course, assume that Douglas voted in the Hughes case, or in other cases, on the basis of his personal friendship with Clifford. While today's rules would prohibit a judge from accepting a gift or assistance from a lawyer who appears before him, the federal rules governing the conduct of judges were not as strict at the time. Judges were not required to disclose their financial holdings or outside income, and it was left to the individual judge to determine when a conflict of interest required that he disqualify himself from a particular case.

However, even then judges generally were expected to excuse themselves from hearing matters that involved close personal friends. The expectation of bowing out of a case was even higher when it involved people with whom the judge had a financial relationship. Yet Douglas clearly saw no need to disqualify himself when it came to his friend Clifford, and he also saw no need to disclose the extent of their relationship.

As for Clifford, he clearly felt he was above the usual rules governing conflicts of interest or appearances of impropriety. When asked years later about his relationship with Douglas and its possible effect on the justice's decisions from the bench, Clifford wrinkled his brow in mild indignation, steepled his long fingers together, and ever so slowly and thoughtfully pronounced, "I have always been able to separate my public affairs from my private affairs."

Yet the financial relationship between Clifford and Douglas remained buried for decades. It was a secret that could have destroyed Douglas's career and damaged Clifford's. Because of his outspoken liberal and judicial views and his unorthodox lifestyle, there were four attempts to impeach Douglas during his thirty-six years on the Supreme Court. The first attempt was petty and political. In 1966, after Douglas married his fourth wife, there was a brief flurry of calls from Republicans in Congress for an investigation of his moral character, but it quickly died. The next attempt was far more serious, and it revolved around the justice's financial troubles.

Late in 1966, Ronald J. Ostrow, a respected reporter with the *Los Angeles Times,* wrote an article revealing that Douglas had been receiving $12,000 a year from the Parvin Foundation, a tax-exempt organization that financed fellowships and scholarships to study international peace.

In defending himself against the accusations concerning his relationship with the Parvin Foundation, Justice Douglas acknowledged that a judge's power to step aside in a case was an important protection against impropriety. But he noted repeatedly that no person or company affiliated with Parvin had an interest before the Supreme Court. As a result, he said, his financial relationship with the foundation had no effect on his job as a justice.

When Republicans in Congress challenged the propriety of the arrangement, Chief Justice Warren echoed Douglas. Warren rebuffed the critics by saying that the payments were a personal matter with no connection to any business before the court. With Lyndon Johnson, a friendly Democrat, in the White House, the matter went no further.

The financial relationship between Justice Douglas and the Parvin Foundation surfaced again in harsher political times, during the administration of President Richard M. Nixon. Eager to get the liberal Douglas off the court and make room for a conservative jurist, the administration prodded Congress into launching a full investigation of the justice's finances. The effort was led by Representative Gerald Ford, the Michigan Republican who later became president of the United States.

The inquiry was exhaustive. However, the basic finding was that, since the foundation had no business before the Supreme Court, there was no wrongdoing by Douglas. While stopping the impeachment talk, the 1971 report did raise questions about the propriety of Douglas's conduct. Among the criticisms was that Douglas had tried to borrow money from Albert Parvin, who had turned him down because he thought the loan might eventually be embarrassing to the justice. Douglas was also criticized because he and his wife had accepted expensive gifts from Parvin.

What the Republicans and their investigators missed could easily have changed the course of the investigation and the composition of the Supreme Court itself. Nowhere in the 924-page congressional report was there a mention that Justice Douglas had, by that time, borrowed money from Clark Clifford, the prominent Washington lawyer. Unlike the Parvin Foundation, Clifford's interests had come before Douglas and the court several times over the years. In the Phillips Petroleum case, for instance, Douglas had voted with the majority in favor of the oil company, saving Phillips $1 million. Never had Douglas bowed out of a decision involving Clifford. Never had he disclosed his financial debts to Clifford. President Nixon despised Clifford every bit as much as he did Douglas. Had the Republicans uncovered the long-standing financial ties between the justice and the prominent Democratic lawyer and antiwar critic, events would have taken a different turn for both men.

There is no way to know now exactly how much influence his financial dependence on Clifford had on Justice Douglas, for he died in 1980. Clifford says he is certain that it had no influence, that Douglas was as able as Clifford to compartmentalize his life. While Clifford's opinion certainly deserves consideration, it must be weighed alongside not only his own self-interest but the entire breadth of his career in Washington.

The relationship between these two powerful figures transcends friendship and resonates with the force of revelation. This is how Washington works: two men of power and influence see nothing wrong when their private lives intertwine with their public roles. As men of affairs, they define conflicts of interest on their own terms.

The pattern of his relationship with Douglas, which was repeated often with other powerful men throughout Clifford's career, is essential in understanding both how a nonpareil lawyer operated during a critical period in the nation's political history and how other men like him defined the country's interests on their own terms. By developing and nurturing relationships with friends in high places, Clifford became one of the most influential and talked-about public figures in the newly preeminent capital city.

Clifford's life both illuminated and shaped his times. In the phrase of his friend Dean Acheson, he was "present at the creation." While Acheson was referring to the start of the cold war, Clifford also was present at — and integral to — the creation of the permanent shadow government of lawyers and lobbyists who have come to dominate Washington. He was a charter member of those unelected courtiers who have come to wield as much power as the men and women elected to govern the nation.

Clifford arrived in Washington in 1945 as a pragmatic and experienced young trial lawyer from St. Louis. Through hard work and intelligence, he rose quickly from assistant naval aide in the White House to President Truman's counsel. He was at Truman's right hand in the postwar years that helped to shape America's destiny. By the time he left the Truman administration in 1950 to start his own law firm just blocks from the White House, Clifford had already earned a place in the nation's history.

For forty years as a lawyer, Clifford was an integral part of the fabric of Washington. His path was marked by public adulation and private wealth. Before the name was on the door of his law firm, Howard Hughes and Phillips Petroleum had hired him. With time, his list of corporate clients — Standard Oil, Du Pont, ABC, McDonnell Douglas, Firestone, Republic Steel, J. P. Stevens Textile Company, Kerr-McGee, General Electric — became the envy of every lawyer in town. The annual retainers paid by these and other elite clients meant that the bills and salaries of Clifford's law firm were covered on January 1 of every year. All the other fees collected over the next twelve months were extra. And there was plenty of extra.

From the start of the firm in 1950, Clifford never earned less than $500,000 a year. It was an extraordinary sum for a lawyer in those days, or even a Hollywood star. Many years, he earned far more. In 1967, for instance, he earned $1.3 million. For one case alone in the early 1960s, Du Pont paid Clifford $990,000 — the equivalent of $4 million in 1995 dollars. And, while the fee went to the firm, it is important to recognize that there were only four lawyers at that point, and Clifford claimed more than half of its revenue for himself each year.

No lawyer dominated an era the way Clark Clifford dominated his. And none who stood so squarely at the intersection of politics, finance, and commerce ever seemed so invulnerable. He became an intimate adviser to Democratic presidents and other prominent Democratic politicians and a legal strategist and counselor to the titans of American business and industry. For decades, Clifford was part of the select club of lawyers whose power and prestige derived from their closeness to prominent political figures as much as their skills as courtroom advocates. And within this informal club, favors and friendships were the coin of the realm.

If there appeared to be any conflict of interest in Clifford offering counsel to a president or key senator while his clients had cases pending before the federal government, no one seemed to mind except the occasional conspiracy theorist or do-gooder who was easily dismissed by Clifford's liberal friends. Ralph Nader and his ilk could complain all they liked. Clifford seemed to be above the fray.

Long after he had helped craft American policy toward the Soviet Union and organized Harry Truman's poker games, he handled sensitive matters as John F. Kennedy's personal lawyer before Kennedy was elected president. After Kennedy's election, Clifford continued to provide advice to him while negotiating with federal agencies on behalf of corporate clients.

Clifford was one of President Johnson's most trusted confidants for years before LBJ made him secretary of defense, and Clifford had many clients whose businesses were significantly affected by decisions of the Johnson administration. In the words of George Reedy, who was LBJ's press secretary, Clifford had the "ability to compartmentalize" everything.

It was as secretary of defense that Clifford showed true courage. He challenged President Johnson — and much of corporate America, his bread-and-butter clients — over the war and played a central role in turning the president against the conflict. After the election of Richard Nixon, Clifford decried the military escalation in Vietnam, becoming one of the most outspoken and influential opponents of the war. He was a hero to thousands of Americans who shared his anger and frustration over the war. *Parade* magazine called him one of the thirty most influential people in the country. Indeed, his popularity during the Vietnam War even kindled a brief, little-known ambition in Clifford to run for president himself, although he had never held elected office.

During the presidency of Jimmy Carter, although his star had waned and business had begun to slack off, Clifford was a personal emissary for the Democrat from Georgia at the same time he represented McDonnell Douglas Corporation in a major case before Carter's Justice Department. Washington defense lawyer Seymour Glanzer remembered a meeting in which several lawyers were trying to devise a strategy to stop the federal government from indicting McDonnell Douglas for paying bribes to sell its planes in Pakistan. Clifford could not attend the session. When he telephoned Glanzer and courteously apologized for his absence, Clifford explained that he had to leave the country on an emergency mission for President Carter. Within hours, Clifford was on a plane bound for India and a meeting with Prime Minister Indira Gandhi to discuss how to respond to Soviet aggression in Afghanistan.

These relationships formed the central theme of Clifford's life in Washington. They also provide an intriguing window on the way Washington works. In an obvious sense, relationships were endemic to how Clifford practiced law. His clients paid him an annual retainer for his general advisory help in navigating the shoals of Washington. At the same time, Clifford maintained relationships with powerful figures in the government. These relationships were clearly two-way streets: they could be used from both ends. Clifford could and did use relationships that he had with the White House and other government officials. And others, such as Presidents Kennedy and Johnson, could and did use their relationships with Clifford.

Clifford's uncanny ability to operate simultaneously inside and outside government extended to his activities in the corporate world, too. While there is no strict prohibition against it, most lawyers refrain from serving as directors of companies that they represent as attorneys. Tradition dictates that a lawyer remain on the sidelines, counseling the client, rather than participating in a client's operations. Yet Clifford served on the boards of two of his biggest clients, Phillips Petroleum and the Knight-Ridder publishing empire. He was not the only lawyer to do so. Many recognized such service as a means of ensuring steady business from a client. But Clifford took the practice a step further. Throughout the eighties, he was chairman of First American Bankshares, Washington's biggest banking company. At the same time he was actively running the bank, it was a major client of his law firm.

Rather than criticism, Clifford reaped esteem. Even now it surprises most people to learn that he spent only six of his fifty years in Washington actually working in the government. The vast majority of his time was spent as a private lawyer, representing private clients. Yet more than any other figure from his era, Clifford represented the shadowy bridge between public and private. His name became synonymous with the politics and power that defined the city. He was portrayed as a miracle worker who could offer sage advice to presidents or guide his clients unerringly through the bureaucracy and intrigue of Washington.

His stature and grandeur rose with each passing decade, to the envy of many and mystification of some. When the well-known Washington lawyer-lobbyist Tommy Boggs complained to a colleague that they did the work and Clifford got the money and glory, the colleague laughed and said, "That's because he's smarter than we are, Tommy."

Describing Clifford in the early seventies, one of his competitors offered this summary: "Clark Clifford — the secret there is he intimidates people. He doesn't make statements, he pronounces judgments. It's a lot like talking to God — or listening to God, to be more accurate. He draws himself up and he says these things, and you have to believe him, yeah, you want to believe him, for anyone who speaks with such authority must be right." Many who have known and respected Clifford have observed that *the way* he says things is often as significant as *what* he says.

Clifford was exalted by Washington and he exulted in it. As he stood at the center of the great social occasions of the day or rose to deliver a speech, he seemed to exude a power more akin to courts of royalty than courts of law. He was a great storyteller, vivid and persuasive. Over the years, he repeated his stories hundreds of times to adoring audiences and accepting journalists. The tales formed the fabric of his legend, even if not all of them were entirely accurate. For many, the image was more important than the truth anyway.

Postwar Washington anointed Clifford as one of the most influential men of the century. He became the de facto chairman of the capital's political-legal establishment, a peerless figure in the nation's permanent government, untouchable by the electorate and out of reach of such passing fancies as term limits. He reshaped the way lobbying worked in the nation's capital, making it respectable and even desirable to trade quietly on relationships with government officials while telling clients with a straight face that he had no influence.

In Washington, he was regarded as a living monument. He was rich, handsome, articulate. He reflected the culture of the city that lionized him and made all of those people in its permanent elite feel better about themselves. He outlived and, in some cases, even eclipsed senators, presidents, and justices.

When the time came to retire with grace and dignity, Clifford was unable to leave the stage. At the age of seventy-five, his peers either dead or retired and his law practice flagging, Clifford embarked on a second career. He became the chairman of First American Bankshares. He reveled in this new power and in the opportunity to demonstrate that he was a smarter businessman than so many of the men he had represented. Clifford set out to prove that he was not yet ready to be written off as an irrelevancy. In staying too long and being too eager for another challenge and another affirmation of his stature in Washington, Clifford sowed the seeds of his own downfall. It was not the first time he had rented his prestige and influence. But this time was different. Flattered by foreign bankers and unwilling to retire, Clifford was blind to the warning signals that this was not just another big case. He could not see that the men from the Bank of Credit and Commerce International and their wealthy Arab associates were pandering to an aging lion's pride.

In the end, Clifford was far from infallible. If he was sometimes heroic, he was not a hero. He was a man of complexity. He had his foibles, his rationalizations, his self-delusions. Over the years, he had come to believe those who praised him and listened to him so carefully. He had come to accept that somehow he had been granted immunity from the rules that governed the behavior of others, even when the rules changed and he did not. He operated above the mores that restrained others, safe in the assurance that his own judgment and wisdom would keep him out of trouble. He accepted a mythical status.

In the end, after so many years walking the quiet corridors of power in Washington and helping guide the United States through the cold war and the Vietnam War, Clifford believed that his interests and those of his clients were concurrent with the interests of good government and the country itself. Like the establishment that he came to epitomize, Clifford believed it was his definition of what was right that counted. Like so many in Washington in the era he came to represent, the myth became more important than reality for Clark Clifford.

2

A Victorian Childhood

As DUSK FELL along Laurel Avenue, the lamplighter would begin his rounds. With four or five neighborhood boys trailing, he would ignite the gas lights and kindle their reassuring glow. Then someone's mother would call out, "Dinner time," and off the children would run toward their homes. Anyone who glanced out a window and saw them racing through the twilight could pick out the Clifford boy. His golden curls and angelic face set him apart, even if he was smeared with dirt from a day's play. He always stood out in a crowd, even as a youngster.

Clark Clifford lived in a rented house on Laurel Avenue with his older sister, Alice, and his parents, Frank and Georgia Clifford. Laurel Avenue was in the fashionable west end of St. Louis. However, it was several blocks from the mansions of the trading and manufacturing tycoons who represented the cream of the city's society in those years following the turn of the century. Although in later times Clifford would be described most frequently as coming from a well-to-do family, the fact is that the family existed on the edge of prosperity and his parents did not buy their first home until both children had completed college and were on their own.

Frank Clifford, a railroad auditor, was one of eight children of Andrew Clifford, a wholesale grocer in Alton, Illinois, which was just across the Mississippi River from St. Louis. Andrew was English and his wife was a German who ran the house with military precision and regulation. Frank would later confide in his son that his mother had been so strict that she squeezed the love right out of the family. Frank and his siblings grew up with ambitions no larger than escaping home.

It had been Frank Clifford's lasting good fortune to court and marry Georgia McAdams, a strikingly beautiful and vibrant young woman. She, too, was one of eight children in an Alton family, but the similarities between the families ended there.

Georgia's mother, Annie Curtis McAdams, was the daughter of a successful Illinois farmer. Georgia's father, William Douglas McAdams, was of Scottish ancestry. A large man with a full, chestnut beard, McAdams worked as a geologist for the State of Illinois. However, his passion was American Indians. He was an authority on Indian artifacts and had written a book about his study of the region's Indian tribes.

While Frank grew up with little encouragement or joy, Georgia and her brothers and sisters were showered with love and instilled with unlimited ambition. The eldest son, Clark McAdams, would become the crusading editor of Joseph Pulitzer's flagship newspaper, the *St. Louis Post-Dispatch*. Another, William, became a prominent advertising executive and founded his own agency in New York City. And John became the owner and editor of Alton's newspaper. Maggie was a published poet, and Bessie an accomplished pianist. Georgia, too, would bloom.

After a tour in the U.S. Cavalry, Frank Clifford had married Georgia McAdams and joined the Missouri Pacific Railroad. It was the late 1800s and America's railroads were thriving. He worked as an auditor at the company's headquarters in St. Louis. In the middle of 1906, Clifford was sent to Fort Scott, Kansas, a small outpost on the Missouri border, to perform an extensive audit of the railroad's division headquarters there. Because the task was expected to take several months, he took his wife and four-year-old daughter, Alice, with him. On Christmas Day 1906, Georgia Clifford gave birth to a son, who was named Clark McAdams Clifford, after his uncle.

It was two more years before the audit was completed. The family returned to St. Louis and rented a small house. By 1910, they could afford to rent a slightly larger house, which was in a modest, middle-class neighborhood on Laurel Avenue.

St. Louis was the nation's fourth-largest city in the early part of the twentieth century, a manufacturing center and gateway to the West. But Laurel Avenue was a wonderfully cozy and tranquil neighborhood. The pavement ended at the streetcar tracks a half block from the Clifford home, which meant it was quiet and safe for youngsters. Often, the only traffic was the arrival of the milkman and the iceman, both of whom plied their trade from horse-drawn wagons. In winter, the Cliffords joined neighborhood children to skate on the icy street. In summer, they raced their bicycles up and down its length and played games in the vacant lot next door to the Clifford house.

Clark went to kindergarten at the Dozier School, just two blocks away. Even closer was St. Rose's Catholic Church, where his father attended services. Not much farther away was the Presbyterian church, where his mother could be found each Sunday morning.

The Cliffords had reached an early accommodation on religion. Frank would continue to practice Catholicism and Georgia would go her way as a Presbyterian. Both children were baptized as Catholics, but they would alternate Sundays at the Catholic and Presbyterian churches. Eventually, Clark and Alice would decide on their own to split the difference. They both became Episcopalians, but Clark was never a religious man.

When it came to education, however, there was no alternating. Georgia insisted that the children attend the city's public schools, which she felt were superior to the parochial schools.

This insistence was only one of the many ways in which Georgia Clifford dominated the family and became the primary influence in her son's life. Her husband was a quiet man, well liked in the neighborhood and known for his faultless manners and good nature. His limited ambitions and gentle personality paled beside those of his vibrant wife and he lived without complaint in her shadow, seeming to accept that she was somehow higher and finer than he.

Years later, his son would have this recollection: "The outstanding characteristic I remember about my father was his complete preoccupation with my mother. She was pretty much his life. It was interesting. When you get that kind of love and attention, you can take it for granted. Maybe she did to a certain extent. He admired her a great deal. He'd say, 'Have you seen your mother this evening? She's perfectly beautiful.' "

If she ever yearned for more out of life, for the aspirations she had left behind, Georgia was too genteel a product of her times to mention it. Instead, she developed her own career and instilled an abiding love of language and a strong ambition in her son. It was her spirit and the tradition of accomplishment in her family that would spur her son to greatness. Even as an old man, Clifford could recite the accomplishments of the McAdams family, but he could not even recall his grandmother Clifford's maiden name, let alone the fates of his seven uncles and aunts from that side of the family.

Georgia had grown up listening to her father's stories about the Indian tribes that had once roamed the Midwest. She had a gift for language and a flair for drama. So it was only natural that she would fashion her father's stories into tales of her own, which she recounted as a professional storyteller and author of children's books. By the 1930s, she had a program on CBS Radio and eventually she was president of the National Storyteller's League.

Each summer, the family rented a cottage for two weeks on the Mississippi River, about fifteen miles north of Alton, Illinois. The cottage was part of a small community called Chautauqua, an offshoot of the more famous public forum in western New York State known as the Chautauqua Institution. The original Chautauqua was founded by Lewis Miller, a son-in-law of Thomas Alva Edison, as a public forum in the Victorian era. It operated as a nonprofit educational center for the study of the arts and religion, attracting speakers from around the world. Some of the speakers would then travel a circuit of Chautauquas to deliver their talks. For young Clifford, however, the summers along the Mississippi were chiefly times to indulge his growing passion for tennis. Years later, his sharpest memory of those long, lazy days would be of the tennis courts a stone's throw from the river.

At home on Laurel Avenue, mealtimes at the Clifford house were English-language tutorials, conducted by Georgia while her husband sat silent. She would instruct her children in the fundamentals of grammar and, each night at the dinner table, introduce them to a new word that had caught her fancy. This was all done with a naturalness and affection that made it fun for the children. Unless they should misspeak.

"If my sister or I would say, 'Well, I saw Joe today and he came up and spoke to Susie and I,' a chill would come into the air," Clark recalled vividly many years later. "My mother would say, 'Will you repeat that sentence?' And I'd say, 'Joe came up and spoke to Susie and I.' She'd say, 'He came up and spoke to whom?' I'd say, 'Ohhh. He came up and spoke to Susie and me.' "

These were the beginnings of a love affair with language that would continue throughout Clark Clifford's life, providing him with one of his most distinctive and valuable gifts. Clifford was not born to success. His path was not eased by money or family connections. But he was fortunate enough to be born to parents who each, in their way, made it possible for him to succeed. From his mother came the skills that would be essential to his career. From his father, Clifford learned the early lessons in how to utilize those tools.

From the age of five, Clark was given regular chores by his father. He swept the porch and walk, emptied the ash from the coal furnace. He was a neighborhood fixture as a small boy, selling the *Saturday Evening Post* door to door and, later, delivering groceries for the local market from the back of a wagon drawn by a horse named Daisy. During high school summers, he worked as a camp counselor in Wisconsin. "Learn habits of industry rather than habits of indolence," his father used to tell young Clark.

It was a philosophy that the son would embrace for the remainder of his life, one of the many pieces of wisdom shared with him by a warm father who seemed always to be there with good advice. As a teenager, Clifford had received a copy of Rudyard Kipling's classic poem "If" from his father. With the poem came the father's suggestion that his son might find value in its message about modesty in the midst of success and integrity in the face of hardship. And it was from his father's own hardship that the young Clifford learned a valuable lesson that remained with him the rest of his life.

Soon after the end of World War I, a man named Louis Egan was hired as vice president and general manager of the Missouri Pacific Railroad. He took a liking to Frank Clifford, promoted him to his assistant, and began grooming him as a successor. No longer relegated to accounting, Clifford was shifted through different phases of the railroad's operation to develop the overview required of a senior manager. For the first time, his ambition seemed to extend beyond his wife. There was a new lilt in his voice, a spring in his step as he left for work in the morning. Sunday mornings would often find him leaving ungrudgingly for the office to meet with Egan. "He's off to watch the trains with Mr. Egan," Georgia Clifford used to joke.

After three or four years of steady progress, Clifford came home from work one day crestfallen. Egan's secretary had gone into his office and discovered her boss slumped over his desk, dead of a heart attack.

Frank Clifford was devastated. The loss of his mentor was soon magnified. The railroad board of directors hired an executive from another railroad to fill Egan's spot, and the new man brought his own top assistants. Frank Clifford's career died with Louis Egan. To his teenage son, "It was just like somebody let the air out of my father's balloon."

By this time, Clark had graduated from Soldan High School in 1922 at the age of fifteen. He had been a fair student. What he had excelled in was tennis, a game that he had learned on the private tennis court at the home of his uncle, Clark McAdams. In his senior year, Clifford's team won fifteen of its sixteen matches and captured the city's interscholastic team title. However, over the years, the team would be remembered for another reason, too — the prominence of two of its members: Clifford and his doubles partner, William McChesney Martin, the son of a wealthy St. Louis family, who would go on to become chairman of the Federal Reserve Board at the age of thirty-one.

Clifford's parents were Democrats, but they were not active in politics. His uncle's home was where the young Clifford was schooled in politics. McAdams and his wife had no children, so he spent a considerable amount of time with his namesake. In him he instilled his sturdy liberal precept that government existed to help people and protect civil liberties. A byproduct of Clifford's close relationship with his uncle was his appreciation of the good life. While his own family lived modestly, Uncle Clark enjoyed the accoutrements of power and money that did not go unnoticed by his young nephew.

Following high school, Clifford's father insisted that he spend some time in a clerical job at the railroad. He enjoyed receiving a regular paycheck, but he had no desire to follow in his father's footsteps professionally. In the fall of 1923, he enrolled at Washington University, a school with a strong academic reputation and within walking distance of the apartment where the Cliffords were then living. As had his sister before him, Clark continued to live at home, partly to save money, partly because of the convenience.

Tall and handsome, Clark Clifford was well known on the campus of Washington University. He was a member of the Kappa Alpha fraternity, an athlete, an actor, and a prankster. While his stint on the football team was cut short when four of his front teeth were knocked loose, he played varsity tennis. Clifford was not an outstanding student as an undergraduate, but he exhibited plenty of that lofty McAdams ambition: he determined quickly that he wanted to be either a surgeon or a lawyer.

It was his father who gently guided him toward the law, employing the lesson of his own disappointment to instruct his son. A lawyer, he said, does not have to depend on anyone else for his future. He can establish his own practice and survive on his own abilities. If he becomes disenchanted with the legal profession, his skills will serve him well in business.

Clifford's mother had urged him to become involved in dramatics at Washington University, something he had ignored in high school. "It is very important for everyone, especially for a young male, to learn to speak in front of people and to be at ease," she counseled. "Try out for different dramatic things. It won't interfere with your studies or your tennis."

So the son joined the school glee club and Thyrsus, the dramatic club. He tried out for parts in school plays and soon won leading-man roles, setting off heated competitions among co-eds to play opposite him. When classmates later reflected on his success as a lawyer, they confessed that they had expected Clifford's good looks and talent for drama to take him to Hollywood, not Washington.

Even after graduating, Clifford remained involved in the theater, playing roles in acclaimed musical comedies staged in the late 1920s and early 1930s by the Quadrangle Club, a local organization. He was the leading man in the group's 1928 production of *High Hat* at the American Theater in downtown St. Louis. The next year, he was assistant director of a production of *Ship Ahoy!*

Clifford's drama was not restricted to the stage. He and his closest college friend, Carleton Hadley, developed a reputation as campus pranksters. Although Clifford denied responsibility for decades, they were the authors of a renowned practical joke on the hapless soul who was superintendent of grounds and security at Washington University.

Near deadline one night, they telephoned the campus newspaper with news of the superintendent's death, which they said had occurred while he was dining out. They provided a virtually complete obituary, but the details were skewed enough to alert any careful reader. For instance, the maiden name of the man's wife was that of the university's dean of women and his surviving children had the names of other campus figures. The superintendent himself, Clifford said later, was "an ass" who deserved to be the butt of the prank.

Although he lived at home, Clifford's social life centered on the Kappa Alpha fraternity, where he often ate lunch and spent many evenings. He also sang bass in the fraternity's popular quartet, which performed at parties and picnics. The motto at Kappa Alpha was "God and the Ladies," and Clifford and his fraternity brothers devoted far more of their time to the latter.

In the fall of 1925, after two years as an undergraduate, Clifford followed custom and transferred to Washington University's law school for a three-year course. It was during those years that two important changes occurred in Clifford.

First, he developed his academic skills, improving his grades each year as his interest in the law grew. Second, his love of drama kindled a passion to become not just a lawyer, but a litigator. He wanted to perform for juries, to sway them with his language and voice. The two great influences of his life, his father's urging to become a lawyer and his mother's interest in drama, had converged.

In his final year of law school, Clifford's favorite class was a seminar taught by Jacob Lashly, a partner in one of the city's preeminent law firms and an outstanding trial lawyer. As he recounted his courtroom victories and outlined his strategies, Lashly took on heroic stature in the eyes of Clark Clifford. Here was a man who had accomplished all that the young law student wanted. Not only would Clifford become a trial lawyer. He decided that he would join Lashly's firm.

Between his twenty-first birthday in December 1927 and his graduation from law school the following May, Clifford went to Jefferson City, the state capital, and took the bar examination. A friend later told Frank Clifford that his son had ranked second among the three hundred and fifty who took the bar, although Clifford never confirmed it. When he was admitted as a practicing lawyer on June 1, 1928, he was not yet twenty-two years old. That same month, he made an appointment with Jacob Lashly and went to the downtown offices of Holland, Lashly, and Donnell.

"Mr. Lashly, I enjoyed your course so much," Clifford said politely. "I would like very much to come into your firm."

Lashly had undoubtedly entertained many such requests from star-struck young students. He kindly replied that he appreciated the commendation, but there were no openings at the firm at the time. Further, the young son of the chief justice of the Missouri Supreme Court was scheduled to join the firm in the fall.

Clifford's disappointment grew as he tried other law firms without success. Business was slow in the summer and no one was hiring. So he demonstrated some real ingenuity. He telephoned Lashly and asked for a second appointment, promising to present his case in ten minutes. Lashly agreed.

"I'll tell you what I want to do," Clifford said when they met again. "I can't find a location just now and I would like to come here for the summer. On Labor Day, I'll leave. But in the meantime, I can run errands for the firm. I'll learn how to file, learn about different courts. I'll keep the books put away in the library."

Lashly was intrigued by the prospect of this eager young law school graduate, but he truly did not have a spot in his firm. "We aren't in a position to pay you for it," he said.

"I don't expect to get paid," replied Clifford. "I just want the experience."

So began the law career of a man who would someday command million-dollar fees. Young Clifford was indeed eager and willing to work. He had learned good work habits and strong Midwestern values from his father. Law school had sharpened his mind and focused his intelligence. And under his mother's influence, Clifford had developed a keen sense that his prospects were unlimited.

3

Best in the Midwest

A GREAT TRIAL LAWYER must be able to persuade juries with compelling rhetoric. However, a mastery of the rules of evidence and legal strategy is more important in winning a case than a dramatic closing argument. This was a lesson Clifford learned at the expense of so many of his early clients that his colleagues joked about dedicating a "Clifford wing" at the Missouri State Penitentiary in Jefferson City.

His first summer at Holland, Lashly, and Donnell was spent filing papers and running errands for the other lawyers in the firm. Lacking the permanency of a desk, Clifford used the firm's library as his make-shift office. As promised, when Labor Day came, the young lawyer walked into Jacob Lashly's office, thanked him for the opportunity, and said he would be moving on.

"Where are you going?" asked Lashly.

"I am going out to find a job," replied Clifford.

"Don't you like it here?" asked the older man.

"I love it here. But this was our original agreement."

"You've learned how the men like to do things. If I were you, I'd just stay here."

So he stayed. Financially, the arrangement was hardly better than working for no pay. Clifford would receive a small hourly wage for research and other work done for the other lawyers. In the first six months, he earned $30. Half of it came from handling a divorce for the friend of a secretary. He augmented the pay by teaching a class in contract law at a night law school, and survived on his meager earnings by continuing to live with his parents.

Money was not important at this juncture in his young career. What was essential was the opportunity to practice law, to stand before a jury and convince them of his client's innocence. The firm specialized in civil litigation, defending insurance companies against personal injury claims and corporations against all manner of lawsuits. It was a rigid place, where apprenticeships could be lengthy. Beginning lawyers could toil for years doing research and writing briefs before conducting an actual trial. Indeed, that first summer Clifford learned that one of the lawyers, Oliver Miller, had worked for Robert Holland, the senior partner, for ten years before he was permitted to try a case.

Clifford was too impatient for such a process. There was still no desk for him, let alone an office, so he remained in the library. But he was determined to try cases. Not long after Labor Day, he called on the clerks in the city's criminal courts, where he had been filing papers during the summer. He explained that he was new to the bar and was willing to represent defendants unable to afford a lawyer. This was in the days before court-appointed lawyers were paid by the court. The only benefit for Clifford would be experience.

A short time later, Clifford received a call from a judge's clerk. He had been appointed to defend an accused car thief named John Piper. In the following weeks, Clifford spent many hours with Piper in the city jail, going over the details of the case and trying to build a defense. The matter was grave for the defendant. Although only a few years older than his lawyer, Piper had two previous felony convictions and faced a stiff sentence as a habitual offender if found guilty.

The case was tough. Piper had been arrested with a set of burglary tools on the front seat of his car. Clifford had collected a library of two hundred books by and about trial lawyers and their practice and he pored over them as well as over statutes on car theft. He woke up nights thinking about the case and how he might present his evidence and arguments to the jury.

The trial lasted two and a half days, closing with Clifford's stirring plea to set Piper free. Scarcely had the young lawyer finished congratulating himself on his performance than the jury was back. After deliberating less than half an hour, they found Piper guilty. He was sentenced to twenty-five years in prison.

Clifford was stunned. It was the blackest day of his young life. The disappointment must have been evident because the judge, John W. Calhoun, summoned the young lawyer to the bench.

"Well, that didn't turn out very well, did it?" he said.

"That's the understatement of my life," replied Clifford.

"You made a lot of mistakes," the judge said. "Why did you let that policeman testify about the burglary tools?"

"I didn't know how to keep it out," Clifford explained.

"You'll learn," said Calhoun.

With that, the judge told the young lawyer that he would assign him another case immediately. Clifford protested, saying he might prefer appellate work. But the judge insisted, telling him, "If you get thrown from a horse, the thing for you to do is to get up, dust yourself off, and get back on that horse. If you don't, you'll be horse-shy the rest of your life."

The judge was as good as his word. Within a week, Calhoun's clerk had telephoned with another case. While the lawyer thought his technique had improved, the second trial also ended with a conviction and a prison term for the defendant, albeit a shorter one than Piper's. Clerks for other judges called with assignments. The guilty verdicts piled up. Clifford lost his first fourteen cases, finding solace only in the fact that he was getting better each time.

"If I had become a surgeon, they would have had a whole section at the local cemetery," Clifford later mused.

Winning a case became an obsession with him. He felt as though his very sanity depended on it. Finally, on his fifteenth attempt, a jury returned a verdict of not guilty. Clifford was elated. The victory was sweeter than he had imagined.

Not long after, Robert Holland was arguing a civil motion before Judge Moses Hartman, who had presided over Clifford's victory. At the conclusion of the hearing, Hartman called Holland aside to praise the splendid verdict won by a young man from Holland's firm. When Holland asked the lawyer's name, the judge said it was Clifford. Puzzled, Holland thought a bit, and then said there was no one at the firm by that name. The judge described the tall young lawyer with wavy yellow hair.

"Oh," said Holland. "That's that young man who sits in the library."

Hard as he worked, the law was not Clifford's only interest. He had been dating a young woman named Dorothy Ladd for some time. It seemed likely they would soon become engaged and he would settle into domesticity. First came one last adventure as a bachelor.

In those days before air-conditioning, most courtrooms in the city conducted limited operations in the sultry summer. So when Louis McKeown, another young lawyer at the firm, proposed that Clifford join him on a lengthy trip to Europe, he jumped at the chance. It was dubbed, naturally, "the Louis and Clark expedition."

In this era before transatlantic airplane flights, the pair took a ship to London and spent several days touring the landmarks and examining the British courts. Clifford, with his flair for drama, was particularly impressed by the dignity lent to the trial process by the English barristers in their powdered wigs.

Next stop was Paris, which was followed by Germany, where they visited Heidelberg and the cathedral city of Cologne. Because Prohibition restricted drinking to speakeasies and discreet flasks in the United States, the two young men found particular pleasure in inexpensive French wine and good German beer.

In Cologne, they joined a group of young Germans at an open-air beer garden and spent a long and happy night drinking and singing. The following morning, they intended to catch the eight o'clock steamer for a day trip on the Rhine River. However, as Clifford would later tell it, McKeown had overindulged and could not be roused in time for the early passage. Instead, they wound up on the nine o'clock boat, where they soon spotted a group of young American women and their chaperone. Clifford's eye quickly fixed on a willowy, beautiful blonde who was sitting at a table playing bridge.

"Why, I haven't seen a good game of bridge since I left the United States," said Clifford as he walked over to the table where the women were playing.

The young blonde looked up at him and said, "That's a very poor start."

Clifford, somewhat surprised by the sharpness of the response, quickly introduced himself to the young woman and her companions. The blonde who had caught his eye said that her name was Margery Kimball, but friends called her Marny.

Marny Kimball was the cultured daughter of a Massachusetts businessman. As a twenty-first birthday present, her father had sent her to Europe with a group of young women from Wellesley College, although she had not attended school there. Instead, she had studied piano at a private school in Bryn Mawr, Pennsylvania, and later at a conservatory in Boston.

As she looked over the tall man standing beside her chair, she thought to herself, "He looks like a Greek god. He may be a little too handsome." But after a morning of conversation, her impression changed. Young Clark Clifford seemed to be one of the nicest, most straightforward men she had ever met. By chance, they shared a hometown: Marny had been born in St. Louis. Her father had spent three years there on business, and in the midst of the sojourn she had been born, in 1908. The family had eventually returned to New England.

In the meantime, McKeown had struck up a conversation with a redhead from Pittsburgh named Angela Higgins, who was part of the group. By the end of the voyage, Clifford and McKeown had persuaded Marny and Angela to give them a copy of the party's itinerary and were making plans to meet up with the women again.

The two young lawyers arrived in Rome at the same time as the American women and invited Marny and Angela to dinner. Florence was next, and again the two young men showed up. In Venice, Clifford and McKeown hired a singing gondolier and took the two women for a romantic ride along the canals. Then came a week in the south of France and a final good-bye party in Paris, which ended at five in the morning with steaming bowls of onion soup in a small bistro. The women headed for home while the men planned to remain in Europe a short time longer.

Europe was not the same for Clifford once Marny Kimball departed. Unfortunately, he could not really hope to see her again. She had explained that she was engaged to someone back in Boston and further contact between them would be improper. And, of course, Dorothy Ladd was waiting for him in St. Louis. So the moonstruck lawyer headed back to his home and his work.

As he began his second year at Holland, Lashly, and Donnell, Clifford's ingenuity began to pay off. The firm started assigning him minor trials. They were small civil cases, usually involving the defense of businesses against personal injury lawsuits and insurance companies against various claims. It was not as dramatic as trying to save John Piper from prison. Still, he was trying cases, examining witnesses, applying the rules of law and evidence, crafting closing arguments.

The appeal of litigation, which he had first sensed in law school, blossomed. Clifford could not get enough of the courtroom. He became engrossed in his preparation and polished both his legal strategy and his presentation. Long gone were the days of fourteen consecutive losses. He was winning cases regularly now, although no trial lawyer wins them all. Jacob Lashly and other partners at the firm were pleased with him. And Clifford was pleased with himself. His goal had once been to become a trial attorney. Now he raised his sights: he would become the best trial attorney in the Midwest.

Success did not come without frustration. The firm was a formal, almost stodgy place. The tone was set by Robert Holland, the very stern, older lawyer who wore Herbert Hoover collars and was referred to by partners and judges alike as "Mr. Holland." It was Holland who determined the compensation of the lawyers in the firm. To Clifford, who was earning only about $150 a month, it seemed that a disproportionate amount went to older men who were not nearly as hardworking or successful as he. Pay seemed tied more to age and time at the bar than to performance.

This grievance was aggravated by the dim prospects for advancement. The firm had a bizarre policy of not elevating its young lawyers to partner, where they would share in the wealth and be more secure. Instead, they hired laterally, bringing in experienced attorneys from other firms, and routinely let their young lawyers go after a number of years. It was a policy Clark Clifford was determined to breach.

Clifford also was uncomfortable with the size of Holland, Lashly, and Donnell. With fifty or more lawyers, it seemed big and impersonal. If he ever had his own firm, he decided, he would keep it small. The practice of law, he thought, should be extremely personal.

These early years fixed Clifford's character. Work would always take supremacy over everything else. He was a young man on the rise and nothing would stand in his way.

Yet there was a sense that something was missing. It had been a year since Clifford's return from Europe, but he still thought often of Marny Kimball. His relationship with Dorothy Ladd had seemed bland by comparison, and he had broken it off soon after his return. Yet he had no hope of ever seeing Marny again. He had written her a letter months ago, but she had never responded. She was probably married by now.

In the fall of 1930, Clifford was returning from court one afternoon when he bumped into Ben Lang, an acquaintance he had not seen for some time.

"I'm glad I saw you," said Lang. "I was in Maine this summer and ran into a friend of yours."

"What was his name?" asked Clifford.

"It wasn't a man. It was a woman. Her name was Marny Kimball."

"What's her name now?"

"Marny Kimball."

"Isn't she married?"

"No," said Lang.

"I'll be damned," exclaimed Clifford.

Hurrying through his good-bye, Clifford rushed back to his office, found her name and address in his files, picked up the telephone, and called the Kimball home in the Boston suburb of Woburn. She was not in, but he left his number. The following morning, Marny called back. It was true. She was not married. It just hadn't seemed the same with her young man after she returned from Europe and she had broken off her engagement. She had not contacted Clifford because she assumed that he was married to Dorothy by this time. He assured her that he was not.

"We should not leave it in this fashion," Clifford said. "Do you think that you could come here for a football game at the university? You could stay with my family."

Marny's parents refused to let their daughter travel to St. Louis and stay with a family they had never met. Undaunted, Clifford proposed that he break away from his busy law practice and come to see her.

"I could get away between Christmas and New Year," he said. "If you thought well of it, I could come up and visit you."

"I think very well of it," said Marny.

A day after Christmas, which had been his twenty-fourth birthday, Clifford arrived at South Station in Boston in a heavy snowstorm. Marny met him and they drove to her house in Woburn. The door to the large house was opened by Marny's father, Willis Grove Carlton Kimball. The elder Kimball had been a partner in a prosperous leather-goods business, but had lost the company in the stock market crash the year before. Since then, he had turned his hobby, collecting antique firearms, into a way to support his family in the depression.

Clifford spent two warm days with the Kimballs, then he and Marny took a day trip to visit one of his aunts in Portland, Maine. During the leisurely drive up and back, Clifford and Marny reached an understanding. When they arrived back at the Kimball home that evening, Marny asked her parents to sit down with them in the parlor.

The young couple explained their experience abroad and how it had affected their lives in the same way although they had not seen each other for more than a year. Over these last few days, they said, they had picked up the pieces exactly where they had left off. Now they were seeking permission for formal courting. Marny's parents were pleased and immediately gave their consent.

A month later, both sets of parents were in New York and had dinner together, sealing the courtship. Clifford made several trips to Boston, and Marny visited him in St. Louis in the spring. Soon after, they announced their engagement.

On October 3, 1931, they were married in Winchester, Massachusetts. Clifford's best man was Carleton Hadley, his closest friend since college and now a lawyer for the Wabash Railroad. At the wedding reception, Oswald Jacoby, the well-known bridge player and a persistent suitor of Marny, offered a toast to the smiling bridegroom. "As a semifinalist to a finalist, I'd like to congratulate you," he said.

The newlyweds would have loved to return to Europe, where they had met, for their honeymoon, but it was the depression and Clifford had to return to work. So they settled for a brief drive through Quebec, where they enjoyed the fall foliage and stayed at the Chateau Frontenac.

Back in St. Louis, the new couple set up housekeeping in a third-floor walk-up apartment over the noisy tracks of the electric trolley. The quarters were cramped, reflecting Clifford's earnings, which were about $175 a month. He was paid by the case rather than a set salary, so his new wife could be expected to chalk up his longer and longer working hours as the price of keeping the money flowing and his career moving forward. Although she had no way of knowing it, Marny Clifford was actually seeing the future for both of them.

Clifford had always enjoyed a measure of social standing in St. Louis because of his uncle, Clark McAdams. However, his rising career as a lawyer and his marriage to a beautiful, cultured woman enhanced his position. He joined the St. Louis Racquet Club, where he played good games of tennis and squash. He and Marny became sought-after guests at parties and dinners. With their blond good looks, it was inevitable that the Cliffords became known as "the golden couple" in St. Louis society.

Clifford had always been conscious of his good looks. Now, as his social standing rose, he was paying closer attention to his dress despite having to skimp on expenses at home. He started wearing the square-shouldered, double-breasted suits favored by successful lawyers and businessmen at the time. It was a style that fit his broad-shouldered, trim build well and one that he would never change.

Once, as he was leaving court, he bumped into a former law professor from Washington University. Noticing Clifford's affluent, tailored look, he suggested less imposing attire might make a better impression with a jury.

"No, I'm too much known as a careful dresser," Clifford replied seriously. "If I dressed differently in court, the jury would think I was trying to put something over on it."

The couple's primary outside interest was music. Marny was an accomplished pianist who had been something of a child prodigy. She gave a few recitals in St. Louis and quickly immersed herself in the city's musical scene. With her encouragement, both became involved with the board of the St. Louis Symphony Society.

The couple's first daughter, Margery, who was called Gery, was born in 1932, ten months after the marriage of her parents. Thirteen months later, Joyce was born. Eventually, the Cliffords bought their first home, a small house at 5608 Westminster.

Not long after buying the house, Marny Clifford was passing the storefront office of a woman who advertised herself as a psychic. Years before, a gypsy who had stayed for a short time on her father's property had foretold that Marny would meet a tall, handsome man in Europe and later marry him. That fortune had come true. So she decided to see what her future now held.

Many years later, Marny still remembered the prediction vividly. "She looked at me and said, 'You are going to move away from here. A little man with gray hair is going to offer your husband a job and you are going to move away from here. You are going to have another baby. I can't tell if it will be a boy or a girl. You will live outside a city in a big, white, rambling house.' "

A few years later, in 1940, the Cliffords had a third child, a daughter whom they named Randall. Marny thought briefly about the psychic's prediction and wondered what else would come true.

By the middle 1930s, Clifford's law career was thriving. His long hours were the product of his deep desire to succeed and his deep fear of financial insecurity. His father's career had been stunted by dependence on another man. His wife's father had lost almost everything in the stock market crash of 1929. And, if he needed another lesson to drive home the message, the depression had recently taken a personal toll. Albert Kurrus, who had married Clifford's sister, Alice, had seen his family's savings wiped out and his job as a bank executive disappear in the financial catastrophe that was engulfing the country. Kurrus had been out of work for months and finally had been forced to move his family to Springfield, Illinois, the only place he could find a job.

"His experience brought me face to face with the economic period we were in," Clifford said later.

No such fate would befall Clifford. Gone were the no-fee criminal cases, but he was trying as many as thirty civil cases a year. Although initially the trials were generally short, he was busy by day in court and by night preparing for the next case. As time went on, he took on more and more complicated matters. This meant fewer trials, but longer ones. He began to travel to other parts of Missouri as well as southern Illinois and farther.

The work ethic, coupled with Clifford's own passion for the law and obsession with financial security, caused friction at home. Marny began to wonder whether she and their daughters were as important to Clifford as his law career. Many nights, his dinner sat warming in the oven until close to midnight. Weekends were spent at the office, too. On the nights when he was home in time to read a bedtime story to his young daughters, a rare treat for the girls, they often would have to poke their father to keep him awake, giggling as they called softly, "Poppy, Poppy. Wake up and finish the story."

Clifford was convinced that he could not reach his lofty goal of becoming the best trial lawyer in the Midwest unless he devoted everything to his job. By the middle thirties, he was not working constantly because he had to. Although still an associate paid by the hour, he was earning a good living. He worked so hard because he wanted to. "If you try the other system, of trying to lead a normal life, it won't be long before you change and you are not winning your cases," he said.

Once, when Clifford tried to explain this to his wife by describing how his father had instilled a commitment to work in him, Marny replied sharply, "It was a pretty good idea, but I think your father overdid it."

But as Clifford saw the problem, the resolution must come from the other side of the marriage. His wife would simply have to grow accustomed to not being the center of his attentions.

"She was an only child and that caused some adjustments when we were first married," Clifford said later. "When you are an only child, you get a great deal of attention. She adjusted to it after a while. It was a good idea for her to leave her house and move to my home in St. Louis. I made a private commitment to myself that we certainly would not have an only child."

Marny Clifford realized that she needed to make adjustments to her husband's career. She also recognized that nothing could deter him from his job. The carefree young man with whom she had fallen in love in Europe was gone. In his place was a dedicated lawyer determined to become the best trial lawyer in the Midwest. The pattern for the marriage was established, and it would endure to the end. Marny made her peace with a life in which Clark was rarely home in the evenings or even on weekend days.

In this way, Clifford differed from his father. While Frank Clifford instilled a strong work ethic in his son, the elder man had always put his wife and family first. For years, the son had marveled at his father's adoration of his mother. But it was not the way Clark Clifford chose to live his life. The son was a determined man who never ceased to seek fulfillment of his own ambitions.

"I soon learned that Clark was happiest when he was busiest," said his wife years later.

In these years of trial after trial, Clifford was developing the skills and philosophy that would allow him to attain his goal. Later, he explained how a trial lawyer must approach his task: "First, he is confronted by a voluminous collection of facts. What he has to do is winnow through them and find which are most salient. He must organize them so he can understand them and put them into an orderly, logical sequence. Then comes the burden of proving his case — that is, presenting the facts as articulately and persuasively as possible, in an effort to guide those who are going to make a decision."

From Clifford's point of view, the devotion paid off. In 1938, at the age of thirty-one, he defied tradition and was named a partner at Holland, Lashly, and Donnell. For the first time, he would no longer be paid by the hour. Instead, he began collecting a handsome salary of about $25,000 a year. As a young man on the way up, he had recently been appointed to the State Social Security Commission and he was active in the St. Louis Bar Association.

During this period, Clifford sometimes stopped off at the St. Louis Racquet Club for a game of squash on his way home from work. One evening, an acquaintance introduced him to Stuart Symington, a business executive, who had arrived recently from New York City and was living at the club temporarily.

Clifford and Symington hit it off immediately. Both were in their thirties, tall and remarkably handsome, intelligent and unfailingly charming. Symington had come to St. Louis with great fanfare to rescue Emerson Electric Manufacturing Company, the state's largest employer, which was on the brink of collapse. The relationship between Clifford and Symington would span one of the most tumultuous periods in American history. Both men would find great success, not along the banks of Mississippi, but along another river in another city.

With the encouragement of Jacob Lashly, Clifford also began to dabble in politics and civic affairs. He was vice chairman of a St. Louis mayoral campaign, and he helped a colleague from the law firm run for local office. His politics were mainstream Democrat, reflecting his uncle and the remainder of his family. But Clifford's real passion remained his growing law practice.

Yet for all of Clark Clifford's talent and ambition, it was a man he met through his wife's interest in music who would open the door to greatness for him.

James K. Vardaman Jr., known to friend and foe as Jake, was a prominent St. Louis banker and business executive. He was born in Mississippi, where his father had been governor and a United States senator. Jake's ample Southern charms contrasted with a short temper that often erupted in a string of accented expletives. He was, Clifford would later learn, a man who made enemies.

Vardaman was a major backer of Harry Truman's successful campaign for the United States Senate in 1934. He and Truman had become friends, and Vardaman was rewarded with an appointment as regional manager for the Reconstruction Finance Organization.

Vardaman also was active in the Symphony Society, and it was through that organization that he met the Cliffords. He and Marny Clifford lamented the absence of opera in the city, so the two of them founded the Grand Opera Guild of St. Louis, which was to bring opera to the city on a regular basis. This shared interest put the Cliffords on the guest list for regular Saturday luncheons hosted by Vardaman and his wife at their farm outside St. Louis. Following the meal, the guests would gather round a bulky Capehart radio and listen to broadcasts of the Metropolitan Opera from New York. At one of these gatherings, the young lawyer was introduced to Senator Harry Truman.

When the Japanese attacked Pearl Harbor on December 7, 1941, Clark Clifford was as shocked and angered as any other American. His first impulse was to join the armed forces, although, just shy of his thirty-fifth birthday, he was too old to worry about the draft. His desire was held back, however, by the necessity of providing for his wife and three young daughters. The overriding obstacle, however, was his father's poor health.

Frank Clifford had been ill for several years and in 1941 he was diagnosed with colon cancer. His son could not think of leaving St. Louis. Every night for a year, Clifford stopped to visit his father on the way home from his law office. Sometimes he was met there by his older daughters, Gery and Joyce, both of whom doted on the warmth and affection of their grandfather, Poppy Clifford. By that time, Clifford's parents lived only a few blocks from Clifford and his family. Each evening, the son would bring his father up to date on the day's news about the war, and watch sadly as Frank Clifford slipped away, slowly and inevitably.

Finally, in 1942, his father died. Clifford had loved his father dearly, but in one respect the death lifted a burden: Clifford could now follow his instinct and join the military. Befitting a man of his caution, Clifford's first step was a small one. He enlisted in the Missouri National Guard as an infantryman. What he wound up doing was shuffling legal papers on weekends.

Jake Vardaman had enlisted in the navy soon after Pearl Harbor with the rank of commander. In his absence, he appointed Clifford as his personal and business attorney. Soon after Vardaman's departure a scandal erupted at one of his former businesses, the Vardaman Shoe Company.

Several years earlier, Vardaman had sold the shoe company to a man named Frank O. Bittner for slightly less than $10,000. Bittner complained that the company's inventory had been padded and he demanded reimbursement. In an attempt to settle the affair, Vardaman had signed over his farm outside St. Louis to Bittner. After the settlement, however, there were allegations that sworn affidavits attesting to the inventory padding were destroyed, perhaps as part of the settlement.

Clifford did not take over Vardaman's interests until after the settlement was reached. But, because his primary duty was to see that the shoe company's creditors were paid off, he found himself in the middle of the controversy. He claimed that he had no knowledge of the destruction of any documents and eventually the matter was dropped in St. Louis. However, the issue would arise again for both men.

Soon after he joined the National Guard, Clifford began talking about enlisting in the army or the navy. The war in the Pacific was not going well and Clifford felt guilty. Symington tried hard to talk him out of going to war.

"You don't have to do it," said Symington. "You are better off here. You are a major in the National Guard and you've got a job to do here at home. This is a war for boys in their early twenties. You're just not up to it. You are expecting a little too much of yourself."

As a young man of seventeen, Symington had joined the army as a private during World War I. He was later commissioned a second lieutenant, but the war ended before he saw action. After the war, he had gone to Yale College, but left for the business world before he got a degree.

Since arriving in St. Louis, Symington was enjoying enormous success in turning around Emerson Electric. When President Franklin Delano Roosevelt called on America to turn from manufacturing plows to swords, Emerson Electric began furiously turning out gun turrets for B-17 and B-24 bombers. But Symington's caution to Clifford fell on deaf ears.

In the fall of 1943, Clifford decided finally that the National Guard was not enough. He would enlist in the navy. Clifford was earning a handsome $30,000 a year as a partner in the law firm, but the family had not had enough time to accumulate any real wealth. Marny said she would take the children back to Boston and stay with her family. The Cliffords' house in St. Louis would be rented.

On April 28, 1944, at the age of thirty-seven, Clifford enlisted in the U.S. Navy Reserves and was commissioned a lieutenant, junior grade. A few days later, he received orders to report to the Office of the Chief of Naval Operations in Washington, D.C.

Marny Clifford packed up their three daughters and a few belongings and moved back to Woburn, where she would spend the remainder of the war living with her family. The house in St. Louis was rented to another family. Just before leaving, Marny Clifford remembered the prediction of the psychic years before. Part of it was coming true. She was moving away from St. Louis.

In the late spring of 1944, the city that greeted Clifford when he arrived by train at Washington's ornate Union Station was far different from the quiet place he had visited a few times before on business trips. The city was alive with urgency and excitement, awakening from its small-town ways to become a growing, vibrant metropolis. It was a historic moment as the violence and upheaval and vitality of the war were transforming Washington into the epicenter of American power.

He found a bunk at the Navy League Club on 21st Street in northwest Washington and performed routine staff chores in the temporary buildings that had been set up along the Mall to accommodate the influx of military personnel.

In July 1944, not long after D-Day in Western Europe, Clifford and another officer were dispatched to San Francisco to conduct a survey of supplies and logistics on the West Coast in preparation for the push against Japan. There, Clifford worked at a desk job under Admiral Royal Ingersoll, the commander of the Western Sea Frontier. His assignment was to oversee the distribution of vast amounts of supplies among the various naval task forces in the Pacific. His organizational skills and ability to think under pressure made him well suited for the task, and he was soon promoted to full lieutenant.

The month Clifford was sent to San Francisco, the Democrats held their presidential convention in Chicago They renominated Roosevelt for a historic fourth term. But Vice President Henry Wallace was dumped from the ticket as too liberal and Senator Harry S. Truman of Missouri, a more conservative figure, was nominated to be Roosevelt's running mate. In the final decision about the vice presidential candidate, Truman was chosen over William O. Douglas, whom Roosevelt had named a justice of the Supreme Court.

Truman's selection came as a surprise to the public, but it had been plotted carefully for more than a year by a handful of the most powerful men in the Democratic Party who disliked Henry Wallace and feared his liberalism. The choice was viewed as extremely important by these men because they feared that Roosevelt's poor health might make the vice president the next president of the United States. Among those backroom plotters was George E. Allen, a Washington lobbyist, businessman, and national party secretary, who would later play a major role in the career of another Missourian, Clark Clifford.

Following a rough-and-tumble campaign against Republican Thomas Dewey, the Roosevelt-Truman ticket won by three million votes, carrying thirty-six of the forty-eight states. The margin was actually quite narrow. As Truman biographer David McCullough noted, a swing of just three hundred thousand votes in the right states would have put Dewey in the White House.

In recognition of Roosevelt's fragile health, the inauguration on January 20, 1945, was short and somber. Less than three months later, on April 12, 1945, Franklin D. Roosevelt died at Warm Springs, Georgia, and Harry S. Truman became president of United States.

Shortly after FDR's death, Clifford was on duty in San Francisco when Jake Vardaman telephoned. He was in town and asked Clifford to come by his hotel. Vardaman, who had been wounded during the invasion of Sicily, explained that he was becoming the president's chief naval aide. A navy reservist like Clifford, Vardaman distrusted regular navy officers. He suggested that Clifford might join him in Washington as his assistant.

Clifford was intrigued, but he did not then take the offer seriously. Vardaman returned to San Francisco in late June with a presidential advance team to prepare for the signing of the United Nations Charter. Vardaman said he would soon be traveling to a suburb of Berlin called Potsdam, where Truman was going to meet with Joseph Stalin of the Soviet Union and Winston Churchill of Great Britain to discuss the future of postwar Europe. Vardaman did not want to leave a regular navy officer in charge at the White House and informed Clifford that he had arranged for him to be posted to Washington as his White House assistant for a few weeks.

Clifford gladly accepted what he assumed would be temporary duty until Vardaman returned from Potsdam with Truman. With the new post came the temporary rank of lieutenant commander. Clifford expected the job and the promotion to be short lived. After the war, he intended to return to St. Louis and his law practice.

But Clark Clifford, the handsome lawyer from the hinterlands, was about to walk onto a stage where the lights of power and politics sparkled brighter than anything he had imagined. Clifford had no experience with life in the limelight or with the trappings and influence of politics. In many ways, however, he was well prepared for Washington. At thirty-eight, he was energetic and eager without being green or youthful. He was accustomed to working long hours. His experience in preparing for a trial and presenting his evidence to a jury had trained him to sift through complex material in search of logical interpretations and explanations that favored the position of his client. Even the manner in which he had arrived in Washington, through the intercession of a friend, would prove good training for life in a city where who you know is so often more important than what you know. But no one could have predicted how this lawyer from the Midwest would succeed in the wilds of Washington.

4

"Big Fella, Ain't He"

HARRY S. TRUMAN became the thirty-fourth president of the United States under what were possibly the most difficult circumstances of anyone to assume the office. The man he replaced had led the country for thirteen years and was a national idol. Even Truman was uncertain that he was up to replacing FDR in the Oval Office. As vice president for less than a year, he had had only one meeting with Roosevelt. When Truman took office, world events were moving rapidly. The war was ending in Europe, and the Soviet Union, an ally during the fighting, was changing into a dangerous adversary. Then there was the top-secret atomic bomb. Truman had not even known of its existence until he became president, and he soon faced the decision of whether to unleash its fearsome power.

In the midst of the turbulent postwar years, the difficult decisions made by Truman and the men around him shaped the world and the nation for more than forty years. Clifford was present at most of these decisive moments in the country's history. In many of them, both foreign and domestic, he played a pivotal role. As a result, the four and a half years he spent in the Truman administration, rising from assistant naval aide to counsel to the president, reshaped Clifford's world, too.

It was a typically muggy day when Clifford arrived in Washington from San Francisco on July 10, 1945. Unlike his last time in the city, however, he would not be performing routine staff chores in a makeshift office on the mall. Clifford was going to the White House, even if it was only temporary duty. Two days after his arrival, Vardaman ushered Clifford into the Oval Office to meet the president.

Truman was busy going over papers on his desk and did not rise to greet the new staff member. He did not seem to recall that he had met Clifford a few years earlier at Vardaman's farm. All that Clifford would remember was the president looking up at him from behind his thick glasses and saying, "Big fella, ain't he." Clifford shook Truman's hand, thanked him, and left. Still fresh from the Midwest and new to Washington, Clifford was excited at meeting the president. However, it would not be long until the thirty-eight-year-old lawyer from St. Louis would make an impression on his fellow Missourian and become far more comfortable in the ways of the White House.

The White House staff in those days was small. No one had the title chief of staff, but the de facto job was held by Judge Samuel I. Rosenman, a New York lawyer who had been called from the bench to Washington by Roosevelt and remained as a holdover in the Truman administration. He also retained the title Roosevelt had given him, special counsel to the president, and had an expansive office in the West Wing of the White House.

Vardaman introduced Clifford to Judge Rosenman, saying that the young navy officer had been his lawyer in St. Louis. The day after Truman and his entourage left to redraw the map of Europe at the Potsdam conference, Rosenman approached Clifford.

"You have much to do over there in the naval aide's office?" he asked.

"Not very much," replied Clifford.

"My impression is that you are kind of a potted palm standing around," said Rosenman. "If you have extra time, I'm way behind and I could use some help."

The first project Rosenman handed to the assistant naval aide was researching and drafting a message for Truman to deliver to Congress seeking universal military training. So when Rosenman went off to Potsdam to join the president to discuss peace settlements and create a Council of Foreign Ministers to work out the details, Clifford was left to prepare for the next war.

Clifford was working in his White House office on August 6, 1945, when he learned that the United States had dropped the atomic bomb on the Japanese city of Hiroshima. The second bomb was dropped on Nagasaki three days later. The following day, August 10, the Japanese government capitulated. The war was over.

Marny Clifford had remained in Massachusetts with their daughters. By chance, she was visiting her husband in Washington on V-J day. The two of them went for a stroll late that afternoon, staying out until past dinnertime to soak up the momentous excitement and relief that accompanied the end of the war. Although neither of the Cliffords knew it, the city was on the brink of enormous change, and they would spend the rest of their lives in the midst of it.

David Brinkley, a young journalist at the time, captured the moment when he wrote: "The city had come out of the war as the capital of the only major country in the world on the winning side, or any side, to survive without a scratch, but those looking to the return of the quiet, easy Washington life they had known in peacetime would not find it. That world was gone."

When Truman returned from Potsdam on August 7, Rosenman asked for permission to continue using Clifford. The president agreed, and Clifford began spending most of his time working alongside Rosenman in his big West Wing office. A month later, Clifford was transferred officially to the White House and his rank as lieutenant commander became permanent.

The ties that Clifford formed in those early days with Rosenman were invaluable to him. But it was the relationship that he began to develop with Truman that became the touchstone for his power and influence. As assistant naval aide, Clifford had the task of organizing cruises on the refurbished presidential yacht, the *Williamsburg*. Some of the voyages went as far as Bermuda. More often, however, Truman would take a bunch of his pals on a trip down the Potomac for an evening of poker, bourbon, and relaxation.

Part of Clifford's job was organizing the president's famous poker games, a task he continued on dry land. Truman loved to play eight-handed poker and he had a core group of regulars, which included Fred Vinson, his secretary of the treasury and later chief justice of the United States, businessman George Allen (possibly the best player), agriculture secretary Clinton Anderson, and Stuart Symington. In 1945, Symington had been summoned from St. Louis by Truman to become chairman of the Surplus Property Board, which was to dispose of American stockpiles abroad. Clifford and Symington had happily renewed their friendship on this new turf.

Initially, Clifford simply organized the games. Eventually, however, Truman offered him a seat at the table. In his typical fashion, Clifford bought a book on poker and researched the game. He played conservatively, collecting small winnings that went a long way in augmenting the meager salary of $400 a month paid to him as a navy officer. On one occasion near the end of 1945, Clifford hit the jackpot, winning more than $50.

The real value of these games to Clifford was the ability to develop a relationship with Truman. Part of Clifford's appeal to Truman was the fact that the young lawyer was from Missouri. Truman, a failed haberdasher and product of Kansas City's Pendergast political machine, knew that most of the Roosevelt New Dealers had opposed his selection as vice president in 1944 and he was never comfortable with them. He once complained to Clifford that Roosevelt had surrounded himself with figures from the "lunatic fringe." Nor did Truman ever feel completely at ease with the patrician Easterners who were his own close advisers, although he had deep respect for men such as Dean Acheson, who eventually became his secretary of state; W. Averell Harriman, who would become secretary of commerce, and Robert A. Lovett, an undersecretary of state.

By November 1945, when British Prime Minister Clement Attlee and his Canadian counterpart, Mackenzie King, came to the White House for a postwar summit on atomic energy, Clifford found himself sitting in for the absent Jake Vardaman. He wrote a breathless letter to his mother back in St. Louis: "I had such an interesting weekend that I knew you would be glad to have the details. J.K. has been gone for a week so I had the opportunity to serve as acting naval aide in his absence. It came at a most propitious time. The President invited me to the formal state dinner which was held Saturday night for Prime Minister Attlee of England and Prime Minister King of Canada. There were fifty-five guests, and the table was arranged in the shape of a horseshoe in the State Dining Room."

Vardaman's absence would soon become permanent. His abrasive style had created numerous enemies for the St. Louis businessman. Among them was James V. Forrestal, the secretary of the navy and a powerful man in Washington. Even worse, Vardaman had angered Bess Truman, the president's wife, a fact later recorded by Margaret Truman Daniel in her biography of her father: "In the White House, Mr. Vardaman proceeded to stick his nose into almost every office and tell them how it should be run. Then he made the blunder of all blunders. He descended upon Mother's side of the White House and started telling *them* how to do the job. That was the end of Mr. Vardaman as naval aide."

In January 1946, Truman wanted to get Vardaman out of the White House, so he nominated him to a fourteen-year term as a governor of the Federal Reserve Board. Clifford would be elevated to naval aide, but first he would have to earn it by helping the former occupant win confirmation by the Senate.

Vardaman's past returned to haunt him at his confirmation hearings. The Republicans, who controlled both the Senate and the House, attacked his record as a banker and as a businessman in St. Louis. One of the issues they raised was the questionable circumstances surrounding the sale of his shoe company. Truman enlisted Clifford to smooth the way on Capitol Hill, providing the young lawyer with the first in his many encounters with the legislative branch.

For six weeks, he lobbied Republican and Democratic senators and their aides, trying to persuade them to overlook Vardaman's foibles and approve his nomination. In the end, Clifford's defense even required him to testify before the Senate Banking Committee that, as his former lawyer, he was aware of nothing that Vardaman had done wrong in connection with the shoe company. Ultimately, Vardaman's nomination was approved by a vote of 66 to 9 in April. Clifford became acting naval aide.

During this same period, Clifford came to the assistance of Stuart Symington, another old friend. In January 1946, Symington submitted his resignation as surplus property administrator. Truman wanted him to remain in the administration and proposed appointing him assistant secretary of the navy. Symington had another job in mind. He had gained experience with the Army Air Corps in supplying gun turrets for big bombers during the war. He wanted to be assistant secretary of war for air. Clifford carried the request to Truman, who agreed, and Symington got the appointment.

Symington would continue with the administration and emerge as a key Clifford ally. However, the departure of Vardaman from the White House was accompanied by a second departure that affected Clifford. Rosenman, who had left the bench grudgingly to serve Roosevelt, told Truman in late 1945 that he wanted to return to New York to practice law. In the beginning of 1946, Truman accepted Rosenman's resignation. However, the president did not immediately accept the New York judge's recommendation that Clifford succeed him as special counsel. The young naval aide, Truman decided, needed more seasoning.

*   *   *

This was the period when a small group of powerful men constructed a new, outward-looking foreign policy for the United States and established the sweeping commitments that formed the parameters of the coming cold war. They brought shape to the postwar world and to the diplomacy of the nation. In doing so, this elite circle later gave rise to the popular and apt phrase "the establishment."

They were decidedly Eastern, bankers and lawyers from Wall Street who had attended Yale and Harvard. Dean Acheson and W. Averell Harriman had attended Groton and Yale together. Robert Lovett grew up playing games on the Harriman estate, where his father worked alongside Harriman's father, a railroad tycoon. Charles Bohlen graduated from Harvard, and John McCloy Jr. went from Harvard Law School to Wall Street. George Kennan, although a native of Milwaukee, was a Princeton man. They were, as described by Walter Isaacson and Evan Thomas in *The Wise Men*, "the architects of the American century."

If Clifford, the son of a railroad auditor, born and educated in the Midwest, did not sit at the drafting table with them, he was rarely far away. Even though some would later disdain him as one who achieved his eminence through government service — rather than on Wall Street — it would not diminish the role he played in those critical years. For in the end, no one would be able to deny that Clifford exerted his own influence over critical events during those years and that, in so doing, he earned his place in the establishment.

Already Clifford had recognized the critical importance of relationships in Washington. His closeness to Vardaman had brought him to the White House, where Rosenman had taken him under his wing. In taking a liking to him, Truman had bestowed a measure of influence on the young aide. So he set about forming his own relationships. While some of them would last a lifetime, often they were not friendships in the traditional sense. Rather, they were alliances, which often pass for friendship in Washington.

An early alliance was formed with Forrestal, the wealthy Wall Street businessman whose skills had built the navy into the powerful force that conquered its Japanese counterpart and provided critical support for the amphibious landings in Europe and North Africa. He had remained in the administration as Truman's secretary of war, where his vision of military power in the postwar years was considered invaluable.

Because Forrestal did not like Jake Vardaman, he turned to Clifford for assistance almost from the start of Clifford's tenure in the White House. He and the young aide lunched together regularly, and Clifford became a sounding board for Forrestal as well as a source of information for him about what was going on inside the White House. He provided Forrestal with intelligence on Truman's mood and predictions about how the president might react to the upcoming installment of Forrestal's constant push to increase defense spending. In turn, Clifford passed on Forrestal's views to his boss in the Oval Office.

In much the same way, Clifford cultivated and was cultivated by Dean Acheson, who at the time was undersecretary of state, the number two position at the State Department. Acheson had enjoyed a distinguished law career, and he and Clifford hit it off well. Again, the naval aide served as an unofficial conduit between the White House and the State Department.

Forrestal and Acheson, like so many of the other senior officials in Washington, had come to the administration as successful lawyers or businessmen. But Clifford had not had time to amass any wealth, and he was struggling to get by on a navy salary. That was one reason he had delayed moving his wife and children to Washington from Boston. It was just too expensive.

He was rescued through another relationship. Alfred Lansing was a businessman in St. Louis whose wide interests in the insurance industry had brought him in contact with Clifford when he was practicing law. Lansing, who had only daughters, had taken a fatherly interest in Clifford. Soon after Clifford went to work at the White House, he had a meeting with Lansing, who was visiting Washington. The younger man complained about trying to make ends meet on his navy pay, which was less than $10,000 a year.

"If you need to stay here," offered Lansing, "I will finance you."

Over the next five years, Clifford received regular payments from Lansing. Each time, Clifford would write out a promissory note, sign it, and mail it to his benefactor. By the time he would leave government service, Clifford would be almost $35,000 in debt to Lansing — the equivalent of nearly three years' salary. It was a highly unusual relationship, and one that would certainly be challenged as improper by the press today. But in those years, before senior federal employees were required to disclose their finances to avoid just such apparent conflicts of interest, few people even knew about the loans.

Clifford's nascent interest in foreign affairs took root late on the night of March 5, 1946, as the presidential train rumbled along the tracks on its return to Washington from the college town of Fulton, Missouri. The nightly poker game was over and, sitting in the leather seats of the private, armor-plated presidential car, the *Ferdinand Magellan,* were the last three men who were awake — Clifford, Truman press secretary Charlie Ross, and Winston Churchill, the former British prime minister.

Earlier that day, Churchill had delivered his soon-to-be-famous "Iron Curtain" speech in tiny Fulton. He had warned sternly about the threat of Soviet expansionism and called for closer American-British cooperation as a countermeasure. As he sat in a blue zipper suit, which Clifford thought resembled a bunny outfit, Churchill sipped scotch and mused that Britain had seen its best days. Now, he told the two Americans, the mantle of leading the free world must be taken up by the United States. Clifford was in wide-eyed awe of Churchill, one of the world's most revered men. Indeed, Churchill's challenge to postwar America made a lasting and important impression on Clifford, who was inexperienced in foreign affairs. He would pick up the gauntlet thrown down by Churchill in ways that would help to shape American relations with the Soviet Union for decades to come.

Before Clifford, or Truman for that matter, could save the world from Soviet aggression, there were two domestic crises with which they had to deal. It was his role in these two events that elevated Clifford to the position of one of Truman's most trusted and important advisers.

On March 31, 1946, about 400,000 members of the United Mine Workers went on strike. Their demands for higher wages and better working conditions had been deferred during the war. They would wait no longer. Coal was still the most important source of energy in the United States, providing the power for most of its electricity and heating as well as keeping the all-important trains rolling.

The strike created a domestic crisis at a time when Truman could ill afford problems as the nation's economy struggled to recover from the war effort. His economic adviser, John Steelman, urged Truman to negotiate a settlement with the mine workers. Clifford, who was still a naval aide, argued that the president needed to stand and fight. The advice appealed to Truman's sense of power politics as much as to economic necessities, and he refused to settle. Seven weeks into the strike, when talks between the mine owners and the union broke down, the president seized control of the soft-coal mines and ordered the workers back into the tunnels. It was a bold stroke, which was greeted with wide political acclaim for Truman.

The same week that he took over the mines, a general railroad strike threatened to shut down the nation's commerce. His patience already worn thin by the coal strike, Truman was furious when attempts at government mediation failed to avert the rail strike. He went on nationwide radio and implied that he might draft the rail workers to keep the trains running. Then he decided to ask Congress for power to seize the railroads, too, and effectively make them government property. With steely determination, the president set about writing his own speech.

Never an eloquent writer, an angry, unrestrained Truman scribbled down his thoughts, calling the union leaders communists and liars. He denounced the Republican-controlled Congress as "weak-kneed" for its failure to approve sweeping labor legislation. Finally, he declared, "Let's give the country back to the people. Let's . . . hang a few traitors and make our country safe for democracy. Come on, boys, let's do the job."

Charlie Ross, the press secretary, was stunned when Truman handed him the remarks. Recognizing that the invective would only inflame the sensitive situation, Ross suggested to Truman that the speech needed some editing. He received permission to pass it on to Clifford, who had already shown that he was a good hand at crafting speeches for Truman.

Rather than a simple refinement, Clifford rewrote the speech entirely, deleting the name-calling and adding a tone of dignity. He also invoked a theme that was to become his favorite: national security. Comparing the rail strike to Pearl Harbor, Clifford suggested that it would wreak havoc on the nation. The only solution, Truman would tell Congress, was that he be granted additional power to halt the strike.

The drama reached its climax in late May. The talks had reached an impasse, and Truman was determined to seek authority to force workers back to the job. At four o'clock on Saturday afternoon, May 25, Truman was scheduled to deliver his message to a rare joint session of Congress. A few minutes before Truman left for the Capitol, John Steelman, the economic adviser, who was involved in last-ditch talks with the leaders of the rail unions, reported that there was a chance of settlement. Public pressure had been mounting since Truman had gone on nationwide radio the day before to berate the strikers. Now Clifford was prepared for a possible last-minute settlement; he had prepared alternative pages that could be inserted into Truman's remarks if the impasse was resolved.

A few minutes after four o'clock, Truman walked into the chamber of the House of Representatives and began his speech. He attacked the union leaders for "obstinate arrogance" and asked for emergency legislation that would let him deal with the national crisis. Among other tough provisions, the legislation would allow the president to seize industries and subject labor leaders to court proceedings, fines, and even criminal charges.

Clifford was waiting anxiously in an anteroom off the House floor, hoping for a call from Steelman. Finally, as Truman was winding up, the phone rang. "We have an agreement," shouted Steelman. "The men are going back, on the president's terms." Clifford scribbled a note for Truman, which was passed to him as he stood at the podium.

"Word has just been received," Truman told Congress in dramatic tones, "that the railroad strike has been settled, on terms provided by the president."

Frank Capra could not have scripted a more dramatic moment for Truman. The chamber erupted in the loudest and longest applause Truman had ever received from Congress. To many, coming on top of the coal strike settlement, the victory marked a turning point for Truman. He emerged from the shadow of Roosevelt and showed himself to be a strong leader in his own right. He even demonstrated a willingness to oppose organized labor, one of his chief sources of political strength.

Clifford also reaped benefits. A week after the speech, on June 1, Truman ordered Clifford to leave the navy and become special counsel to the president. Along with Rosenman's salary of $12,000, the highest on the White House staff, Clifford got the judge's former office, three doors from the Oval Office. On the paneled walls, Clifford hung a series of pastels depicting naval engagements and an autographed photograph of Harry Truman.

The promotion meant new responsibilities and longer hours for Clifford. From the start, he had worked six days a week. Now he added Sundays to his regular schedule as he balanced speech writing, drafting legislation, offering political advice, and playing a role in major decisions. It also meant that Clifford could afford to move Marny and the three girls to Washington.

During two years in Massachusetts, Marny Clifford had, almost by chance, found a way to support the young family. Her father's antique business had boomed and one day she was minding the booth at an antiques exhibition at the Copley Plaza Hotel in Boston when a woman struck up a conversation with her about some items on display. The woman turned out to be Lillian Smith, the author of a popular and somewhat scandalous novel, *Strange Fruit*. She purchased several expensive pieces of furniture and then came up with a surprising proposition.

"I have just acquired an apartment in New York City," said Miss Smith. "How would you like to decorate it?"

"What a silly notion," replied Marny Clifford. "You've only just met me."

"Yes," replied Miss Smith. "But I like the way this booth looks and I want you to do it. You will have carte blanche."

For Marny, who had borrowed money from her father to support her children the past two years, the offer was a grand opportunity. She accepted and spent several months buying fine furniture and other items to decorate the Smith apartment in Brooklyn Heights. With what she earned, she was able to repay her father and set aside some money to help with the move to Washington.

In the summer of 1946, the Clifford family rented a thirteen-room, furnished house next to the exclusive Chevy Chase Club in northwest Washington. They sold their house in St. Louis and, to save moving costs, loaned the furniture to various friends there.

Clifford had begun to shed his awestruck Midwestern attitude as he grew accustomed to Washington and to brushing shoulders with the powerful and famous. Indeed, even before his appointment as special counsel, he cut something of a dashing figure on the city's social scene. His good looks and courtly manners, accompanied by his increasing power at the White House, had made him a conspicuous and sought-after dinner guest. Often, he could be found dining at the home of Pauline Davis, the leading hostess on the Washington social scene and wife of Dwight Davis, a former secretary of war. Not everyone, however, was a fan of the smooth young lawyer.

Alice Longworth, the daughter of President Theodore Roosevelt and widow of the powerful congressman Nicholas Longworth, was known on the Washington social scene for her biting gossip. On the party circuit, she often introduced herself by saying gaily, "If you don't have anything nice to say about anyone, come and sit next to me."

When it came to Clifford, she took such a strong dislike to the newcomer that she dubbed him "Pauline's counter jumper." The disparaging term was a reference to the nineteenth-century male department store clerks who were hired for their good looks and ability to attract female customers.

While he still played tennis, Clifford found time in 1946 to take up a new, more social sport. With characteristic discipline, he read instructional books on golf and took lessons from a professional. His natural athleticism and competitive drive made him an accomplished player in a matter of months. However, his character also made him a deliberate player. For years, his partners, as well as anyone playing behind him, bemoaned the number of practice swings and moments of contemplation employed by Clifford.

Gradually, Marny Clifford found her way into Washington society just as so many matrons had before her — in the wake of her husband. They began to host parties for a circle of bright young professionals and policymakers. Among the regular guests were Stuart and Evelyn Symington, Supreme Court Justice William O. Douglas, and Washington lawyer Eugene Carusi and his attractive wife, Ceci. These gatherings often concluded with Clifford singing while his wife played the piano.

On several occasions, the Cliffords were guests at the White House. In addition, the president and his wife bestowed the ultimate Washington honor on Marny Clifford by dining at the Clifford home several times. Truman shared Marny's love of the piano, and he also took a special liking to Randall, the youngest Clifford daughter. In fact, it was while Truman was having dinner at the Cliffords that the next major crisis arose in his administration.

5

Counsel to the President

HISTORIANS SOMETIMES DISAGREE on the precise date, but there is no dispute that the cold war began in the Truman administration. Clifford dates the start more precisely: September 24, 1946, the day he turned over to the president a startling and far-reaching report on the future of relations between the United States and the Soviet Union. It was a landmark document that helped to chart the course of the United States at a critical time in its history.

The country was struggling to fulfill its strategic role in the world as the tenuous wartime cooperation with the Soviet Union deteriorated. It was a pendulum that many historians believe swung too far, causing both nations to forsake the language of cooperation and locking them in a costly, four-decades-long arms race that wasted hundreds of billions of dollars and spawned countless conflicts around the globe.

In the aftermath of the war, the United States expected to continue its wartime alliance with Joseph Stalin and his government. Truman himself had returned from the Potsdam conference in 1945 and told Clifford, "I think I can work with old Joe." In the blush of early romance, there were even plans to cooperate on a project that would speed the development of atomic energy by the Soviets. However, as the months wore on, the Soviets grew increasingly wary of an American-led peace. The specter of encirclement by the British, French, and other American allies gave rise to fears of invasion on the part of the Russians, who sought to increase their security by creating a buffer of occupation around them.

Most Americans, including Secretary of State James Byrnes and Secretary of the Navy James Forrestal, argued for a hard line against Soviet expansionism. Secretary of Commerce Henry Wallace was part of a minority that championed the view that the only way to avoid a catastrophic war was to cooperate with the Soviet Union. Wallace's position of cooperation set the stage for a showdown that helped harden the American attitude toward the Soviets, and cost Wallace his job.

Wallace had served as secretary of agriculture under President Roosevelt and then as vice president. In 1944, Wallace had been replaced on the ticket by Truman, largely in response to conservative pressure, but he had stayed in the administration as secretary of commerce. After Roosevelt's death, Wallace became increasingly concerned about the direction of American foreign policy, and he was scheduled to deliver a major address on the topic at Madison Square Garden in New York City on September 12, 1946. Two days earlier, he had taken a draft of his speech to Truman for his approval. Wallace later said that he had sat in the Oval Office while Truman thumbed through the speech and gave his okay.

On the night of September 12, Truman was having dinner at Clifford's home when the telephone rang. It was John O'Sullivan, who was acting secretary of state while Byrnes was out of the country. The State Department had just seen a copy of the Wallace speech. O'Sullivan insisted that Truman halt Wallace's address. Truman talked it over with Clifford and Charlie Ross, his press secretary. They agreed that an attempt to muzzle Wallace would do more harm than the speech.

The following night, Wallace went before a packed house and publicly decried the emerging "get tough" policy in some quarters of the Truman administration. "The tougher we get, the tougher the Russians will get," he said.

The following morning, Truman and Clifford discovered how wrong they had been. As Clifford later recalled, "All hell broke loose." The press demanded to know if the speech represented a shift in U.S. policy. Secretary of State Byrnes demanded the same thing, and threatened to resign if it were true.

The White House moved quickly to try to control the damage. Clifford and Ross tried to protect Truman by leaking stories to the press that the president had been interrupted during his meeting with Wallace and had not actually read the speech. When that failed, they suggested that Truman tell the press that he had approved only Wallace's right to deliver the speech, not the content. Clifford later admitted that was "a clumsy lie."

After a damaging week, Truman met with Clifford and Ross. He was so distraught that he said he would rather be anything than president. "Please don't say that," pleaded Clifford. Truman said he had concluded that his only choice was to fire Wallace. Clifford agreed, believing that the secretary of commerce had become a political liability, particularly with the 1946 congressional elections approaching.

Into this highly charged atmosphere came a report destined to shift the president's thinking into an even tougher mode and weaken any opportunity for cooperation with the Soviets.

Earlier in 1946, a little-known U.S. diplomat stationed in Moscow named George F. Kennan had written an 8,000-word telegram laying out what he saw as the expansionist ambitions of the Soviet Union. Truman had been alarmed by the document, which would become famous in foreign policy circles as "the long telegram." However, the president was reluctant to abandon the war-era collaboration with the Soviets. In July, responding to Kennan's warning, Truman had asked Clifford to prepare a list of Soviet violations of international treaties.

Clifford was swamped. For assistance, he turned to George M. Elsey, a young lieutenant in naval intelligence who had spent much of the war assigned to the top-secret Map Room at the White House. When Clifford had moved up, Elsey had assumed his former position as White House naval aide.

The relationship between Clifford and Elsey was informal and discreet because Clifford said he did not want to be perceived as an empire builder. So, just as Clifford had worked quietly with Rosenman, Elsey had evolved into Clifford's assistant. The senior man had even asked that Elsey remain in his naval uniform so he would not appear beholden to him.

"Could you do a study of treaties that the Soviets have broken?" Clifford asked. "The president wants it."

"The president is missing the point," said Elsey. "The problem is that the relationship between the United States and the Soviets is broken. The president needs more than a study of treaties."

Clifford returned to Truman and got permission for a wider-ranging study, which would include interviewing key administration officials with an eye toward producing a comprehensive analysis of U.S.-Soviet relations. Clifford gave Elsey the green light and then accompanied Truman on a cruise to Bermuda aboard the *Williamsburg*.

By the time Clifford returned, the study was well under way. The special counsel conducted a couple of key interviews and gave his notes to Elsey. Over several weeks, Elsey produced a fifty-page report, which at one point he submitted to George Kennan for comments. In September, Elsey turned the completed document over to Clifford, who edited it and submitted it to Truman under his own signature and without mention of the roles played by Elsey and Kennan.

On the night of September 24, 1946, Truman read the study, entitled "American Relations with the Soviet Union," with shock and concern. While obviously influenced by Kennan's "long telegram," the report was even more blunt and alarming. The potential for real hostility between the two countries, the two presidential advisers had written, was increasing. Indeed, Clifford and Elsey were so frightened by the course of relations between the two emerging superpowers that they invoked the possibility of employing both germ warfare and nuclear weapons against the Soviets.

"Therefore, in order to maintain our strength at a level which will be effective in restraining the Soviet Union, the United States must be prepared to wage atomic and biological warfare," said the report. "Whether it would actually be in the country's interest to employ atomic and biological weapons against the Soviet Union in the event of hostilities is a question which would require careful consideration in the light of the circumstances prevailing at the time. . . . But the important point is that the United States must be prepared to wage atomic and biological warfare if necessary."

According to Walter Isaacson and Evan Thomas in *The Wise Men*, the tempering sentence about "circumstances prevailing at this time" was actually added by Kennan. Even with that caveat, the passage creates a disquieting portrait of Clifford's willingness to use the ultimate military power.

Another alarming element in the report contrasts with Clifford's life-long image as a dovish liberal and foreshadowed the anti-Communist paranoia fomented by Senator Joseph McCarthy that would soon grip the country. In the memo, the authors warned Truman that the Soviet military was trying to expand its influence and control in satellite countries as part of a worldwide expansion of Communism. "There is continuous Communist propaganda within the United States Army and from without to promote left-wing sentiment among soldiers. Strong and continuous efforts are being made to infiltrate the educational service of the Army and to color the material used in indoctrination and education of the troops," declared the report. "A definite campaign, in the making at present, is being sponsored by the Communist Party to indoctrinate soldiers to refuse to act in the event the United States Army is called on to suppress domestic disturbances, to take over essential industries, or to operate public utilities."

While acknowledging that the United States should strive for peace with the Soviet Union, the report rejected the notion of a negotiated coexistence and relied instead on the prescription that became the bitter medicine of the cold war: "The general pattern of the Soviet system is too firmly established to be altered suddenly by any individual — even Stalin. Conferences and negotiations may continue to attain individual objectives but we cannot talk the Soviets into changing the character of their philosophy and society. If they can be influenced in ways beneficial to our interests, it will be primarily by what we do rather than what we say, and it will not happen suddenly."

In preparation for defense of American interests, Clifford and Elsey provided the motivation that Truman would later employ in uniting the armed forces under a single Department of Defense. They advocated unifying the military and bringing civil policies into line with a tough stance toward the Soviet Union. Among the policies they urged Truman to adopt was universal military training, the draft.

In analyzing the report almost fifty years later, as the Soviet Union was dissolving before the eyes of the world, historian Garry Wills observed, "What Clifford was calling for was the remobilization of America on a wartime basis only a year after the Second World War had ended."

Small wonder that President Truman was shocked by the blunt assessment. In the early hours of the following morning, he telephoned Clifford at home.

"How many copies of that memo do you have?" Truman demanded.

"I think there are nine others," said Clifford.

"Get down here first thing. I want all those copies gathered together and I want them delivered to me. If this got out now, it'd blow the roof of the White House."

The memo's impact on Truman was great. Along with Kennan's famous "long memo," the Clifford-Elsey report helped coalesce an uncertain attitude toward the Soviets. It became part of the blueprint for Truman's postwar strategic planning. It played a role in creating the

North Atlantic Treaty Organization, defending South Korea, and reorganizing the military of the United States.

Elsey sensed that the memo also had a tremendous effect on Clifford. "This was the first time he had immersed himself in an international matter," said Elsey. "From that point on, he became a pretty key player."

Much as the steel crisis had catapulted Clifford into a more public position, the memo on Soviet relations was a rite of passage into the heart of foreign policy matters for someone who just a short time before had been a complete neophyte on such matters. The man whose highest ambition had been to become the best trial lawyer in the Midwest now found himself in the midst of momentous forces that were reshaping the world. Certainly Clifford was in good company when it came to viewing the Soviets as a threat; Acheson and his mandarin colleagues had done so, too. Clifford may have sometimes shared the lofty visions of his more experienced colleagues. At other times he seemed intent on nothing grander than accumulating power and enhancing his own reputation. In this way, Clifford represented a new breed of more ambitious power players who have since become the hallmark of Washington.

As for the memo itself, twenty years would pass before it became public. Despite Truman's order, Clifford had not given him all the copies. In 1966, he provided a copy to Arthur Krock, the *New York Times* columnist, who was a frequent recipient of Clifford leaks for more than two decades. Krock reprinted the entire memo in his memoirs two years later, crediting Clifford solely as "the aide who prepared the 1946 memorandum." Elsey has since been given credit by historians.

But it was a mark of Clifford's ambition that he tried to claim sole responsibility. Clifford later maintained that he had given the memo to Krock "on background" so that the columnist could refer to its contents. His actions, however, amounted to an attempt to enlarge his own role in the planning of the cold war by taking sole credit for the memo.

Just as he advocated a hard line with the Soviets, Clifford urged the president to get tough with organized labor when the crisis over the coal mines erupted again. Just two weeks before the November elections, John L. Lewis of the United Mine Workers repudiated the contract worked out the previous spring and threatened a new strike by the

400,000 mine workers. Lewis, the most powerful union leader in the country, anticipated that Truman's fears of voters going to the polls in the midst of a widespread strike would force him to reopen the earlier settlement. Steelman, who had urged a compromise the first time around, did so again. Clifford again urged the president to stand firm against "the Lord of Labor."

Days of debate ensued and the election came and went. Finally the dispute climaxed in the family quarters of the White House around midnight on November 16, a Saturday. In a session attended by Clifford, Steelman, Attorney General Tom Clark, Interior Secretary Julius Krug, and the president, Steelman argued in favor of minor concessions to avert a strike. Clark advised the president that Lewis had the legal authority to reopen the negotiations at will. But Clifford again advised Truman not to capitulate. "The President [will] have to take him on sooner or later, and the longer we put it off, the worse it [will] be," said the special counsel.

As he had in the last face-off with Steelman, Clifford carried the day. Truman agreed that the attorney general and the Justice Department should take action against Lewis and the union to stop a strike. On Monday, Justice Department lawyers went into federal court and obtained an order directing Lewis to call off the planned strike. Two days later, on November 20, the union boss ignored the order and called a nationwide strike.

In early December, with the nation running low on coal and winter approaching, the Justice Department returned to court and received an order citing Lewis and the union for contempt of court for violating the November ruling. A $3.5 million fine was imposed on the UMW and a $10,000 fine on Lewis himself.

At several points, Lewis tried to contact the president for a face-saving compromise. On Clifford's advice, Truman refused to take telephone calls from the union leader in November and early December. With the December 7 anniversary of Pearl Harbor approaching, Clifford returned to the theme that had worked in the railroad strike. He prepared a speech for Truman comparing the coal strike to the still-emotional disaster in the Pacific. The speech was to be delivered on Sunday, December 8, but it never was. The day before, Lewis called a press conference and announced that he was ending the strike and workers would return to their jobs under the old contract.

Truman's victory in the shootout with John L. Lewis was a seminal event. Roosevelt himself had never been able to defeat the union boss. And the showdown marked a sharp change in the relationship between Washington and the labor movement. Even before passage of the tough Taft-Hartley Act of 1947, which outlawed the closed shop and restricted union political activities, the hard line advocated by Clifford against Lewis marked the beginning of the emasculation of American labor.

It also marked a turning point for Clifford. Until that time, he had kept a fairly low profile in the White House. He had followed the advice he received from his predecessor, Judge Rosenman: the White House staff exists for the sole purpose of serving the president. Indeed, up until this time, Clifford's relations with the press had been confined to promoting his boss and the administration's policies through well-placed leaks to prominent journalists.

But his role in facing down big labor had brought Clifford to the attention of the press in a far more public fashion. Typical of the stories was a front-page article in the *New York Sun* on December 9. Beneath the headline "Truman's Young Counsel Hailed as Lewis's Nemesis," White House correspondent Edward Nellor began: "Clark McAdams Clifford, the 39-year-old special counsel to President Truman, emerges as a new national figure of importance today, credited in Washington with having won almost single-handed a public slugging match with John L. Lewis and his corps of lawyers. Lewis, without a doubt, quit cold in the face of granite-nerved White House strategy and called his miners back to the pits."

Clifford had gone from relative obscurity to the front page, where he would remain for the rest of his life. When asked by a reporter about Clifford's role at the White House in December, Charlie Ross joked, "All I do around here is answer questions about the great Clark Clifford."

There was some truth to the remark, as Eban Ayers, who was Ross's assistant, observed in his diary at the time: "Newspaper and magazine writers are beginning to devote attention to Clark Clifford. Suddenly, they discover someone that may have been performing similar work for months, and they immediately see him as the primary influence in all the decisions by the President."

Life magazine published a flattering profile of Clifford in June 1947, devoting several paragraphs to his good looks and impeccable tailoring. He also had, the magazine noted, a voice that resonated with authority.

The *Saturday Evening Post* found a Boy Scout quality in the president's counsel, observing, "He seems determined to keep his reputation as spotless as party politics permits while at the same time doing everything to embellish Truman's reputation." And syndicated columnists Robert Allen and William Shannon wrote: "Glamorous Clark Clifford is one of those people who is too good to be true. His face is too handsome, his blond hair too evenly waved, his smile too dazzling, his voice too resonant, his manner too patently sincere. Somewhere there must be a flaw, a glaring weakness, an idiosyncrasy. But so far Washington hasn't discovered it."

Clifford was too discreet to actively seek publicity. He gave no speeches and never went on radio or television while he worked in the White House. The shrewd and genial Clifford did, however, develop relationships with key reporters and use them to leak stories.

"You could always get to Clark Clifford and he would always tell you things," recalled Robert Donovan, who covered the White House for the influential *New York Herald-Tribune* and later wrote a highly regarded biography of Truman. "They were things that would build him up of course. He very smoothly used the press to build himself up."

Of course Clifford was not unique in courting the press. The grand waltz between the Washington press corps and the men who govern the country had been playing for many years. Few practitioners, however, had executed the steps as well as the lawyer from St. Louis.

This coziness with the press turned mildly embarrassing for Clifford in the spring of 1947. Every March, Washington's senior journalists put on a farcical theatrical review called the Gridiron Dinner. At the 1947 installment, a journalist portraying Clifford sat on stage with a dummy of Harry Truman in his lap. Sitting in the audience, Clifford cringed at the performance. Later, he apologized profusely to the president. Truman brushed off the incident, saying, "It's not your fault, Clark. They're just jumping over your back to get at me."

Clifford's rising prominence alienated some members of the White House staff. Particularly unhappy was John Steelman, the older, voluble economic adviser who had found himself offering the wrong advice for a second time in the coal crisis. Steelman, a former economics professor and labor expert, was actually closer to Truman than Clifford. He did not hide his displeasure with the president's counsel. To assuage Steelman and keep peace, Truman tried to compensate the older man by giving him a new title, "The Assistant to the President." However, Steelman got no new authority. The result was that he and Clifford remained roughly equal in terms of power, fostering an inevitable competition over who would have the most power inside the White House.

Over the next three and a half years, Steelman sought to diminish Clifford's influence with the president. George Elsey said that he never heard Clifford utter a word against Steelman, but the former professor criticized Clifford frequently and gossiped about him to the press. *Life,* for instance, disclosed that Clifford's "enemies" had been spreading the silly rumor that he had his hair curled. White House insiders were certain Steelman was the source.

As Elsey observed the rivalry, he thought that some of Steelman's animosity stemmed from his jealousy over the glamour and social standing of the Cliffords. Not all of Steelman's dislike was so superficial. He was more conservative than Clifford and, despite Clifford's opposition to the expansion of Communism and tough stance against organized labor, he found the White Houe lawyer too liberal for his tastes. In this view, he was joined by Truman's long-time friend John Snyder and other members of the Missouri gang who had been with the president for years.

Margaret Truman, the president's strong-willed daughter, shared some of the same concerns, as she confided at a dinner party one night when seated next to Stuart Symington. The following day, Symington called his old friend from St. Louis and said, "I think I ought to tell you Margaret really has her gun sights aimed at you. I got one hell of a speech last night about how since you came into her father's White House you've been getting all the good publicity."

Aware of the hostility from various quarters within the White House, Clifford countered by bringing what one observer described as "a bedside manner to the starkest political situations and . . . an attaché case full of tricks."

Among those tricks was vigorously guarding his personal relationship with Truman. He made a point of having lunch with the president two or three times a week at the mess in the White House basement, and he continued to organize and participate in the regular poker games. In addition, Clifford's long hours often made him the last to leave the White House, which gave him the chance to be the last to see Truman at the end of the day.

Clifford also remained protective of Truman. One night in the fall of 1946, the president's regular poker game was hosted by James Forrestal. The guests included many of the regulars, such as Averell Harriman, the U.S. ambassador to Moscow, Supreme Court Chief Justice Fred Vinson, and Clifford. Forrestal did not enjoy poker and was not very good at it, so he had a naval aide sit in for him much of the night. When the final tally was made, Forrestal's stand-in had won $300 and the president had lost $700. As Truman started to write a check to cover his loss, Clifford intervened. "No checks, Mr. President," he said. "I'll take care of this and you can take care of me tomorrow."

Clifford's influence with Truman was clearly rising, and the tenets of the new relationship with the Soviet Union that he had outlined in his 1946 memo got their first test early the following year. In February 1947, the British government announced that it was withdrawing military and financial aid from both Greece and Turkey. The decision brought a steady stream of warnings flowing into the White House from American diplomats and others that both countries could fall into Soviet hands unless the United States stepped in. General George Marshall, the Army chief of staff throughout World War II and a man lionized by Truman, had become secretary of state in January 1947. He made it plain to Truman that he had to act or lose Greece and Turkey to the Soviets.

Truman grappled with the matter throughout February. In early March, he went to Mexico for a four-day state visit. While he was there, the State Department received an urgent communiqué from the government of Greece. It said that Communist support for the insurgents in the civil war there had become a serious threat to national stability.

At a cabinet meeting on March 7, the day after Truman's return, Dean Acheson, the undersecretary of state, said the disintegration of Greece was only weeks away. Acheson advocated assistance to Greece, but he realized the gravity of such a step. The Greeks needed at least $250 million for the remainder of 1947, which would be only the beginning of American assistance to countries facing a Soviet threat. Truman decided that he would go before Congress and lay out the dangers and his proposals.

The State Department drafted the first copy of the speech and sent it over to the White House. Truman gave it to Clifford for revisions. Clifford decided to make the language stronger, stressing that American foreign policy would not stand for Soviet interference in the internal politics of other countries.

Marshall, who was in Paris when he received a copy of the new draft, thought Clifford had gone too far. There was too much "rhetoric" and too little recognition of the nuances of foreign policy. Most offensive to the secretary of state was Clifford's reference to "a worldwide trend away from free enterprise toward state-controlled economies," which disregarded the United Nations support of greater government economic controls. On Marshall's instructions and using his name, Acheson persuaded Clifford to withdraw the potentially offensive language and approve the speech in essentially its original form.

This was not Marshall's first confrontation with what he viewed as Clifford's lack of sophistication and disregard for the nuances of foreign policy. A few weeks earlier, preparations had been under way for one of Truman's addresses to Congress, and Marshall attended the final drafting session with the president and other cabinet members. Several times during the discussion, Marshall pulled a document from his pocket and read remarks that he thought should be included in the speech. Eventually Clifford interrupted and asked, "General, may I ask what is that document from which you are reading?" Marshall replied sharply, "It's a copy of the draft I sent you as my recommendation as to what the message should say."

These relatively minor disputes foreshadowed a far more explosive and monumental showdown between the war hero and the White House lawyer. But first, Clifford helped the president and secretary of state lay the foundation for the postwar era.

On March 12, 1947, Truman spoke for eighteen minutes before a joint session of Congress. Despite Marshall's tempering changes, it was a strong speech. The government of Greece was in great need of American assistance, Truman told his audience, and so was Turkey. American policy, he declared, must ensure that these and other nations be allowed to decide internal matters free of outside coercion.

"At the present moment in world history nearly every nation must choose between alternative ways of life," he told the hushed audience. "The choice is too often not a free one . . . I believe that it must be the policy of the United States to support free peoples who are resisting attempted subjugation by armed minorities or by outside pressure."

Warning that "resolute action" must be taken immediately, Truman asked for $400 million in aid for Greece and Turkey. "If we falter in our leadership," he said in conclusion, "we may endanger the peace of the world, and we shall surely endanger the welfare of this nation."

The Truman Doctrine had been launched and the American sphere of influence had been expanded dramatically. The House chamber broke into applause, and the cheers were echoed by the nation's press. The tone was set by the *New York Times*, which compared the speech to the Monroe Doctrine, the statement in 1823 by President James Monroe that warned European nations not to interfere in the affairs of the Americas. And *Newsweek* recognized that a turning point had been reached: "If words could shape the future of nations, these unquestionably would. They had clearly put America into power politics to stay."

Nine days later, Truman followed up his speech by issuing an executive order establishing an elaborate Federal Employees Loyalty and Security Program. The executive order had been drafted by J. Edgar Hoover, the red-baiting FBI director, and Attorney General Tom Clark.

Years later, Clifford said he did not believe there was a serious loyalty problem, despite the strong reference to the threat in his own 1946 report on U.S.-Soviet relations. Rather, he said, he thought the issue was being manufactured and Truman had been forced to respond to political pressure.

"We had a presidential campaign ahead of us and here was a great issue, a very damaging issue, so he [Truman] set up this whole kind of machinery," Clifford later recalled, adding that he regretted not making a strong effort to kill the loyalty program.

Not until safely after the miraculous 1948 election would Clifford write the following eloquent memo to Truman: "It is one thing for a nation to take basic counter-espionage and security measures necessary to protect its existence. That it must do. It is another thing to urge or tolerate heresy hunts at every stump and crossroads to smoke out and punish non-conformists of every shade and stripe of opinion different than that of the majority. I'm afraid we are moving increasingly in that direction."

Another legacy of the Truman administration was unveiled in that momentous spring of 1947. All across Europe that winter, the wreckage of the war still inflicted casualties. Nineteen thousand Berliners died of frostbite and hunger. Residents of the cities starved because bridges were unrepaired and railroads in shambles and food could not be transported from the farms. Europe, said Winston Churchill, is "a rubble heap, a charnel house, a breeding ground of pestilence and hate."

In a speech at Harvard University, Marshall outlined an ambitious program to provide massive economic aid to U.S. allies in Europe. The purpose, Marshall insisted, was to restore the health and economy there, not to fight the spread of Communism. Dean Acheson would later describe the proposal as "one of the greatest and most honorable adventures in history."

The details were worked out by Marshall, with the assistance of George Kennan and another senior State Department official, Chip Bohlen. But it was Clifford and Acheson who translated the proposal into legislation. The potential greatness of the program was evident to Clifford and he conveyed his sense of it to the president.

"This is going to be one of the great accomplishments of your administration," he told Truman. "Let's make sure that in some way it bears your name."

But the president, confronting the reality of a Republican-controlled Congress and his election campaign the next year, responded, "If anything goes up there with the Truman name on it, it'll quiver a couple of times and then turn on its belly and die."

The lesson was that there is no limit to what a man can accomplish if he doesn't care who gets the credit. It took another year, but eventually the Marshall Plan was adopted by Congress, signed into law by Truman, and millions of dollars began flowing to help Europe rebuild from the rubble of World War II.

Truman's wisdom in sharing credit was a lesson that Clifford apparently did not learn. Already he had claimed authorship of Elsey's memo on the Soviets. Soon he would make an ever bolder grab for glory, appropriating the work of another man to take credit for the century's greatest political upset.

Clifford believed that the creation of a modern national defense and security apparatus was integral to executing the Truman Doctrine and establishing the military structure needed for a strong response to the Soviet threat. Once again, Clifford's closeness to Truman brought him considerable influence.

The unification of the nation's armed forces had been a simmering controversy since Truman took office. At one point, the president remarked to Clifford that, had the armed forces fought as hard against Germany as they did against unification, the war would have ended sooner. Truman initially sought to combine the land, sea, and air forces. As the largest of the services, the army greeted the proposal warmly. That deepened suspicions in the navy and marine corps, both of which were concerned about being relegated to second-class status in a system dominated by the men in green.

Truman had first tried in late 1945 to create a single Department of National Defense, with a secretary overseeing branches for land, naval, and air forces. The revolt against the legislation was led by James Forrestal, the secretary of the navy, and his supporters in Congress.

Clifford had an ally in Stuart Symington, the assistant secretary for air, and his relationship with Forrestal remained good, too, despite their differences over the new department. However, Clifford was unable to overcome Forrestal's fears that the navy would become a stepchild to the army under the proposed arrangement.

The impasse dragged on until late 1946, when Truman demanded an agreement. However, the president's ability to force a plan through Congress over objections from Forrestal and his backers was highly doubtful. In November, the Republicans had won control of the 80th Congress.

In early 1947, a compromise was worked out between Forrestal and General Dwight D. Eisenhower of the army. There would be a secretary of national defense, but the departments of the army, navy, and air force would function independently and the head of each would have direct access to the president. This was an inherent flaw, but it was the best that the administration could achieve. The National Security Act of 1947 was passed in July.

In an inspired move, Truman foisted the job of running the new department on the man who had done the most to weaken his plan. In September, James V. Forrestal was sworn in as the first secretary of defense of the United States.

In the months that followed, Clifford regularly had lunch at the Pentagon with Forrestal, who had initially resisted taking the job. Six months into it, he confessed to Clifford that it was not working. He did not have the authority essential to managing all three branches of the service. It was the opening for which Clifford and Truman had been poised.

"Let me make an appointment for you to see the president," urged Clifford. "Let's do it today. Come over and see the president and tell him."

It took two years, but new legislation signed into law in 1949 provided the secretary of defense with more authority and became the blueprint for today's Department of Defense.

The glare of publicity surrounding the creation of the Department of Defense obscured a small section of the National Security Act of 1947, which also would have a far-reaching effect on American policy. The section created the nation's first formal, proactive intelligence operation. It was called the Central Intelligence Agency.

Truman had disbanded the Office of Strategic Services in 1945, largely because he did not like the man who had run its famed intelligence operations during the war, General William Donovan. The absence left a vacuum. There was no coordinated approach to intelligence gathering. The problem was remedied initially in January 1946 when the post of director of central intelligence was created to coordinate a Central Intelligence Group. The CIG in turn would correlate and evaluate intelligence from the various branches of government.

Clifford, who helped draft the executive order establishing the CIG, also persuaded Truman to give the first director's job to Admiral Sidney Souers, a friend of Clifford's from his St. Louis days. In midyear, Souers resigned and was succeeded as director of central intelligence by Lieutentant General Hoyt Vandenberg, a flamboyant World War II aviator.

Vandenberg immediately set about expanding his job by advocating the creation of the Central Intelligence Agency. As he envisioned the CIA, the organization would go far beyond coordinating intelligence from other sources. It would actively seek foreign intelligence and mount intelligence operations in other countries. Through Stuart Symington, Vandenberg arranged to meet with Clifford.

While the White House counsel had some reservations, Clifford agreed in principle with Vandenberg's view of the necessity of creating an intelligence organization commensurate with the new strategic role of the United States. As a result, he helped draft a section of the National Security Act that created the CIA.

Couched in the obfuscating language of the bureaucracy was Section

102. It created the statutory authority for the new agency to carry out covert actions. The era of American innocence was over, and the final capabilities for conducting the cold war were in place.

In three years at the White House, Clark Clifford had undergone an amazing transformation. From the giddy letter home to his mother about his first state dinner, he had matured quickly into a significant figure in the Truman White House. He had grasped the importance of establishing and nurturing relationships in Washington and of how to use them to accrue power. He largely remained in the background, allowing Truman to receive his due. And for the young lawyer, the best was yet to come.

6

A Dubious Authorship

A S SUMMER TURNED TO FALL in 1947, Clifford seemed to be living his father's axiom that a man who enjoys his work enjoys his life. One night over dinner, he described his transformation to David Lilienthal. A graduate of DePauw University in Indiana and Harvard Law School, Lilienthal had been one of the few members of the Roosevelt administration to stay on with Truman, and the president had recently nominated him as the first chairman of the Atomic Energy Commission. Clifford developed a true liking for his fellow Midwesterner and, over the next years, would unburden himself to Lilienthal. That night in 1947, Clifford explained that before coming to the White House, he had wanted only to make a lot of money, live in a big house, and have servants. Now, he confided, those goals seemed mundane compared with the satisfaction of public service.

While he no doubt loved his work, Clifford may have been putting on a bit of a bold face for Lilienthal. His salary of $12,000 a year was less than half what he had made in private practice. The profits from the sale of his house in St. Louis a year earlier had helped, but they were disappearing. There were still the loans from Alfred Lansing, but the prospect of living in a rented house and scraping by on limited income was not enticing. In a letter to another friend, Justice Douglas, Clifford wrote, half in jest, "The only regret about my personal condition is that I have never deserved more and got less in my life."

Clifford's success at the White House was remarkable because he went into his new role with so little preparation. He had no experience in foreign affairs until 1946, when he had received a crash course at an epic turning point in American relations with the Soviet Union. In the same way, Clifford had entered the White House as a political neophyte and learned on the job. His only political experience had been on the periphery of a handful of local races in Missouri. Nothing had prepared him for the pressures and stakes of the 1948 presidential campaign.

Clifford's debut in the role of political adviser was a dismal failure.

With a dramatist's instinct, he grasped that television, still in its infancy, was emerging as an important vehicle for communication. As such, it could be useful in the upcoming election. The Truman Doctrine and decisive action to avert a long coal strike had sent the president to new levels of popularity by the summer of 1947. Noting his 60 percent approval rating, *Time* suggested that the president had adopted a new formula: "Be natural." Television might be the means to sustain Truman's popularity by enabling him to reach the American public directly. If only a way could be discovered to make the president appear "natural" on camera.

Truman was anything but telegenic. He had not gone beyond high school, spoke with a flat, Midwestern accent, and depended on a typed speech. The result was a very wooden delivery. So one day, Clifford prepared several large placards on which he wrote a few lines of large print. He hoped that, instead of reading from a text on his desk and showing television viewers the top of his head, Truman would appear more at ease as he read the large cue cards while looking into the camera. The experiment was a flop. Truman was so nearsighted that he could barely see even the cards.

The 1948 presidential campaign came into sharp focus for Clifford on September 18, 1947, when he received a thirty-three-page, single-spaced memorandum written by James Rowe, a Washington lawyer. A former aide to Roosevelt, Rowe had left government in 1945, but he had not left politics. His law partner was Thomas "Tommy the Cork" Corcoran, another former New Dealer and a legendary wheeler-dealer in Washington political circles. Rowe himself had keen political instincts.

Truman's popularity was still high with the public. However, there were serious obstacles to victory in 1948. The Republicans controlled the Congress, and they were appealing to the nation's strong isolationist sentiment and insinuating that Truman's administration was riddled with Communists. Henry Wallace, the jilted former secretary of commerce, could siphon off key liberal votes from Truman if he ran as a third-party candidate, although conventional wisdom discounted the likelihood of his candidacy. After two decades in power, the Democratic national leadership was weak and uninspired. And Southern Democrats in Congress were bristling at Truman's efforts to strengthen civil rights programs.

Sooner than anyone else, Rowe foresaw the potential threats and developed a strategy to surmount them. After consulting with a number of labor leaders and others about the obstacles facing Truman, he wrote a detailed outline for a course of action for the upcoming election. It would prove remarkably prescient.

The Republican nominee, he predicted, would be Thomas Dewey, the New York governor defeated by Roosevelt in 1944. Rowe called Dewey "resourceful" and "highly dangerous," warning that this time around he would be harder to defeat. Contrary to popular opinion, Rowe said, Wallace would run as a third-party candidate and likely win important votes from the left.

The Republicans in Congress would do everything in their power to block Truman's programs, Rowe said, so the president must run against Congress and be willing to forgo any compromises with the Republicans. At the same time, he said, Truman had to maintain the party's alliance in the South and the West and strengthen his base among farmers. Also, Truman should work to retain support among Catholics, liberals, and northern blacks.

With the exception of Woodrow Wilson in 1916, no candidate had lost New York and won the presidency since 1836. Truman's prospects there looked dim; it was Dewey's home state and a stronghold for Wallace. Contrary to the popular view, Rowe believed that Truman could lose New York and other big states and still win the election. Nonetheless, New York's forty-seven electoral votes were a prize that Truman could not afford to turn his back on.

To have a chance there required a strong turnout among Jewish voters. The single most important issue in that community was the fate of Palestine. Yet there was no unanimity among American Jews about whether Palestine should be placed under a United Nations trusteeship or recognized as an independent Jewish homeland. Because of this division, Rowe saw no profit in pandering. Instead, he suggested that "there is likely to be greater gain if the Palestine problem is approached on the basis of reaching decisions founded upon intrinsic merit."

Rowe sent the memo to James Webb, the director of Truman's Bureau of the Budget, with a request that it be passed to the president. Webb had an aide deliver it to Clifford three doors from the Oval Office. The White House counsel was impressed by Rowe's political acumen. Further, the memo coincided with a recommendation from George

Elsey that the White House begin considering issues to build Truman's platform for 1948.

Instead of forwarding the memo to Truman, Clifford kept it in his desk. During the next several weeks, he discussed the concepts in the Rowe memo with Elsey and with some trusted political strategists. Among them were the other administration members who formed the "Monday Night Group," which drew its name from their regular Monday night meetings at the Wardman Park Hotel in Washington. These men were at the sub-cabinet level and they were more liberal than the conservatives who dominated the senior positions in the administration. Among the members of the Monday Night Group were Leon Keyserling, the intellectual vice chairman of the President's Council of Economic Advisers; David Morse, an assistant secretary of labor; and Charles Brannan, assistant secretary of agriculture. After enlisting their suggestions, Clifford reworked the memo in very minor ways, adding paragraphs on civil rights and foreign policy, tinkering with the language, and changing some of the dates.

On November 19, Clifford gave the president the revised version of Jim Rowe's memo. The chief difference, as would be noted years later by an archivist at the Truman Presidential Library, was that Clifford's version was forty-three pages; it had been double-spaced. At the bottom of the last page were the name Clark M. Clifford and the initials C.M.C. There was no reference to Jim Rowe.

The actual impact of the memo on the campaign is difficult to weigh. Truman, a product of the rough-and-tumble era of Missouri's Pendergast machine, was more experienced at politics than either Clifford or Rowe. Yet the document proved cannily accurate, both as a predictor of what would happen and as a strategy for countering Dewey and Wallace. A year later, after Truman's come-from-behind victory, it would be Clifford, not Rowe, who reaped the glory for having devised the remarkable political strategy. In a singular way, the memo became Clifford's political calling card. He became known as the man who engineered Truman's upset win over Dewey, and he would advise every Democratic president for the next three decades on that basis.

As Clifford explained it later, he believed that submitting the memo in Rowe's name would have undercut its powerful message. Because of Rowe's association with Corcoran, whom Truman roundly disliked, the president might not have paid as much attention, explained Clifford.

Webb later agreed, saying the memo would not have had the same effect without Clifford's name.

But there is evidence that Clifford's view is more convenient after-thought than truth. Less than a month after delivering the political memo to the Oval Office, Clifford had passed on to the president a three-page analysis of the Securities and Exchange Commission prepared by Rowe. In a letter thanking Rowe for the SEC memo, something he had never done with regard to the political analysis, Clifford wrote that he had passed on the second document to the president. There was no mention of the political memo. The SEC was clearly far less important than the 1948 campaign, so perhaps Clifford simply was not as concerned about watering down the impact of that second Rowe document.

The stronger evidence indicates that Clifford baldly claimed credit for an important strategy developed by someone else in order to improve his own standing with the president. After his supposed authorship of the memo had lifted him to new levels of fame, it was too late to con-fess. So even after the 1948 victory, when disclosure of the true author-ship of the memo would not have harmed anyone except Clark Clifford, he remained silent, just as he had done with the Elsey report on Soviet relations. As for Rowe, he was far too modest and mild-mannered to challenge Clifford publicly.

It was years before journalists learned that Jim Rowe had come up with the odds-defying strategy. As late as the 1980s, Clifford still claimed authorship. In one lengthy interview with a reporter in 1982, he took a tentative step toward the truth, describing the document as an "assem-bly job." However, when he listed the political strategists he had con-sulted in assembling the document, Rowe was not even mentioned. And by this time, Clifford had dined out on the memo for more than three decades. John Kennedy had sought Clifford's political advice in 1960 on the basis of his supposed role as architect of Truman's upset victory. Lyndon Johnson drew Clifford into his inner circle because he wanted to be closer to the man who had created the winner in '48.

Clifford's reluctance to give full credit to Rowe was even evident in 1991 when Clifford wrote his own memoir. By this time, Jim Rowe was dead and there had been mentions of Rowe's role in the press, but the complete story of the memo's origin remained hidden.

In May 1991, the *New Yorker* serialized Clifford's memoir before publication of the book. The magazine used a version of Clifford's manuscript for three lengthy installments. In discussing the 1948 memo, Clifford offered this explanation: "The memorandum was an extensive revision of a draft originally prepared by James Rowe, one of the most brilliant political thinkers of the New Deal era. Unfortunately, President Truman disliked Rowe, and had refused to read the draft, suggesting that it be given to me. Since President Truman would have refused my memorandum, too, if he had known that it was associated with Rowe, I did not refer to his role in its drafting." By the time *Counsel to the President* was published, Clifford had taken a step closer to the truth: he dropped the claim that he had extensively rewritten the memo. This meager approach came only after Rowe's son, James, complained through intermediaries that Clifford was still claiming credit for his father's work.

When Rowe wrote his memo in 1947, he touched on the complicated, emotionally charged issue of what to do about Palestine. Years later, Margaret Truman would say that Palestine was probably her father's most difficult dilemma. For Clifford, it was a matter of conscience and politics, climaxed by a battle of wills with one of the most powerful men in government, General George Marshall.

Since the end of the war, thousands of Jews had been pouring into Palestine, their biblical homeland, and demanding their own country. Fervent opposition by the Arabs led to bloodshed on both sides, with Arabs attacking Jewish settlers and Jewish terrorists blowing up the King David Hotel in Jerusalem in 1946.

The British had seized control of Palestine at the end of World War I and administered the territory under a League of Nations mandate. In the 1917 Balfour Declaration, the British government formally recognized that the land would someday become a permanent Jewish state. However, in 1939, the British backed away from the homeland pledge and promised to limit Jewish immigration to Palestine. After the end of World War II, the British faced a battered economy at home and rising violence against their soldiers in Palestine. So the Attlee government said in 1947 that it would withdraw from Palestine, as it was doing in Greece and Turkey. Control over the narrow strip of land would be turned over to the fledgling United Nations in 1948.

In the spring of 1947, the United Nations created a special committee to study Palestine. Four months later, the committee issued a majority report proposing the partition of Palestine into Arab and Jewish states, which would become independent at the end of two years.

Pressure on Truman to express public support for the partition proposal was enormous. Thousands of letters and postcards poured into the White House. The president was sympathetic to the plight of the Jews and their suffering at the hands of the Nazis in the Holocaust. As a senator, he had said on many occasions that he favored a Jewish homeland once the war ended. In the White House, he also felt tugged by the human side of the question.

The most ardent supporters of partition on the White House staff were Clifford and David Niles, who was Truman's assistant for minority affairs and himself a Jew. Clifford viewed the issue on many levels. On the surface, he simply wanted to carry out Truman's wishes, as a lawyer would advocate for a client. However, he also saw a Jewish state as a possible bulwark against Soviet expansion. Finally, with the election looming, he analyzed the dilemma from a political standpoint.

While only about four percent of the nation's voters were Jewish, Clifford was keenly aware of what Rowe had written about the significance of the Jewish bloc in New York and other states with large electoral votes. Moreover, prominent Jews traditionally had been strong financial backers of the Democratic Party. The money could be more important than the votes.

But the president's senior foreign policy advisers adamantly and unanimously opposed creating a separate Zionist state. Marshall, Acheson, Forrestal, and Lovett all argued that siding with the Zionists would antagonize the Arabs and threaten U.S. national security. To them, the prospect of cutting off the flow of Mideast oil and possibly pushing the Arab states into the Soviet fold outweighed humanitarian sentiment. Further, Loy Henderson, the State Department expert on the Middle East, wrote a report warning that American troops might be required to enforce any attempt to partition Palestine.

On a Saturday in early October, Judge Sam Rosenman returned to the White House from New York. Truman's first White House special counsel wanted to meet personally with his successor and urge Clifford to persuade Truman to support the recommendation for partition publically. At the staff meeting the following Monday, Clifford described the meeting to Truman and urged him to release a statement of support for the United Nations plan. Eben Ayers, the assistant White House press secretary, sat in on the meeting and noted in his diary later that "Clifford and Rosenman urged this for political reasons if no other."

After conferring with Marshall and others, Truman decided that the United States would support the partition recommendation. However, he stressed, American assistance would be economic, not military. The U.S. backing was announced on October 11 and, on November 30, the United Nations General Assembly adopted the resolution recommending partition.

Two days after the historic vote, Clifford described to Truman a conversation he had had with a prominent Jewish Democrat. In contrast to Roosevelt, who had promised recognition but never delivered, the Democrat said, American Jews were impressed by Truman's commitment. This view was bound to translate into financial support for the campaign, Clifford reported enthusiastically. Truman brushed off the value of such a promise, cautioning Clifford that the Jews would be asking what he had done for them lately when November 1948 rolled around. In fact, the issue was far from decided.

Early in 1948, Henry Wallace announced his third-party candidacy. His campaign was based on the twin planks of civil rights at home and improved relations with the Soviet Union abroad. He also began chipping away at Truman's Jewish support by strongly advocating a Jewish state. Adopting Rowe's strategy, Clifford advised Truman to isolate Wallace as a Communist sympathizer. The counsel then set about trying to recapture the Jewish vote — and money — by encouraging Truman to be more forceful in support of a Jewish homeland.

Truman was reluctant to speak out, partly because of the strong counterarguments posed by Marshall and others at the State Department. The Arab nations had vowed to wage war against any United Nations force sent to enforce partition, and the State Department feared the Arabs would turn to the Soviets for help. Clifford countered that the threat was minimal from what he referred to as "a few nomadic tribes."

On March 18, Truman met with Chaim Weizmann, an author of the Balfour Declaration. Weizmann, an aging and eloquent spokesman for a Jewish state, had come to Washington from London for the sole purpose of seeing Truman. At first, the president refused to meet with him. Eventually, though, he relented and he found Weizmann's arguments persuasive. Once again, he committed himself to the creation of a Jewish homeland.

No sooner had Weizmann left the White House than chaos erupted. The following day, Warren Austin, the U.S. ambassador to the United Nations, rose to address the Security Council. "My government," he declared, "believes that a temporary trusteeship of the United Nations should be established to maintain the peace and afford the Jews and Arabs of Palestine, who must live together, further opportunity to reach agreement regarding the future government of that country."

Austin's remarks followed a series of discussions between Truman and Marshall in February, while Truman was vacationing in Key West, Florida. But there had been a grave misunderstanding. Truman had agreed that the United States would support the weaker concept of a trusteeship only if a vote on partition failed.

The next morning, Clifford's home phone rang at 7:30. "Can you come down here right away?" asked the president. "There's a story in the papers on Palestine and I don't know what's happened." Clifford finished dressing and rushed out to pick up the newspaper. He was furious as he read that the United States had retreated on partition. "There was no God-damned reason on earth why they changed," he muttered. It crossed his mind that the State Department had timed the speech to embarrass Truman in the aftermath of the visit from Weizmann.

At the White House, Clifford found Truman as disturbed as he had ever seen him. "How could this have happened?" fumed the president. "I assured Chaim Weizmann that we would stick to it. He must think I'm a shitass."

Truman's popularity had dropped sharply since the previous year, partly because the Republicans had succeeded in portraying him as indecisive. This episode only buttressed the image. Clifford fingered the State Department, believing that those who opposed partition had tried to make an end run around the White House. Clifford felt strongly that the State Department would do anything to undermine the Jewish state. Some at Foggy Bottom, he surmised, were even anti-Semitic. Truman respected Marshall almost above all living Americans and refused to believe that the secretary of state had had anything to do with Austin's speech. He told Clifford to investigate.

Marshall and his undersecretary, Robert Lovett, were out of town, so Clifford sent for Dean Rusk, then director of U.N. Affairs at the State Department, and "Chip" Bohlen, another top official. The normally composed Clifford was in a fury. "He was looking for somebody's neck to be sliced," Rusk later recalled.

When Clifford demanded an explanation, Bohlen opened his briefcase and handed him the original telegram relaying the instructions to the United Nations delegation. In the upper right-hand corner, Marshall had noted "approved by the President." Clifford was not assuaged. Even if Truman had signed off on the concept of trusteeship, he insisted, the president had given explicit instructions that he wanted to see the text of any speech Austin proposed to make on partition.

Attempts to craft a statement clarifying the White House position and mitigating the political damage to Truman seemed fruitless. While acknowledging that the trustee concept had originated at the State Department, Marshall would go no further. There was a policy rift between State and the White House, and the controversy refused to die.

Truman called an Oval Office meeting to see what could be done to put his Palestine policy back on track. But the meeting degenerated into name-calling. Loy Henderson suggested that perhaps all that was needed was a publicity campaign for a new policy of trusteeship. Clifford thought the idea was ridiculous. Employing a courtroom technique reminiscent of his trial attorney days, he peppered the State Department official with questions that Henderson believed were "designed to humiliate me and break me down in the presence of the president." Fed up with the bickering and suffering political damage, Truman interceded and told Clifford to prepare a statement for the press that reconciled the trusteeship proposal with continued support for partition.

Through the night, Clifford, Niles, and another White House aide, Max Lowenthal, worked to craft a statement for Truman. "Our policy is to back up the United Nations in the trusteeship by every means necessary," Clifford wrote. "The purpose of trusteeship was the preservation of the peace in the aid of partition."

The following day, 172 reporters jammed the Oval Office and adjoining hallway. It was the largest press contingent in memory. They were not satisfied as they listened to Truman read Clifford's words. "Partition could not be carried out by peaceful means," he said, "and we could not impose this solution on the people of Palestine by use of American troops." Because large-scale fighting appeared inevitable if partition proceeded, Truman offered trusteeship to "fill the vacuum" soon to be left by the British withdrawal.

No one was happy. Jewish Americans flooded the White House with telegrams, letters, and telephone calls imploring Truman not to back down from his support for partition.

By early May, with British withdrawal set for midnight on May 14 and five Arab armies poised to invade, the question was stark: Would the United States recognize the Jewish government, giving it the chance to survive, or ignore it, possibly condemning the new nation? Clifford and Niles beseeched Truman to approve the new homeland in advance. Truman gave a partial green light, telling Clifford to draft a statement for him. When Truman saw the statement on May 12, his reaction was favorable. However, he wanted to talk with Marshall before releasing it. Later that day, Marshall, Lovett, and two assistants met with Truman, Clifford, and Niles.

The meeting had been called, Truman said, to consider recognition of a Jewish state. Opening the debate, Marshall argued forcefully that the attempt at partition had failed. The Jews and Arabs would be pushed over the brink into war by such a drastic action. Trusteeship, he argued, was necessary to buy time. Recognition of a Jewish state was out of the question. Lovett followed with similar logic, contending that the United States should wait until the situation in Palestine was clarified.

Truman had instructed Clifford to organize his presentation as if he were arguing before the Supreme Court. In a fifteen-minute talk, Clifford traced the history of the Balfour Declaration, the treatment of the Jews by the Nazis, and the commitments to a homeland made by Roosevelt and Truman. "It is unrealistic to pretend that there will be no Jewish state," Clifford said.

As Clifford spoke, he noticed Marshall's face growing redder and redder. Finally, the hero of World War II could stand it no longer. "Mr. President," he exploded, "this is not a matter to be determined on the basis of politics. Unless political questions were involved, Mr. Clifford would not even be at this conference. This is a serious matter of foreign policy determination and the question of politics and political opinion does not enter into it."

Clifford knew that public opinion did matter, and so did Jewish votes. No presidential policy could survive without political support, no matter how right it might be. But he had not made any mention of those considerations during his talk. "Mr. President," Clifford responded, "I am not conscious that I in any way touched on politics. I have tried to speak of the merits of the matter."

Marshall returned fire with a startling ultimatum. "In an effort to let you know how strongly I feel about this issue," he told Truman, "if you were to adopt the policy that is recommended by Clifford, I would be unable to vote for you in this fall's election. What is Clifford doing here anyway?"

The room fell silent. The man Truman depended on for his foreign policy, a man he respected enormously, had threatened to abandon him. Truman tried to play peacemaker, saying, "General, I see you feel very strongly about it. I understand that. There is great merit to your position." Marshall, Lovett, and their two assistants excused themselves and left.

Clifford sat in silence. Then, as he gathered his papers and rose to leave, he said to Truman, "Well, Mr. President, I didn't expect to win all my cases anyway. But it sure doesn't look like I won this one."

"Let's let the dust settle," said Truman, trying to buoy his lawyer's spirits. Still shocked by Marshall's outburst, the president added, "I've never seen the general like this before. I have never seen him evidence any emotion. He must feel terribly strongly about this."

Late that afternoon, the phone rang in Clifford's office. It was Lovett. "Clark," he said, "that was the worst meeting I ever attended. We can't just leave it that way." When Clifford said he agreed, Lovett asked him to stop by his house in the Kalorama district of the city on the way home that night.

As the two men sipped drinks in Lovett's elegant living room, Clifford was surprised by what he heard. Lovett, who revered Marshall, said he feared the secretary of state would resign, creating a diplomatic catastrophe. He told Clifford that it was the White House counsel's job to bring the president around to the old soldier's point of view. Clifford did not interrupt, and when Lovett finished, he said, "Bob, I listened to that, but that's not the problem. Marshall is a great man and I admire him enormously, but he isn't the president. It is the president who has made this decision. I know how the president feels about it. So, it is you, Bob, who has to talk. It is your job to bring Marshall around. The president is not going to budge."

Clifford had learned the art of a bluff from his nights at Truman's poker table. He overstated Truman's position, shifting the burden for compromise away from the White House and back to Marshall. Lovett and Clifford exchanged several telephone calls the following day, a Thursday. Neither side was moving. There seemed to be no middle ground, and matters were growing tense. British control of Palestine would expire at midnight on Friday, May 14 — six o'clock at night in Washington.

On Friday morning, Clifford met with Truman and they discussed a new idea. Perhaps they did not need Marshall's support. All they needed was for him not to oppose the president's position. Clifford broached the notion with Lovett that Marshall simply remain silent in public. Lovett called back. Clifford should meet him at the F Street Club for lunch. They might be able to work out a deal. So Clifford took a copy of the statement he had prepared for Truman and met with Lovett. It was four o'clock before Lovett called back. But the news was good. Marshall had agreed to remain silent. In the end, the stern general had done his duty, accepting Lovett's explanation that the decision ultimately belonged to the president.

That did not mean Marshall had to like it. Clifford asked if the secretary of state would call the president to deliver the decision. Stubborn to the end, Marshall refused. So it was left to Lovett to relay word to Truman that Marshall would go along quietly. As for Clifford, Marshall never spoke to him again.

At 5:40 p.m., Clifford telephoned Lovett and said that Truman would recognize the Jewish homeland at 6 p.m. By then, the White House had learned that the new state would be called Israel. Lovett protested that there was not enough time to notify the U.S. delegation at the United Nations. Clifford said he would check with the president. To have maximum impact, Clifford felt recognition had to be immediate. Again he bluffed his good friend, drumming his fingers on his desk for three minutes before calling Lovett back to say that Truman was adamant. Recognition of the new government would come at six o'clock.

As the British mandate expired, the provisional Zionist government declared the existence of Israel. Eleven minutes after six o'clock, Charlie Ross, the White House press secretary, read the statement written by Clark Clifford saying that the president of the United States "recognizes the provisional government as the de facto authority of the new State of Israel."

In Tel Aviv, the new nation's first prime minister, David Ben-Gurion, was awakened to hear the news of Truman's recognition. Throwing a coat over his pajamas, he was driven to a radio center, where he broadcast his thanks to the United Nations and Truman and pleaded for help to keep the new nation alive. As Ben-Gurion delivered his plea, Arab planes could be heard bombing Tel Aviv.

Truman's recognition established the American policy that ensured Israel's existence and established the course of United States relations with the region for the remainder of the century. This time, Clifford deserved an enormous amount of credit. He had argued staunchly, against one of the most respected men in the country, for a policy that he believed to be morally and politically right. He had helped to shape American policy on the Mideast in a way that is still felt today.

7

Spoils of Victory

O N JUNE 3, 1948, Harry Truman stepped from the concrete platform at Washington's Union Station and boarded the seventeen-
car presidential special. Photographers, newspapermen, and Truman's
campaign staff clambered aboard the train for a two-week journey
across the country. The trip was described officially as nonpolitical, since
Truman was to go to the University of California at Berkeley to receive
an honorary degree. But everyone knew it was a campaign trip, a pre-
lude to the Democratic convention in July and the general election in
November.

Truman trailed badly in the polls behind the certain Republican candidate, Governor Thomas Dewey of New York. Political pundits were
already predicting that Truman had no chance to win. This trip was vital
to show the American people that they had a strong, confident president. Clifford rode along to write the speeches for the president and
organize the stops.

During the two weeks, Truman delivered seventy-three speeches and
traveled more than nine thousand miles through eighteen states.
Crowds were surprisingly large. In Los Angeles, a million people lined
the route between the railroad station and the Ambassador Hotel. But
the trip was not flawless. Truman stumbled in Oregon. In response to a
question about relations with the Soviet Union, he said, "I like old Joe.
He's a decent fellow." Despite the gaffe, the trip succeeded in halting
Truman's slide in the polls and gave him firmer ground going into the
convention.

A week after his return, it was the Soviets who presented Truman
with an opportunity to demonstrate to the world — and the American
voter — that he was a leader willing to act decisively and dramatically.
On June 24, the Russians set up a blockade of all rail and highway traffic
in and out of Berlin. The city had enough food to last only a month, and
its coal supply would be exhausted in six weeks. Two and a half million
people faced the prospect of starvation.

Since the end of the war, the Soviets had shared control over the German city with the British, French, and Americans. Russian troops in Berlin far outnumbered those of the other three countries, and the blockade was a clear attempt to push the other countries out of the city. Rejecting suggestions that ranged from military retaliation to turning his back on Berlin and pulling out the three thousand American troops there, Truman responded that night by ordering that a cable be sent to the U.S. ambassador in London. It read simply, "We stay in Berlin."

Four days later, Truman ordered a full-scale airlift of food and other supplies to Berlin. To sustain the city, American planes flew in as much as 1,450 tons in a single day. At one point, 30,000 residents of Berlin cleared rubble from a deserted World War II airfield to prepare a landing site for the U.S. aircraft. The decision to remain in Berlin, and to feed its residents, was made by Truman alone. George Elsey later pointed out that the president had not consulted anyone on the White House staff. Political strategists were not asked for their opinions on how it would make him look. The State Department was not consulted on ramifications with other countries.

The Democratic convention opened in Philadelphia on July 11, two weeks after the Republicans had met there to nominate Dewey. It was sweltering in the Pennsylvania city, and the Democratic convention itself was a listless affair.

The only drama was picking a candidate for vice president. Before the convention, the president had decided on William O. Douglas. The young associate justice of the Supreme Court would offer a strong liberal balance to the ticket. Douglas had earlier turned down a request to become Truman's secretary of the interior, so this time the president dispatched Clifford to persuade the justice to join the ticket.

Douglas was one of the first people Clifford had come to know when he arrived in Washington to work temporarily for the navy in 1944. With an introduction provided by a mutual friend in St. Louis, the two bright young lawyers had hit it off immediately and the friendship had grown to the point where Clifford considered the justice one of his closest friends. He socialized with Douglas and occasionally invited him to participate in Truman's poker games. From their conversations, Clifford knew that Douglas harbored a deep ambition to be president himself, and the vice presidency would be a big step in that direction.

But Douglas was reluctant. Reflecting the wisdom of the day, Douglas confided in Clifford that he felt it was unlikely Truman would win. He feared that he would wind up out of government for good if he gave up his lifetime appointment on the Supreme Court to run. Clifford withheld the justice's political assessment, reporting back to Truman only that Douglas had reservations and had asked for three days to consider the offer. At Truman's suggestion, Clifford sought help from Eleanor Roosevelt, whose husband had appointed Douglas to the court. Mrs. Roosevelt also was unable to persuade Douglas to join the ticket. When the justice called Truman to tell him he was not taking the job, he kindly said it was because he preferred to remain on the Supreme Court, not because he felt Truman had almost no chance to win.

So, the president few expected to win went into the convention without even a choice for vice president.

The keynote speech in Philadelphia was delivered by Alben Barkley, a popular senator from Kentucky who had been majority leader of the Senate. He brought the convention to life with a rousing attack on the Republicans and a defense of Democratic policies that had kept the nation prosperous. As the audience stomped and cheered, Truman sat in Washington, watching on a new television set with a twelve-inch screen. He was impressed, too, although it occurred to him that Barkley might be campaigning for the top spot, rather than vice president. Most Democratic officials thought that speech had made Barkley the strongest candidate for the number two spot on the ticket, despite the fact that he was seventy-one years old. Truman agreed and, after a bit of sparring over the telephone the next day, Barkley accepted.

Following the convention, the president's staff began planning a final, cross-country blitz by train. Clifford focused on galvanizing organized labor, which he knew was a key component in the coalition the Democrats had to assemble to win. In mid-August, he met with James Carey, the secretary-treasurer of the CIO. Carey and the rest of organized labor had wavered over Truman's toughness with the unions. But he told Clifford the dismal labor record of the Republicans would keep organized labor in the Truman camp. Then Clifford brought John Gibson, assistant secretary of labor, to the White House to provide substance for Truman's Labor Day speech at Cadillac Square in Detroit.

Truman faced a difficult battle. The Democratic Party was divided among Truman, conservative Dixiecrats, and Wallace. In the crucial farm states, a Gallup Poll put Dewey ten points ahead of Truman. In the west, only Arizona, with four electoral votes, appeared to be a certainty for the Truman column. In early September, a Roper Poll showed Dewey leading Truman by thirteen percentage points. "My whole inclination is to predict the election of Thomas E. Dewey by a heavy margin and devote my time and efforts to other things," said Elmo Roper. Newspaper columnist Marquis Childs wrote that the obstacles to a Truman victory "loomed as large as the Rocky Mountains."

The gloomy atmosphere made it especially difficult for Truman to raise campaign money. In near-desperation, he invited about twenty Democratic contributors to the White House and asked them to finance the cross-country train trip.

"Boys, if I had the money to bet on this race, I would put it on myself," he told them. "If I could make a trip across the country and see the people face to face, I know I could win."

Truman wanted $100,000, but when the potential benefactors returned to Democratic National Committee headquarters, the atmosphere was gloomy. Into the vacuum stepped Abraham Feinberg, a wealthy clothing manufacturer from New York, who had ardently supported the creation of a Jewish homeland. Clifford had dealt with Feinberg on the homeland issue several times since becoming Truman's counsel. But Clifford was a neophyte at political fund-raising and the call inviting the wealthy businessman to the White House meeting had been made by the president himself.

"Look," Feinberg told the group after they returned to Democratic headquarters, "I have to get back to New York. I promise, in light of Mr. Truman's activities toward Israel, that I will come up with this money. If you give me two weeks, I can get the $100,000."

Feinberg demonstrated why he became a legendary Democratic fund-raiser. Within two days, he had collected the $100,000 and forwarded it to the Democratic committee. As a thank you, Truman later sent Feinberg one of the seven pens he had used to sign the official recognition of Israel.

With the money in place, Truman took a step that threw the campaign staff into turmoil. Wanting to muster all the talent he could, the president reached outside the White House and hired two young speechwriters, David Noyes and Albert Carr. They immediately began to tinker with the speeches that Clifford had been working on for the whistle-stop tour. Soon, competing drafts were in circulation.

Angered by what he viewed as outside interference and the challenge to his position in the Truman hierarchy, Clifford took his complaints directly to the president. It was a measure of Clifford's rise to power within the administration that he would argue with Truman over what the president thought was best for the campaign, but argue he did. In the midst of the political fight of his life, Truman had little patience for what he viewed simply as a staff dispute. "Clifford has gone prima donna on me," he wrote in his diary. Adding that he had to force Clifford to accept the new speechwriters, Truman wrote, "I get a headache over it. But a good night's sleep will cure it."

The campaign journey began on September 17, with the president's private car, the *Ferdinand Magellan*, at the end of a seventeen-car train. The pace in June had been hectic, but this trip was outright frenetic. The schedule called for covering 31,000 miles in thirty-three days, with the president delivering nearly one hundred and fifty addresses.

A speech at the national plowing contest in Dexter, Iowa, set the tone early. As the train rolled through Ohio, Clifford had been given a story from the Dayton newspaper describing how the Republican Congress had passed legislation extending the charter of the Commodity Credit Corporation, an arm of the Agriculture Department that financed overseas sales of American grain. However, the bill prohibited the agency from acquiring new storage bins for grain awaiting shipment. As the train passed the bountiful cornfields of the Midwest, it was obvious that the farmers had a lot to lose if they could not store their bumper crop.

Ken Hechler, a White House staff member, later described what happened: "Clifford received copies of the news story, and it wasn't too long before the whole episode was portrayed as a Republican plot dreamed up by the big grain dealers' lobby in conjunction with the GOP." In his speech in the heart of Iowa farm country, Truman referred to the GOP as "Gluttons of Privilege." The phrase was emblazoned across the front page of the *New York Times* the next day. Truman drove the message home the rest of the trip, attacking Congress and appealing to the farm vote.

In retrospect, Clifford did not want to take full credit for what some viewed as a melodramatic appeal, but he also did not want to disassociate himself from the plaudits earned in other quarters. So all he would say was that he had something to do with coining the phrase "Gluttons of Privilege." Whoever originated it, the phrase served the purpose of the Truman campaign.

Having overcome his initial dismay over the intrusion by Noyes and Carr, Clifford became the good soldier and immersed himself in the campaign. He was constantly writing and revising speeches, receiving intelligence from Elsey and others back at the White House, and working on the logistics for the next stop. When he was not planning the next day's message, he was jawboning with reporters in the press car.

Sometimes during the long trip, the tall, handsome Clifford would slip off the presidential train at a stop and mingle with the crowd. If no one was shouting the campaign rallying cry, all of a sudden Clifford's deep voice would boom out, "Give 'em hell, Harry."

On October 1, two weeks into the trip, the stage was set for Truman to deliver what the staff billed as a major foreign policy address in Oklahoma City. The speech was to be carried live on a radio network, but on September 28 the network demanded that the campaign pay the $60,000 advertising fee in advance because of rumors about Truman's dwindling finances.

The money from Feinberg and his contributors was almost all gone, so Truman and the Democratic National Committee began a desperate search for funds. After rejections from a number of party patrons, they returned to Feinberg. Once again, the New York clothier promised to tap his list of friends to keep Truman going. The Jewish vote had not yet been counted, but Jewish money played a major role. Truman was able to deliver a critical speech countering the rising cry from the Republicans that his administration was filled with Communists. The charges, he said, were a "smoke screen" to hide the failure of the Republican-controlled Congress to deal with real problems, such as housing and price controls. The speech kept Truman's head above water as Dewey threatened to wash him away.

Despite what the campaign believed was a very successful trip, few outsiders expected Harry Truman to retain the presidency. In mid-October, *Newsweek* took a poll of fifty political writers about the outcome of the election. All fifty predicted that Dewey would win.

Worried that it might upset Truman, Clifford tried to hide the magazine from him. But when the president discovered it, he was undisturbed. "I know every one of these fifty fellows," he assured Clifford. "There isn't one of them has enough sense to pound sand in a rat hole."

A few days before the election, Clifford left the president's side for the first time in months. Truman headed home to Independence, Missouri, to vote, and Clifford flew to St. Louis. Despite living in Washington, he was still registered to vote in his hometown.

After voting and visiting his mother briefly on November 2, election day, Clifford arrived back in Washington, exhausted and worried. Momentum had swung toward Truman in the last weeks of the campaign, he felt, but he seemed to be in a lonely minority. His mood did not brighten when Robert Lovett telephoned. The undersecretary of state stressed the need for an orderly transition to the Dewey administration to prevent the Soviets from taking advantage of a "spectacle of terrible uncertainty" after the election.

That night, Clifford had a rare dinner at home with his wife and three children. The returns trickled in slowly. Leaving the girls at home, Clifford and Marny went to the home of a neighbor to watch the first-ever television coverage of a presidential election. At five o'clock in the morning, they went home and to bed, the outcome still uncertain.

Four hours later, the telephone rang. President Truman was calling from Independence. Returns just in from Ohio and Illinois put both states in his column and California appeared to have gone for Truman. He had won. Despite the Wallace movement, which had siphoned off enough votes to cost Truman New York and Michigan, and Dixiecrat victories in four Southern states, the president had beaten Dewey in an extraordinary triumph.

As Clifford put the phone down, he was ecstatic. Truman had pulled off the political upset of the century, and Clark Clifford had been at his side every step of the way. Yet only a few minutes passed before he felt a physical and emotional weariness that seemed to go right to his bones. With barely enough time to catch his breath, he would be returning to the unrelenting work of the White House.

To savor the victory, Truman and his campaign advisers flew to Key West for a much-needed rest. Clifford, who had been running on adrenalin for weeks, abandoned his double-breasted suits for khaki shorts. He wandered barefoot, grew a blond stubble on his face, and soaked up the sunshine. In a letter to Jacob Lashly, Clifford's former law partner, the president wrote, "You'll have to help me keep Clark Clifford from floating away. He's far more elated than I am." Naturally, evenings in Key West were devoted to serious poker playing.

The election made Clifford a genuine celebrity. Billed as the mastermind of the upset victory, he received fan mail from across the country. Clifford certainly deserved credit for his role in the campaign. He had been a loyal soldier, sticking with Truman when others had their doubts and working long hours on speeches and strategy. That some of the acclaim actually belonged to James Rowe was known to only a handful of people.

The excitement of the election faded with Clifford's suntan when he returned to the White House in early December and found himself immersed in internecine staff feuding. Too many people in the White House, buoyed by the certainty of four more years of a Democratic administration, seemed to him to be interested only in self-promotion. The idea that some might have seen him as one of those interested in promoting himself was not the sort of thought that would occur to Clifford.

A source of constant tension for Clifford was Harry Vaughn, the president's friend and military aide. Observing what he called "terrific jealousy" on the staff, Noyes, who had stayed on after the campaign, said flatly, "Vaughn hates Clark Clifford." It did not stop there for the hero of the election. Clifford continued to cross swords with John Steelman, his conservative nemesis; and Matt Connelly, the president's appointments secretary, whispered to the press that Clifford was too ambitious.

Robert Donovan, a Truman biographer who covered the White House in the forties and fifties for the *New York Herald-Tribune*, came to regard Clifford as an important figure in the White House, but one whose influence never reached the levels described by a fawning press. "Truman was a marvelous politician in his own right and he would have known everything Clark Clifford would have known and more," said Donovan. "Clifford was in no way a big mover. He was not Harry Truman's type. There was no pretense about Truman. Clifford had studied drama. He was on stage all the time. Appearances were much with Clark. But I would never deny that he was very shrewd."

★   ★   ★

Since Clifford had helped with his appointment as chairman of the Atomic Energy Commission, David Lilienthal had become a confidant for the White House counsel. At a long dinner on December 10, Clifford poured out his disillusionment. Despite the rest in Florida and the thrill of the victory, he told Lilienthal that he was emotionally and psychologically worn out. He was sick of the petty infighting at the White House. The grand vision of public service that Clifford had described to Lilienthal just a year before during a similar dinner had faded. "Clark seemed tired and very thoughtful. He spoke in a worried tone — quite unusual for him," Lilienthal recorded in his journal.

For the first time in front of Lilienthal, Clifford talked of leaving government. Along with a break from the pressure of the White House, he said he needed to earn more money. His daughters were growing older. The family needed a larger, nicer house. And Clifford, approaching his forty-second birthday, was entering what should have been the prime earning period of his life. He expressed ambivalence about returning to his former life in St. Louis, but he did not come right out and say that he wanted to go into practice in Washington.

Lilienthal later recalled, "I knew what he had in mind: He wanted me to comment on whether it would be proper for him to practice law in Washington. I said of course he shouldn't go to St. Louis, that the fact that others had been greedy and not too principled in how they practiced law didn't mean that he needed to be, nor would he."

This was the confirmation for which Clifford had been fishing. He was still a little unsure of himself and his place in the Washington establishment, but he knew this was the perfect time to leap into private practice, with his role in the campaign still fresh in the minds of grateful Democrats and prospective clients.

Truman would not be told for several weeks, but Clifford began to plan for his departure. He asked Dean Acheson to put him up for membership at the Metropolitan Club, Washington's oldest and most venerable men's club, with a membership roster that had included such names as Elihu Root, Robert Todd Lincoln, and six presidents — Ulysses S. Grant, William Howard Taft, Warren G. Harding, Herbert Hoover, Theodore Roosevelt, and Franklin D. Roosevelt. Stuart Symington and George Smathers, a Democratic senator from Florida and frequent golfing partner, helped Clifford join the exclusive Burning Tree Country Club, where the men who ran Washington got together for golf and dealmaking.

Most of his time, however, was still spent on White House business. Since 1946, Clifford had helped Truman prepare the two key presidential speeches each year, the State of the Union address and the annual budget report. But in 1949, another important message was added to the list of his chores — the president's inauguration speech.

In early January, the speechwriting team was still having a difficult time putting together an address that did not have the ring of recycled campaign promises. Clifford understood that Truman needed something fresh and provocative. As Clifford put it years later, "Most of his program was old hat . . . in a public relations sense." Clifford and Truman agreed that the speech should concentrate on foreign policy so the president could make the transition back to statesman from politician.

About this time, George Elsey passed on to Clifford a memorandum he had received months before from a mid-level State Department Latin America expert named Louis Hardy. The memo described a modest technical assistance program under way in Latin America and suggested that it be applied worldwide. The concept struck Clifford as a good one, something that could be massaged into the inaugural speech. "Fine, put it in and we'll work out the details later," Truman told him when Clifford outlined the program.

These were the days before the professional politicians and the spin doctors who turned presidential politics into a surreal profession on behalf of men like Ronald Reagan and Bill Clinton. In many ways, Clifford was the godfather of the current breed of campaign gurus. Unencumbered by a strong ideology and possessing a true gift for drama and eloquence, he became the master of what would play to the audience. Expanding the modest Latin assistance program, he decided, offered a perfect means for attracting attention in the president's inaugural speech.

The responsibility for fleshing out the concept was left to Elsey. Summoning information and ideas from various departments and agencies, the loyal staff man wrote seventeen drafts of the inaugural speech for Truman from his office in the East Wing of the White House. As the speech changed and grew, the new assistance program became a crucial leg of a four-pronged policy proposal to be offered by Truman. Thus, it became known as Point Four. After Elsey submitted his final version to Clifford, the White House counsel added his own flourishes and passed it on to the president.

By that last draft, the fourth point had been pumped into a major foreign policy initiative: the United States would provide technical assistance to help its allies build strong economies. However, pragmatic officials at the State Department were reluctant to include such an ambitious program in the speech without working out the details in advance. Paul Nitze at State, who had worked on the reconstruction of Europe, liked the idea but feared it might raise expectations too soon. Years later, he said he considered Point Four "a publicity and propaganda effort."

Nitze and his State Department colleague Chip Bohlen advised holding up the plan for further study. Clifford objected, arguing that Nitze and Bohlen were behaving like bureaucrats and threatening to "bury it through inaction." In the end, because Clifford had ultimate control of the speech and Truman liked the idea and trusted his lawyer's judgment, Point Four stayed in.

On January 20, under a brilliant blue winter sky, Truman delivered his inaugural address to an estimated one million people who had gathered on the grounds of the Capitol Building. Confidently, he laid out a global view built on four cornerstones: the United Nations, the Marshall Plan, the North Atlantic Alliance (a forerunner of NATO), and his bold new plan for technical assistance.

Reaction to the speech was positive, especially to Point Four. The only problem was, when people wanted the details, there were few to provide. Gradually, the State Department and the Agriculture Department started a program that, Nitze said, accomplished little. However, technical assistance eventually became an integral part of American foreign policy, and Point Four was a forerunner of the successful Agency for International Development. Clifford's flair for the dramatic actually turned into a worthy American aid program.

In April, Truman assigned Clifford to head off a showdown with a freshman Democrat in the Senate by the name of Robert Kerr. A wealthy oilman, chairman of Kerr-McGee Oil Industries, and former governor of Oklahoma, Kerr had been elected the previous November and was just learning to play power politics in Washington. A fast learner, he soon emerged as one of the most powerful men in the Senate, dubbed its uncrowned king by many. Kerr also would become enormously important to Clifford.

Kerr had come to Truman's attention when he tried to force the president to withdraw the nomination of Leland Olds to the Federal Power Commission, which regulated the natural gas industry, a major Oklahoma business. Olds favored stricter regulation and, when Truman refused to pull the nomination, Kerr introduced legislation to reduce the ability of the commission to regulate the gas industry. Truman refused to budge, threatening to veto the bill and sticking with Olds.

In an attempt to break the impasse, Clifford held several meetings with Kerr and others, including another freshman Democrat in the Senate, former Congressman Lyndon Baines Johnson of Texas. At one point, Clifford suggested a compromise: Truman would consider signing the legislation if the Olds nomination were approved. But there was no deal. Kerr and his oil-state colleagues from the Democratic side of the aisle joined with Republicans to defeat Olds, and Truman, as promised, vetoed the bill. Clifford, however, had made a lasting impression on the ambitious new senator from Oklahoma, and Kerr was destined to play a central role in Clifford's life before long.

Early in the summer of 1949, another kind of problem required Clifford's intervention. Washington in those days was still very much a Southern city. Jim Crow segregation reigned, and the nation's leaders appeared to be unwilling to change the situation in their own city. In the summer of 1949, liberals and blacks were up in arms over the refusal to integrate the public swimming pools in Washington. The Department of the Interior, which ran the pools, decided to integrate one of the all-white pools. The result was a melee in which two hundred whites battled two hundred blacks and whites from the remnants of Henry Wallace's Progressive Party.

The *Washington Post* assigned the story to a bright young reporter named Benjamin Bradlee. While tame by latter-day standards, the melee was a brutal confrontation between blacks and whites, with mounted officers from the U.S. Park Police vainly struggling to maintain order. Bradlee was exhilarated, rushing back to the newsroom with a colleague, Jack London, to bang out a detailed account of the riot on deadline.

Excited at the prospect of a front-page story, Bradlee stayed in the newsroom until the newspapers came off the presses. His story was not on page one. It was nowhere in the front section of the paper. Finally, buried deep in the second section, he found three paragraphs that downplayed what had occurred, even substituting "incident" for "riot."

Bradlee stormed around the newsroom, filled with indignation and shouting about betrayal. "This great fucking liberal newspaper can't even say what happened," shouted Bradlee.

Suddenly the young reporter felt a tap on his shoulder. He turned around and found himself face-to-face with Philip Graham, the publisher.

"That's enough, buster," demanded Graham, who was wearing a tuxedo. "Come with me."

Bradlee followed him to the executive offices, giving Graham the full, uncensored account of what he had seen at the pool. Inside Graham's office, Bradlee found three other men, all in tuxedos. They were Julius Krug, the secretary of the interior; his deputy, Oscar Chapman; and Clark Clifford. Krug and Chapman had jurisdiction over the pools and, as even the cub reporter knew that night, Clifford could speak for the man who sat in the Oval Office.

"Tell them what you just told me," said Graham.

The other men did not say much. They just listened. After Bradlee recounted the riot, Graham dismissed him. Later, the young reporter learned that Graham had made a deal. The publisher and Clifford were already good friends who saw each other socially and who respected their mutual access to power. The *Post* dropped the story, and Clifford and Krug saw to it that the pools were desegregated. Ben Bradlee, who went on to become the most renowned editor in Washington history, had learned a lesson in the quiet, backroom workings of Washington.

By the summer of '49, Clifford had decided to tell Truman he would be leaving. The timing still seemed excellent, at least from Clifford's vantage point. His reputation had actually risen since the hoopla after the 1948 election. He had been on the cover of *Time* the previous year. Now, in August 1949, he was the subject of a flattering cover story in *Newsweek*, which described him as the president's most creative and influential adviser. In addition, Clifford needed the money he could earn in private practice more than ever.

Along with his debt to Alfred Lansing, which exceeded $30,000, he had borrowed about $20,000 from George Allen, a poker-playing friend of the president's who was involved with several corporations and was the secretary of the Democratic National Committee. Clifford had justified the Lansing loans to himself by saying that Lansing's business interests did not intersect with the federal government. But it should have been a more troubling matter when it came to George Allen, whose varied businesses often came in contact with the federal government. Many of the large corporations Allen represented or where he served on boards were either regulated by the government or did business with the government. Nonetheless, Clifford had borrowed a substantial amount from Allen, too.

After four years in the White House, Clifford's combined debts were more than $50,000, which far exceeded the salary he had drawn from the navy and then as special counsel for the same period. The borrowing was a highly unusual practice, one that would certainly have provoked protests had it been widely known at the time. But there was no requirement that senior federal employees disclose their financial assets and liabilities, so there was no one to ask questions about Clifford's relationship with Allen or Lansing.

For the president, Clifford cast his decision to resign in economic terms, but Truman was spared any information about the loans. Instead, Clifford explained that the money from the sale of his house in St. Louis had run out, his daughters were growing older and approaching college age, and his salary was no longer enough to provide a comfortable life for his family.

"I hate to have you go," Truman said. "We've worked together so well, but I understand it well. You pick the time." Then, the president quickly added, "I'll depend on you to get the early-year messages out, so I think you'd better stay through the first of the year."

The next step was deciding what to do when he left. For a man of Clifford's standing, the opportunities seemed endless. Truman had hinted that he might appoint him to the Supreme Court, but justices did not make much money. His former partners in St. Louis assumed that Clifford would rejoin the firm. Dean Acheson had left the State Department and returned to his former Washington law firm, the prestigious Covington and Burling; he proffered an invitation, too. Symington and other St. Louis friends tried to entice him back to Missouri to pursue a political career, perhaps a run for the United States Senate. But Clifford had his own ideas.

Clifford had not come to Washington as an idealist. He was a practical man, and it was that talent for seeing a situation logically and clearly that had enabled him to help the president. The same pragmatism would keep him in Washington.

Elsey, after working closely with Clifford for three years, never expected him to go home again. "He recognized that a return to St. Louis would be pretty dull after the experience he had had in Washington," Elsey said later. "He was a man who could see long term and he knew the kind of law he could practice in Washington would go far beyond the law he would return to in St. Louis. Clifford recognized the sea change had shifted the center of gravity in the country to Washington and he would stay on to reap the benefits."

Marny Clifford had come to love much about Washington. She enjoyed the beauty of the city, particularly in the spring when the cherry blossoms lined the Potomac Basin around the Jefferson Memorial. And she and the girls had developed strong friendships.

"We had come under the best auspices, working for Harry Truman, and I loved Washington in the beginning," she remembered later, after events had poisoned much of the city for her. "It was a benign city. It was nice and old and the people were very nice."

What she did not like was the way men dominated the city. She used to tell her husband, "Washington is for men. Men make all the decisions and women just kind of tag along behind." Once she told him that if she were to write a book about the city, she would call it *The Invisible Wives of Washington*. It was a view that was hard to dispute in those days. While Roosevelt had appointed a woman, Frances Perkins, as secretary of labor, there were no women in the Truman cabinet. There were really none in responsible positions of the government. And government was what Washington was about.

But Marny had made her peace with the city and with the demands of her husband's career. And she would not dream of interfering with the decision on where he was to renew his law practice.

"I never said much about anything related to his job," she said. "I think a decision like that is Clark's, not mine. I wanted to stay because my children's friends were here and so were mine. They had made new friends and it seemed to me a pretty good idea that we stay. But the decison was his."

In its March 1948 cover story, *Time* had portrayed Clifford as a "model father" and "the kind of husband women wish their husbands would try to be." In the style of the times, he was probably as good a model as any. His wife supervised the upbringing of the children. She was a strict disciplinarian, who often spanked her lively daughters. Clifford backed her up when things got out of hand, but otherwise he concentrated on his work.

The office was where he defined himself. In some ways, his commitment to getting ahead reflected the times, too. The years immediately after World War II offered great promise for the nation, and Clifford was one of the many men who seized that opportunity. But, as he always had, Clifford seemed to go further, devoting himself completely to his career and leaving the raising of his daughters to the patient and uncomplaining Marny.

Clifford was rarely home for meals with his family. He left early in the morning and returned home late at night. His wife had a special warming oven installed in the kitchen of their house so his dinner would stay heated. Saturdays were regular workdays at the White House. Although the Cliffords were members of All Saints Episcopal Church in Chevy Chase, Maryland, and regular donors to the church coffers, they were not regular churchgoers. On Sundays, after spending the morning on the golf course at Burning Tree with Symington or George Smathers, Clifford often returned to work.

While Marny Clifford put up a bold front for the sake of publicity, in private she told stories about the rare occasions when she and her husband ate dinner together. Usually, she would say, they took their meal in front of the television and Clifford was so worn out that he invariably fell asleep in his favorite wingback chair. Sometimes his absence wore on her, but she rarely complained.

Too, Marny had come to discover that her husband depended on her in a strange way. Late at night, he would discuss his work with her. Not so much the issues as the personalities, for he found her to have an unerring sense of people. Clifford's natural inclination was to trust the people he came in contact with, which his wife saw as a potentially dangerous byproduct of his Midwestern upbringing.

"I come from a long line of New Englanders, and we are pretty good at spotting phonies," she said later. "Clark always depended on me to provide him with good advice when it came to people."

For the girls, Clifford was a figure as much of awe as of warmth. They knew that he was at the center of important events and that his position meant important and interesting people swept through their lives regularly. There was pride, but little presence.

"I was always sure of his love and concern for us, but it was over a distance," recalled Joyce, the middle daughter, who would go on to become a successful clinical psychologist. "He was the worldly figure who stood alone in the family. We girls and Mother had a different role. He also was on track all the time. Up in the morning, dressed, ready. His life was orderly, planned, the result of enormous discipline. Everything got done that he said would get done."

But his absence took a toll. At one point during Truman's 1948 campaign, Joyce told her mother that she was going to write a book.

"That's a fine ambition," said Marny Clifford. "What are you going to call it?"

" 'Life Without Father,' " replied the fifteen-year-old with a sigh.

The demands of this orderly, disciplined life took a physical toll on Clifford, too. For the first time in his life, he developed an ulcer in 1948. Immediately, he acted to guard his health, forgoing alcohol and coffee for a time and instituting a strict diet. He kept promising to take time off, but one crisis after another interrupted him. In nearly five years at the White House, he had never taken a vacation except for occasional one-week golf outings to Florida with other powerful men and the post-election trip to Key West.

When he did find time to be with his daughters, Clifford could be loving and funny. In each of them, he found something different and appealing. Clifford was fond of saying that Gery was "the prettiest child I ever saw." As a young girl, she was bright and funny, with an excellent singing voice. She grew into an accomplished singer and a stunningly attractive, tall young woman. Joyce, who in later years would be closest to her father, was the brainy child, the one who loved to listen to his pronouncements on foreign policy and domestic economics. In Randall, the youngest, Clifford saw signs of his own youthful athleticism. She was a terrific tennis and field hockey player. "She moved a great deal like Joe DiMaggio when he was in the outfield," Clifford later recalled.

More often, however, Clifford was preoccupied, a distant father with the problems of the country on his mind. Later, he would voice regrets about the time he lost with his children. And the eldest daughter, Margery, would grow estranged from her father and the rest of her family.

Despite the demands of her husband's job, Marny accepted his decision that the family should remain in Washington. She knew that the chances he would mellow back in St. Louis were no better than here, and the economic prospects were better in Washington. The girls were in school, happy and seemingly unaffected by their father's growing fame. The pattern of their lives was established. So, as Clifford said later, Marny "adjusted herself to it," constructing a life for herself and the children that was, in many ways, separate from that of her husband.

Clark Clifford never acted on impulse. As he did in the law and the White House, he weighed each option carefully, listing for himself its pros and cons, plotting his strategy as if he were preparing a case for the jury. A political career held little interest. He had already wielded more power than all but the most elite politicians. Covington and Burling held little appeal, since his experience with the impersonal nature of a big firm in St. Louis had left unpleasant memories. As for his hometown itself, Clifford never seriously considered going back to St. Louis. He wanted independence, both of a financial and professional nature, and the prospects for that appeared to be best in Washington.

Remaining in the nation's capital, however, meant breaking the news to Jacob Lashly, the man Clifford had idolized as a law student and who had given him his big break in the law. When Clifford told him that he would be leaving the White House, Lashly had come to Washington to persuade him to return to the firm.

"Our firm has been doing well, but it could use some additional impetus," Lashly told his former partner. "You have become really quite well known. If you came back to St. Louis now, the excellent reputation you have in government would do a great deal for the firm."

Then came the closing argument. Lashly said he was getting older. Retirement was not too far away. The firm, he told Clifford, would someday belong to him.

As he listened to the prospect of controlling the firm where he had started as an unpaid lawyer, the truth was clear to Clifford. "Washington is the big league," he thought. "St. Louis is a minor league player." He told Lashly that he thought he should remain in Washington, for the sake of his family and his career. There was no need to speak the words, but Clifford knew he was ready for the big leagues.

Once he had made the decision, Clifford contacted Edward Miller, a senior attorney in the antitrust division at the Justice Department. Miller was from St. Louis, where he and Clifford had been acquaintances. By coincidence, the two men had lived for a time in the same Connecticut Avenue apartment building in Washington. Miller, too, was ready to leave government, so he readily agreed when Clifford proposed that they start their own firm. Miller offered three important attributes — he knew how the Justice Department worked from the inside, he had the type of trial experience that big businesses needed, and he would not upstage Clifford. The latter was an essential element in the partnership. From the outset, Miller would be the technician and Clifford the acknowledged senior partner, the star who would attract most of the clients and command the firm. It was a position to which Clifford felt entitled, given his prominence and the experience he had gained at the White House. After all, few people in the country had ever heard of Ed Miller, but Clark Clifford, if not exactly a household name, certainly had the credentials to draw clients.

Clifford had matured as a lawyer over the five years he had been in the White House. He had gone to the White House with a litigator's skills — the ability to analyze facts and develop a logical strategy. Now, he had added an understanding of how Washington worked and, something far more important, how power worked. He had dealt with some of the most powerful men in the world at a critical time in the nation's history, and he had proven himself their equal in many ways. He was ready to move on.

Clifford and Miller met often on chilly evenings in November and December 1949, discussing potential clients and searching for office space. Eventually they found a small suite of offices at 1523 L Street, just a few blocks from the White House. Miller left the Justice Department at the first of the year and moved into the offices. He hired the clerical help and recruited a young lawyer named William Dorsey as the firm's first associate. Everything was set for Clifford's arrival.

On December 22, three days before Clifford's forty-third birthday in 1949, the president invited the White House press corps into the Oval Office. With Clifford sitting to his left, he announced that his special counsel was leaving government. His replacement would be Charles Murphy, an able lawyer but one who lacked Clifford's charisma. A reporter whispered to a colleague that Clifford looked like a Greek god and Murphy like your next-door neighbor. Another newsman gave a low whistle.

Clifford's departure was mourned in the press. The liberal *Nation* called him "the mainstay of the Fair Deal, the author of the best presidential speeches, and the originator of its most impressive strategies." The like-minded *New Republic* worried, "Clifford's retirement further weakens our side in the White House. . . . Clifford knew the score. In some ways he was the strongest liberal influence in the presidential entourage."

The president was genuinely sorry to see Clifford leave. While he never was part of his Missouri gang, Truman recognized the value of Clifford's work. Moreover, he liked Clifford and his family. On the credenza behind his desk, he kept a photograph of Clifford's youngest daughter, Randall, who had become a favorite of Truman.

In a letter accepting his resignation, Truman thanked Clifford for devoting his "talents and superb abilities to your country's welfare." He praised his memoranda as "models of brevity and accuracy, as well as clarity and strength." And he recognized the sacrifice, writing that the "years of public service" had been "potentially among the most fruitful of your professional life."

Clifford was a private man who rarely showed emotion, but the president's letter struck a deep chord. Although he was not one of the Truman loyalists who remained until the end, and despite the fact that he had nourished his own ambitions while in the White House, Clifford felt a genuine affection for the president. In responding that day with his own letter, Clifford wrote, "During my father's lifetime, he and I were very close and I felt sure I would never feel toward any man what I felt toward him. I was wrong. For you now occupy that place in my heart that he held for so many years."

January 31, 1950, was Clifford's last day at the White House. That evening, George Elsey organized a small farewell dinner for him at the Cosmos Club, the exclusive men's club founded in 1878 by a group of scientists. While the Metropolitan Club, with its stately building two blocks from the White House, prided itself on the stark power of its membership list, the Cosmos Club tried to project a more intellectual atmosphere. Its membership was limited to people it considered distinguished in science, art, public service, or professional work — so long as those distinguished people were male, of course. Along with Presidents Taft, Hoover, and Wilson, the club boasted more than two dozen Nobel and Pulitzer prize winners.

For Clifford's dinner at the club's stately turn-of-the-century stone mansion, the guest list included Stuart Symington and some of Clifford's allies from the liberal Monday Night Group and the White House, such as Leon Keyserling and Charles Brannan. They called themselves "the little wheels," and they concluded their five-course meal in a private dining room by toasting Clifford and throwing their champagne glasses into the fireplace.

If Harry Truman's letter had been right about Clifford's value to him, the president was clearly mistaken about the most fruitful years of Clifford's professional life. Those were about to begin. Clifford was going to become a big wheel, but he would not do it as a public servant.

Somewhere between the night in 1947 when he had described the satisfactions of public service to his friend David Lilienthal and this day, Clifford had changed his dream once more. Although his career would be forever intertwined with government, he would not rejoin public service for nearly two decades. In the meantime, he would pursue something closer to that original ambition of making a lot of money and living in a big house, although he would never live ostentatiously. As for the power and influence he had wielded in the White House, Clifford had learned enough about Washington to understand that it could be exercised outside the confines of 1600 Pennsylvania Avenue, too. He was not the first to leave government service intent on using what he had learned to make money. But he would prove to be the best at it.

8

"I Have No Influence"

FROM THE BROAD WINDOW of his office at the White House, Clark Clifford could not quite see the building on L Street where he and Ed Miller had rented their first law offices. What he could see was the life he had chosen, the careful journey toward success that was mapped in his mind's eye. Others might have opted for the safety of St. Louis, where he knew the job, where his place was established. Washington was a risk, but the downside was hedged by the relationships he had cultivated while in the White House, and, most of all, by his own clear-eyed determination.

In the month between Truman's announcement that the White House lawyer was retiring and his actual departure on February 1, 1950, Clifford began to see that his gamble was going to pay off. He had been contacted by several prospective clients. Clients from the old days in St. Louis, such as Allied Chemical and Dye Company, were eager to hire him. New clients, attracted by his fame and presumed influence, also contacted the White House lawyer. Naturally, Clifford said that he could not discuss any legal matters until he left the administration. He did not want to do anything that would tarnish his image. But in at least one case he did step into a dangerous area when he referred a prospective client to Miller.

Everyone seemed to want to be Clifford's friend. No potion is stronger in the nation's capital than being a winner. Clifford's reputation as the strategist of the 1948 Truman victory was like a magnet. Senator Robert Kerr, who had set about developing a friendship with Clifford soon after the election, told him he could count on a retainer from Kerr's friends in the oil business. Secretary of Defense Louis Johnson wrote a score of letters recommending Clifford to some of the nation's big defense contractors.

Still, no one could guarantee success. The legal business in the city was dominated by large firms, such as Covington and Burling, Hogan and Hartson, and Arnold, Porter and Fortas. Competition also would come from other bright young lawyers who were striking out on their own, men such as Edward Bennett Williams, who just the year before had left Hogan and Hartson to form his own firm. But with vision akin to genius, Clifford had recognized the transformation that was occurring in Washington after World War II. He saw the slow-moving Southern town growing more urbane and vital as the United States assumed its place across the table from the Soviet Union, the world's other super-power. He recognized, too, that the straightforward workings of the federal government were being overtaken by a complexity and sophis-tication unseen before in the country. It was a historic transformation that translated into opportunity for a well-positioned lawyer with the proper credentials and skills. Clifford saw a place for himself, an oppor-tunity to turn his White House experience into a new type of law firm that would become a lucrative bridge between business and govern-ment. He believed that he could corner the market in advising corporate America on its dealings with the fast-growing federal government.

Years later Clifford described his strategy this way: "Instead of being a broad-range law firm, we were more like a boutique. Somebody says, 'My God, I have a real tough problem. It involves Washington.' That's when they ought to come to Clifford."

The firm would take advantage of the lessons he had learned from the Olympian view at the White House. He did not care to get bogged down in the time-consuming demands of trials or appearances before regulatory commissions. His time in the courtroom had been exhilarat-ing in St. Louis, but Clifford had a broader vision of the law now. In establishing his own practice, he would offer advice and counsel to cor-porate clients on how to navigate the sometimes-turbulent waters of Washington. With Clifford's contacts and experience, he could help cli-ents understand how the White House might react to a certain proposal, what steps the Justice Department was likely to take in a particular sort of case, and whom to contact in Congress to block or speed up legislation.

"An advisory firm," he described it, one that would stay small and personal. "From the very beginning, I thought, 'I don't want a firm of more than twenty lawyers,'" Clifford recalled later. "In that way, I could keep informed about everything going on in the firm. In those big law firms, you don't have any real idea about what other partners and associates are doing. Sometimes you learn about it when you pick up the morning paper. I said to myself that I didn't want to take that chance. I had seen a lot about how Washington operates. I had some idea about where the minefields were. And I wanted to proceed with great caution. So we started very small."

Clients would pay not by the case but by the year. For an annual retainer, they would buy the privilege of calling on Clifford for advice at any point. Particularly complex cases, or walk-ins from the street, would pay higher fees. And the culture of the firm — the mixture of personality, values, goals, and business practices — would be defined by Clifford himself.

The key element of this culture would be discretion. Rather than a public advocate in the courtroom, Clifford wanted to convey the image of a wise man who understood the need for privacy. However, he could not afford a reputation as just another influence peddler and fixer. Rules covering contacts with officials by lobbyists and lawyers had not kept pace with the rising power of the federal government. A handful of influential committee chairmen in the House and Senate controlled legislation, and a whisper in the right ear could a move bill or stall it. Too many times at the White House, Clifford had listened to Truman rail about Tommy Corcoran's blatant attempts to influence government policy or call in favors from colleagues from the Roosevelt years. Corcoran did not seem to care about his reputation as a fixer, but Clifford knew intuitively that his own long-term success would depend on the perception that he was an honest man who would not abuse his access to Truman and other former colleagues.

Clifford had another model in those early days. George Allen, Truman's poker-playing friend and one of the men who had helped him secure the vice presidency under Roosevelt, was a prominent lawyer-lobbyist in Washington. He also was something of a patron to Clifford, coaching the younger lawyer on the ways of Truman and lending him the money to supplement his government salary. While serving in an unsalaried position in the Truman administration, Allen sat on several corporate boards and represented many of the nation's biggest businesses. Many regarded him as a backslapper who used his associations with powerful politicians to help his clients.

His fees and his ego were legendary. Allen once boasted that he would not even talk to a client on a serious basis for less than $5,000. When asked to defend the practice, the man who would call his autobiography *Presidents Who Knew Me* shot back, "If there is anything wrong with that statement, it's because it is on the low side." To ameliorate his brash reputation, Allen liked to assure people that he had neither access to nor influence with those in government. He only offered them counsel on occasion.

To what he saw in Corcoran and Allen, Clifford added refinements adopted from another prominent lawyer, Dean Acheson. The patrician and scrupulously honest Acheson presented the image of a citizen-statesman, moving smoothly between government and private practice without raising eyebrows or eliciting whispers about conflicts of interest or influence peddling. From watching Acheson, Clifford began to develop his own philosophy. He became convinced that his continuing contact with government officials provided a service to them as well as to his own clients.

As part of this philosophy, Clifford developed a speech that outlined the type of service he would offer. Over the next four decades, he would deliver this homily so regularly that associates in his law firm could recite it word for word. Simultaneously a graceful protest against influence peddling and a convenient fiction, the speech was designed to create the perception that Clifford would never trade on his access. There is no way of knowing how many of the corporate titans who hired Clifford believed the speech, but perception is as important as reality in Washington. And the first to hear it, one of the world's richest men, was not deterred.

The telephone started ringing the first day that Clifford was in the new offices on L Street. His departure from the White House had been widely publicized and there was a long list of people eager to hire the president's former special counsel. For the first time in his life, Clifford began to look forward to a sense of financial security. Years later, he would think back fondly on those early days and say, "The phone rang fairly steadily. Really, it would be nice to say that we got through a tough period, but we didn't have any tough period. It just took right off."

On the first or second day, Clifford's secretary buzzed him. Howard Hughes was calling from California. Orphaned and a millionaire at eighteen, Hughes had turned the patent on an oil drilling bit developed by his father into an ever-expanding empire that included Hughes Tool Company, Hughes Aircraft Company, TransWorld Airlines, and RKO Motion Picture Company. Hughes also had raced airplanes around the world, cavorted with starlets, and been accused by the United States Senate of war profiteering and political payoffs.

"I've followed your career in government, Mr. Clifford, and I need advice in Washington," said Hughes. "I would like to retain you. I want to retain you on behalf of three of my companies, Hughes Tool, TWA, and RKO. Would you be interested?"

Clifford was surprised and pleased. While he was confident of his ability to attract clients, and the ones he was signing up already seemed to bear out his optimism, Hughes represented a level that Clifford had only dreamed of attaining. He assured Hughes that he was interested in representing him, explaining his belief that establishing a Washington presence would be a major trend for American businesses. Hughes, who was already showing signs of the irrational behavior that would eventually make him the world's most famous recluse, mumbled his agreement and then told Clifford sternly never to take orders from anyone except Hughes himself or Noah Dietrich, his primary assistant.

Near the conclusion of the conversation, Clifford delivered the speech he had been rehearsing for all the prospective clients he expected to come calling.

"Mr. Hughes," he said, "I look forward to our association. But before we proceed, there is one point I must make clear. I do not consider that this firm will have any influence of any kind here in Washington. I cannot, and will not, represent any client before the president or before any of his staff. If you want influence, you should consider going elsewhere. What we can offer you is an extensive knowledge of how to deal with the government on your problems. We will be able to give you advice on how best to present your position to the appropriate departments and agencies of government."

Hughes listened patiently to the speech and said he still wanted to hire Clifford. By that time, Clifford knew enough about the law and Washington to realize that a lawyer often does not know exactly why he is hired. It was Clifford's impression that Hughes had hired him for general matters. This view reflected a certain naïveté in the neophyte Washington lawyer that would eventually be replaced by a more cold-eyed view of the city. But even after forty years of practicing his brand of advisory law in Washington, Clifford would still voice the notion that he was not an influence peddler.

Hughes, like the others who came to Clifford in those days, did not object to Clifford's harmless homily. He was enough of a realist to recognize its hollowness, even if the man speaking the words did not. He was hiring Clifford because Clifford knew not only the president but the people who worked for the president. He was their former colleague and their friend. He was a man who could open virtually any door in Washington. The savvy billionaire had a few specific doors in mind that day in early 1950 when he called Clifford.

Hughes wanted to move part of his burgeoning aircraft company from Los Angeles, where taxes were high, to Nevada, where there was no state income tax. The site that Hughes wanted for his new research laboratory and any future production facility was 25,000 acres, roughly ten square miles, on the western edge of Las Vegas, the fast-growing gambling capital. Like much of the state, the site was owned by the federal government.

Secret negotiations had already started. Hughes planned to swap the government 73,000 acres that he owned in five remote counties of northern Nevada for the land he wanted near Las Vegas. However, there were questions about whether the Hughes tracts were equal in value to the land near Las Vegas. To overcome any potential resistance, Hughes intended to muster support from the company's biggest customer, the U.S. Air Force. At the time, the secretary of the air force was Stuart Symington, Clifford's old friend from St. Louis.

Husite Company, a subsidiary formed for the land swap, filed a formal application with the Bureau of Land Management at the Department of the Interior on July 19, 1950. The application, which was drawn up by Clifford's firm, said the company was developing new radar and guided-missile devices and production needed to be moved from the West Coast location where the company said it was "too vulnerable to attack."

Federal regulations required that the BLM evaluate the trade to make sure that the parcels of land were of equal value. But the air force initially tried to persuade the bureau to waive the statutory requirements. When that effort was rebuffed, the air force tried to expedite the decision.

"Since this project is of interest to the Air Force, it would be greatly appreciated if the Bureau of Land Management would advance the application of the Husite Company on its calendar for an early consideration of the merits of the case," an Air Force colonel at the Pentagon wrote in September 1950.

By this time, Clifford's firm was also pushing the Interior Department and the BLM for an early decision in favor of the trade. In a letter to a senior BLM official, Clifford associate Bill Dorsey sought to speed up the investigation being conducted in Nevada to evaluate whether the two tracts were of equal value.

The initial study said the lands involved appeared to be of near-equal value. However, a field examiner for the Interior Department objected vigorously to the findings, claiming that the Hughes land was in a remote area and the government's site was far more valuable because of the likelihood of development in Las Vegas.

With the help of Clifford, other powerful Washington lawyers, and the air force, however, Hughes had little trouble overcoming the low-level opposition and the transaction was eventually approved by the Interior Department.

Over the following two and a half decades, Clifford and his firm would continue to represent Hughes in a variety of matters, from intervening with the president of the United States to try to stop atomic tests in the Nevada desert to helping smooth the way for one of the most profitable stock sales in history.

Despite the long relationship, Clifford says that he never met Hughes, whose bizarre eccentricity had become legendary by the time he died in 1976. Instead, they communicated solely by telephone. Even then, Hughes sometimes wound up talking with Marny Clifford and not her husband because of one of her husband's ironclad rules.

As his law practice increased and the hours grew more demanding, Clifford refused to accept business calls at home. This did not fit well with Hughes's schedule or his temperament. Even given the time difference between California and Washington, Hughes kept odd hours and demanded that his employees be on call twenty-four hours a day. But Clifford never relented, and when the billionaire called his house in the middle of the night, he invariably wound up speaking with Marny. They developed a friendship and she took notes so that her husband could return the telephone call the next day.

Even more important to the immediate success of Clifford's private practice was Senator Robert Kerr. Born in a log cabin in the Territory of Oklahoma, Kerr had told his father as a youth that he wanted three things — to marry a beautiful woman, earn a fortune, and become governor of Oklahoma. His father's prudent advice was to achieve those goals in that order, which was precisely what Kerr had done. The fortune had come from Kerr-McGee Oil Company, which started as a drilling company and went on to become one of the country's most prosperous oil and uranium businesses. Kerr became governor of Oklahoma in 1942, and in 1948 he was elected to the Senate. But he was not content to be a rich senator. A large man with large ambitions, he brought to Washington a deep, burning aspiration to become president of the United States.

Bobby Baker was the top aide to another member of the Senate's Class of '48, Lyndon Baines Johnson of Texas. Kerr and Johnson formed a quick and lasting alliance, and their relationship gave Baker a rare window from which he could watch the brawny oil baron in action.

"His answer to everything was money," Baker later recalled. "If you had enough of it, you could do anything you wanted." On one occasion, Kerr told Baker, "A man who doesn't have money can't operate. Why, if I don't have at least $5,000 on me as pocket change, I'm afraid the taxi drivers won't pick me up."

But Kerr was more complex. He never viewed money as an end, but rather a means to an end. His fortune had enabled him to come to Washington with a legislative agenda that put protecting his home state's interests first. That those interests often paralleled the interests of Kerr-McGee was in many ways a happy coincidence.

When he decided early on that Clark Clifford was the man to help him get to the presidency, Kerr's wealth and his powerful connections served to bind Clifford to him. His courtship of Clifford began after the White House lawyer helped engineer Truman's 1948 victory and escalated once he left the administration.

They were an unlikely pair, the ultimate in Washington contradictions. Kerr was brash and seldom couched his opinions in gentle words. He was impossible to classify politically, and he enraged conservatives and liberals alike with his bitter, sometimes personal attacks. Clifford was silky smooth as he cultivated and exercised power, creating as few ripples as possible. He used persuasion and flattery. Despite his increasing alliance with big business, Clifford's public reputation remained that of an unflinching liberal. Theirs was, of course, the prototypical Washington relationship. Each man had something to offer the other and, contradictions aside, favors were exchanged as part of what evolved into a genuine friendship. For both, it became a matter of loyalty.

The tone was set while Clifford still occupied an office three doors from Truman's, when Kerr introduced him to Kenneth Adams, the president of Phillips Petroleum Company of Bartlesville, Oklahoma. Kerr had started in the oil business drilling wells for Frank Phillips, the founder of Phillips Petroleum, and he had maintained close relations with Adams. Known as "Boots" to one and all, Adams was a loyal friend of Kerr's and the senator wanted him to become a great friend of Clifford's, too.

The first week Clifford was sitting in his new law office, Kerr walked through the door with Adams in tow. Adams wanted to hire Clifford to represent Phillips Petroleum in Washington, explained Kerr. To seal the relationship, Kerr had planned a fishing trip to Florida for all three men. There was never a question of a busy man saying no, and so off Clifford went to a river in Florida. The three men spent a week fishing, talking, and playing gin rummy. By the time he returned, Clifford had secured a client whose business and fees would flow into his office for the next forty years.

"Kerr wanted Phillips Petroleum to be important to me and it was," Clifford recalled later. "We did a lot of work for them. He wanted to be my friend. And he was doing anything he could to direct law business to me, which was perfectly all right with me. I was just brand-new, getting started."

Phillips Petroleum was not the only tie that bound Clifford to Kerr. The senator sent other clients to him, including Standard Oil and Kerr-McGee itself. To fulfill his part of the unspoken bargain, Clifford spent hours schooling Kerr on how Truman had won in 1948. For many years, Kerr picked Clifford up at his home on his way to work in the mornings and they discussed politics.

Clifford also traveled to Oklahoma with the senator, where he was a firsthand witness to an amazing political transformation. When he touched the soil of his home state, Kerr was a different man. He could talk weather and ranching and oil with any workingman who crossed his path. They all knew Kerr and he knew most of them. As his son William said years later, Oklahoma was Bob Kerr's mistress and it was a relationship that served them both very well. As for Clifford, back in Washington, he used his contacts and charm to smooth Kerr's way into Washington society, a must for a potential presidential candidate.

The society aspect of Clifford's role led to a funny story that he loved to tell after Kerr's death. The self-made man from Oklahoma was accustomed to being a big shot. Along with being immensely wealthy, he had been the most powerful man in Oklahoma when he was governor. Since his arrival in Washington, however, he did not think he was meeting the right people or traveling in the proper social circles. One day he confided in Clifford that he wanted to host a party for the movers and shakers. But Kerr, a devout Baptist and Sunday school teacher, was a teetotaler who had been schooled in prohibition by his mother. He refused even to have liquor in his house and once made his daughter dispose of a bottle of Chianti she had brought home from Wellesley.

For Kerr's party, Clifford arranged an impressive guest list, which included House Speaker Sam Rayburn and Connecticut Senator Brien McMahon. However, at Clifford's suggestion, the guests met first for drinks at Stuart Symington's house. Knowing that there would be no liquor at Kerr's house, the guests quickly downed a night's worth of drinks. By the time they arrived at the Kerrs', everyone was slightly tipsy. The dinner conversation was highlighted by raucous laughter and even a few tears as Sam Rayburn delivered an inebriated account of his poverty-stricken childhood.

Kerr apparently attributed the good humor to a festive atmosphere, not predinner imbibing. Early the next morning, the senator telephoned Clifford at home to thank him. "Well, Clifford, it just goes to show," crowed Kerr. "You don't have to serve liquor to have a good time."

The relationship with Kerr opened Clifford up for criticism in the press within months of entering private practice. The allegations centered on whether Clifford had lobbied the Truman administration on behalf of legislation to curtail the ability of the Federal Power Commission to regulate gas prices, which was supported by the senator and natural gas interests. Clifford denied the accusations, saying it was "wholly and unequivocally untrue" that he had lobbied the administration. He said his sole work in the energy area involved assisting one of his clients who wanted to buy a synthetic rubber plant from the government. "Whether he has any interest in natural gas or the Kerr amendment, I don't know," said Clifford.

Clifford did not identify the client interested in buying the rubber plant, although records show that it was Phillips Petroleum. At the time, Phillips was far and away the nation's largest natural gas company and it stood to benefit dramatically from the Kerr legislation.

By 1952, Clifford had spent enough time with Kerr to have concerns about the senator's penchant for associating with high-rollers. Despite doubts that a rich oil man could be elected, Clifford would champion the Oklahoma senator's presidential candidacy with his friend the outgoing Harry Truman. It was partly out of loyalty and friendship. But part of the relationship was an unwritten business arrangement: Kerr delivered the clients and helped Clifford with matters in Congress from time to time, and Clifford would serve as his political adviser.

In the meantime, Clifford's law practice prospered. Within weeks, Miller had hired Carson Glass, a colleague from antitrust at the Justice Department, to help with the growing caseload. Clifford also needed a lawyer to assist him. For a recommendation, he turned to George Allen, who suggested hiring one of his own former protégés, Samuel McIlwain. "He's a good Washington utility man," said Allen.

McIlwain was born in the tiny Mississippi town of Waynesboro, the son of a country doctor. After graduating from the University of Mississippi in Oxford, he came north to Washington in 1934 on a lark. His first job was clipping newspapers for George Allen when the older man was running the District of Columbia government. He remained at Allen's side until the war, completing law school at night.

During the war, McIlwain enlisted in the navy and Allen arranged for him to be appointed an assistant naval aide at the White House. There he worked with George Elsey and briefly met his predecessor, Clark Clifford. After the war, McIlwain worked with Allen at the federal Reconstruction Finance Corporation and then he went to work as a government land lawyer back in Mississippi.

In the spring of 1950, he got a call from Clifford. "Ed Miller and I have formed this law firm," said Clifford. "We are getting more business than we originally thought and I need some help. Would you be interested in coming up to talk with me about coming with the firm?"

McIlwain caught the next plane to Washington, met with Clifford, and started his new job by the end of April. He spent the next thirty years as an associate and partner in Clifford's firm. During those years, McIlwain did his share of legal work. However, his primary assignment was as executive assistant to Clifford, arranging details of the law practice and organizing much of Clifford's personal life.

Clifford's relationship with George Allen also proved to be a major bonus for bringing clients to the fledgling firm. Allen, a founder of the March of Dimes charity, at one time sat on thirty corporate boards. This gave him influence over a considerable amount of corporate legal business, and he referred clients regularly to Clifford's firm. Among the big early referrals from Allen were Republic Steel and Radio Corporation of America, later known simply as RCA.

"He was our runner," McIlwain later recalled of Allen. "He sent us case after case after case. He thought Clark was one of the ablest people he had ever known. Allen was a pragmatist. If he sat in a board meeting and heard directors talking about problems they were having, he had no hesitancy in sending for Mr. Clifford."

For his part, Clifford had no hesitancy in casting himself as a friend of big business. While he had a reputation in the Truman White House as a liberal, Clifford was not an idealist, but a pragmatist. He was driven not just by the need to succeed but to be secure. If this meant siding with big business, Clifford was eager to do so.

"We must do everything in our power to preserve the free enterprise system," he told a meeting of the Executives Club in Chicago in March 1950. "It isn't going to be preserved unless government and business can join together in a joint enterprise and preserve it."

The only way to provide a decent standard of living for American workers was to expand the economy, he told the audience. And the only way to do that was through a government-financed expansion of overseas markets and a massive program to rebuild the country's military.

As Clifford was describing this strategy in Chicago, the White House was in the process of approving a document that he had helped to write before leaving the administration, National Security Council resolution 68. The paper envisioned a quadrupling of the defense budget. It was signed by Truman in April 1950, but the dramatic expansion of military spending was not unveiled to the public until the outbreak of the Korean War two months later.

The relationship between government and business became a familiar theme as Clifford gave speeches around the country. Promotion of free enterprise, he argued in this era of rising fears of the Soviet Union, was integral to defeating communism. Along with endearing him to big business, this viewpoint fostered Clifford's own belief that there was some quasi-state purpose to whatever he was doing in his private law practice.

And that practice was booming his first year. The average retainer for the Clifford firm was $25,000, a sizable sum in 1950. And there was no shortage of clients willing to pay it. But the financial success was marred by sadness. Early in the spring, Ed Miller became ill and was placed under a physician's care. Then in June, at the age of forty-three, Miller died of a heart attack. Suddenly Clifford, who had been working longer hours than ever before, faced a new and daunting challenge.

Dorsey, Glass, and McIlwain lacked the seasoning and stature to become partners. Clifford's first choice to replace Miller was his close friend Justice William Douglas of the Supreme Court. Despite being in the midst of the financial woes that plagued him throughout his life, Douglas was not interested in leaving the court.

Next, Clifford turned to John J. McCloy, the former Wall Street lawyer, who was preparing to step down as Truman's high commissioner for Germany. McCloy expressed an interest, so Clifford did the politic thing. He paid a visit to President Truman at the White House and asked his approval. Truman agreed that McCloy would make a good partner, but he said he wanted him to stay on for another year as director of the American effort to rebuild Germany. So Clifford pressed ahead on his own, determined to continue building his law firm.

Whether they are in government or in the business of influencing government, few people reach the upper echelon in Washington without climbing the social ladder, too. Dinner-party guest lists have traditionally delineated the city's power structure. Connections are made or cemented at social functions. Insider knowledge is traded like any other commodity as trays of canapés are passed among guests.

During the war and the years immediately following it, there was a slump in the business of entertaining. Washington's hostesses did not join Rosie the Riveter on the nation's assembly lines, but they tightened their belts and cut down on the caviar and champagne.

The 1950 social season, however, marked a renaissance of lavish entertaining that reflected the city's newfound power. With their own prosperity on the rise, the Cliffords assumed a greater role in the city's social life.

Only a month after he started his practice, Clifford and his wife opened the Washington social season with a party for Vice President Alben Barkley and his new bride. During the 1948 presidential campaign, the Cliffords had introduced Barkley to Jane Hadley, the widow of Clifford's best friend from college. Although Barkley was much older, the couple had married and the Cliffords' party was a belated wedding gift and an introduction to Washington society for Jane Barkley.

It was a lavish affair, held in the ballroom of a rented mansion on Massachusetts Avenue and catered by Ridgewell's, the city's leading society caterer. An orchestra was hired and Rosa Ponselle, a distinguished opera singer who had become friends with Marny when she ran the St. Louis opera guild, was brought down from New York to entertain the five hundred guests. The party was so grand that it was featured in *Life* as part of a series called Life Goes to a Party. *U.S. News and World Report* offered the astounding estimate that the affair cost between $10,000 and $15,000 — roughly equal to Clifford's salary at the White House the previous year and enough to buy a small house in Washington at the time.

For Clifford, however, the most important part of his social life revolved around President Truman. Even if he never asked the president for a favor, it was essential that he continue to be perceived in public as someone who had access to Truman.

So Clifford was glad to continue organizing the president's regular poker games, which kept him in contact with Truman's inner circle as well. And Truman remained fond of his former lawyer. In March 1950, when Clifford had to go through the formality of joining the District of Columbia bar, Truman wrote a letter attesting to his former counsel's fitness. "His reputation, character, and legal ability are all that can be desired," wrote the president.

In the same vein that Clifford remained helpful to Truman, he retained his connections to his former colleagues in government. He often met at the Cosmos Club or Metropolitan Club with members of the Monday Night Group for dinner and conversation dominated by policy and politics. And, as he had been at the White House, Clifford was available to provide advice to any Democrat in Congress who asked. Unlike McCloy and Robert Lovett and others who had served with him in the Truman administration, however, Clifford was not bipartisan. He stuck with the party that brought him to Washington, evincing his strong belief that the two-party system — and the United States itself — could not flourish without such unstinting loyalty.

"I say, pick your party, work for it, and stay with it," Clifford said later. "Those people who say they don't belong and they are nonpartisan, I don't really have any regard for them. If we can keep a good, strong two-party system, we can keep our form of democracy alive."

So when Senator Lyndon Johnson or Speaker Sam Rayburn or some other Democrat called, Clifford happily went to Capitol Hill to offer his advice. When a new Democrat arrived in Congress, he often called on the gracious lawyer who had served President Truman and the party so ably. The newer politicians offered to come to Clifford's office, but he flattered them with his assurance that he would be pleased to come up to the Hill to see them. Along the way, Clifford built a bank of favors on which he could draw, with discretion, should the need arise.

In a matter of months, Clifford appeared to have made a successful transition from public life to private practice. His new status required a new home. In May 1950, the Cliffords discovered a rambling house along Rockville Pike in Bethesda, Maryland, just across the district's northern border. The fourteen-room, former farmhouse was nestled beneath towering white ash and locust trees on three acres of land. It was built in the early 1800s and once served as the temporary headquarters for a Union general during the Civil War.

The house had been empty for three years and it was in a dismal state. But Marny, with a decorator's eye, saw the possibilities. And she remembered the psychic's prediction: she would live in a white house outside a city. Well, she thought, much of what the psychic had said had already come true. She had left St. Louis and her husband had gone to work for a little man with gray hair, although Harry Truman did not have too much hair. So that month the Cliffords paid $40,000 for the house and spent twice as much renovating it, under the supervision of Sam McIlwain.

After moving from their rented home in the District of Columbia, they began to host parties at the house and occasionally the president was among the guests. However, the social aspirations of the Cliffords did not meet with complete approval in Washington, which was still infused with a stuffy combination of Southern rigidity and Eastern snobbism.

Having inherited or earned their fortunes long before, the upper reaches of society could afford to care more for power than money. As a result, a segment of the upper crust disapproved of Clifford's obvious profiting from his years at the White House. Some wags dubbed him a "five percenter," denoting the percentage of money that some wheeler-dealers raked off the top of business transactions.

Introducing young women to society at a debutante ball was de rigueur in Washington. The Cliffords were eager to present their eldest daughter, Margery, who would be eighteen in the summer of 1950, but there was a hitch. Some of the doyennes of society objected to conferring such a high honor on the daughter of Clark Clifford. To the rescue came Phyllis Pratt Nitze, a Standard Oil heiress and the wife of Paul Nitze, a brilliant diplomat and former Wall Street investment banker, who knew Clifford from the administration.

"Phyllis was somewhat of a friend of Mrs. Clifford's," explained Nitze years later. "The Cliffords' eldest daughter wanted to be a debutante and there was some concern over whether she should be approved. Many of the senior people had a dim view of what Clark was doing, of Clark being a five percenter. He was not respected by some people in Washington."

Eventually, Phyllis Nitze prevailed. Margery Clifford was presented to society on June 21, 1950, at a party hosted by her parents. Her escort was Bill Lanagan, a handsome marine officer who was stationed at the White House as an aide. He and Gery had met a few months earlier when she had been queen of the President's Regatta and Lanagan had been her escort. Before the year was out, they were married. President Truman accorded the Cliffords a rare social honor when he attended the wedding in December 1950 at All Saints Episcopal Church in Chevy Chase, Maryland.

Two years after Gery's debut, Truman and his daughter, Margaret, were among the four hundred and fifty guests at a lavish dinner party hosted by the Cliffords for the debut of their second daughter, Joyce. By this time, Clifford's rising prominence as a lawyer, his wife's quick wit and charm, and their continuing friendship with the Trumans had earned the Cliffords a place on the social scene. Newspaper society pages gushed about the elegant affair, remarking that it was the first time in the annals of Washington that a president had attended a coming-out party.

The next day, Clifford wrote a characteristically warm note to Truman:

"In your very full life you have done a great many kind and thoughtful things for others. But never, I repeat never, have you ever brought as many people the happiness that you brought our family on Saturday evening. We were very proud that you came. . . . Thank you so much and don't forget how much we all love you."

Clifford's reputation grew, and so did the roster of corporate clients willing to pay handsomely for his advice. Leaving the White House had not meant shorter hours. Instead, he found himself working harder. Much of the work involved counseling corporate executives and advising politicians. But part of it was devoted to building the Clifford legend.

"Clifford could do anything, or he could convince you he could do anything," mused Sam McIlwain. "When he took a job on, he did it right and he got results. He had an ability to impress people who came in to see him. A natural ability. He is quite an egotistical fellow, and you have to be that to be successful the way he was. Of course, having been counsel to the president of the United States and familiar with the Washington scene helped. He got a reputation for getting the job done. People just kept coming in."

Clients who came to see Clifford on L Street were ushered into his office and greeted by a man who rose to his full height from behind a desk covered with neat stacks of papers and said, "I am Clark Clifford." It was the knowing voice that clients had heard on the radio or even the new television programs, such as NBC-TV's *Meet the Press*, where Clifford had appeared occasionally since leaving government.

As the businessmen talked, Clifford listened intently, sometimes steepling his long fingers together or pressing them to his temples, deep in thought. Everything said that this powerful man was thinking of nothing but the matter in front of him. Clifford scratched notes on a pad of paper, then placed them carefully in one of the neat stacks on his desk. Occasionally he told a funny story about Truman or described something that had occurred during his government years. Invariably, new clients listened to the speech about the lack of influence. Invariably, they hired him anyway.

Clifford detested the word "lobbying," yet few definitions of the word would exclude him from the ranks of lobbyists. However, he was far more subtle than any of his predecessors or contemporaries. Calling a senior official at a federal agency, he might only express an interest in an issue or ask for a briefing. Never was there anything so brash as asking for a favor or any special treatment. As far as contacting a president directly, that was crass and unnecessary. Clifford merely had to let it be known at the right level whose side he was on.

The value of these sorts of contacts was demonstrated late in 1950, when Clifford was hired by RCA at George Allen's suggestion. The stakes were huge — who would build the first generation of color television sets. CBS-TV was fighting for its own system, which would transmit color through attachments to existing sets. RCA and most manufacturers of black-and-white sets wanted the technology to receive color to be contained in new sets. The matter was to be decided by the Federal Communications Commission, and the focus of the lobbying effort was Wayne Coy, the commission chairman.

To get its viewpoint across, RCA mobilized a sizable contingent from Truman's poker gang. Along with Clifford and Allen, former agriculture secretary Clinton Anderson, executive vice chairman of the Democratic National Party and another Truman poker pal, was hired.

Soon after he was retained, Clifford contacted Coy, a friend from his years in the administration. His new client, RCA, Clifford explained, wanted him to familiarize himself with the color television controversy as quickly as possible. He asked Coy to provide him with an informal briefing. Coy agreed, and Clifford also attended one or two commission sessions on the subject. Clifford did not attempt to influence Coy. He simply let him know that he represented RCA.

At the same time, Allen contacted Coy and made it clear that he had discussed the color issue with Truman. In fact, said Allen, it was Truman who had suggested he raise the matter with Coy. As for Anderson, he let Coy know that the decision would mean political problems if television set owners were required to buy the CBS gadgets for their sets.

Coy said that he did not feel unduly pressured, but he went to the White House and let Truman know that a hot political issue was about to be decided at the commmission. Truman listened and indicated that Coy should decide the matter on its merits. On October 10, 1950, the commission issued an order favoring CBS. However, the order was not implemented.

While Clifford himself never broached the color TV issue with Truman, a few weeks later he wrote the president a letter reminding him that RCA's president, General David Sarnoff, was hard at work developing an early-warning radar system for the country. It had nothing to do with the fight against CBS, of course, unless the president decided that a patriot like Sarnoff should be thrown a bone.

In the end, the CBS victory was short-lived. The development of color television was restricted to free up materials and labor for defense production for the Korean War.

Even if RCA did not get its way with the Federal Communications Commission, the episode illustrated the ability of a major corporation to muster powerful forces in Washington that could ensure its views were heard at the top levels of government, including the Oval Office. Lobbying was coming of age, and so was Clark Clifford.

His list of clients was the envy of every corporate lawyer in the city. Along with Phillips Petroleum and Howard Hughes, the roster included Standard Oil, American Telephone & Telegraph, the Pennsylvania Railroad, and the government of Indonesia. Right from the start, Clifford won his share of cases for these clients. He even succeeded in winning the Pennsylvania Railroad an increase in the cost of using a railroad toilet to a dime from a nickel.

Because Clifford's firm was small (there were never more than four lawyers throughout the fifties), he often farmed out complex work. But he still felt entitled to the lion's share of the fees. For instance, in preparing a case for the Supreme Court for one of his clients, the actual writing of the brief was done by another firm with expertise in tax matters selected by Clifford. When the client paid Clifford $40,000, he passed on $5,000 to the other firm. His name had apparently added an enormous value to the brief.

Sometimes Clifford's access backfired. Howard Hughes wanted desperately to block the acquisition of American Overseas Airlines by Pan American Airlines. Pan Am was already the archrival of Hughes's TWA. Hughes feared that the deal would give his competitor a major edge in the growing area of transatlantic air travel.

Clifford succeeded in persuading the Civil Aeronautics Board to block the merger. But Truman, wary of the appearance of a backroom deal, forced the board to reverse its decision. Not only did Pan Am get approval for the acquisition, it received permission to compete directly with TWA on routes to Paris and Frankfurt.

*   *   *

Dean Acheson, who had returned to government as Truman's secretary of state, used the phrase "present at the creation" to describe those heady postwar years when America's foreign policy was born. It is just as apt to say that Clifford was present at the creation of a new breed of Washington lawyer.

As Clifford had learned as a young trial lawyer in St. Louis, you don't win all your cases. But by the end of his first year in private practice, he had won enough to more than keep the doors open. Along the way, he had begun to change the way lawyers operated in Washington.

In St. Louis, Clifford had been a trial lawyer, but in Washington, his access to the administration and his reputation as an insider gave him instant status as a dealmaker, someone who could get the ear of anyone in government, right up to the president himself. Clifford prided himself on never exercising any influence, but no amount of care could erase the fact that he prospered through the perception that he had access to the decision makers in the administration. Over the years, the perception would become the reality.

In that first year of private practice, Clifford grossed $500,000. For the next four decades, he would never earn less. Many years, he would earn more. For one case alone, he would earn twice that amount. These fees were paid because he had reinvented the genre *Washington lawyer*. He patrolled the corridors of power on behalf of his elite clientele with discretion and efficiency. He avoided the crassness of his predecessors, such as Tommy Corcoran. He was perfectly respectable, smooth-tongued, handsome, and accessible to the press. He was persuasive and he had access to those who needed to be persuaded. No private figure in Washington would be as listened to, or talked about, as Clifford at the height of his fame. Yet, in a city where power is often a blunt instrument, Clifford exercised his influence with tact and shrewdness. Along the way, Clifford did what no one before had managed to accomplish. He made it honorable to profit from access to top government officials. He became the model for generations of lawyers who would follow him into government service and out the revolving door into private practice.

The money that first year was almost more than Clifford could fathom. More surprising was the discovery that he had little left at year's end. He was able to repay the loans to Alfred Lansing and George Allen that had carried him and his family through the lean White House years.

And he paid cash for his house. But the government had collected a huge amount in taxes. Clifford vowed to himself that that would never happen again. It was vital to provide financial security for himself and his family, so he began to spend an increasing amount of time on his personal finances. The answer, he decided, was to search for tax shelters. For the first time, he gave serious consideration to investing in some oil ventures suggested by his friend Senator Kerr. The tax incentives might help him avoid becoming, mused Clifford, "a tax collector for the government."

Clifford was not acting out of greed. Rather, he sought financial security and independence. He had grown up in a family that always seemed to be on the edge of prosperity but was never better than modestly middle-class. He also had seen how his father-in-law had been wiped out in the depression and had to start a new business from scratch. From his father's experience in the railroad business, Clifford had learned never to trust the benevolence of fate or to be dependent on another person. Relationships such as Clifford's with Truman and Kerr were very important, but they were no substitute for discipline, intelligence, and hard work. Instead of taking comfort from the prosperity of his first year, Clifford fine-tuned his ambitions. He was determined to be not just wealthy, but financially secure. Only he could judge when that security was reached. And only he could know when he was truly independent.

Moving relentlessly forward that first year took an enormous personal toll on Clifford. Although his facade of composure and serenity never seemed to crack, Clifford let his guard slip one day over lunch with his old confessor David Lilienthal.

"He told me the whole details of his last year, his first year of law practice after leaving the White House," Lilienthal recounted in his journal. "It is a simply unbelievable story. He practices alone. His law partner died two and a half months after they began; he hired four young lawyers, five stenographers. In this establishment — a one-man performance — he earned probably as much as any professional man in the country, amusement field included, and more than any lawyer. He said he came out even on the year, after paying off his debts incurred for living costs while he was in government service, buying a house, outfitting a law office, et cetera. He was uneasy about what will happen when Truman is out, if he is; wonders if he will keep any of his clients, which is nonsense, as he is a very able man with or without Truman."

The physical price was evident to Lilienthal. The man across the table from him, barely forty-four years old, had aged ten years in twelve months. He complained of stomach problems, of waking at three o'clock in the morning, of nerves that never allowed him to relax. But Clifford rebuffed his friend's suggestions that he slow down and pay attention to his health and his family. No, Clifford countered, he had to make a success of his law practice.

With the razor-sharp insight of an anxious and trusted friend, Lilienthal wrote in his journal, "He has a sense of insecurity (financial) that is hard to fathom, considering the facts."

9

The Smear Artists

FEW MEN OF PROMINENCE ever worked harder to maintain a pristine image than Clifford. Despite those assiduous efforts, his reputation sustained a blemish early in his career as a private lawyer in Washington. The episode attracted a small amount of attention when it first broke and then quickly subsided. But it is instructive as an example of how, even in those early days out of the White House, Clifford was seen in some quarters as a man willing to use his relationships with government officials to help clients.

The incident occurred in the middle of 1952. Investigators for a House of Representatives committee were digging into activities at the Justice Department when they discovered an intriguing nugget. Clifford's firm had received a $25,000 fee from a Detroit businessman to negotiate what appeared to be a sweetheart settlement with the federal government.

The matter was dangerous to Clifford for several reasons. One was the sleazy nature of the allegations against his client. The owner of a Detroit trade school was accused of overcharging the government for training soldiers during World War II. Another was the image of Clifford, Harry Truman's golden-boy lawyer, profiteering in his own way during his final days in the White House. Clifford had referred the businessman to his soon-to-be law partner while still on the government payroll and then benefitted when the client's case was decided favorably by a friend of Clifford's at the Justice Department.

Further, and potentially most damaging to Clifford, the allegations arose at a particularly sensitive time for the Truman administration. The "red scare" fueled by Senator Joseph McCarthy was keeping the administration on the defensive, and so were a handful of other scandals and inquiries that cast doubt on the honesty of administration officials. Among them was a report issued a year earlier by a Senate subcommittee that implied misconduct in the operations of the Reconstruction Finance Corporation, which dispensed low-interest loans to business. White House aide Donald Dawson and Democratic Party chairman

William Boyle were implicated, giving rise to speculation in the press that favoritism in giving out loans was linked to the White House. *Time* used the occasion of the loan inquiry to write a study of the "peculiar Washington species known as the influence peddlers. The finest specimens claim Missouri as their habitat, have at least a nodding acquaintance with Harry Truman, a much chummier relationship with his aides and advisers, and can buzz in and out of the White House at will."

Such allegations left Truman's staff fuming over the damage being done to the president and his reputation by "chiselers" inside the administration. And the Republicans were clearly gleeful at the prospect of raising corruption as a campaign issue in the fall. For Clifford's burgeoning law career, the possibility of being portrayed as one of those specimens was far more dangerous than the allegations themselves.

The dispute began when the United States comptroller general's office accused the Michigan School of Trades of overbilling the government by $1.3 million for training soldiers. The comptroller general asked the Justice Department to recover the money and prosecute the case on grounds of "brazen and flagrant fraud and corruption." Joseph Peters, the owner of the school, denied the charges and hired a politically powerful Detroit lawyer to fight the case.

Peters, a chunky and talkative man, described what happened next in testimony before a congressional hearing in June 1952. He said that he had read in a magazine in late 1949 that Clifford was leaving the White House to open a private law practice in Washington. Peters said he went to Washington, met with Clifford at the White House, and described the dispute to him. Peters testified that Clifford said there was nothing he could do at the moment. However, Peters recounted, Clifford suggested that, if his problem needed immediate attention, he should see Ed Miller, who would soon become Clifford's law partner. So, Peters said, he visited Miller in January 1950 and paid him an initial $10,000 retainer to take over negotiations with the federal government.

A year later, after Miller had died and Clifford had taken charge of the case, the Justice Department agreed to settle the case for $125,000. The department also declined to prosecute. In examining the sequence of events that led to the favorable settlement for Peters, congressional investigators found that it was first approved by Holmes Baldridge, an assistant attorney general. Then it was given final approval by Howard McGrath, the attorney general. The involvement of these two senior officials gave rise to questions from congressmen about the propriety of the settlement. Not only had Clark Clifford referred the case to his law partner while he was still in the White House, Clifford had been friends with McGrath and Baldridge for years. He had even recommended Baldridge for a promotion at the Justice Department.

Baldridge was called to testify before the committee. When asked if his relationship with Clifford should have disqualified him from the matter, the assistant attorney general said it should not because he had never discussed the case with Clifford. Further, Baldridge defended the merits of the settlement. Rather than the $1.3 million demanded by the comptroller general's office, Baldridge said, the Justice Department had determined that Peters's school owed only $141,000. Thus, he said, the $125,000 settlement seemed prudent.

Clifford was not called to testify. However, he was questioned by a reporter from the *Washington Post*. So it was that, on the steamy morning of June 7, 1952, the lawyer who prided himself on his good name awoke to find it in the headlines in a most unfavorable fashion. Clifford had confirmed that Miller had received the $10,000 retainer and that the firm later had been paid more. But he had denied ever working personally on the case. After Miller's death in June 1950, Clifford said, the case was handled by Carson Glass, who had been Miller's assistant. Clifford acknowledged speaking with Attorney General Howard McGrath about promoting Baldridge while Clifford was in the White House, but he said Baldridge had not gotten the job he had suggested for him.

It was precisely the sort of publicity that Clifford had feared from the day he opened his practice. On June 9, two days after the article appeared, Clifford sought to defuse the accusation and defend himself in a letter to Truman, who had complained so vigorously about influence peddling by Tommy Corcoran and others.

"The smear artists have finally gotten around to me," he wrote in a "Dear Boss" letter. The settlement, he explained, had been negotiated without his involvement. Therefore any accusation of influence peddling was unfounded. "I will not labor the details any more," Clifford concluded, "but I prize so greatly your good opinion of me that I did not want it to be affected in any way by this smear job."

Truman responded the following day with an encouraging note, which said: "Dear Clark: I read your letter of the ninth with a lot of interest. Don't worry about these smear artists. So far as I am concerned they can't hurt you." At the bottom of the page, Truman scrawled: "Never admit to anything — swing from the ground and tell 'em to go to hell."

There is no evidence that Clifford was personally involved in negotiating the settlement with his friends in the Justice Department. But the case illustrated the dangers involved any time the law firm bearing his name dealt with the administration he had once served so publicly and ably. Indeed, it was just the sort of case that would crop up over and over during Clifford's dual career as a Washington lawyer and a government insider.

Lobbying had not yet changed much in Washington. In the 1940s, there had been a lot of talk about influence peddling, and Corcoran had come to symbolize the underside of lobbying in the press and some quarters of Congress. However, most deals were really cut in the smoke-filled backrooms on Capitol Hill, where a few powerful men in the Senate and House maintained an iron grip on the legislative branch of American government. Access to those men, and their equivalents in the executive branch, was the lifeblood of the lobbyists and others who sought to influence government. Washington still thrived on the clubbiness of the old-boy network, and Clifford was building the sorts of relationships that would ensure his place in the club.

The very nature of Clifford's law practice kept him involved with politicians and politics, so naturally he wanted a big role in the main event of 1952, the presidential election. His business required access, the most prized commodity in Washington by those seeking favors. Clifford knew that he had a lot at stake if Truman left the White House, although he had cultivated and won over enough insiders that his fortunes no longer depended solely on the man in the Oval Office. Beyond the needs of his business, however, Clifford wanted to remain an insider. He cherished his proximity to power and the prestige it conveyed. Soon his primary sponsor would be retiring to Missouri, and Clifford would get the chance to find out whether, in David Lilienthal's phrase, he could be more than "Harry Truman's helper."

As the 1952 election approached, the country was in turmoil. The conflict in Korea threatened to escalate into another world war when China entered on the side of North Korea. At home, the economy was stagnant and the Truman administration continued to be tainted by a scandal of petty graft among White House aides. Adding to the darkness was Senator Joseph McCarthy of Wisconsin, who was ranting about Communist infiltration of the State Department and other government agencies.

By the summer of 1951, Truman had decided not to seek reelection. However, the president wanted to choose his successor, a capable Democrat whom he trusted to run the country. Initially, he settled on his friend Fred Vinson, the Chief Justice of the United States. Vinson had been out of politics for a long time and he liked serving on the high court, so he declined politely. In an attempt to persuade him to change his mind, Truman dispatched Clifford to meet with Vinson. However, the jurist said he did not feel up to the rigors of a nationwide campaign and he again refused.

Briefly, Truman reconsidered his own candidacy, fueling public speculation that he might seek another term. Clifford knew, however, that the president was tired and wanted nothing more than to return to his home in Independence, Missouri. So, while he certainly would have joined a Truman reelection bid, Clifford embarked on the repayment of his debt to Kerr. He became the Oklahoma senator's chief campaign strategist in the full expectation that Truman would not run again.

Truman and Kerr shared some attributes. Both had a folksy, homespun nature that appealed to voters, both hailed from the heartland, and both could play hardball politics. However, Truman had grave doubts about whether Kerr could be elected. In Truman's mind, Kerr was too beholden to the oil interests to win a national election. Secretly, Clifford had the same concern, but he set aside his doubts and plunged into the Kerr campaign. Since the senator was relatively unknown outside Oklahoma, Clifford advised him to launch a full-scale campaign and run in as many Democratic primaries as possible. Clifford also wrote strategy papers for Kerr, touted him to Democratic national committeemen, and, most important, tried to persuade Truman that Kerr was the man most capable of following in his footsteps.

Privately, Truman had decided that the best choice after Vinson was Adlai Stevenson, the cerebral governor of Illinois. Stevenson had shown no signs of seeking the job, but Truman believed he would be a formidable national candidate. In late January, he invited Stevenson to the White House and told him that he could get him nominated, whether Stevenson wanted the job or not. Stevenson was greatly surprised and flattered, but he told the president he was not interested.

Three weeks later, Truman convened his closest political advisers at Blair House for dinner and a discussion of the upcoming campaign. Clifford, of course, was on hand. Among the others were Vinson, John Steelman, Bill Hasset, who had been with Roosevelt when he died and had stayed on to serve Truman, and Charles Murphy, who had replaced Clifford as White House special counsel. Vinson urged Truman to run himself, arguing that the president could not refuse another term. Murphy, who knew Truman's heart was not in another race, pushed for another approach to Stevenson.

When Clifford's turn came, he proposed that the president throw his weight behind Kerr. Truman did not react favorably. Not only was Kerr too close to the oil and gas interests, but Truman believed that labor was likely to oppose him. The president refused to commit to Kerr, and the evening ended with Truman more uncertain than ever about what he should do.

By March, Senator Estes Kefauver, the Tennessee populist, was gathering momentum in his race for the presidency. He seemed to be moving into position to grab the Democratic nomination. Truman worried that Kefauver was too liberal for the country and he feared that his nomination would drive the Southern Democrats from the party, splitting it and and ensuring its defeat in November. Moreover, Truman did not like Kefauver personally, referring to him in private as "Senator Cowfever," a play on both the sound of his name and his populist philosophy.

On March 15, Clifford wrote to Truman, again urging him to endorse Kerr. Aware of the president's concerns about Kefauver, Clifford opened his letter by setting up the Tennessean as the bogeyman, noting that he had gotten a "real shot in the arm" from his strong performance in the New Hampshire primary. The Nebraska primary on April 1, said Clifford, offered an opportunity for Truman to jump into the race and sweep away any of Kefauver's chances. "On the other hand," wrote Clifford, "if you do not run again, a victory by Kerr over Kefauver would lend great impetus to Kerr's candidacy and seriously damage Kefauver's."

There was no way to counter Truman's reservations about Kerr's oil and gas ties, particularly since Clifford himself now represented those same interests. However, he did try to assuage Truman on the question of labor. Declaring that he had looked into the issue, Clifford wrote that he was "pleased to report that he has very substantial labor support." He enclosed a copy of a supportive letter to Kerr from the president of the Oklahoma Federation of Labor and an article from the Labor Party newspaper in Omaha, Nebraska.

Truman, tired of living in what he referred to derisively as "the great white jail" and uncertain of his chances anyway, decided finally not to run again. But he withheld any endorsement in Nebraska, dooming Kerr to finish second to Kefauver in what should have been a strong state for the Oklahoma senator. Clifford then persuaded Kerr that his hope lay in a deadlocked convention, where he might emerge as a unity candidate in the face of a clash between conservative southerners and northern liberals. It was wishful thinking. On July 6, two weeks before the convention in Chicago, Vice President Alben Barkley announced that he would seek the nomination in the name of party unity. The next week, Truman endorsed Barkley and the pundits agreed that a deadlocked convention would turn to the vice president, not Kerr.

Clifford and his wife arrived at the Democratic convention in Chicago on July 20, checking into the Blackstone Hotel, where they met their good friends the Symingtons. Stuart Symington had just come from Missouri, where he was the Democratic candidate for the United States Senate. Clifford knew that Kerr still had hopes of winning the nomination, but Clifford recognized that the senator had no chance. Nonetheless, Kerr arranged for Clifford to be an honorary assistant sergeant-at-arms, which gave him access to the convention floor to plot strategy for a last-ditch effort.

Kefauver came to Chicago with a commanding lead of 257 delegates, followed by Senator Richard Russell of Georgia, the last-minute southern candidate, with 161, Averell Harriman with 112, and Stevenson with 41. Kerr had no committed delegates, but when the time came to nominate him, the convention floor erupted in a massive demonstration. A band played and women volunteers passed out buttons picturing the log cabin in which Kerr was born. Washington columnists Drew Pearson and Jack Anderson later described the show for Kerr as "the biggest, best financed, and least sincere."

Despite Kefauver's big lead in delegates, Truman and the Democratic hierarchy gathered in the back rooms and worked to deny him the nomination. After two ballots and still no winner, Harriman released his delegates and most jumped on the Stevenson bandwagon, which had been gathering steam since the opening gavel. In the end, the Democrats nominated the reluctant Stevenson to oppose the Republican nominee, General Dwight David Eisenhower. Kerr had not even been a factor at the convention.

In the wake of the convention, Clifford sought to mend political fences. He wrote a letter to Harriman praising the skill and dignity of his campaign, and he praised Barkley in a letter, saying his speech at the convention was "the most magnificent I have ever heard." To his own candidate, Clifford wrote of "how deeply affected and impressed" he had been by Kerr's campaign. And he vowed that they would start planning earlier for 1956.

As usual, Clifford's highest praise was for Truman. "My heartiest congratulations for the superb job which you did at the Chicago convention," he wrote. "I thought your speech was excellent and that you delivered it magnificently."

During the election, the man who had ridden the campaign train to fame and glory four years earlier was relegated to a back seat. Aside from briefing Stevenson's staff on Truman's upset victory in 1948, Clifford was ignored. There was little he or anyone else could have done anyway. Eisenhower, the hero of World War II who campaigned as a nonpolitician under the slogan "Time for a Change," trounced Stevenson. He carried thirty-nine of the forty-eight states, including Stevenson's Illinois and Truman's Missouri. The country had a Republican president for the first time in twenty years.

The 1952 election was not a total loss for Clifford. Symington had been elected to the Senate from Missouri. And in Massachusetts, a young congressman named John F. Kennedy had knocked off the incumbent Republican senator, Henry Cabot Lodge. For Clifford and the country, this little-noticed victory would prove to be of monumental significance.

Truman's departure from Washington was unsettling to Clifford. He feared that he was facing his own years of exile. In the reflected glow of his patron in the White House and the memory of his service to Truman, Clifford had prospered. Moreover, even when Clifford had played it close to the edge in the Michigan Trade School case, the president had forgiven him. With the Truman administration dismantled and a potentially hostile Republican administration in its place, it seemed possible that Clifford's own stature — and prosperity — would be diminished.

His worst fears seemed to be realized right away. Within months of Eisenhower's taking office, a friend of Clifford's who was a career lawyer at the Justice Department came across a memo indicating that the department should open an investigation into whether Clifford had used his influence in any illegal ways. Clifford was startled. He had seen hardball politics in the Truman White House, but the attempt to get something on him went beyond his experience. He chose not to react to the memo, and there was no record that an investigation was ever conducted. However, the hostility toward Clifford and the other Truman cronies remained in some quarters of the Eisenhower administration.

The Eisenhower years were a time of strengthening old alliances and building new ones for Clifford. No longer would he organize poker games for the president of the United States or be summoned to the White House for a critical consultation. His focus shifted to Congress, where he remained very friendly with Kerr, drew closer to the rising star Lyndon Johnson, and renewed his friendship with Stuart Symington. As he had once served as Truman's adviser, now he offered his counsel to these and other powerful Democrats in Congress. The transition would be from insider at the White House to insider on Capitol Hill.

Symington, a former secretary of the air force and defense contractor, had been appointed to the Senate Armed Services Committee after his election. However, he also drew an assignment on the Senate Committee on Investigations, where Senator Joseph McCarthy of Wisconsin was conducting his long-running inquiry into allegations of anti-American activities.

During the Truman administration, McCarthy had concentrated on officials he charged were "soft" on Communism. He had succeeded in hounding several into resigning. Now, with a Republican administration elected after running on a platform that stressed opposition to "Godless Communism," the Wisconsin Republican's dark power was in danger of waning. So he had turned his attention to Communist infiltration of the armed forces and opened a new phase in his witch-hunt, the Army-McCarthy hearings. The army fought back and seemed to have McCarthy on the ropes when he came up with the case of Major Irving Peress.

Peress was a dentist who had been drafted into the army as a captain. After receiving his commission, he had refused to answer questions from a loyalty and security board about alleged associations with Communists. Although he was marked as a security risk, Peress was promoted to the rank of major because it corresponded with his civilian pay. Just as Peress was scheduled to leave the army in a routine discharge, McCarthy learned about his refusal to answer the loyalty questions and obtained a subpoena for his testimony.

Peress appeared before McCarthy's one-man subcommittee on January 30, 1954, and refused to answer any questions, asserting his constitutional rights. McCarthy demanded that Secretary of the Army Robert T. Stevens court-martial the major. Three days later, however, Peress was granted his honorable discharge before anything could be done about a possible court-martial. McCarthy was enraged and demanded a public explanation from Stevens and Brigadier General Ralph Zwicker, who had been the dentist's commanding officer.

Stevens, who knew Symington from his days at the Defense Department, turned to the Democratic senator for help on a Saturday in February 1954. Symington already had clashed with McCarthy. After listening to Stevens's concerns about McCarthy tearing down the army, the senator warned him to stay away from the hearing. Instead, he suggested, Stevens should launch his own counterattack on McCarthy.

"I would suggest two things to you, old fellow," said Symington. "One, let's counterpunch this stuff and not lead." The Missouri senator also said to Stevens about McCarthy: "This fellow might be sick, you know. If you are going to play with McCarthy, you have to forget about any of these Marquis of Queensbury rules."

He then suggested that Stevens not appear before McCarthy. "I wouldn't go," he said. "Let me talk to Clifford about it and I will call you."

Twenty minutes later that Saturday morning, Symington telephoned Stevens. "I talked to our legal friend," he explained. "He thinks it would be a mistake for you to talk to Mac." Symington then suggested that Stevens talk directly to Clifford.

McCarthy's antics had been distasteful to Clifford since the days of the loyalty oath in the Truman administration. However, he had avoided any public criticism of the volatile senator. When Stevens telephoned him at home the following Sunday morning, Clifford was calm and reserved. Unlike Symington, he did not attack McCarthy. But he did advise Stevens that neither he nor Zwicker should appear before the senator.

Unfortunately for Clifford and Symington, Stevens had had his telephone conversations with them monitored by army officials, who took verbatim notes of the talks. When the transcripts of the conversations were disclosed in early June 1954, Senator McCarthy turned his anger on Symington and Clifford. He accused them of conspiring to destroy the Republican Party and he demanded that Symington disqualify himself from participating in the Army-McCarthy hearings and that Clifford be subpoenaed to testify.

The last thing Clifford wanted to do was offer himself up to Joe McCarthy. Trying to avoid antagonizing the senator further, he wrote a careful letter. "In the event that the Subcommittee should believe that my testimony would be relevant to the issues under consideration, I am available at all times," he wrote. But Clifford said he saw no reason why he should have to appear and suggested that he might invoke the attorney-client privilege should he be asked about his conversation with Stevens. The mercurial McCarthy continued to complain about Clifford, but he did not force him to testify.

Symington refused to step down from the subcommittee hearings. Instead, he turned to Clifford for his insights. Symington wanted to challenge McCarthy one last time, but Clifford suggested that he avoid a direct confrontation. He proposed that Symington say the hearings had been inconclusive and that the record would have to be studied before any final determination. While not directly condemning McCarthy, Clifford offered two lines of attack. McCarthy, suggested Clifford, had tried to distort the record by limiting testimony by witnesses. Also, McCarthy had threatened the constitutional separation of powers doctrine by demanding that employees of the executive branch provide him with confidential information.

Symington delivered a strong speech at the closing hearing in June, criticizing McCarthy for distorting the truth and defending Clifford's role in the Stevens affair. Symington's outspoken opposition to McCarthy helped to establish him as a man who was not afraid to stand up for his principles. However, while Symington went on to become chairman of the Armed Services Committee and a highly regarded senator, he never developed the raw power of Clifford's other close friends in the Senate, Robert Kerr and Lyndon Johnson.

Clifford first met Johnson when the rangy Texan climbed aboard Truman's campaign train as it rolled into Texas during the 1948 campaign. With Johnson's own election to the Senate that year, he had begun a meteoric rise from the obscurity of the House of Representatives to the leadership of the Senate. In 1951, with only two years' tenure, he got the job of majority whip. Two years after that, with the Republicans in control, Johnson became minority leader.

With Johnson's rise in the Senate came a sharp change in his relationship with Clifford. While counsel to Truman, Clifford had occasionally provided advice to the senator from Texas. Even after leaving the White House, Clifford had sometimes been consulted by Johnson. But with his new post as minority leader, Johnson faced a much larger array of problems. Clifford was one of the men he sought out regularly for advice. Thus Clifford often found himself sitting in Johnson's Senate office alongside Abe Fortas, who had risen from bright young New Dealer to become one of the most influential lawyers in Washington; Tommy Corcoran; and James Rowe, another former New Dealer, whose memo had been so important to Clifford's own rise.

The personalities of Clifford and Johnson were too different for the men to be truly close friends. Johnson was loud and profane, given to bluster and intimidation. Clifford was measured and deliberate, although he could be counted on for the occasional off-color joke. However, the distance between Johnson and Clifford was bridged by their common love of power, even if they obtained and exercised it in different manners.

In Clifford, Johnson saw two things he wanted. First, Clifford was a winner. Often the wily Texan confided to associates that he liked the polished lawyer because of Clifford's role in engineering Truman's victory in '48. Second, and equally important, Clifford's clients included some of America's most powerful corporations. In seeking advice from the lawyer, Johnson could reach into the thinking of big-time corporate executives.

Clifford and Fortas became sounding boards for Johnson. They would be invited to his office to offer their opinions on subjects ranging from civil rights legislation to tax issues. Fortas later described the sessions with

Johnson this way: "Contrary to the way that he's portrayed, he wanted desperately to get all sides of the issue on every question. And so, on occasion, he would meet with his advisers and he would call up someone in whom he trusted — usually either me or Clark Clifford — and he would say, 'Everyone's telling me this. Give me the opposing argument.' Whether I believed it or not, I was to just lay out the opposing argument so he could see what the issues were."

What Clifford thought Johnson relished the most in those sessions was when the two lawyers disagreed. Johnson would lean back in his chair and grin as the two advocates argued it out, then he would make his own decison on which way to go.

Along with soliciting his opinions and advice, Johnson began to use Clifford to try to lobby Kerr on specific pieces of legislation. Johnson and Kerr were often allies and both were extremely powerful in the Senate. But Johnson also used Clifford to lobby the Oklahoma senator if Kerr was obstructing some piece of Johnson's legislative agenda. "Why don't you call him up and straighten him out?" Johnson would tell Clifford. "He's driving me crazy on this bill. Find out what he wants in return."

After Johnson suffered a heart attack in 1955, Kerr and Clifford went together to visit him as he recuperated at his Texas ranch. Clifford remembered how Johnson was eager to rejoin the fray in Washington, which he did as soon as he got permission from his doctor. Within months of Johnson's return to the Senate, Oregon's independent Wayne Morse declared himself a Democrat, giving the Democrats a majority in the Senate and allowing Johnson to become majority leader.

In a letter to former President Truman in December 1956, Clifford recounted an hour-long discussion with Johnson about the Democratic legislative agenda for the coming session. "Perhaps the greatest service I can render to the [Democratic] party is in being of assistance to him," Clifford wrote. "He is going to need plenty of help at this next session."

But Clifford's motivation was not entirely altruistic. George Reedy, who was Johnson's press secretary, found that Clifford and some of Johnson's other advisers used their relationship with the majority leader to assist their clients. Each, however, had a different style, as Reedy noted when he compared Corcoran, Fortas, and Clifford.

"If Tommy was going to steal a hot stove, he'd tell you about it, and then when he went back for the ashes, he would also tell you he was going back for the ashes," said Reedy. "Whereas Fortas, if he were going to steal a hot stove . . . would give you quite a story about how he was recovering an ancient relic from the infidel and restoring it to its rightful place." As for Clifford, Reedy said he would tell a tale similar to that of Fortas, but he would tell it so convincingly that, when he finished, "you'd go and help him take it."

With such powerful friends in Congress, it was no wonder that Clifford wound up with a client in the middle of one of the most interesting congressional investigations of the decade. The client was Charles Revson, the chairman of Revlon Corporation. Revlon was a sponsor of the television quiz show *Twenty One,* to which the nation had been riveted, watching a string of victories by a young Easterner named Charles Van Doren. When it was discovered that the questions were rigged, Revson was summoned to Washington to testify before Congress about what he knew of the scandal.

Max Kampelman, who had recently left the staff of Minnesota Senator Hubert Humphrey, was hired to represent Revlon Corporation in early 1956 when the congressional committee initially began investigating allegations that Van Doren and other contestants on the show had been provided the answers to questions. Responding to the public outcry, the investigators wanted to know whether the sponsors were aware of the rigging.

Kampelman met with Revson, who ran the company with his brother Martin. After questioning him and examining the company's files, Kampelman was convinced that Revlon had been duped along with the American public. In fact, Revson himself was a regular viewer of the weekly show, cheering for contestants and believing that the program was honest. Despite this, Kampelman advised Revson not to appear when his testimony was sought by the congressional committee.

"Revson looked slick on his good days, slippery on his bad days, and I felt he would add nothing to the inquiry," said Kampelman. Instead, the lawyer thought he could stop the inquiry into Revlon by opening up the company files to the committee staff.

A short time later, Revson called Kampelman and said he was rejecting the lawyer's advice. He said that his public relations staff had convinced him to testify so that he could clear the company's name in public. Unable to persuade him to remain silent, Kampelman said Revson would have to hire another attorney to represent him personally for his appearance, since Kampelman's client was the company. When asked for a recommendation, Kampelman suggested Clark Clifford.

A short time later, Revson appeared before the committee, with Clifford at his side. But Congress was out for blood and there was no room for Revson's version of events in an atmosphere of public indignation. "The committee clobbered Revson," Kampelman remembered. "They kicked his brains out."

Clifford was unfazed by the bruising of his client. A few days after the debacle, he called Kampelman and asked what Kampelman thought he should charge for the small amount of time he had put in trying to prepare Revson for his testimony. When Kampelman said he had no idea, Clifford suggested $25,000. Kampelman whistled in disbelief, but Clifford, in his most reassuring tones, said, "Max, Revson will be unhappy with my bill, and he's going to tell you it's highway robbery. But he'll pay it and next winter when he's playing pinochle with his cronies in Miami he'll talk about his Washington lawyer Clark Clifford."

Kampelman learned an important lesson. "Name-dropping as well as aggravation seemed billable," he concluded. "I increased my own bill."

For a time in the 1950s, Clifford also collected rent from the Federal Bureau of Investigation. It was an unusual and highly secret arrangement that illustrated not only Clifford's patriotism but his pragmatism and ability to get along with people he disliked as well.

Clifford had had little use for J. Edgar Hoover, the legendary FBI director, since his days in the Truman White House, when Hoover was promoting his anti-Communist loyalty oath. But one day after Clifford had opened his law practice on L Street, the FBI director telephoned him.

"I'd like to talk to you," said Hoover.

"I'll come right up," replied Clifford.

Actually, Hoover said, he would prefer to come to Clifford's office.

When the FBI director arrived, he explained that the bureau wanted to improve its surveillance of the Soviet Embassy, which was near the rear of the office building. "I understand you have an office here that might be useful," said Hoover.

So the two men went to a room at the rear of Clifford's suite of offices. Sure enough, the window looked down directly on the rear entrance to the embassy, offering a clear view of anyone who entered or exited. At the height of American fears about the Soviet Union, it was a priceless observation point for monitoring the comings and goings at the embassy. Clifford agreed to clear the office and turn it over to the FBI. Agents moved in sophisticated surveillance gear and staffed the room twenty-four hours a day. The bureau paid rent to the law firm and the office was still in use as a surveillance post when Clifford moved out years later.

"It was never politic for me to say, 'Mr. Hoover, I don't like you,' " Clifford said later. "That wouldn't make any sense."

The best vantage point for witnessing Clifford's extraordinary political connections throughout the decade of the fifties was at the annual New Year's Day party he and Marny threw. Invitations were coveted and the guest list embraced Supreme Court justices, administration officials, congressional leaders, and many of the most prominent lawyers in Washington. While the parties were not ostentatious, the rambling house was decorated warmly for the holidays and the entertainment was unique and elaborate.

Planning was a family task. Beginning in October, a good part of each Sunday was devoted to planning the coming year's entertainment. All three daughters — and eventually their husbands — participated in writing lyrics for songs and scenarios for skits. Margery, who had a glorious singing voice, would be counted on to handle the toughest songs. Joyce, always the smartest of the daughters, came up with the sort of satire that tickled her father's fancy. And Randall, the charmer of the group, brought her own vibrancy to the occasion. The leader, of course, was Clifford himself. With his mother's flair for the dramatic and his own college training, he was invariably cast as the star of the humorous skits, and it was he who delivered the final number each year, the State of the Union address.

In the years when his daughters lived at home, the planning sessions for these parties were one of the few times the family worked together as a whole. By the early 1950s, Marny Clifford was developing her own life, clearly separate from that of her husband. In her husband's word, she had "adjusted" to marriage to a man whose first priority, unlike that of his father, was work.

Mrs. Clifford spent summers with the girls at her parents' summer home in New Hampshire. Later, as her husband's law practice prospered, she found a house she loved on Nantucket Island, off the Massachusetts coast of Cape Cod, and persuaded Clifford to buy it. Financial success had brought a better life in other ways. Gery and Joyce had been debutantes, and Randall was about to graduate from Foxcroft, an elite girl's boarding school in the horse country of Middleburg, Virginia.

There also was enough money for Marny Clifford to indulge one of her lifelong passions. Before the depression, she had traveled often to Europe with her father and mother. In the early years of her marriage, there had not been enough money for such extravagances. But now, with her daughters becoming independent and money worries over, she began taking long cruises.

"Clark was very generous with me," she would say years later. "I have seen most of the world two or three times. I love it."

But it was a passion she indulged without her husband. Clifford hated the confinement of a ship. Even worse, he could not abide being away from work for any length of time. So he never accompanied her. "He has no curiosity about anything to do with looking at anything," his wife explained. "One time I accompanied him on a business trip for the government. We were on a train going through Europe and I was hanging out the window looking at the world going by. He was asleep."

It was not an unusual marriage by the conventional standards of the day. Clifford was the breadwinner and provider. From the earliest days following their honeymoon, Marny Clifford had known that her husband's work was his first love. For years, she had confined herself to raising their three daughters, managing the couple's social life, and pursuing her own interests, such as advising friends on interior decorating and assembling her own recipes and those of her friends to eventually publish a cookbook.

But those Sundays leading up to the holidays when the family pooled their skills and humor were rich times, and the results became nothing less than legend in Washington social circles. The grand piano and all of the furniture were removed from the large living room at the south end of the house. A smaller upright piano was rented and a small stage was erected for the performers. As the family members sang their songs or performed in the skits, they could look across the room and see Lyndon Johnson lounging in a corner, Justice Douglas sipping a whisky on a couch, and his colleague Justice Stanley Reed in his favorite spot, propped against the upright piano where Marny Clifford was playing. As the years went on, the crowd grew, spilling into the adjoining library and the small room where the bar was set up. Once guests were invited one year, they never stopped coming, whether or not they received another invitation. Eventually, the overflow was so large that speakers were installed in other rooms of the house.

In one memorable skit, Clifford stepped onto the five-foot by six-foot stage and began to recite "Invictus," a popular nineteenth-century poem. As Clifford spoke the words, "My head is bloody but unbowed," his two sons-in-law, Bill Lanagan and Dick Barrett, walked onto the stage and began wrapping him in gauze bandages, from the feet up. Finally, as the famous baritone voice came to the ending lines, "I am the master of my fate/I am the captain of my soul," the only space left uncovered was Clifford's mouth. The two men then carried their father-in-law from the stage to the laughter and applause of the audience.

Barrett, a banker who married Joyce after she graduated from Vassar, remembers his former father-in-law as a man who always seemed to speak as though he were on television or before a congressional committee. He was never impulsive or intemperate, and his formal manner extended to his daughters. "He had a unique relationship with his daughters," recalled Barrett. "He is an absorbed individual. It wasn't a close relationship. They respected his privacy enormously. It's difficult to describe. He was so frequently occupied by great thoughts."

Sometimes during those years, Clifford shared his thoughts with Joyce and her husband in an intriguing ritual known as the Wednesday seminars. While Marny Clifford was on Nantucket each summer, Clifford would go to dinner at the home of Joyce and Dick every Wednesday. After dinner, he would lead a three-person seminar on a pre-chosen topic. One summer, the topic was the economy. Another summer it was foreign policy, and later it was the oil business. "He really knew the oil business," said Joyce later. "He had an encyclopedic grasp of things and, of course, Poppy loves an audience."

So it was that the whole family had its audience each year on New Year's Day, too. In the warmth of his home, surrounded by family and friends, Clifford seemed to let down his guard once each year. The skits he devised often demonstrated great wit as well as an ability to mock himself. These seemed to be the rare occasions when Clifford thoroughly enjoyed himself.

*   *   *

The vast majority of Clifford's energy and time was devoted to building his law practice, which he did methodically and conscientiously. Fears of lean times early in the Eisenhower administration had long since passed. George Allen, whose law firm was dominated by Republicans, kept business flowing to Clifford. Phillips Petroleum continued to pay its retainer, as did about two dozen other big corporations. Howard Hughes kept the firm on his payroll, too, although he gave more of his Washington business to the bigger firm of Hogan and Hartson.

Hughes himself was uncertain of Clifford's loyalties. In 1956, when he hired a former FBI agent named Robert Maheu as his newest eyes and ears in Washington, Hughes gave Maheu a piece of advice about how to deal with Clifford. "Use him only when it is real necessary, but don't ever tell him more than you have to," Hughes instructed. "Remember, this is a smoothie who tries to be all things to all people. Use him but watch him."

Hughes, on his way to becoming a phobic, bedridden paranoid, was in a distinct minority. Among the many who had no such doubts about Clifford's loyalty was Senator Robert Kerr. Along with continuing to refer clients to Clifford, Kerr and his friend, Boots Adams of Phillips Petroleum, suggested oil and gas drilling ventures in which the lawyer could invest. Kerr often assembled the partnerships and included those from whom he wanted favors. In addition to Clifford, Kerr arranged for one of his Senate colleagues, Allen Frear of Delaware, to become an investor in at least one oil-and-gas venture. Clifford always put up his own money, a few thousand for each investment, and as the years went on, he invested in twenty-five or twenty-six oil drilling ventures and earned millions of dollars in profits.

Years later one of his law partners was at Phillips Petroleum on business when he came across some papers that cast a new light on Clifford's investments. When an oil company selects land for geological exploration, they map the area out in grids and then select the most promising grid to begin sinking wells. If a gusher is found in one grid, it is highly likely that the other grids in closest proximity will also produce oil, although the amount will probably be less. These neighboring grids are called "farm outs." As his law partner examined the records at Phillips headquarters in Bartlesville, Oklahoma, he discovered that Clifford's investments had been concentrated in farm outs. As a result, his investments had entailed far less risk than a normal investor would have faced.

Clifford displayed his gratitude to Kerr one Christmas. Clifford usually sent lawmakers small gifts, such as candy or scarves. But for Kerr one year, he paid several hundred dollars to install a state-of-the-art intercom system in the senator's office. It was called an "Executive Control Intercommunication System," and Clifford wrote Kerr that the gift was for "the one man who is busier than I am." He added, "I want you to know how sincerely I appreciate your fine friendship."

In those years, Clifford's law work also had an international flavor. For a time, he represented a millionaire New York businessman and former Hollywood mogul named Matthew Fox in his dealings with the government of Indonesia and the American government.

Early in his life, Fox had made a fortune as a young executive with Universal Pictures and RKO Theaters. He was credited with making fundamental improvements in Hollywood's business practices and pioneered the use of motion picture films on television. But he was most famous as the "economic godfather of Indonesia."

After the Dutch began their forced withdrawal from Indonesia in 1948, Fox emerged as a spokesman for the fledgling nation's economic interests in the United States. By 1949, Fox's American Indonesia Corporation had a contract to handle all Indonesian government buying and selling in the United States. He also was granted extensive rights to develop oil and other natural resources in Indonesia. He had obtained the lucrative franchise in exchange for loaning the cash-strapped new government about $40 million worth of gold bullion to support its new currency. But Fox's would-be monopoly ran into strong criticism from the American State Department and the Dutch government, and he was forced to tear up the contract to handle imports and exports. Fox managed to hold onto his oil development rights. When it came time to permit the development, however, Indonesia tried to get out of the deal and Fox called on Clifford.

Fox's business operated out of a building at 445 Park Avenue in New York City, where Fox also maintained a penthouse apartment. One day Clifford visited Fox in his Manhattan penthouse and as they chatted in the living room, the lawyer noticed a photograph of a stunning woman on a side table.

"That is the most beautiful woman I have ever seen," he said. "Who is she?"

Fox smiled and replied, "That is my wife."

Yolande Betbeze Fox was indeed a beauty. Born in Mississippi, she had married the short, balding Fox in 1953, two years after she had been crowned Miss America. Clifford always admired attractive people, both men and women, and he did not forget that photograph. Not long after her husband's death in 1963, the former Miss America would move to Washington, renew her acquaintanceship with Clifford, and help him land an intriguing client.

As for Fox, he never did get to develop Indonesia's vast oil resources, but with Clifford's help, he eventually got back his $40 million in gold from the Indonesians. In fact, Fox was so impressed by Clifford's skills that he suggested that the Indonesian government hire the lawyer to represent its interests in Washington, which he did for several years in the fifties.

But Clifford's most important corporate work throughout that first decade in business was for Phillips Petroleum. Before Truman left office, Clifford had lobbied hard in Congress for passage of Kerr-backed legislation that allowed Phillips and other companies to raise the price of natural gas. When Truman vetoed the measure, Clifford appeared before the Federal Power Commission and convinced regulators that the companies had the power to raise prices without the legislation.

At the time, columnist Joseph Alsop charged that Kerr had bought the support of the federal commission by providing lucrative gas leases to key people. When a congressional committee investigated the case, they discovered Clifford's involvement in lobbying the commission. It turned out that he had been friends with one of the commissioners, Frederick Stueck, when they were at Washington University law school together. Records showed that the two men had had lunch together eight times while the Phillips case was pending before the commission. But Stueck told the committee that he and Clifford never discussed the issue. They only talked about old times in St. Louis. As he had during the Detroit trade school debate earlier in the decade, Clifford avoided testifying before Congress and the matter eventually subsided.

It was during this period that Clifford's representation of Phillips also led him to an appearance before his friend on the Supreme Court, Justice Douglas. In the fall of 1959, Clifford argued on behalf of Phillips before the Supreme Court in a case involving an attempt by a Texas school district to collect more than $1 million in taxes. The school district contended that Phillips owed the property taxes for a plant the company owned. Phillips contended that the plant was on land leased from the federal government and therefore could not be taxed. The Texas Supreme Court had agreed with the school district, but Phillips appealed to the United States Supreme Court.

In his appearance before the court, Clifford repeated the arguments made by other lawyers for the company in the lower courts. A few months later the court ruled in favor of Phillips, saving $1 million for Clifford's most important client. Justice Douglas voted in favor of Phillips.

10

The Kennedy Connection

ON A SATURDAY NIGHT, December 7, 1957, Jack Kennedy was sitting in his home in Washington's affluent Georgetown neighborhood watching television when he erupted in anger. On the ABC-TV program *Mike Wallace Interview*, the prominent Washington columnist Drew Pearson was accusing Kennedy of plagiarism. *Profiles in Courage*, the book for which Kennedy had won the Pulitzer Prize, was actually ghost-written, claimed Pearson.

Early on Monday morning, the young Democratic senator from Massachusetts telephoned Clark Clifford. "I want to come see you," said Kennedy.

"I'll come see you immediately, senator," offered Clifford, sensing that Kennedy was highly agitated.

"No," insisted Kennedy. "I'll come to you. I'll be there in about twenty minutes."

Clifford's contacts with the Massachusetts senator had been minimal. Like many other seasoned Washington observers, he had concluded that there was not much depth to the young man from one of the nation's richest families.

When Kennedy arrived at Clifford's law office on L Street, he got straight to the point. He described Pearson's accusation and denied it.

"It is very damaging to me," said Kennedy. "It goes to my credibility, my honesty, my concept of ethics. I accepted the Pulitzer Prize. We must do something about it."

Kennedy said that he wanted to explain to Clifford how the book had come to be written, but he said that he expected to be interrupted soon. "Sometime during this meeting my father will call you," said the senator. "I told him I was coming to see you."

Describing how he had been recuperating from back surgery in Florida when he came up with the idea of writing the book to pass the time, Kennedy said he began by jotting his thoughts into notebooks, outlining how he would organize the manuscript and the issues he wanted to raise.

"Can you produce these notebooks?" asked Clifford.

Kennedy said he could. Theodore C. Sorensen, an aide to Kennedy, and others had provided him with considerable assistance in the research and polishing the writing, Kennedy acknowledged, but he insisted that it was his book and that Pearson's charge was rubbish.

In the midst of this explanation, Joseph Kennedy, the former ambassador to England and patriarch of the Kennedy clan, called to talk to his son. Clifford watched as the senator listened to his father. After a few minutes, Kennedy said, "No, Dad. I don't think so." Then Kennedy said, "Dad, let me put you on the line with Clark."

When Clifford picked up the phone, the first words he heard were "Sue the bastards for $50 million. Goddamn them. They're trying to destroy my boy."

"Mr. Ambassador," Clifford said calmly, "I'm not sure . . ."

"Sue them," interrupted the furious elder Kennedy. "That's all these people do. Give them the best you've got."

"Well, we'll think about it, Mr. Ambassador," said Clifford. "But that isn't quite the way to go about it."

From years of practice and gut instinct, Clifford knew that a legal victory for political figures means not just winning in court, but preserving their reputations and minimizing negative publicity. Once Joseph Kennedy hung up, the lawyer turned to Kennedy and said, "That's the worst possible thing to do. You get it back on the front page again, and you go back through the whole Pearson testimony again. It inflates the whole thing. It keeps it alive. These libel suits last forever."

"Well," said Kennedy, "you can convince me. I agree that is the worst thing to do. What should we do?"

"As soon as we can, we ought to get up there and see the head of ABC. He'll have his lawyer there and others, and it will be up to us to convince them that they have made a mistake. What we need here is a retraction and that takes care of it. But by God, to throw the thing into court, and then every step gets it back in the papers, Pearson would love that."

Kennedy left with instructions to assemble all of the original material for the book that he could find. Clifford said that he would arrange a meeting as soon as possible with Leonard Goldenson, the chairman and founder of ABC.

Before the day was out and before he had anything more than Kennedy's word that he had written the book, Clifford had called Goldenson. He said that Kennedy felt strongly that he had been libeled. Unless Goldenson met with them and listened to the senator's evidence, they would be forced to file a lawsuit. Goldenson agreed to listen and the meeting was arranged for ten o'clock in the morning on Thursday, December 12, in New York. Joseph Kennedy also would be sending his own lawyer to the session, undoubtedly to press for a lawsuit.

Before going to New York, Clifford met with his friend Phil Graham, the publisher of the *Washington Post*, where Pearson's column appeared. Clifford tried to persuade Graham to get Pearson to retract the allegation in a forthcoming column, but Graham said he had no control over Pearson's column. He was not a staff member, but an independent, syndicated columnist.

A heavy snowstorm blanketed the Northeast on the afternoon of December 11. Clifford decided to take the train from Washington that evening, in case the airports were closed in the morning. Indeed, no planes were landing in New York the morning of the twelfth and Joseph Kennedy's lawyer was stuck in Boston.

The meeting at ABC's executive suites with Goldenson and his lawyers lasted most of the day. Kennedy did not attend, so Clifford argued his case. Key details were corroborated by Ted Sorensen, who had brought along the written evidence he said showed that the senator had actually conceived and written the book. Around four in the afternoon, Goldenson and Oliver Treyz, an ABC executive, asked to discuss the matter with their lawyers. When they returned to the conference room, Goldenson said that ABC was prepared to work out a settlement.

"That is very good," said Clifford. "Now give me a little time to talk on the phone with Senator Kennedy. I would like to prepare a suggested statement that would be satisfactory to my client."

Clifford crafted a masterful retraction. The denunciation of Pearson's claim would not come from Kennedy, but from ABC itself. After a more thorough investigation of the allegation, ABC would tell its audience, on the same show on the upcoming Sunday, that the network had determined that Pearson was in error. Senator Kennedy had written *Profiles in Courage*. Then came what Clifford laughingly referred to later as "the stinger": ABC would apologize not just to Kennedy but to the Pulitzer Prize committee.

On Saturday, December 14, Oliver Treyz of ABC read the statement at the beginning of *Mike Wallace Interview*, apologizing to both Kennedy and the Pulitzer Prize committee. It was a retraction that angered Wallace, already regarded as the leading interviewer on television. Years later, he was still complaining that ABC should have called Kennedy's bluff.

Kennedy was extremely pleased with the outcome. Clifford, too, was satisfied. But the lawyer was puzzled that Kennedy's father had so clearly overreacted to the allegation. After the retraction was broadcast, Clifford asked Kennedy why his father had been so angry over the Pearson allegation.

"I have something to tell you in great confidence," John Fitzgerald Kennedy told him. "We have had a lot of family meetings about it and I am going to run for president. We thought the charge would be a real burden in the campaign."

Clifford had earned at least a partial admittance to the Kennedy inner circle, a place reserved for family members and the most trusted aides. He also had seen how carefully the Kennedy clan was planning the senator's rise. A few weeks later, he got another glimpse when he received a letter from the young senator.

In the letter, Kennedy asked for Clifford's assistance in preparing his speech at the upcoming Gridiron Dinner. The dinner, which is sponsored by the elite of the Washington press corps, is a lighthearted affair at which the press pokes fun at the high and mighty. But Kennedy prepared for his own speech with the thoroughness that would mark his upcoming presidential campaign. Clifford joined several others, including Sorensen and Joseph Kennedy, in tossing around ideas for the talk. By Clifford's count, they voted on 112 jokes and other humorous suggestions. The result, which Kennedy delivered on March 15, 1958, was a grand success.

In remarks that would prove cannily prescient, the senator spoke following a sketch in which his wealthy father had been lampooned for buying him his Senate seat. Reaching into his breast pocket, Kennedy withdrew a slip of paper and said he had just received a telegram from his father. "Dear Jack," it supposedly read. "Don't buy a single vote more than is necessary. I'll be damned if I'm going to pay for a landslide."

During the next three years, Clifford was involved in other legal matters for Kennedy leading up to an election that was far from a landslide. Some of those matters were quite sensitive in nature and demonstrated that Kennedy had enormous trust in Clifford. Even in later years, Clifford refused to discuss these matters, saying that he would take the late president's secrets to the grave with him. In 1960, however trusted he was, Clifford would be unable to support the senator's bid for the Democratic nomination because his primary loyalty was elsewhere.

With President Eisenhower approaching the end of his second term, the Democrats were confident that they could recapture the White House in 1960. The midterm elections of 1958 had buoyed their fortunes, giving them the largest majority in the Senate since before World War II. As the presidential campaign neared, a number of Democrats were scrambling for the right to oppose the anticipated Republican candidate, Vice President Richard M. Nixon.

Senator Kerr had tried in vain to wrest the 1956 nomination from Adlai Stevenson. Kerr appeared to have no better chance this time around, although he had difficulty abandoning his aspirations. The Senate, however, had provided the leading candidates — Kennedy, Lyndon Johnson of Texas, Hubert Humphrey of Minnesota, and Stuart Symington of Missouri.

In early January 1959, Symington and his wife went to dinner at the Cliffords' house on Rockville Pike. The two couples dined regularly, but this was a special occasion, a farewell dinner for Marny Clifford, who was leaving by herself on a two-month Mediterranean cruise. But something else was launched that night.

Since their meeting in St. Louis more than twenty years before, the two men had remained close personal friends. Their families spent many holidays together, and Clifford and Symington were frequent golfing and card-playing companions. After the meal, the two men adjourned to Clifford's upstairs den and talked until past one o'clock in the morning. It was a long and sober discussion.

Symington, who had been reelected to the Senate the previous fall, told his old friend that he was considering running for president and asked Clifford for an honest assessment. Clifford said that Symington faced a tough race, particularly against a well-financed Kennedy campaign. But the man credited with engineering Harry Truman's upset victory more than a decade earlier left no doubt about where he stood. He was in Symington's corner. For Clifford, personal loyalty was one of the highest attributes to which a person could aspire. He and Symington were simply too close for the lawyer to do anything but throw himself wholeheartedly into his friend's campaign, even if success was unlikely.

Symington, little known outside Washington and Missouri, was a long shot. As Clifford evaluated the campaign, Symington seemed to be everyone's second choice. Therefore, Clifford reasoned, let Johnson, Kennedy, and Humphrey battle it out in the primaries. By the time of the convention, no one would have a clear majority and Symington, rested and unbloodied from the intraparty warfare, could step in as the consensus candidate.

The strategy of appearing to be the candidate everyone could live with extended to Symington's actions in the Senate. In February 1959, one of the senator's aides learned that Kennedy intended to vote against legislation to provide federal financial assistance to parochial schools. The aide proposed that Symington drive a wedge in Kennedy's Catholic support by voting for the bill. Symington pondered the issue and told the aide to consult with Clifford. After listening to the plan, Clifford rejected it. "We don't play politics with that sort of thing," he said. The idea was dropped.

While the refusal to politicize parochial education was the honorable course, keeping the Symington campaign out of the mud also meant that Clifford would not be burning his bridges in the event of a Kennedy victory, which most people even then thought far more likely than a Symington win.

Central to Clifford's strategy for Symington was that the Missouri senator stay out of the Democratic primaries. "Your strength is to be everybody's second choice," Clifford repeated to Symington. "By not entering the primaries, you will be fresh and untouched."

Skipping the primaries was strongly opposed by Symington's professional political advisers, as well as his two sons, Stuart Jr. and James. They believed that precisely because he was not well known across the country he needed to demonstrate that he could attract voters outside his home state and go to the convention with delegates in hand. The Democratic primary in Indiana, a state with a political temperament akin to that of Missouri, offered what they felt was a good opportunity for Symington to get on the national map. In the spring of 1960, his sons and other advisers urged Symington to reject Clifford's advice and enter the Indiana primary.

"You young men had better understand something," the senator said, leaning back in his chair and smiling indulgently. "Mr. Clifford and Mr. Truman knew something about winning elections."

Symington's son James, who later was elected to Congress himself, thought his father could win Indiana, Maryland, and certainly Missouri. But he discovered that it was Clark Clifford whose advice was, as he phrased it later, "seminal and controlling."

It soon proved to be the wrong strategy. The decision left the door open for the Kennedy campaign to fulfill its plan of sweeping every single Democratic primary. When Kennedy won Indiana in April, Lawrence O'Brien, one of his closest advisers, said it proved that a young Catholic could win in the Midwest. O'Brien offered public thanks to Symington, who, he said, had chosen not to enter Indiana "for reasons only known to God."

Charlie Brown, Symington's official campaign manager, knew why his candidate has passed up Indiana. "It was because of that goddamned Clifford," he moaned. "His advice was just so bad."

Although there would be whispers later that Clifford had sabotaged the Symington campaign in a clandestine effort to help Kennedy, nothing could be more outrageously mistaken. Clifford had given his best advice to a man he truly regarded as a friend. Clifford can be criticized for his political instincts, but not for his loyalty.

What Clifford brought the Symington campaign was an aura of experience and success. No one was more aware of that aura than Hugh Sidey, the chief political correspondent in Washington for *Time*, the most powerful force in journalism in the nation at the time.

When he first came to Washington in 1957, Sidey moved into a house about half a mile from the Clifford home. "To the neighbors, his house was like a shrine," recalled Sidey later. "Everyone talked about where Clark Clifford lived."

The charter of *Time* correspondents in those days was to get as close as possible to the powerful people they covered. They had lavish expense accounts and belonged to the same exclusive private clubs frequented by Washington's elite. For Sidey, as a political writer, this meant getting close to Clifford.

It was not a difficult task. Sidey, the son of an Iowa newspaper family, shared Clifford's Midwestern roots and his liberal Democratic politics.

For his part, Clifford had learned long ago that relationships with key people in the press were invaluable to anyone who held or desired power in Washington. And he and his family loved the buzz and excitement that journalists often brought to their house. The two men formed a lasting and mutually beneficial friendship. Over the years, Sidey earned a reputation as one of the most influential journalists in the nation's capital and an expert on the presidency. The man he quoted more than any other in his columns was Clark Clifford. The relationship endured and flourished even though Sidey's first impression of Clifford was to wonder what all the fuss was about.

"I remember one of the first times I interviewed him," said Sidey later. "I came out and looked at my notebook and read the notes and I thought to myself, 'These are the most simple and commonsense observations. There is nothing clever or brilliant in what Clifford said.' But I soon came to realize that this was his genius: he didn't try to do anything that fancy, he just provided commonsense advice. There was always a stark logic to his expositions."

When Sidey shared his observation with a more experienced Washington hand, the man told him, "The longer you are in this city, the more you will understand that logic and common sense are the rarest of commodities."

So it was with logic and common sense that Clifford sought to explain to Sidey in 1959 how Stuart Symington could win the Democratic nomination for president. Sidey had been assigned to do a cover story on Symington's candidacy for *Life*, the sister publication of *Time*. He spent hours in Clifford's office, going over a scenario in which Kennedy would fail to win the nomination on the first ballot, throwing open the convention and paving the way for Symington. Clifford and Sidey, both from the Protestant-dominated Midwest, expected Kennedy's Catholicism to doom his candidacy.

While agreeing that Clifford's strategy made sense, Sidey was puzzled by his support for Symington. He knew that Clifford had represented Kennedy, the hands-on front-runner, and that he had been a longtime confidant of Lyndon Johnson, also a stronger candidate than Symington.

"Why are you working for Senator Symington? Why Symington and not Kennedy or Johnson?" Sidey asked Clifford during one of their interviews.

"He's been my best friend over these years, and when he asked me, there was no way I could refuse him," responded Clifford.

Sidey, who harbored his own doubts that Symington was the best man for the job, sensed that Clifford probably agreed with his sentiments. But loyalty stopped Clifford from saying anything bad about his friend, the same way it committed him to helping him seek the nomination. Of course, if Symington's long shot came in, Clifford would find himself in a very opportune position with a Symington White House, whether he joined the administration or sought favors from it as a private lawyer.

Unfortunately for Symington and Clifford, conservative publishing magnate Henry Luce decided he did not want to give the Democrats too much publicity in advance of the election and killed the cover story. It was a harbinger of things to come for the senator from Missouri.

Despite his role as Symington's principal adviser, Clifford continued to walk a political tightrope by performing sensitive legal work for Kennedy and offering advice to him. Just weeks before the Democratic national convention, Clifford helped keep the lid on a matter that he later admitted could have destroyed Kennedy's chance for the presidency.

Even long years after Kennedy's death, Clifford refused to discuss the subject. Shaking his head gravely, he would say only, "We had troubled matters. I was called in. His father was in. They were rather sensitive matters. I privately said that I felt it was a tribute to the fact that I would be wholly discreet and totally reliable."

Indeed, bringing him in on a politically explosive secret at a time when he was running a rival's campaign seemed the ultimate compliment to Clifford's discretion.

The "troubled matters" most likely involved a claim by a woman that she had been engaged to Kennedy in 1951, but that Kennedy's father had forced him to break off the relationship because of her Polish-Jewish background. For reasons that remain unknown, the allegations were never made public. Years later, however, J. Edgar Hoover, the FBI director, wrote to Robert F. Kennedy that the bureau's files contained evidence that a $500,000 settlement had been paid to the woman.

At another point, Kennedy complained to Clifford that former President Truman had been openly denouncing him, partly because he was Catholic, and asked if Clifford would intercede. Because of his role in the

Symington campaign, Clifford was reluctant to approach Truman himself at this point. So he raised the issue with Dean Acheson and Acheson agreed, in the name of party unity, to speak to Truman.

A month before the Democratic convention, Kennedy telephoned Clifford and asked him to drop by his house the next morning. When he arrived at eight o'clock, Kennedy went straight to the point. "I'm not interested in Adlai's two campaigns in which we lost," Kennedy said. "I want to talk about the campaign in which we won. I want to go back to the '48 campaign of Harry Truman. Start in at the beginning and tell me what decisions you made and why you made them."

Clifford spent the next four hours recounting the strategy that won the presidency for Truman in 1948, the strategy actually devised by Jim Rowe but widely accepted as Clifford's. He described the basics of the Democratic coalition — blacks, organized labor, the farmers. Kennedy occasionally interrupted with questions, but mostly Clifford's deep, confident voice went on and on.

As Clifford concluded, Kennedy brought the discussion to the present. "We've analyzed with care the coming convention and we think we have enough, but we are not sure," he said. "It would put us over if Senator Symington would throw his strength to me."

"I'd be glad to talk to him, but the possibility of that happening is remote," replied Clifford. "He has worked hard and our friends have raised money and I don't think he feels in the position just to say that he is giving up without even going to the convention."

When Clifford raised the issue with Symington, the senator laughed and said, "You go back and say to him that we would like to have Senator Kennedy throw his strength to Senator Symington." Clifford dutifully called with his candidate's answer and Kennedy took the rebuff in the good spirit that was intended.

Two weeks later, Clifford was back before Kennedy at the senator's request. This time, Kennedy said, his campaign was within striking distance of sewing up the nomination. "If you can see your way clear to throw Senator Symington's strength to us, we might consider selecting him as the number two man on the ticket," said Kennedy.

Again, Symington rejected the offer, but in a softer fashion. He was clearly enticed by the prospect of the vice presidency, and Clifford thought it likely that Kennedy would offer the job to him.

The Democratic convention was held in Los Angeles in mid-July.

Kennedy appeared to have amassed enough delegates to win the nomination, but his victory was not certain. And the matter of a running mate was still undecided. Early in the convention, Kennedy summoned Clifford to a private room at the Biltmore Hotel, away from his main suite, which was surrounded by reporters.

"We are thinking seriously about Senator Symington on the ticket," said Kennedy. "Do you think you might persuade him to throw his strength to us? As we analyze it, he can't win."

Clifford said Symington might want to take the chance on a deadlocked convention, but he promised to present Kennedy's offer once again. Symington rejected the proposal late that night. The next afternoon, July 14, Kennedy telephoned Clifford and offered the vice presidency to Symington. Clifford said he would convey the message and respond later that evening.

Over dinner and a long meeting in his suite, Symington debated the offer with his wife, Evelyn, his sons Stuart Jr. and James, and Clifford. Symington's family opposed accepting the nomination, arguing that he should remain in the Senate rather than accept the relative obscurity of the vice presidency. When it came his turn, Clifford said, "I don't see how he can refuse. He'd like to be president. This has been said many times before: the vice president is just one heartbeat away. He must not turn this down." Clifford and Symington adjourned to the bedroom of the suite, where the senator said that he would accept Kennedy's offer. Clifford got Kennedy on the telephone, relayed the acceptance to him, and went to sleep assuming that the deal was settled.

Throughout the night, however, House Speaker Sam Rayburn and a group of other conservative Democrats kept up the pressure on Kennedy to give the number two spot to Senator Lyndon Johnson of Texas. No one in the Kennedy family liked Johnson. Robert F. Kennedy argued the most vehemently against Johnson at the family meeting later that night. But at seven o'clock the next morning, the phone in Clifford's hotel room rang. Kennedy wanted to see him immediately.

Without shaving, Clifford rushed to Kennedy's suite. "I must do something now that I have never done before in my life," said Kennedy. "I am going back on my solemn commitment. I acknowledge that I made it. I meant it at the time. I have been persuaded that I made a mistake and I must rectify it. I am withdrawing the offer I made to

Senator Symington and I would appreciate it if you would take that message to him."

Surprised, Clifford returned to his room and relayed the decision to Symington. While his old friend was surprised, too, Clifford did not sense any huge disappointment on Symington's part. After all, his sons had argued against accepting the nomination and Symington would remain a powerful figure in the Senate.

The announcement of the vice presidential nominee was scheduled for that night, and Robert Kennedy spent much of the day continuing his fight against Johnson. Clifford, however, had seen that putting Johnson on the ticket was inevitable. So he demonstrated the pragmatic flexibility that was a Clifford hallmark. With his man sidetracked, Clifford hurried to get aboard the next train leaving the station. So while Bobby Kennedy still fought against putting the Texan on the ticket, Clifford telephoned John Kennedy and urged him to stick with Johnson. "This is disastrous," Clifford told Kennedy. "You've got to take him."

It was an astute maneuver, one that signaled to the nominee that Clifford was now on his team. The day after Kennedy won the nomination, with Lyndon Johnson as his running mate, Clifford moved to solidify his position with Kennedy. He offered his congratulations and his services during the general election campaign. Kennedy promised to be in touch. A week later, Clifford reiterated his offer in a letter to Kennedy, proposing that they meet to discuss the best way to persuade Truman to become active in the campaign, particularly to counter what Clifford expected to be a larger anti-Catholic sentiment. "The fact that he is a Baptist and a thirty-third-degree Mason is important," wrote Clifford.

Writing back, Kennedy said that he had asked Sargent Shriver, his brother-in-law and one of his campaign aides, to call Clifford for advice. Kennedy also said he hoped to meet with Clifford in early August in Washington to discuss strategy. As for enlisting Truman, the matter on which one would assume Clifford might be most valuable, Kennedy passed him over. He wrote that he had dispatched Johnson to meet with the former president.

When Clifford met Kennedy for breakfast at the nominee's home in Georgetown in early August, Kennedy had an assignment for him. He said that he had heard about a study done by the Brookings Institution, a Washington think tank, that criticized presidential transitions. Praising

Clifford's experience in the executive branch, Kennedy asked him to prepare a blueprint for an orderly transition. With his customary diligence, Clifford set about researching and writing a lengthy memorandum.

Clifford was to play no greater role in the campaign. The trump card that had drawn Democrats to him for twelve years, his role in Truman's victory, did not play well with the Kennedys, despite the candidate's early interest in the '48 race. The Kennedys hated Truman because they were certain he was not doing enough for Jack's campaign. Clifford was viewed as part of Truman's organization, not the Kennedys'.

Not long after his breakfast with Jack Kennedy, Clifford went to the senator's office for a sandwich with Bobby, who was managing his brother's campaign. The chill was obvious to Clifford, who recognized that Bobby felt strongly that Truman was not helping. But Clifford believed that Bobby was also jealous of Clifford's closeness to his brother. Whatever the reason, Clifford left the brief lunch with the understanding that he would play a minimal role in the campaign.

John Fitzgerald Kennedy defeated Richard Milhous Nixon and was elected president of the United States on November 8, 1960, in the closest presidential election in American history. It was a signal of the political reality to come that part of Kennedy's success stemmed from the fact that he looked so much better than Nixon in televised debates.

The day after the election, the president-elect telephoned Clifford and asked if the transition paper was ready. Clifford assured him that it was. Before the day was out, he was on his way to the Kennedy compound at Hyannisport, Massachusetts, for a meeting with the president-elect and his top advisers.

Kennedy found Clifford's paper to be shrewd and helpful on the mechanics of the transition. But this was only mechanics. Now he needed to find the right people for the key jobs in his new administration. As a result, the first position he sought to fill was transition chief, the person who would collect the names of possible cabinet members and other key posts. Kennedy turned first to James Landis, a former Roosevelt New Dealer. Landis refused, saying he did not have the right kind of experience. Kennedy then asked Clifford, who readily accepted.

It was a canny appointment. Clifford was, as Ted Sorensen remembered, "one of the few Democrats around who had experience at the highest levels of government." He had links to the Truman crowd and to Symington, who represented the center of the Democratic Party. More important, Clifford was viewed as someone of stature who, while a liberal, understood big business and knew its leaders, who were very skeptical of Kennedy.

Clifford said he took the post with the understanding that he would not be considered for a position in the new administration. Rather than serving, he would recommend the officials with whom he was bound to come in contact as a lawyer over the next four years. As head of the transition team, Clifford's job was to facilitate the changeover from the Eisenhower administration and suggest candidates for various jobs. However, he actually had relatively little to do with the hiring process. The president and his brother Bobby chose the cabinet. Sargent Shriver and Stephen Smith were responsible for filling most of the second-tier and third-tier spots.

When a new president and his retinue come to Washington, every event and nuance is scrutinized and analyzed by the press and the powers in the city. Rumors about who will get which job are as valuable as a season ticket on the fifty-yard line at a Redskins game. So even if Clifford was not directly deciding the final make-up of the new administration, his role as chief of the transition and a Kennedy confidant gave him a profile that was invaluable to a Washington power broker in the days leading up to the inauguration. He was often at Kennedy's residence in Georgetown or down in Palm Beach, Florida, poolside with the president-elect. He flew to New York and tried to persuade investment banker Douglas Dillon to join the new administration. He also accompanied Kennedy to his first meeting at the White House with President Eisenhower on December 4. As one reporter wrote of Clifford's position with Kennedy, "This wasn't going to hurt his rating with Dun and Bradstreet."

Clifford was, however, called on to play a role in the appointment of the attorney general, albeit an unsuccessful one. Joseph Kennedy was insisting that Bobby get the post. The president-elect worried that his brother, at thirty-five, was too young and inexperienced for the nation's top law enforcement post. According to his wife, Ethel, Bobby was worn out by the campaign and did not really want the job. When President-elect Kennedy asked for Clifford's advice, Clifford said he was concerned less about Bobby's fatigue than his qualifications. Clifford argued that Bobby's lack of experience as a lawyer, combined with the certain charges of nepotism that would follow his appointment, would damage the new president.

The president-elect asked Clifford to fly to New York and present his argument to his father. Clifford was greeted warmly by the former ambassador, who listened politely as Clifford made a case for Bobby starting elsewhere in the administration. When Clifford was done, the Kennedy patriarch thanked him and said, "Now, I want Bobby to be attorney general and that is final."

It was not the last time that Clifford would wrestle with a problem involving Robert F. Kennedy.

On January 19, 1961, the day before his inauguration, Kennedy went to the White House for a final meeting with the outgoing president. The only noncabinet official to accompany him was Clifford. As the young senator and the old general settled into a lengthy discussion of foreign policy issues, Clifford dutifully took notes. The conversation he recorded contained the seeds for two significant foreign policy initiatives. One would prove to be the president's most costly foreign policy blunder; the other would ultimately plunge the nation into the turbulence and violence of Vietnam and lead to Clark Clifford's finest hour.

One of Kennedy's first questions that day concerned U.S. support for Cubans who had fled their country when Fidel Castro seized power and were now plotting anti-Castro activities. Clifford's notes reflect that Eisenhower urged the incoming president to continue United States backing for the Cubans and help them find a moderate leader to displace Castro and his Communist regime. It was Kennedy's "responsibility" to do "whatever is necessary" to help the anti-Castro forces, said Eisenhower. Clifford said that he sensed no reluctance on Ike's part to back an invasion of Cuba. Five days after the meeting, Clifford sent a memorandum to Kennedy reminding him that Eisenhower had said it was United States policy to help the Cubans.

At another point, the conversation turned to Southeast Asia. Communist-backed guerrillas, led by Ho Chi Minh, had driven the French out of Vietnam and were threatening to expand a civil war to neighboring countries, such as Laos and Cambodia. Clifford noted that everyone in the room, including Kennedy, was profoundly influenced by Ike's argument that Communist forces were poised to overrun Southeast

Asia. Should one country fall, Clifford's notes show Eisenhower saying, others in the region would follow "like dominoes."

Following the inauguration, Clifford returned full-time to his law practice, but not before President Kennedy had a bit of fun at his expense. Two days after his swearing in, Kennedy appeared as the guest of honor at the annual dinner thrown by the Alfalfa Club. Named for the thirsty plant with long roots always in need of replenishing, the Alfalfa Club was an elite, all-male organization that had existed since 1913 solely for the purpose of holding a white-tie, boy's-night-out dinner once a year. Among the guests at that 1961 edition of the dinner were former President Truman, Vice President Johnson, most of the Supreme Court, and a host of other Washington luminaries. Clifford was to be elected president of the club, and the traditional nominating speech was delivered by the master of ceremonies for the evening, comedian Bob Hope.

"You don't hear of Clifford running around nights," said Hope, looking over at the man seated to his left. "You don't hear of Clifford stealing. You don't read about Clifford in *Confidential* magazine. That's what I like about Clifford. He never gets caught."

When it was the president's turn, he picked up where Hope had left off. He joked that Clifford had chosen the cabinet, the sub-cabinet, and even ridden a buffalo in the inaugural parade. Pausing, Kennedy said that many in the audience probably wondered why Clifford himself had not received a job in the new administration.

"Well," said Kennedy with a smile, "the only thing Clark Clifford asked for was to have the name of his law firm printed on the back of the dollar bill."

Clifford remembered the remarks fondly, and the new president clearly intended them as a humorous barb. But there were indications that Kennedy was not pleased with the appearance that Clifford was profiting from his role as the new administration's transition chief. Former *Boston Globe* newsman and Kennedy friend Robert Healy remembered Kennedy complaining about the people who were hiring Clifford because of the lawyer's ties to another Democratic White House.

The Kennedy administration and his close association with the president was a watershed period for Clifford and his law firm. A decade had passed since he had left the Truman White House in a burst of glory. In those years, Clifford had capitalized on his reputation and continuing ties to the powerful. He had displayed great skill as an adviser and nego-tiator and nurtured the close relationships with other influential politi-cians on which his practice depended, men like Senators Johnson and Kerr and Justice Douglas. By the end of the fifties and two administra-tions of President Eisenhower, Clifford had built a prosperous practice and a stable of blue-chip clients. He had demonstrated convincingly that he could be more than Harry Truman's helper. But his firm remained small, with only three other lawyers, and in some ways his influence was overstated.

It was the connection to the fabled Kennedys that propelled Clifford back to the top of the Washington power scene. His practice expanded sharply as corporations saw him as a conduit to the president and his subordinates. New lawyers were brought in to handle the growing busi-ness. And added to the growing roster of clients were President John F. Kennedy and First Lady Jacqueline Kennedy.

Clifford was poised to enter a new stage in his career. He had spent the fifties cementing relationships with key members of Congress and continuing his prosperous law practice. It had been easy in a sense be-cause, despite the growth of government, Washington had remained, as Alice Roosevelt Longworth observed, "a small, cozy town, global in scope." Now, with a graceful and youthful new president and his stylish wife setting the tone, Washington was on the cusp of great change.

Journalist Haynes Johnson has called Kennedy "our first television president." And he made Washington the world's first television capital. From their living rooms, Americans would watch the telegenic young president from the pageantry of his swearing-in ceremony to the solem-nity of his funeral. The city would become the focus of the great civil rights demonstration in the middle of the decade. And, at the decade's close, antiwar protesters would fill its streets. All of it would be captured on television for the American people. Historian Alan K. Henrikson would later write, "Watching network television news every night, they often knew more about what had happened in the nation's capital than they knew about what had occurred in their own local communities."

Clark Clifford began the sixties determined to continue building his law practice. Before the decade's end, his handsome, lined face would loom large in the living rooms of millions of Americans and he would be, for the first time since coming to Washington, his own man.

11

Matters of Influence

CLIFFORD?" BARKED THE VOICE on the other end of the telephone line.

"Yes, senator," replied Clifford, recognizing the bulldog tone of Senator Robert Kerr of Oklahoma.

"A fellow will be calling you," said Kerr. "You may find it interesting."

"Who's that, senator?" asked Clifford.

"Name is Crawford Greenwalt."

Anyone as attuned to business as Clifford in those days knew the name. Greenwalt was the chairman of E. I. Du Pont de Nemours & Company, the Delaware-based empire of the Du Pont family. A noted ornithologist, he had married into the Du Pont family and gone on to become a well-regarded corporate executive.

The matter that would bring Greenwalt to Clifford's office a few days later would turn out to be one of the most complex and lucrative cases of Clifford's career. Were those the only two factors involved, the case might not deserve a full illumination, for Clifford had many prominent cases and, by the time of the call in early 1961, he was a wealthy man. However, the Du Pont case provides a rare window on the strategies, relationships, and influence of this exceptional lawyer as he was rising to the height of his power. A new president was in office and Clifford was close to him. The lawyer's relationships with men like Kerr and Vice President Johnson were mature and solidified, and so was his network of connections elsewhere in the bureaucracy. His method of dealing with Washington matters was sophisticated and silky smooth. Before the drama was over, Clifford would invent a lobbying technique that would be copied for decades, save the Du Ponts half a billion dollars, and collect a staggering fee.

Few historians have appreciated the power that Robert Kerr wielded in the United States Senate. For much of his career, he operated in the shadow of the domineering figure of Lyndon Johnson, the Senate majority leader. But when the Texan moved to the White House as vice president in 1961, Kerr jumped in to fill the power void. As liberal Democratic Senator Paul Douglas of Illinois, an archenemy of Kerr, phrased it, he became "the uncrowned king of the Senate." Unlike the scholarly Democratic Senator Mike Mansfield of Montana, who replaced Johnson as majority leader, Kerr never hesitated to exert his considerable influence.

Defying classification as either a liberal or a conservative, Kerr specialized in protecting the interests of his home state and the energy companies that dominated it. Although he was nominally second in command to Virginia Democrat Harry F. Byrd, it was Kerr who controlled the Finance Committee and its tax-writing functions. As Kerr himself once said, "I don't need to be the mule if I can hold the reins." For seven years, he punished the liberal Douglas by denying him a seat on the committee. Once Douglas got onto Finance in 1960, his administrative aide, Howard Shulman, observed firsthand what others had long known: "Kerr ran the committee."

The Oklahoman exercised a similar degree of influence as chairman of the Public Works Subcommittee. There, Kerr controlled the spending of millions of dollars a year on new highways, including the interstate system then crisscrossing the country, at the time the largest public works project in the country's history. For each dip into the pork barrel by one of his colleagues, he was sure to extract allegiance and favors in kind. In Senate circles, Kerr was famous for the line "I'm against any deal I'm not in on." Regarded as one of the most effective and fiercest debaters in the Senate, Kerr once referred to Senator Homer Capehart of Indiana as "a tub of rancid ignorance."

As the *Wall Street Journal* described the situation in the early sixties, Kerr supported the Kennedy administration "only when their goals coincided or when the White House was willing to pay the price for his support on one matter by making a concession on another." Because of his control of key committees and his ability to call on favors from his colleagues, the Kennedy administration was usually willing to pay his price.

Clifford had remained so close to Kerr over the years that he had loaned one of his attorneys, Sam McIlwain, to the senator and the Finance Committee for twenty months in 1957 and 1958. Often, Kerr and Clifford drove to work together and sometimes the pair, two of the most powerful men in Washington, were seen eating lunch together in the Senate cafeteria. So it was natural for them to join forces on behalf of the Du Pont family, just as it was natural that Kerr would see an advantage for Du Pont and for himself in Clifford's closeness to the president.

The Du Pont case had a long and tortured history before Clifford ever got involved. In 1949, the Department of Justice had filed a complaint in United States District Court in Chicago seeking to force E. I. Du Pont de Nemours & Company and Christiana Securities Company to sell 63 million shares of stock in General Motors Corporation. Christiana Securities was a holding company for the Du Pont family, who controlled E. I. Du Pont. Du Pont provided much of the paint used by General Motors for its automobiles. The government argued that Du Pont's ownership of so much General Motors stock gave it undue influence over the company's selection of paint suppliers. After a protracted litigation, the U.S. Supreme Court directed the court in Chicago to order Du Pont to sell its GM shares over a ten-year period.

The order presented enormous tax consequences for the Du Pont family members. The stock had been purchased in 1916 and 1917 at an average cost of $2.16 per share. By the time the courts ordered the sale of the stock, it was trading at $43 a share. The capital gain for the Du Pont shareholders was a staggering figure, roughly $2.5 billion. Unless they could find relief, they would face a tax bill exceeding $1 billion. With their day in court exhausted, they turned to Congress and sought a federal law cutting their tax bill.

Such specialized legislation, which creates loopholes in the tax law tailored for a specific company or other powerful interests, was not uncommon then or now. Tax legislation is riddled with seemingly insignificant, carefully worded passages that benefit these powerful interests. Over the years, Congress and the presidents have enacted so many of these specialized laws that, as authors Donald L. Barlett and James B. Steele wrote in *America: What Went Wrong?* the country has two separate tax systems — one for the rich and powerful and another for everyone else. However, the size of this loophole set it apart from other specialized incentives for the wealthy.

The Supreme Court portion of the case had been handled primarily by Covington and Burling, the big Washington law firm. Du Pont first turned to those same lawyers to craft a strategy for winning congressional approval of tax relief, but questions soon arose about whether Covington and Burling was up to the task. The dilemma was complicated because Delaware's two United States senators, John Williams and Allen Frear, although steadfastly in the corner of their home state's wealthiest family, were not strong enough to carry the bill in the Senate. So one day in early 1961 Crawford Greenwalt had gone with Frear to see the man who controlled the tax-writing committee and could push their bill through to passage: Robert Kerr.

"I don't give a shit about Du Pont or you, Greenwalt, but I'd shovel shit for Allen Frear," Kerr boomed as the two men sat in his office. This was part of Kerr's standard country hocum. If anyone was going to shovel manure for anyone else in the room that day, it would be the diminutive Frear cleaning out the stables for Kerr. However, there was a bond of loyalty between the two men, cemented in part by the oil ventures into which Kerr put Frear years earlier. By pumping up the Delaware senator in front of Greenwalt, the crafty strategist from Oklahoma boosted his friend and opened the way for his own suggestion about how Du Pont could win in Congress.

Kerr agreed to oversee the passage of a tax measure aimed at reducing the bill owed by the Du Ponts. For help in getting the right kind of bill written and assuring its passage, he suggested that Greenwalt might want to augment the services of Covington and Burling with those of another Washington law firm. Kerr suggested that Greenwalt pay a visit to his friend Clark Clifford.

A few days after Kerr's introductory phone call, Greenwalt sat in Clifford's office on L Street. As Greenwalt described the problem to him, Clifford began to craft his strategy. This must not be described as a measure to help the Du Ponts, whose vast wealth and power would win them little sympathy in the House and Senate. Rather, he decided, they would stress the impact of the court's divestiture order on Du Pont's small shareholders, average people who could ill afford the inevitable drop in Du Pont stock that would follow the massive sell-off and resulting tax bill. The actual task of drawing up the legislation was farmed out to another law firm that had more lawyers and specialized in tax matters, and Senator Kerr's staff also contributed their expertise. Creating and executing the strategy was Clifford's department.

The tax legislation that was devised employed a complicated formula that would allow some of the GM stock to be sold tax free while capping the total tax at $470 million. It represented savings of more than $500 million for the Du Pont family and the other shareholders. The measure also was crafted so that Christiana Securities was the only corporation in America that could take advantage of the formula.

Near the middle of 1961, Crawford Greenwalt sat in Clifford's office and listened as the lawyer described his plan for winning approval of the bold measure. It was simple and revolutionary.

"I've been thinking a good deal about it," Clifford said slowly and thoughtfully. "There is just one man in the world who can sell this to Congress."

"Who's that?" asked Greenwalt.

"You," replied Clifford gravely.

"You mean it?" asked Greenwalt. "I don't know how."

Greenwalt had looked down his nose at politicians all his career. Winning passage of bills in Congress was what big business sent its friends to Washington to do — or at least what they hired lobbyists and lawyers to do. Never before had an executive of a major corporation been asked to engage in this kind of door-to-door salesmanship.

Clifford convinced Greenwalt that the stakes were so high that the Du Pont executive would have to pay personal visits to the key members of the House and Senate. No one knew the issues better than Greenwalt. Moreover, he had enormous public prestige and Clifford knew congressmen would be impressed by his vast wealth. It would be up to Greenwalt to convince the legislators that the bill was not just tax relief for one of America's wealthiest families, but something that was good for anyone who owned stock. So Greenwalt agreed, becoming the first of what eventually turned into a long line of corporate executives to do their own lobbying.

In keeping with his practice of not lobbying directly, Clifford did not accompany Greenwalt to the congressional offices. Instead, John Sharon, a partner in Covington and Burling, went with the Du Pont executive on his visits to more than fifty congressmen, including every member of the House Ways and Means Committee and the Senate Finance Committee. They also paid calls on senior administration officials, including Attorney General Robert Kennedy and one of his deputies, future Supreme Court Justice Byron White. Meanwhile, Clifford worked behind the scenes with Kerr.

Sometimes these rifle-shot tax measures slip through unnoticed, because they do not contain the identity of the beneficiary or specify the amount of money involved. This time, however, a cadre of liberals in the Senate, led by Albert Gore of Tennessee (whose son would one day become vice president), discovered what was afoot. By exposing the attempt to public scrutiny, Gore forced Clifford and his allies to try to hedge their bets.

With the measure pending in Congress, Clifford and several other Du Pont lawyers went to see Robert S. Knight, the general counsel at the Treasury Department. At the time, the secretary of the treasury was Douglas Dillon, the New York investment banker whom Clifford, as transition chief, had helped persuade to take the post. The lawyers wanted to line up the Treasury Department's support to push the bill in Congress and counter the attacks by Gore and his liberal allies. Knight was the man who had to be convinced. If that failed, they wanted Treasury to approve a scheme that they had devised for selling the General Motors stock in a manner that would at least minimize the tax impact.

As the lawyers talked in Knight's large office in the Treasury Department building, just a stone's throw from the White House, Knight's secretary opened the door and interrupted.

"The White House is calling," she announced.

Rising immediately, Clifford suggested gravely that he and the others leave the room. Knight required privacy for his call from the president. As the lawyers stood, the embarrassed secretary stopped them.

"No, no," she said. "The president is calling for Mr. Clifford."

It was a classic example of Clifford's influence. He did not need to tell Knight that he was close to the president. He never had to remind Dillon that he had helped him get his job at Treasury. Clifford did not even have to mention directly to Kennedy that he represented Du Pont. All of the power and influence was conveyed in that simple, direct statement, "The president is calling for Mr. Clifford."

A few weeks later, the House of Representatives passed the legislation, but Gore and his liberal colleagues in the Senate managed to delay a vote there. It was only postponing the inevitable. Between them, Kerr, Clifford, and Greenwalt had ensured passage of the measure, with a little help from another old friend of Clifford's.

On September 23, 1961, Senator Stuart Symington rose on the Senate floor to express his backing for passage of the House measure. He echoed Clifford's strategy when he described the legislation as something designed to help the little guy. Disguising tax relief for one of America's wealthiest families, as Clifford had proposed to Greenwalt months earlier, was particularly brazen in Symington's case; the Du Pont company had only 3,443 stockholders in Missouri, and more than two-thirds of all the stock was held by members of the extended Du Pont family. Nonetheless, Symington said, "It is my belief that this proposed legislation should be enacted and should be enacted at this time. Many letters from people in my state who are small holders of stock in the companies in question . . . state the tax provisions of this order for divestiture constitute an arbitrary appropriation of their property."

It was no surprise when Kerr himself spoke strongly in favor of the bill, somehow contorting logic to make it appear that the measure was actually placing an onus on the Du Ponts. "The groups who will pay the most by reason of its passage," he said, "are, first, Christiana Corporation, the majority of which is owned by the Du Pont family, and second, the Du Ponts and their folks who own Du Pont stock."

The legislation passed the Senate and was sent to the White House for the president's signature. There was no reason for Jack Kennedy to do any favors for the Du Ponts. They had opposed his candidacy in 1960, going so far as to provide Richard Nixon with his largest contribution, $125,000. Further, at that very time Kennedy's Treasury Department was crafting an attack on the special preferences and other abuses woven into the federal tax code. Nonetheless, on February 3, 1962, President Kennedy signed the legislation saving the Du Ponts more than half a billion dollars.

There is no direct evidence that Clifford ever approached Kennedy about the measure. But there are convincing indications that the president was briefed on the issue by Clifford or by someone dispatched to the White House under Clifford's auspices. The strongest indication was in Clifford's own hand.

Two days after the president signed the bill, Clifford wrote him a personal note in longhand about the Du Pont legislation. The lawyer expressed his "deep appreciation for the courtesies extended to me with reference to the matter in which I had such a vital interest." Clifford also thanked Kennedy for his "willingness to take the time to understand the facts and the issues involved." And he added that it had "meant a great deal" to him. Clifford closed the letter by offering to express his gratitude "by having you call me for any assistance I might render you."

Even if Clifford did not directly discuss the issue with Kennedy, the president clearly knew the lawyer was involved in the important case. Clifford's interests would by no means have been the only factor in Kennedy's signing the legislation. The president was still eager to mend his fences with the American business community and the bill would go a long way toward bringing the powerful Du Ponts into his corner. But the entire episode stands as a prime example of the advantages conveyed by Clifford's relationship with the president of the United States.

A short time after the bill was signed, there was a dispute over the final impact of its complicated provisions. The resolution required a ruling by the Internal Revenue Service. Knight, who had presented the Treasury Department's position to Congress, recommended that the IRS adopt language capping Du Pont's tax bill at $470 million, the amount used in the congressional debate on the issue.

Finally, the deal seemed to be done, and it was a major victory for Clifford. Unfortunately, from Clifford's viewpoint, the politically charged debate in Congress had made the victory a public one, too. No one knew that Robert Kerr had referred the Du Ponts to Clifford. Indeed, few people in Washington were aware of how close the two men were. And news that Kennedy had called Clifford in the midst of a potentially crucial meeting at the Treasury Department would not be disclosed for years. It was the money that caught the eye of the press and dragged Clifford into the fray — not only the savings to the Du Pont family but also the legal fee for their lawyer.

Rumors circulated that Clifford had charged Du Pont $1 million for his services, ten times the highest annual retainer the firm had ever collected. The speculation embarrassed Clifford, who was never ostentatious about his wealth and was leery of that sort of publicity. When *Time* went so far as to print the $1 million figure, albeit categorizing it as mere rumor, Clifford got on the telephone to his friend Hugh Sidey in the magazine's Washington bureau.

Clifford rarely raised his voice in anger. When someone did or said something irritating, his usual tactic was either to ignore the person or to make his own point very slowly and precisely, as though he were speaking to a slow-witted person.

"Hugh," he said when Sidey answered the phone, "I can't imagine where that figure came from."

Sidey said little as Clifford explained calmly that it had been a case of unfair taxation, even if the Du Ponts were rich, and that Clifford had convinced Greenwalt to come to Washington and carry the day with Congress. It was a very lengthy and complicated matter, one that Covington and Burling had been unable to handle. As for his fee, Clifford assured his friend Sidey that it was not $1 million.

There was other speculation about the Du Pont fee over the years. Some press accounts said that Clifford was granted a $100,000 retainer for ten years from the Du Ponts. The truth is that the magazine was far closer to the mark than Clifford had indicated to his friend Sidey. But the lawyer, trying to anticipate such criticism, had built himself a semantic escape route.

Soon after passage of the legislation, Sam McIlwain had gone into Clifford's office to discuss some of the firm's administrative matters. As McIlwain sat in front of Clifford's desk, he watched Clifford write out the bill for his secretary to send to Du Pont. The amount was $990,000 — more than $4 million in 1995 dollars. "I don't think Mr. Clifford wanted to have the million-dollar figure kicked around, so he came in slightly under that amount," recalled McIlwain. "They paid in two weeks."

During the Du Pont case, Clifford had been impressed with the work of John Sharon, the Covington and Burling lawyer who did most of the actual lobbying. With his own firm short-handed in the face of all the business that was coming in, Clifford decided to hire Sharon. Because of Sharon's stature, he was hired at a senior level. It was a rare divergence from Clifford's pattern. In his days at the Lashly firm in St. Louis, Clifford had seen the frustration in other young lawyers as outsiders were hired above them as partners. Clifford had vowed not to do that in his own firm and, up until the hiring of John Sharon, he had kept the promise to himself. But another lawyer was needed to keep up with the work, so Clifford had bent his own rule. The hiring created some antagonism among the other lawyers, and Sharon, who could be quite abrasive, did nothing to make matters smoother. It would be a few years, however, before Clifford discovered how big a mistake he had made.

*   *   *

Throughout the period that he was working on behalf of the Du Ponts, among numerous other clients, Clifford and his wife were occasional guests of the Kennedys, starting with a private dinner for twelve with the president and first lady following Kennedy's first State of the Union address on January 31, 1961. Then there was all manner of legal matters, large and small, that Clifford handled for the Kennedys. Later, Clifford would estimate that about a third of his time was devoted to working for Kennedy, although the president never considered him a member of his inner circle.

The first crisis of the Kennedy presidency led to Clifford's only formal ties with the administration. On the morning of April 16, 1961, a CIA-trained band of Cuban refugees invaded their former country. Almost all of them were captured or killed in a foreign policy debacle that would forever make the Bay of Pigs synonymous with the word "fiasco." Kennedy blamed the tragedy on bad advice from the CIA, which had predicted that the Cuban people would rise up in support of the invaders.

The president ordered a full-scale investigation of the intelligence agency by the little-known President's Foreign Intelligence Advisory Board. He asked Clifford, who had helped to draft the legislation creating the CIA during the Truman administration, to join the board. Clifford readily accepted the part-time post.

Established in 1956 by President Eisenhower to monitor the various intelligence agencies of the United States government, the board had become moribund, little more than, as McGeorge Bundy phrased it, "a club people want to be a member of [because] it is where you get all the hot dope." Indeed, its members had the highest-level security clearance and were granted access to information unavailable even to most congressmen.

The board's investigation of the Bay of Pigs had little impact on the Central Intelligence Agency, but Clifford enjoyed the access to top-secret information and remained a member of the board for the next seven years.

On a few other occasions, Kennedy summoned Clifford to the White House to discuss a particularly sensitive legal matter with his brother, who had never practiced law. Clifford's presence clearly irritated Robert Kennedy and exacerbated the cool relations between them that had begun during the presidential campaign. The attorney general had little use for Clifford, whom he viewed as part of the Washington establishment. For his part, Clifford once remarked that he found Robert Kennedy "lacking the grace and political maturity of his older brother."

During these years, Clifford was a sought-after source for Washington journalists, and he cultivated them with discreet leaks of information obtained from his vantage point as an insider. Clifford regularly invited prominent journalists to his office for lunch, where they would eat sandwiches and swap information. While he was close to Sidey, Clifford thought nothing of sharing information with his friend's archrivals at *Newsweek*. Kenneth Crawford, an elegant old-timer who ran the Washington bureau of *Newsweek*, was a regular lunchtime guest. Sometimes Crawford invited along Ben Bradlee, who had left the *Post* for a stint in the magazine's Washington office.

"We'd sit there and I'd listen to these two old guys talk about old times and eat miserable sandwiches," recalled Bradlee. "Clifford would send his secretary downstairs to some place for bad sandwiches. And there was no booze. Still, I had the sense that I was in the presence of the Almighty."

These sessions were beneficial to all concerned. From President Kennedy's point of view, Clifford could serve as a safe conduit to the press for information too sensitive to come directly from a White House source. For the press, the insatiable appetite for scoops and inside dope on which Washington journalism has always thrived was satisfied on a regular basis. As for Clifford, there is no better way to win friends and immunity from criticism than providing information to reporters. In important ways, Clifford's care and feeding of the press inoculated him against serious investigation into his private practice and kept his reputation shining brightly.

Jack Anderson, who has written about Washington with a critical eye for four decades, was a regular diner at the Clifford information trough. "Clifford was a leaker," said Anderson. "He knew who to leak to. He leaked to the people who could do him good or do him harm. He leaked to me when I could hurt him. Those who practiced that kind of journalism loved him. You never left his office empty handed."

Because of his close relations with Washington reporters, it was predictable that the press would portray Clifford as perhaps closer to President Kennedy than he actually was. Pumping up a source was a way to inflate the stories they wrote based on leaks from that source and, of course, to keep the spigot open. So it came about that the press dubbed

Clifford "the shadow attorney general," much to the irritation of the real attorney general and those around him. To Robert Kennedy loyalists, the phrase was a misnomer, yet another example of Clifford's subtle attempt to exaggerate his influence within the administration. "Bobby ran the department very completely and was definitely in charge," a Kennedy aide said later. Even Bradlee, who was extremely close to President Kennedy, later observed that Clifford was not quite so important at the Kennedy White House as he was described in the press.

Nonetheless, Clifford was clearly an important outside adviser to President Kennedy on various issues, including some that involved the Justice Department. White House visitor logs show that Clifford and Robert Kennedy attended half a dozen meetings together with the president. The same records show that Clifford had many more private sessions with the president on a variety of subjects.

In 1962, when President Kennedy had his first opportunity to fill a vacancy on the Supreme Court, Robert Kennedy urged his brother to appoint the first black justice. His recommendation was William H. Hastie, a distinguished federal appeals court judge. Clifford argued that the president should appoint the best lawyer he could find. In his opinion, while Hastie was a good man and an adequate judge, he was not the best choice for the court. Persuaded in part by Clifford's logic, Kennedy nominated Byron White, then a deputy attorney general.

Attorney General Kennedy and Clifford also clashed on the handling of the steel crisis in the spring of 1962. In March, management and the unions were negotiating a new contract. Worried about inflationary pressure on the economy, the president stepped in and tried to persuade the unions to forgo a steep increase in wages. Kennedy believed that he had extracted a pledge from the management not to raise steel prices as part of the bargain. However, on April 10, U.S. Steel, the largest steel manufacturer in the country, announced a 12 percent price increase. The other big companies quickly followed suit.

The president was angry, but the attorney general was livid and determined to strike back. A federal grand jury was convened in Washington to investigate whether the industry had violated antitrust laws. The companies were served with subpoenas and a full-scale investigation appeared imminent.

Hoping to avoid a potentially debilitating showdown, the president called in Clifford, who represented Republic Steel, one of the major companies. He instructed Clifford to meet with Roger Blough, the president of U.S. Steel, and persuade him to abandon the price increase or face government action. Clifford had enormous credibility with the steel industry, and it was part of Kennedy's shrewdness that he recognized he had placed the lawyer in a tough situation. "Can't you just see Clifford outlining the possible courses of action the government could take if they showed signs of not moving," the president said to a friend, Paul Fay.

Clifford flew to New York and, after several hours of intense negotiations with Blough, he reported that U.S. Steel would cut its increase in half. The president was adamant; there could be no price hike. Negotiations resumed and Robert Kennedy plowed ahead with his investigation. Finally, after several days, Blough gave in and rescinded the entire increase. The other companies immediately followed his lead and withdrew their increases.

This was a perfect opportunity for Clifford. After serving as the president's middleman to industry, he could argue the case of industry, including his client Republic Steel, to the president. Since the companies had backed off their plans to increase prices, Clifford argued, the antitrust investigation should be shut down. But the attorney general, who viewed Clifford all along as the industry's man inside the tent, advocated continuing the probe. In his diary, Robert Kennedy wrote that Clifford had "expressed himself as very anxious that we do not take action against the companies. I had a strong exchange with him that caused Jack to say later . . . joking I think, 'What we need in this administration is a good attorney general that can be fixed.' "

Robert Kennedy reluctantly dropped the investigation, writing in his diary this time that it was important for the president "to make up to business so that they would not consider him or the administration antibusiness."

Skeptical of President Kennedy from the start, some quarters of the business community still viewed him with contempt. Early in his administration the *Wall Street Journal*, the nation's most powerful business daily and never a friend of Democrats, had written a scathing editorial about the administration's tactics in averting the steel price increases "by the pressure of fear — by naked power, by threats, by agents of the state security policy."

Ted Sorensen remembered that the president again sought out Clifford for advice on how to improve his image with big business. "The truth is that JFK and I knew very few people in the business community," said Sorensen later. "Clifford was seen as a link to the business community." Clifford advised the president to issue a series of periodic statements that would be perceived as pro-business. He also suggested inviting business leaders to the White House for consultation. To a degree, the strategy was a success, but big business never really trusted Kennedy or his brother. In return, Robert Kennedy was never comfortable with Clifford's closeness to big business.

Indeed, Clifford's view of the relationship between government and business was far more conservative than that of either President Kennedy or the attorney general. In a speech in early 1963 to his alma mater, Washington University, Clifford warned that the nation's antitrust law was "not really anti-monopoly so much as it was anti-bigness." He recommended that the president appoint a commission to overhaul the antitrust laws. After Clifford sent him a copy of the speech, President Kennedy suggested that he provide a more detailed study of the matter. The attorney general, who also received a copy of the speech, did not reply.

While Clifford clashed with Robert Kennedy, he got on famously with another Kennedy from the very start. Glamorous Jacqueline Bouvier Kennedy had captivated the nation. Soon after the inauguration, she became determined to transfer some of that radiance to the White House by renovating the dowdy interior of the nation's most famous residence. The cost would run into the millions. Her husband, remembering the public furor when Harry Truman added the famed South Portico to the executive mansion, begged her to leave things alone. Mrs. Kennedy would not be deterred and she devised a plan of her own for financing the project. When she told the president that she wanted to create a private association to raise money for the renovation, he wanted some legal advice. So Clifford was invited to lunch at the White House with President Kennedy and his wife.

Jackie Kennedy explained her plans to restore a sense of history and class to the interior of the White House. Further, she told Clifford, she wanted to get together a group of wealthy donors who would contribute the money necessary for the project.

"I think that is an excellent idea," said Clifford, smiling winningly. "But what you must do, Mrs. Kennedy, is organize this group so that people can legally make tax-deductible gifts. People look at these things realistically."

Mrs. Kennedy adopted Clifford's suggestion, and she had other ideas, too. Realizing that hundreds of thousands of people toured the White House every year, she wanted to sell them postcards depicting the various state rooms of the White House and she wanted to publish an elegant guidebook illustrated with fine photographs.

At Mrs. Kennedy's request, Clifford agreed to draw up the legal papers for the new organization, which would be called the White House Historical Association. Mrs. Kennedy would take care of the guidebook and other matters, and for assistance she contacted Melville Grosvenor, the president of the National Geographic Society, which published the most handsome magazine in the country.

Returning to his office that day, Clifford discussed the fund raising concept with Carson Glass. The problem was that the White House was owned by the government, and Glass was uncertain about whether even the president's wife had the authority to set up such a corporation. So the two lawyers went to the Justice Department for an official opinion. There, the draft of the incorporation papers was polished and approved by Nicholas Katzenbach, the deputy attorney general.

By February 21, 1961, the new organization was official and held its first meeting at the White House, with Mrs. Kennedy presiding. After tea and coffee were served, Mrs. Kennedy got down to business. The committee members should start searching for appropriate furniture and rugs to acquire as donations to the White House. Such gifts, chimed in Clifford, would be completely tax deductible, as would checks sent in lieu of specific articles. In the following months, Clifford marveled at the success of Mrs. Kennedy's idea. The guidebook sold by the thousands, and donations allowed her to furnish the mansion with some of the nation's finest antiques and paintings.

Throughout his legal career, Clifford used his insider status to invoke the issue of national security to lend credence to his arguments. While in some instances it may have been warranted, it more often was an argument of last resort.

One example occurred when Clifford was called on to assist the president and first lady in securing a weekend retreat in the Virginia countryside. They had rented a house, called Glen Ora, while Kennedy was a senator, but the wealthy widow who owned the house planned to occupy it herself following Kennedy's election. The Kennedys wanted to keep the house, so Mrs. Kennedy asked Clifford to persuade its elderly owner, a Mrs. Tartiere, to allow them to remain. Initially, the owner resisted. Then Clifford played his trump card. Adopting his gravest tones, he explained that securing a private country retreat for the president and his wife was a matter of national security. In Clifford's view, the scope of national security apparently extended to anything that might ease the life of the president. Mrs. Tartiere was intimidated by the argument, and the Kennedys remained in the house.

Jackie Kennedy was so pleased that she sent Clifford a sketch of him calling on Mrs. Tartiere with a bouquet in one hand and a sheaf of legal papers in the other. A Valentine-like lace framed the first lady's drawing.

Author Truman Capote, who knew Mrs. Kennedy well in later years, once speculated that she had developed a romantic fixation on Clifford in her White House years. There was never a suggestion that it was anything more than an unfulfilled fancy, but the two remained close friends until Mrs. Kennedy's death in 1994.

Clifford was not as successful when he represented the Kennedys in another real estate transaction. When he was elected president, Kennedy had sold his small brick house on N Street in Georgetown for $110,000, regarded as a somewhat inflated price. However, Mrs. Kennedy changed her mind and wanted the house back. The president hired Clifford as his lawyer and the home's new owner retained Dean Acheson. It was a rare occasion to have two such august attorneys handling a real estate squabble, and a rare loss for Clifford. The sales contract was validated by a judge, and the Kennedys did not get the house back.

On another occasion, Kennedy called upon Clifford for advice after his youngest brother, Edward, had gotten into a scuffle with a photographer while on a ski vacation in Stowe, Vermont. The photographer had taken a picture of young Kennedy with the winner of a local beauty contest. Kennedy, who had recently been elected to the Senate, grabbed the camera, pulled out the film, and exposed it. The photographer worked for William Loeb, a right-wing newspaper publisher who had no use for the Kennedys. Loeb threatened to sue Senator Kennedy and went so far as to hire a former governor of Vermont to represent the photographer.

Faced with the possibility of an embarrassing lawsuit, the president summoned his brother to the White House along with Clifford and some other advisers. After Edward Kennedy explained the situation, the president asked Clifford for his assessment. Clifford intoned that it would have been "better if this had not happened," and suggested that steps be taken to avert the lawsuit. It was the sort of obvious advice that would lead Ted Sorensen years later to say, "Clark has the ability to listen to what you just said and then give it back to you, but make it sound much more powerful." In the end, Edward Kennedy followed Clifford's advice, writing a letter of apology to the photographer and paying for his damaged camera.

The Du Pont family was far from the only important Clifford client with business before the Kennedy administration at the very time Clifford was serving as Kennedy's personal lawyer and adviser, his emissary to big business, and debating Justice Department policy. Faced with a potential financial disaster of unprecedented proportions and the necessity of taming a tough-minded Justice Department, the General Electric Company turned to Clifford in the biggest antitrust case in American history.

In early 1961, General Electric and seven of its officers pleaded guilty to criminal charges of fixing prices and rigging government bids. Twenty-eight other electrical equipment manufacturers were also convicted of violating antitrust laws by fixing prices and rigging bids in sales of equipment to the nation's public utilities, including the Tennessee Valley Authority.

The conspiracy to fix prices and eliminate competition had been extraordinarily brazen. Corporate executives from the companies had devised elaborate schemes to cover their tracks. They met in hotel rooms around the country for what they called "choir practices." They falsified travel expense accounts to conceal the cities where the meetings took place. And they divided the electrical equipment business among themselves on a formula based on each company's market share. General Electric, as the biggest supplier, was accorded the lion's share of most contracts.

The inflated prices, of course, had been passed on by the utilities to their customers. As a result, General Electric's legal problems were compounded by hundreds of civil lawsuits brought in the wake of the plea by the bilked utilities and by federal, state, and local government agencies. The most serious suit was the Justice Department's claim for $70 million in damages.

To plan a defense strategy, General Electric hired its former board chairman, Charles E. Wilson. As vice chairman of the War Production Board during the Truman administration, Wilson had gotten to know Clifford and the two had kept in contact over the years. In the winter of late 1961, Wilson tracked down his old friend, who was on his annual golfing vacation at Hobe Sound, Florida.

"Clark, we have a tough problem and it is getting worse all the time," said Wilson. "I need to talk to you about it."

Wilson insisted on flying down to Florida immediately. Over the course of the next year, Clifford spent at least one day a week at General Electric's headquarters in New York City. He assisted in preparing a legal strategy for dealing with the lawsuits and, more important, helped General Electric deal with an angry Congress and Bobby Kennedy's Justice Department.

Senator Estes Kefauver, the populist Democrat from Tennessee, had taken a sharp interest in the price-fixing case because one of the victims was the Tennessee Valley Authority. As chairman of the Senate Antitrust and Monopoly Committee, he ordered a series of hearings into the episode. As a star witness, he intended to call Ralph Cordiner, the president of General Electric. If Cordiner refused to appear, Kefauver planned to subpoena him.

Naturally, Cordiner did not want to testify and he sought Clifford's help. Clifford assigned the newest lawyer in the firm, a recent law school graduate named John Kovin, to research whether the Senate committee had the legal authority to subpoena a witness. Meanwhile, Clifford went up to Capitol Hill and talked with Kefauver and some of his friends in the Senate about how embarrassing it would be for Cordiner to testify and how anything he might say in public could jeopardize the civil lawsuits still pending against the company. Before Kovin finished his legal research, Kefauver had withdrawn his request for Cordiner's testimony.

The company lost the first two civil cases in court, creating new worries about the ultimate cost of the hundreds of other pending cases. This time, Clifford helped negotiate a settlement of the largest suit, the one brought by the Justice Department on behalf of the federal government. The Justice Department agreed to a payment of $7.7 million, slightly more than 10 percent of the damages it had sought. There is no evidence that Clifford used an undue influence, but he was well known as the First Family's outside lawyer. For General Electric, the agreement was an immensely valuable victory, establishing a pattern that led to the settlement of nearly two thousand other suits brought by various governmental agencies and other customers.

In one final bit of legal dexterity, the Internal Revenue Service was persuaded to allow the company to deduct the payments from its tax bill. On this count, however, Clifford claimed that he played no role. "This was something entirely different," he told an interviewer at the time. "But because you are associated with a company in a particular case, you tend to be associated with every blasted detail."

Clifford's influence with the Kennedy administration also appeared to benefit another client, FMC Corporation. In the middle of 1962, Stauffer Chemical Company had announced its intention to acquire one of its suppliers, American Viscose Company. However, the day after the announcement, the Justice Department threatened to file an antitrust action to block the transaction, claiming that Stauffer was attempting to gain a monopoly. Stauffer immediately backed down.

In January 1963, FMC Corporation picked up where Stauffer had left off, agreeing to buy American Viscose for $116 million. But FMC was smarter. The company's chairman, Paul Davis, called Clark Clifford, introduced himself, and asked Clifford to represent FMC. Although FMC was twice as large as Stauffer and did even more business with American Viscose, the Justice Department did not make any move to block the acquisition.

The transaction would have been relatively routine for Clifford had it not been for investigative reporter Jack Anderson. A protégé of columnist Drew Pearson, Anderson had gotten a tip on Clifford's role from a source inside Clifford's own law firm. After checking it out, Anderson wrote about the case for Pearson's widely read "Washington Merry-Go-Round" column on February 16, 1963. Beneath the headline "It Pays to Hire the Right Lawyer," the story asked, "Why has the Justice Department hesitated to send FMC the same warnings that were sent at once to Stauffer? Insiders claim the big difference is the influence of Clark Clifford."

When Clifford read the piece that Saturday morning, he was furious. Just as he had with the Detroit trade school case, Clifford feared that the allegations would damage his standing with the Kennedy White House unless he defused them immediately. He telephoned the offices of both the president and the attorney general, dictating identical messages to both of the secretaries who answered.

"The inference and conclusions are one hundred percent erroneous," Clifford said. "Even the facts are ninety percent incorrect. An associate of mine has attended one meeting at a staff level at which time the subject was discussed. I have not contacted, or been in touch with, anyone in the Justice Department, or anyone else in the government, with reference to this matter."

It was a common protest by Clifford and, technically, an accurate one. Clifford had not made direct contact. Therefore he had convinced himself that his well-known rapport with President Kennedy had had no impact on the department's decision, just as it had had none on the Du Pont tax matter or the General Electric bid-rigging settlement or other matters large and small.

The protest to Kennedy echoed the speech that Clifford delivered regularly to his clients disclaiming any influence with the government. And it was just as disingenuous. Never had Clifford's influence been stronger in Washington. Far more mature and better connected than in the days when he was first starting out in practice and Harry Truman was in the White House, Clifford had been able to draw on his closeness to Kennedy to attract new clients, such as the Du Pont family, and expand his law practice dramatically.

Direct lobbying by Clifford was never really necessary. Whether it amounted to a telephone call from the president in the midst of a critical meeting on tax policy or the mere presence of a Clifford associate at a Justice Department negotiating session, the impact was the same: Clark Clifford, the president's confidant, is on the case. Tread lightly.

Yet Clifford continued to claim in his pat speech that he had no influence in Washington. Each time he delivered that soliloquy to another corporate executive, Clifford uncoupled his words from his actions. It was a practice fraught with peril. Clifford had started out fooling others. He wound up fooling himself.

12

The President's Adviser

MOST AMERICANS who were alive at the time remember where they were when they heard the news on November 22, 1963. Clark Clifford was sitting down to lunch in the White House mess with other members of the president's Foreign Intelligence Advisory Board. The first reports were sketchy: Gunshots had been fired at the presidential motorcade in Dallas. President Kennedy had been hit. The wound was not serious. Then came the awful truth: John Kennedy had been assassinated. With Jackie Kennedy standing beside him in a pink suit stained with the blood of her dead husband, Lyndon Baines Johnson was sworn in as president aboard *Air Force One* and was en route back to Washington.

Clifford was stunned. He and the others sat in a White House conference room and pondered the ultimate question: Who would want to kill the president? With the Bay of Pigs and the Cuban missile showdown fresh in their minds, the speculation focused on Castro and the Cubans. But there was no consensus. The question remained unanswerable that day, and perhaps forever.

In the days immediately after Kennedy's assassination, Clifford was called upon to help the thirty-four-year-old widow with various legal matters. Among them was arranging for her to receive her husband's final paycheck. The question that Clifford pondered, however, was where he would stand with the new man in the Oval Office. He had been close to Johnson in his Senate days, but things had cooled in recent years as Clifford spent most of his time advising Kennedy and building his law practice. A friend recalled Clifford's concern that his fabled access to the White House had come to an end. "I remember how upset he was," said the friend. "He knew Johnson, but their relations were not close. He said he would never be as close to Johnson as he had been to Kennedy."

For someone who contended that he did not depend on influence with the president, this was a curious concern.

This was one time when Clifford's instincts failed him, and it did not take long to find that out. On November 27, he wrote Johnson a letter lamenting the difficult days the new president was experiencing and offering his services. "The period from November 1963 to November 1964 (the next presidential election) offers a variety of problems which will have to be given prompt and thoughtful consideration," wrote Clifford, whose letter was hand delivered to the White House.

Later that same day, Johnson invited his former adviser in for a private meeting. Sitting alone in the Oval Office, they talked nonstop from four o'clock in the afternoon until nine at night, without even a break for dinner. The main topic was a smooth transition from a Kennedy to a Johnson administration. But the new president had another problem on his mind: Robert Kennedy.

Clifford knew the animosity between Johnson and the late president's younger brother had not waned since the presidential campaign of 1960. After all, he had seen the evidence for himself earlier in 1963. The lawyer had been sitting in the reception room outside the Oval Office talking with Robert Kennedy while they waited to see the president. The door to Kennedy's office opened and Johnson stepped out, fresh from his own consultation with the president. As Clifford and Johnson exchanged greetings, the attorney general refused even to acknowledge the presence of the vice president. To Johnson, who had grown up poor in Texas hill country and amassed political power through hard work and his own genius, such treatment symbolized the high-handedness of the Kennedys. Now, just days into his presidency and confronting a nation convulsed by the assassination, Johnson was already hearing rumors that he was only keeping the seat in the White House warm for the thirty-seven-year-old attorney general.

After their long meeting, Johnson dispatched Clifford to sound out Kennedy on his future intentions. Clifford met with the attorney general a few days later and reported back to Johnson that Kennedy had no plans to leave the administration. Nor was he willing to rule out a run for the presidency. Firing Bobby Kennedy was out of the question. The emotional and political costs would be too high. Johnson and Clifford agreed that there was nothing to do but wait until 1964, when Johnson would run for the presidency and be elected in his own right. Then he would have a mandate to lead, to choose his own government, and to get rid of Bobby Kennedy.

★　　　★　　　★

Clifford's fears of being shut out of the White House proved to be unfounded. Johnson quickly returned to the practice he had followed in the Senate, bringing in Clifford and lawyer Abe Fortas to offer the last word on any crucial decision. George Christian, Johnson's press secretary, referred to the two lawyers as "the Bobbsey twins." To others in the Johnson White House, they became known as the court of last resort. Observed Jack Valenti, one of Johnson's aides: "Clifford and Fortas were first among equals. They carried the heaviest weight."

As it had been with the Trumans and the Kennedys, the Cliffords were often invited to the White House for small dinners as well as state affairs. Lady Bird Johnson and Marny Clifford became close friends. Mrs. Clifford, who was known for her fine eye in interior design, even helped with the decoration of bedrooms at the White House for the Johnson daughters, Lynda Bird and Luci Baines. On occasion, the Cliffords spent the weekend with the Johnsons at Camp David, the presidential retreat in Maryland.

Under Kennedy, Johnson had exercised little power, and although he had controlled the Senate in the fifties, he was not well known by people outside Washington and Texas. He realized that the first major speech of his presidency offered the opportunity to establish his own agenda and his own credibility. So it was natural that he summoned the best and the brightest of his advisers on December 23, 1963, to begin laying out his State of the Union address. Gathered around the Cabinet Room table were Secretary of State Dean Rusk, Secretary of the Interior Stewart Udall, Secretary of Agriculture Orville Freeman, Secretary of Labor Willard Wirtz, Deputy Attorney General Nicholas Katzenbach, National Security Adviser McGeorge Bundy, Walt Rostow of the State Department, speechwriter Ted Sorensen, and presidential aides Jack Valenti and Walter Jenkins. There also were three outsiders: James Rowe, Abe Fortas, and Clark Clifford. After listening to the others, Johnson turned the meeting over to Clifford and Fortas, who began organizing the ideas that had been discussed into the outline of a coherent speech.

The day before Johnson was to deliver the address, an incident that he thought dead threatened to stain the new president's reputation just as he was trying to gather momentum. A few months before, Johnson's former Senate aide Bobby Baker had become embroiled in an influence-peddling scandal. Nicknamed the 101st senator for the power he had amassed, Baker had acquired financial stakes in twenty-two corporations dealing with everything from vending machines to housing developments. He had been forced to resign as secretary of the Senate after allegations were made that he had used his influence to place his vending machines at defense plants around the country.

Now, the Senate Rules Committee had released testimony by an insurance executive named Donald Reynolds that threatened to revive the Baker mess and drag Johnson into it. Acting at Baker's suggestion, Reynolds said, he had sold two life insurance policies to Johnson while he was in the Senate. The fees had been high because Johnson's 1955 heart attack made him a high risk for insurance. In return for arranging the transaction, Reynolds told Senate investigators, Baker was supposed to receive a commission and Reynolds was required to buy advertising time on a radio station owned by Johnson in Austin, Texas. As part of the deal, Reynolds said, he also had sent an expensive stereo set to the Johnsons. To support his allegations, Reynolds had said that Walter Jenkins, another former Johnson Senate aide, who now worked at the White House, knew that he had given the stereo to the Johnsons. The committee wanted to hear from Jenkins.

Johnson was worried that the attorney general might use the testimony to revive the Bobby Baker affair. If there were a public outcry, Kennedy might push hard for an investigation to tarnish Johnson and drive him off the Democratic ticket in 1964. So he brought in Clifford and Fortas to find a way to avoid having Jenkins testify before the Senate. While there seemed little evidence that Johnson even knew about the arrangement between Baker and Reynolds, the two lawyers agreed that the appearance of Jenkins at a public hearing could transform the matter into a full-blown scandal.

Fortas's law firm, Arnold, Porter and Fortas, prepared a twenty-six-page legal brief concluding that Jenkins was covered by executive privilege and could not be compelled to testify. After some cajoling by Clifford, who claimed that Jenkins was too busy with the transition to testify, the Democrat-controlled committee agreed to accept an affidavit in lieu of an appearance. In the document, Jenkins denied the allegations by Reynolds, saying he thought the stereo set was a gift to the Johnsons from Baker. Because he had not gone before the committee, he could not be questioned about the statements or about other matters that he did not address in the affidavit, such as his knowledge about whether Reynolds had been coerced into buying radio advertising time.

At the suggestion of Clifford and Fortas, Johnson then surprised an unprepared press corps by raising the issue himself at a press conference on another matter. He gave a brief history of the insurance policies, omitting the allegation that Reynolds had bought advertising time, and repeating the denials by Jenkins. The controversy subsided. Years later Republicans accused Clifford and Fortas of "conducting a cover-up" of the affair. Given the values of Washington, the charge did nothing to harm Clifford's reputation. Rather, it enhanced his image as a man close to power, an insider.

The attorney general never pursued the accusations by Reynolds. As Nicholas Katzenbach, the deputy attorney general, recalled later, Kennedy "never got much into the details of the case. I don't think he wanted to know a great deal about it." In fact, Kennedy was becoming thoroughly disillusioned at the Justice Department for a variety of reasons. Among them was his belief that FBI Director J. Edgar Hoover took orders only from his friend the president, although he supposedly worked directly for Kennedy. He attributed a series of unflattering items that had appeared in the press about him in recent months to leaks from Hoover. And he concluded that Hoover had probably acted at the urging of Johnson.

On June 11, 1964, Robert Kennedy walked into Clifford's law office and announced that he had sent Johnson a letter asking to be appointed the new ambassador to Vietnam. Kennedy was certain that Clifford could persuade Johnson to give him the post and he asked him to do so. But the lawyer expressed genuine concern about Kennedy's safety in such an environment and said he was extremely reluctant to help him. Privately, Clifford viewed that particular diplomatic post as too critical to Johnson's reelection possibility to entrust to Kennedy, even if it would mean getting him out of the country. After Kennedy left, Clifford contacted Johnson and advised him to politely reject the attorney general's offer. Although Johnson undoubtedly would have liked nothing better than to dispatch Kennedy six thousand miles from Washington, he recognized the dangers of placing Kennedy in such a sensitive and dangerous post. Still, something had to be done about the attorney general. Johnson was not willing to wait much longer.

★   ★   ★

As the Democratic national convention approached in August 1964, the nomination was Johnson's by acclamation. The only drama was picking a vice president. Always a canny politician, LBJ sensed that he had to deal with Kennedy before the convention or face the likelihood of Bobby's momentum sweeping him onto the ticket at the convention. There was impressive support for such a ticket. Richard Daley, the powerful Democratic mayor of Chicago and a longtime pal of the Kennedy clan, was making it known that he wanted Bobby in the vice president's spot. A number of Northern and Midwestern governors and some state party chairman also thought that the Democrats had a stronger chance of winning with a Kennedy on the ballot. There were even reports that Jackie Kennedy, still an immensely popular figure with the American public, was returning from a cruise to attend the convention and champion Bobby's candidacy.

Aside from his strong personal feelings, Johnson had valid political reasons for not wanting the attorney general as his running mate. The businessmen, whose contributions Johnson needed, remained wary of Kennedy. To them, he was a symbol of government intervention, grand jury investigations, and antitrust actions. Further, Kennedy's liberal position on civil rights would not play well in the South, where the conservative Republican presidential candidate, Senator Barry Goldwater of Arizona, was expected to run strong.

Yet Johnson could not openly dismiss Kennedy's candidacy. The memory of his brother was too strong in the country and the party. Clifton Carter, one of Johnson's aides, cautioned him, "Don't ever participate in anything that is anti-Kennedy. If anyone else does, fire him." So, to rid himself of this personal and political problem, Johnson had to cast his decision in the most impersonal and politically palatable terms possible. To help, he called on a master of political discretion who also was no fan of Robert Kennedy. His name was Clark Clifford.

Johnson was a savvy political operator and he saw that Goldwater's nomination provided him with a convenient cover. With Clifford doing the writing, the two men crafted a memorandum that became Johnson's justification for knocking Bobby off the ticket. The fifteen-paragraph memo echoed the 1948 strategy for Harry Truman's presidential campaign, which Clifford had appropriated from Rowe. Now, he would dust it off to eliminate Kennedy.

The memo argued that Goldwater would be strong in the South,

Southwest, and possibly the Middle West. A close race could be decided in the Midwest and the Border States, places where a liberal Easterner would be of little use to the ticket. In one classic sentence, Clifford cast the decision in a manner that would simultaneously remind Bobby Kennedy that the president was aware of Kennedy's opposition to Johnson four years earlier and make it difficult for Kennedy to oppose the decision in public. "I am sure that you will understand the basis of my decision and the factors that have entered into it, because President Kennedy had to make a similar decision in 1960," it read.

On July 29, a Wednesday, the attorney general was summoned to the White House. Johnson delivered his lines and Kennedy said little. The attorney general could see what was afoot and he refused to publicly withdraw his name from consideration. He had never declared his candidacy for the vice presidency, he argued to Johnson, and therefore could see no reason to announce his withdrawal.

This left Johnson in a quandary, as Kennedy no doubt knew it would. He and his advisers had discussed what would happen if Kennedy refused to withdraw gracefully, but it was true that there was no precedent for publicly dumping a potential running mate who had not even declared his candidacy. The thorny problem was heightened by Hugh Sidey, the well-connected *Time* correspondent covering the White House.

Washington was awash with speculation that Johnson would have to put Kennedy on the ticket. Sidey learned of Kennedy's visit to the president the day after it occurred and he began calling his sources within the administration to learn what had been said. By late Friday, he had enough fragments to write a story saying Johnson was dropping Kennedy as a vice presidential contender, but he still needed some official White House confirmation.

"Finally on Saturday night, I had written a story and we were ready to go to press," recalled Sidey. "It was getting hairy because of the deadline. I called one White House official and got him at a party, but he would not confirm or deny it. I called the White House and got Billy Don Moyers [a presidential assistant]. I said, 'Here's the story,' and read him some of it. He sort of paused and said, 'Well, hang on.' Then he came back to the phone and said, 'You will get a call in a few minutes from Clark Clifford and he will talk to you.'"

Sidey, of course, knew Clifford well. The relationship that had begun on the Symington campaign had blossomed into a full friendship, with Clifford recommending Sidey for membership in the exclusive Chevy Chase Club and continuing to feed the journalist scoops and insider insights.

"Hugh, they tell me you have quite a story," Clifford said when he called Sidey a few minutes later, a touch of humor in his voice.

After Sidey described the key elements of the story, Clifford confirmed that the reporter had pieced together an accurate account. Clifford added some details of what had taken place. In fact, he seemed so sure of what had occurred that Sidey thought he might have been in the room with Johnson and Kennedy during the conversation. Clifford also sprang the strategy that had been developed in the event Bobby would not step down himself. The president had decided, he informed Sidey, that none of his cabinet members should be considered for the vice presidency. This was the trick that Johnson and Clifford hoped would avoid the specter of singling out Bobby Kennedy. Of course, Clifford would not be quoted by name or referred to in any way in the article. In the time-honored Washington tradition, he was speaking on background, providing a layer of protection for the president on this touchy matter at the same time he put the desired political spin on the matter.

With Sidey poised to expose the decision on Monday, the White House was scrambling. The administration did not want *Time* to break the story first. So, in an attempt to diffuse the impact of the *Time* story, Johnson issued a brief statement on Sunday, July 30. "I have reached the conclusion that it would be inadvisable for me to recommend to the convention any member of my Cabinet or any of those who meet regularly with the Cabinet," it read.

Sidey had been scooped, although his account contained far more information. But the White House's fig leaf did not conceal much. Kennedy partisans were angered by the abrupt dismissal of their man less than a month before the convention, and so were backers of other potential candidates, such as Secretary of Defense Robert McNamara and Secretary of State Dean Rusk. As columnists Rowland Evans and Robert Novak wrote later, "All of Washington guffawed at the clumsiness and transparency of the ploy."

Johnson knew the Democrats had nowhere else to turn in November. And he had gotten rid of Kennedy, who announced a short time later that he would run for the United States Senate in New York. In his memoirs, *The Vantage Point*, Johnson described the forty-five-minute meeting with Kennedy on July 29 as cordial and cast his decision in statesmanlike terms. Johnson even went so far as to reproduce the Clifford memo in the appendix of the book as his justification for dumping Bobby. But when he had recounted the session not long after it occurred for Sidey, Johnson's tone was decidedly different. He reveled in his dismissal of Kennedy. "That little shit Bobby just sat there with his Adam's apple going up and down," Johnson said with a hearty laugh.

Clifford never had an official role in Johnson's 1964 presidential campaign. Throughout the summer and fall, he continued to act as an important outside adviser. At the Democratic convention in late August, he worked with Walter Reuther, the president of the United Auto Workers and a champion for civil rights, to reach a compromise with blacks from Mississippi who had been denied full participation in the convention. After the convention, Clifford worked as an unofficial consultant on handling the media. Part of his advice was that Johnson should avoid appearing on any of the Sunday morning question-and-answer television programs, such as *Meet the Press* and *Face the Nation*. They were, Clifford maintained, not dignified rostrums for the president.

As he had for John Kennedy, Clifford also dealt with more sensitive matters for Johnson. Thus, his most important moment in the campaign occurred during the second week of October when scandal threatened to derail the momentum the president was gathering to roll over Goldwater.

On October 7, a Wednesday, *Newsweek* threw a party to inaugurate its posh new offices on Pennsylvania Avenue, just a few blocks west of the White House. It was a distinguished gathering, drawing seven cabinet members as well as a large number of legislators, diplomats, and prominent journalists. Also attending was Walter Jenkins, the married father of six children. After leaving the party about seven o'clock, the presidential adviser walked two blocks to the men's room of the YMCA, a well-known meeting place for homosexuals. District of Columbia police had staked out the rest room, using peepholes for surveillance, and thirty-five minutes after Jenkins entered he was arrested. At the police station, he was booked on a disorderly conduct charge and his occupation listed only as "clerk."

The arrest remained unpublicized and unknown until a reporter for the *Washington Evening Star* called the White House for comment the following Tuesday morning, nearly a week after the incident. The *Star* and the city's other afternoon paper, the *Washington Daily News*, had been tipped by an anonymous caller who later turned out to be an official with the Republican Congressional Committee. After digging, the *Star* reporter had discovered that Jenkins also had been arrested five years earlier for a similar sexual offense. In that case, the charge had been "pervert."

The incident had the earmarks of a major disaster for Jenkins and his boss. Johnson was out of town, so Lady Bird Johnson and her press secretary, Liz Carpenter, asked Clifford and Fortas to come to the White House for an emergency meeting to deal with the matter. After that meeting and another later at Fortas's home with Jenkins, Clifford and Fortas decided to try to persuade the newspapers not to publish the story. Theirs was a delicate mission fraught with pitfalls for everyone involved if it blew up.

The first step was to hospitalize Jenkins, who was in a state of near panic. Along with keeping him away from the press, Clifford and Fortas suggested that the move might elicit sympathy from the newspaper editors because homosexuality was regarded in some circles in those days as a disease. Next, Clifford and Fortas paid calls on the editors of the *Star* and the *Daily News* as well as the *Washington Post*. The trick was to get the story killed without asking specifically for it to be killed. A straightforward request to kill a story usually angered editors and pushed the matter onto the front page. So the two lawyers appealed to the editors' sense of decency and compassion.

They started at 10 o'clock on the morning of Wednesday, October 14, at the *Star*, which seemed to be furthest ahead on the story. Newbold Noyes, the editor, recalled that he was told Jenkins was a "sick man, had had a nervous collapse and was going into the hospital, and was not going to return to his job" at the White House. "They made what I would regard as a plea to have us not break the story," said Noyes. "I agreed to go along at that time."

At the *News*, editor John O'Rourke was told the same story. "Our position was that if it was possible to withhold it we were willing to do it provided it didn't break anywhere else," said O'Rourke.

The *Washington Post* did not even know about the arrest until Clifford and Fortas met with its editor, J. R. Wiggins. He refused to make any commitments, although he promised to handle the case in a way that would do the least damage to Jenkins.

Late that afternoon, Clifford telephoned President Johnson, who was at the Waldorf-Astoria in New York City. It was the first the president had heard of the incident. The only reassurance Clifford could offer was that the newspapers seemed willing to lay off, at least for the moment.

Unfortunately for Clifford and the White House, there were too many news organizations in Washington to plug all the potential outlets. About eight o'clock that night, United Press International put the story out over its news wire to hundreds of newspapers across the country. The news service had been tipped that afternoon by a reporter at one of the Washington newspapers who was angered that his publication was holding back. UPI had checked the story with the police and distributed it. With the lid off, the Associated Press put out an account two hours later and the *Post* ran its own story in the morning. The *Star*, which could have broken the story, and the *Daily News* followed with fuller accounts that afternoon.

The press and the Republicans emitted howls of protest. National security was invoked because Jenkins had had a top-secret clearance and had been in charge of background checks on White House employees. The Republicans claimed that he could have been blackmailed by the Soviets. As for Clifford and Fortas, they found themselves portrayed as censors in newspapers around the country. The White House sought vainly to control the damage by distancing itself from Clifford and Fortas. Bill Moyers said President Johnson had not learned of the Jenkins arrest until late on the afternoon of October 14, hours after Clifford and Fortas had visited the editors.

Years later, Clifford tried to blunt the accusations that he tried to suppress the story, saying that he had acted only to ease the pain for Jenkins and his family. But Liz Carpenter remembered that it was Fortas, not Clifford, who showed concern for Jenkins in trying to keep a lid on the arrest. "Fortas was so much more full of heart and compassion, and it was not another case to him," she said later. Jenkins himself would later remember that "Clark was certainly more business. Fortas was more interested in the person as a human, as opposed to an issue."

Clifford's chief instinct had been to protect the president. He had evaluated the dilemma with the dispassion of a lawyer, recognizing that creating sympathy for Jenkins could serve the ultimate goal of protecting Johnson.

As often happens within that closed society, it turned out that Washington had taken the matter far more seriously than the remainder of the country. Most Americans seemed to care little even then about the sexual preferences of a presidential assistant, and the story did not damage Johnson's campaign. The president, with Hubert Humphrey as his running mate, drubbed Barry Goldwater in November and finally earned his own mandate to govern. As for Bobby Kennedy, the attorney general was elected to the United States Senate from New York.

By this time, Clifford's reputation as a lawyer was complete. His insider status at the Kennedy White House had been surpassed by his astonishing closeness to President Johnson. He was one of the most-talked-about attorneys in Washington, on a par with the great trial lawyer Edward Bennett Williams in prestige.

His relationship with Johnson was but one of many that Clifford had nurtured to fruition. He still remained extremely close to Justice Douglas, continuing to serve as his personal attorney and frequent financial adviser. When Douglas ran into marital troubles with his third wife, Joan Martin, he appealed to Clifford to intervene with her on his behalf, and again the lawyer came to the aid of his friend.

Along with marital difficulties, Douglas had recurring financial problems and often turned to Clifford for help with those, too. In the fifties, Clifford had loaned Douglas money so that he could refinance his mortgage. In 1966, Clifford guaranteed a $6,150 loan to the justice from the National Bank of Washington, much as he had assisted Douglas financially in the fifties. At the time, Clifford was a director of the bank, and he arranged the loan by telephoning its chairman, his close personal friend Bernard Colton.

Clifford himself made few appearances before the Supreme Court. However, he often was involved in cases that reached the highest court. In most of those instances, Clifford farmed out the legal work to other firms that specialized in Supreme Court and appeals litigation. Nonetheless, he remained involved in these matters, which were decided with the help of his friend Justice Douglas.

Clifford also maintained friendships with media barons and business tycoons, and they illustrated an interesting Washington symbiosis. In the most obvious way, these men turned to him for advice because they saw that he was close to men such as Johnson and Kennedy. On the other hand, it was Clifford's ability to communicate with America's business leaders that made him more valuable to Kennedy and Johnson. Clifford was always shrewd in managing each of these alliances with care and discretion. His association with senior government officials, and even with the new president, was valuable only so long as he did not abuse it on behalf of his clients. The value was sometimes intangible, but nonetheless very powerful.

Describing the significance of his friends in high places, Clifford spoke with some candor years later when he said, "It would be a psychological value. If clients feel that even privately you are in contact with the country's leaders, that you are keeping up on all that is going on, that perhaps they turn to you for advice, it generally has value in the conduct of one's life in Washington. I would be less than truthful if I were to say that doesn't exist. It does. I did not make a point of it. I did not affirmatively use it. If President Kennedy every now and then would accentuate it by some comment that he made —'I talked to Clifford about it'— well, that was all right with me."

In this atmosphere, Clifford's law practice was prospering. Given Clifford's reputation and power, however, most people in Washington would have been surprised to know that his firm still remained very small and intimate. He ran it as a fiefdom, doling out salaries as he saw fit and even assigning each lawyer a specific seat at the firm meetings held in his office.

Even with the increased demand that had started during the Kennedy administration, in 1964, there were only six lawyers. The firm was still known as Clifford and Miller, although Miller had been dead well over a decade. Along with Clifford, the members of the firm were Carson Glass, Sam McIlwain, John Sharon, Tom Finney, and John Kovin. Glass and McIlwain had been there from the beginning and the others had come in the sixties.

One of the most interesting routes to the law firm had been traveled by Kovin, who had joined the firm in 1961 after graduating from George Washington Law School. He had moved to Washington in the middle fifties from Michigan to attend college. He met Clifford in 1956 while mowing the lawn at Clifford's home along Rockville Pike.

"My brother said he was working for this 'dynamite character' and he asked me if I wanted a job," said Kovin later. "I was in college and needed the money, so I started caring for the lawn, polishing the cars, stacking wood, and doing other chores. My brother and I planted the line of trees that shielded the house from Rockville Pike, which was getting to be a busier street. Mr. Clifford was very engaging. All the boys liked him. The most impressive thing was to go into the barroom in his house, which is behind the dining room, and see all the pictures on the wall. There was Harry Truman and Chief Justice Fred Vinson of the Supreme Court and all these senators and other leaders. And of course the *Time* magazine cover of Mr. Clifford."

When Kovin started law school, Clifford loaned him money for tuition. When he graduated, Kovin was hired by the firm as a lawyer, although he said he spent most of his time in those first years running errands and handling minor matters.

Sharon had come to the firm following the Du Pont victory in 1962. A few months later, Finney had joined. The son of an Oklahoma lawyer, Finney had spent five years as a covert agent for the CIA in Denmark and then worked as a staff assistant to Senator Mike Munroney of Oklahoma. Finney was a bright, well-organized attorney who was widely respected in Congress.

One of those who had gotten to know and respect him in Congress was Lyndon Johnson. In the wake of the Jenkins scandal, Johnson had asked Clifford if Finney could provide some help at the White House. Naturally, Clifford agreed and Finney found himself spending many hours each day filling in for the departed aide. Even after returning to the law firm, Finney helped draft the Johnson administration's trade bill. Throughout all of this, he remained on Clifford's payroll.

As the firm prospered and grew, it outstripped the small offices on L Street. In August 1964, Clifford and Miller moved to a new building at the corner of I Street and Connecticut Avenue. The lawyers and their staff took over half of the 13,000-square-foot twelfth floor, which was the top of the building. The offices were paneled in rich woods, the floors graced by thick carpet. From the spacious windows of his corner office, Clifford could look across Lafayette Square to the White House, where he had started his Washington career. Clifford's personal suite had its own bathroom and a small, private study. The narrow study contained a twin-size bed, where Clifford took the secret afternoon naps that had become a regular part of his long day a few years earlier. Callers would be told that Mr. Clifford was in conference when, in fact, he was sleeping soundly.

Until the move to new quarters, the firm had been run as a sole proprietorship, which meant the other lawyers were paid salaries and Clifford collected the profits at the end of the year. Several of his partners later said that the profits never dropped below $500,000 for Clifford. In 1964, with business booming, Clifford agreed to turn the firm into a more traditional partnership. Finney drew up the partnership agreement, which left Clifford with the largest portion of the firm's ownership and parceled out smaller shares to the new partners — Glass, McIlwain, Sharon, and Finney. Kovin, the youngest and least experienced, remained an associate. Despite this more equitable arrangement, Clifford retained sole control over the distribution of profits. It was a small legal family, with Clifford the patriarch at the head of the table.

Because most clients paid by annual retainers of $25,000 to $50,000, the operation started in the black each January 1. New clients or particularly complex matters that required additional billing of a retainer client during the year only swelled the profits. At the beginning of each year, Clifford would assign each partner a specific percentage of the firm's profits. The number of points was based on Clifford's subjective analysis of the partner's performance the previous year. At year's end, each percentage point would be worth one-hundredth of the firm's profit for the preceding twelve months.

The goal in those first years of the partnership was to gross $2 million, which would be split among the partners after deductions for paying the clerical help, rent, and other expenses. Clifford retained roughly half the ownership points, so his income hovered around $800,000. Still, a sizable amount was left for the other partners and there was little grumbling in the beginning. After all, it was Clifford who brought in most of the business.

Another equally important factor in minimizing dissension was Clifford himself. He was a man of restraint who treated clients and colleagues alike with immense courtliness. McIlwain, who would spend nearly forty years working at his side, would say that he recalled no time when Clifford raised his voice in anger. Other partners quibbled with that assessment in later years, remembering incidents in which Clifford dealt brusquely with some of his colleagues and times when he did display anger. The anger surfaced most often when someone, usually

Kovin, questioned the way in which the partnership's money was allocated.

"Yes, he could get angry," said Kovin, who became a partner in 1970. "He could raise his voice and grimace and scowl. Anyone would know he was angry, although he didn't shout. I guess over the years I made him angry more than anyone else. It usually occurred when I questioned the way he was splitting up the pie at the firm."

But on the whole, it was a small and prospering family in the sixties.

Not long after the move to the new quarters, the Du Pont case came back to life briefly. Since the special tax-relief legislation had passed in 1961, the price of General Motors stock had nearly doubled, rising to $100 a share from $55. The Du Pont family had been selling its shares slowly to avoid disrupting the market for the stock and they still had more than eight million shares to sell. This meant that they were facing a capital gains tax that was nearly twice what they were to have paid under the 1961 legislation.

In early July, Clifford had met with Secretary of the Treasury Douglas Dillon and discussed the matter at a social gathering. Clifford argued the case for a tax-free distribution of the remaining shares, saying that the United States treasury had already received all of the revenue anticipated from the Du Ponts through the earlier sales. Dillon listened carefully and said he would pass on Clifford's proposal to the department's lawyers.

The opportunity to lobby the treasury secretary arose again near the end of July. This time the location was the White House. President Johnson hosted a luncheon for prominent businessmen on July 23 and the guest list included Dillon, Clifford, and Crawford Greenwalt, the Du Pont chairman.

By early fall, the lawyers at the Treasury Department told Clifford they saw no reason to provide any further special relief for the Du Ponts. Clifford met with Fred Smith, who had replaced Robert Knight as general counsel at the Treasury Department, but he got nowhere with his argument for tax leniency. Smith and his staff were clearly prepared to recommend to the Internal Revenue Service that the Du Pont family and related interests be required to pay the full tax on the sale of the remaining stock, a bill that would reach hundreds of millions of dollars.

Faced with almost certain defeat, Clifford turned again to Dillon, whom he had known since the Kennedy administration. Years later,

Clifford remembered it this way: "I went to Doug Dillon, who was secretary of the treasury, and I think I may have sent Greenwalt to Dillon, who had a good business background. Then I think Doug Dillon turned me over to Robert Knight [who] was with a New York law firm. Dillon said Bob Knight knows more about this than anyone else."

Indeed, it was Knight who had issued the helpful interpretation for the Du Ponts two years earlier. Since then, Knight had left government and become a partner at the New York law firm of Shearman and Sterling, a corporate firm with high-powered clients and a low profile. Clifford telephoned Knight at Shearman and Sterling and said that he and the Du Ponts' other lawyers were asking the Treasury Department for a modification of the tax rules.

Since he had interpreted the rules while at Treasury, didn't Mr. Knight agree, suggested Clifford, that raising $470 million in taxes from the Du Ponts on the General Motors sales met the needs of the government as defined under the legislation? And, Clifford continued, would Mr. Knight mind writing a letter for the Treasury Department agreeing with that interpretation?

"I do not feel that it is proper for me, as a private citizen, to comment on what I said in a ruling when I no longer have any responsibility for Treasury," replied Knight. When Clifford pressed, Knight did agree that the rules allowed Du Pont to come in and seek a modification of the regulations.

"Is the Secretary going to call you back [to government] and decide this thing?" asked Clifford.

"I have no idea," replied Knight.

When Clifford hung up, Knight telephoned Dillon in Washington and described his conversation with the lawyer for the Du Ponts. Dillon listened and thanked Knight for his call. Clifford called Knight a second time to discuss the matter further. Later that same day, Dillon also called Knight after talking with Clifford.

The treasury secretary told Knight that his staff was having difficulty deciding the Du Pont case and he inquired about Knight's willingness to return to the department as a temporary consultant to handle the matter. After receiving the okay from his law partners, Knight agreed and returned to the department's headquarters next to the White House on November 4.

Again, there is no direct evidence that Clifford raised the matter with the president. Again, he was more subtle, simply associating himself with the Du Pont name. In early November, Clifford wrote a memorandum to Johnson concerning an upcoming campaign swing through Delaware. Clifford said he had had a long conversation about the trip with Lammont Du Pont Copeland, a member of the Du Pont family and an executive with the Du Pont Company. "He stated he would alert the newspapers in Delaware in which the Du Pont family had an interest and he could guarantee that the President's trip would receive full treatment on the front pages with pictures," wrote Clifford. "He said he would be helpful in assuring the type of coverage we wanted."

During the following two weeks, Knight reviewed the history of the case, read new memoranda written about it, and discussed the issue with lawyers for the Internal Revenue Service and the Du Ponts, including Clifford. On November 20, he submitted a report on his findings to the commissioner of the Internal Revenue Service. Knight recommended that the Du Pont request be granted. It was never the intention of the Treasury Department or the Congress, he wrote, to collect more than $470 million from the Du Pont family and the other shareholders.

Clifford had scored another major victory for the Du Ponts, but this one touched off a furor in Congress. Had Senator Kerr not died on New Year's Day of 1963, he might have been able to head off the controversy over the Du Pont tax case. However, with Kerr gone, the leading Democratic liberals on the Senate Finance Committee, Albert Gore of Tennessee and Paul Douglas of Illinois, demanded a hearing.

In a statement on the Senate floor in late December, Douglas described the ruling by saying, "It seems to me this has been a heads-I-win, tails-you-lose ruling — heads, Du Pont wins, tails, the government loses." Gore followed Douglas, charging that the "last-minute change in the Treasury ruling [was] negotiated and issued in secrecy and contrary to the clear intent of the Congress. Stranger yet was the fact that Knight first learned of his appointment as a special consultant by way of a telephone call from a Washington lawyer for the Du Pont interests, Mr. Clark Clifford."

The Finance Committee held two days of hearings in March 1965. Knight recounted his telephone calls with Clifford and the conversation in which Dillon asked him to review the matter. Dillon did not disclose his meeting in July with Clifford. Instead, he testified that he had asked

Knight to return because the lawyers at Treasury and the IRS were having difficulty with the complex matter.

When Bertrand Harding, the deputy commissioner of the Internal Revenue Service, appeared before the committee, Gore asked if Harding was having any difficulty deciding the Du Pont matter before Knight's arrival.

"I was not, sir, personally," he replied.

"You were prepared to exercise the responsibility of the office which you held with or without the advice of a consultant?" asked Gore.

"Yes, sir," said Harding. "I was prepared to act on the basis of the recommendations of my staff, and the concurrence of the chief counsel."

"Did you request that appointment of a special consultant?" asked Gore.

"No, sir, I did not."

Gore's line of questioning broke down when Harding volunteered that he agreed with Dillon's suggestion that Knight be hired to evaluate the complex matter. As a matter of fact, said Harding, the appointment of Knight had been "absolutely necessary to our proper conclusion of the matter."

The issue of whether Clifford had suggested to Dillon that Knight return to government was left unresolved, and Gore and Douglas were defeated. The issue was dropped, one of America's wealthiest families avoided millions of dollars in taxes, and Washington's most powerful lawyer notched another victory.

Clifford's success as a lawyer enhanced his standing with Lyndon Johnson, who liked accomplished people, particularly those who knew the art of making a deal. At one point, Johnson boasted to reporters covering that White House that "my friend" Clark Clifford had earned $1.3 million the previous year.

As Johnson began 1965, his first year as an elected president, he operated as his own chief of staff with three sets of advisers. One group, led by McNamara and Rusk, had been retained from the Kennedy administration. Another set was composed of hard-core Johnson loyalists, such as Bill Moyers, Jack Valenti, and Joseph Califano. Then there was a troika of outsiders — Clifford, Fortas, and Rowe.

Throughout 1965, Clifford found himself spending increasing amounts of time advising Johnson on a range of issues, from presidential appointments to the nettlesome problem of Vietnam. Often, Clifford and Johnson spoke by telephone five or ten times a day. When Johnson confronted a pressing problem, or simply wanted an audience, he would tell an aide, "See if Clark can come over." Clifford always obliged. Even if he was meeting with an important client, he would excuse himself with the simple explanation: "I'm sorry, if you will excuse me. The president is calling."

Although his office was only a block from the White House and he had an unobstructed view of the executive mansion, Clifford rarely walked to his meetings with Johnson. Instead, he would have his driver take him through the massive wrought-iron gates to the front portico, claiming that he did not want to be seen walking into the White House so often. Nonetheless, the effect was not lost on those who worked there. Walt Rostow, one of Johnson's key aides, remembered Clifford always arriving in a big black car, delivering his views eloquently, and then returning to his law office.

These were the years when Clifford's image was burnished to an unprecedented luster among the lawyers of Washington. His star had risen under Truman and been reestablished in the city's political firmament under Kennedy. But with Johnson in the White House, Clifford found his advice more in demand than ever. He began to take on the characteristics of a statesman, although he had had no official role in government since 1950 aside from the intelligence advisory board.

Still handsome and ever-courtly as he approached his sixties, Clifford cut a dashing figure in the corridors of the White House. He always tipped his head, smiled, and waved to all the secretaries as he made his way to the Oval Office, every bit the Washington wise man. The bond between Clifford and Johnson was strengthened because their wives were genuinely fond of each other. So the two couples often dined together, usually in small, intimate gatherings.

Johnson was a shrewd judge of people. He recognized that part of what came with Clifford was a well-honed presentation, the double-breasted suits, the resonant voice with his deliberate cadences. Out of the presence of Clifford, the president would sometimes mimic the lawyer's mannerisms. Folding his hands and summoning up his best preacher's voice, Johnson would say slowly, "Well, Mr. President, if I were you . . ." Then he would throw back his head and laugh. Still, Johnson valued the advice he received from Clifford as well as that from Fortas, trusting the abilities of both men to see the logical solution to many problems.

Fortas, of course, was around even more than Clifford. Even after Johnson appointed him to the Supreme Court in 1965, a position that should have kept him out of the White House and its partisan dealings, Fortas remained a primary adviser to Johnson. In a famous picture, the two lawyers are bent over Johnson's desk in the Oval Office advising the president on his 1966 State of the Union address.

"All of us looked on Clifford and Fortas as figures who were part of the pantheon of political gods," said Valenti, who went on to become one of the city's most powerful and well-paid lobbyists as president of the Motion Picture Association of America, Hollywood's man in Washington. "Clark and Abe were very careful not to ruffle any feathers, too. So that, rather than resent them, we welcomed them into the inner circle.

"LBJ knew that Clifford had ties to all the corporate giants of the world, but he had political experience, too. Clifford's role in the '48 election was his most important triumph in Johnson's eyes. The greatest shield against criticism in this town is to win. Arrows might hit you, but if you are a winner, they bounce off."

Clifford was sensitive to possible resentments. After all, he had once been a White House staff member himself. So he went out of his way to praise the president's staff. He wrote a letter to Johnson commending a speech written by Jack Valenti, calling it "wonderful" and noting that he had been "impressed by the sincere and heartwarming nature of the tribute." When Joe Califano negotiated a strong agreement with the steel industry, Clifford wrote to LBJ praising Califano as "exceptionally able, tactful, and intelligent." And when Bill Moyers replaced George Reedy as press secretary, Clifford sent Moyers a congratulatory letter saying, "It is wonderfully impressive that when the President is faced with an emergency he turns to you."

In some quarters of the administration, however, there was uneasiness over the unofficial, yet increasingly influential role played by Clifford. Rusk, for example, thought that Clifford was better informed than Fortas, but still offered little advice of real value. And, after an early meeting on Vietnam, Defense Secretary McNamara told Johnson: "I can't see why you bother consulting your experts. For in a pinch, you pick two guys off the street . . . and follow their advice."

Others, however, found Clifford's viewpoint valuable. McGeorge Bundy, the president's national security adviser, remembered Clifford as "a man whom LBJ trusted. Any man who was trusted by LBJ, you wanted to hear from as much as possible." In fact, it was this trust that would convey to Clifford a special role in the darkest days of Johnson's White House years.

13

"An Insider's Insider"

THE VIETNAM WAR began to assume a prominent place in Clifford's life in late June 1965, when the president brought his closest military advisers to Camp David for a series of weekend discussions that extended through July. Just weeks earlier, the military regime of Nguyen Cao Ky had been established in South Vietnam and the president was wrestling with the issue of how many American troops would have to be committed to protecting the Ky government against the Communist forces of North Vietnam, under the leadership of Ho Chi Minh. Clifford attended the meetings in his official capacity as chairman of the Foreign Intelligence Advisory Board, but the real reason for his presence was that Johnson trusted him.

Johnson was not a man who brooked dissent, but Clifford was one of the few who could differ with the president to his face. Zbigniew Brzezinski, who later became President Carter's national security adviser, said that Johnson once described Clifford as a man who gave solid advice and was "not taken in by circumstances or events or even other individuals." Clifford, Johnson told Brzezinski, knew that "in politics, sometimes it's important to grab your opponent by the balls, to squeeze hard and to twist, and not to let go."

At one point during the discussions at Camp David, Clifford questioned General Earle Wheeler, the chairman of the Joint Chiefs of Staff, about the number of troops the United States would need to commit to Vietnam. Clifford ventured that he had heard the figure 75,000 being bandied about. Johnson interrupted and called the number nonsense, but Wheeler acknowledged that protecting South Vietnam might very well require that kind of commitment. Then Clifford, who was skeptical of the military's role in Vietnam, pressed Wheeler on what was in store for the United States in Southeast Asia even if it could win a military victory. The United States, said the general, might have to maintain a standing army there for twenty or thirty years. Clifford was visibly shaken.

On July 25, the last session at Camp David, the president asked each adviser to present his view on the necessity of committing more American troops to Southeast Asia. Although each used a different rationale, all of the advisers said they believed that United States needed to meet the Communist threat. Finally, Johnson turned to Clifford and asked what he thought. Speaking in deep, measured tones, the lawyer who had helped to launch the cold war made the case that the United States could not win a military victory.

"If we send in 100,000 troops, the North Vietnamese will match us," he said. "And when they run out of troops, the Chinese will send in 'volunteers.' Russia and China don't intend for us to win this war." With almost uncanny accuracy, Clifford predicted that the United States would lose 50,000 men and spend billions of dollars on a fruitless war. Pounding his fist on the table for emphasis, Clifford said, "I cannot see anything but disaster for our nation in this area."

Clifford lost the argument. Three days later, President Johnson told the country that he was stepping up the war effort. As he was returning to the White House from the Pentagon after making the decision on July 28, Johnson told his aides he wanted the press corps to have something more than the buildup of troops in Vietnam to report that night. "Let's announce the new head of the Voice of America and the new Supreme Court justice," said Johnson.

Presidential aide Joe Califano was told to write up a statement announcing the two nominations. When it came to describing the Supreme Court nominee, Califano asked whom Johnson had in mind. "Just write a statement that will fit any truly distinguished lawyer and scholar," replied the president. "Someone like Clark Clifford, but make it general and leave the name blank."

The name that was eventually filled in was not Clifford, but Abe Fortas. The appointment, however, did not obscure the news of Vietnam that night, nor would anything else in Johnson's career as president.

By the fall, the United States had 150,000 soldiers in Vietnam. As the war escalated, Clifford put aside his own reservations and fell into line behind the president. In retrospect, Clifford's decision to shelve his objections to the war merit consideration. His actions can be seen partly as loyalty to the commander in chief. Johnson had decided to go forward, and Clifford, ever the lawyer, supported his client. Partly, too, he took the course that would ensure his continued access to Johnson and the White House, an important business commodity for Clifford. But the lawyer also slipped into the same trap as Johnson's other advisers and feared that any sign of retrenchment would be viewed by the world as a sign of weakness. It was the type of foreign policy dilemma that would bedevil Johnson to the shortened end of his presidency.

Even if Clifford had continued to argue against escalation, there is no reason to think that Johnson would have heeded his advice. More likely, Clifford would have found himself shut out by the president, and that would have had an impact that none could have foreseen in 1965.

In late October of that year, the loyal Clifford made his first visit to Vietnam. At Johnson's request, he went in his capacity as chairman of the Foreign Intelligence Advisory Board to determine the likelihood of China entering the war and to assess how the overall intelligence effort might be improved. He stayed at the residence of Ambassador Henry Cabot Lodge, where he met a Harvard professor who was serving as a consultant to the embassy. His name was Henry Kissinger.

During a ten day tour of Vietnam, Clifford met with all of the top military officers. General William Westmoreland, the commander of the American forces, complained to Clifford that Washington was micromanaging the war, right down to selecting the bombing targets. Clifford assured Westmoreland that he would raise the matter upon his return, and, in a testament to Clifford's influence, the general later said that the interference stopped.

The only glitch came when Henry Kissinger invited a group of reporters to lunch and criticized the political maturity and motives of South Vietnam's leaders. A reporter for the *Los Angeles Times* wrote a story about the lunch, but mistakenly attributed the remarks to both Kissinger and Clifford. The result was a diplomatic stir in Saigon and Washington, which Clifford did his best to smooth over with Johnson by explaining in a letter that he had never even met the reporter.

The letter was significant for another reason. Clifford said that he had "formed no opinions with reference to the government of South Vietnam — and expressed none." In other words, Clifford no longer appeared to see any point in arguing over whether the war was worth fighting and the government there worth saving. The decision had been made to fight and the commitment must be to winning. Over the next two years, Clifford advanced that argument in his discussions with Johnson and others. He opposed halting the bombing of the north and he concluded that the United States was "on the right road and our military progress was bringing us closer to resolution of the conflict."

The visit had a more personal fallout for Clifford. A few months after his return from Vietnam, in the early spring of 1966, he became ill. Day after day, he was overcome by fatigue and nausea, accompanied by a steady high temperature. Marny Clifford was on an extended trip to the Virgin Islands, so Clifford's physician, Lawn Thompson, checked him into Georgetown University Hospital in Washington, where he was diagnosed with hepatitis. Presumably he had contracted the illness in Vietnam.

For several weeks, Clifford was confined to bed. It was the first time in his life that he had been incapacitated for any length of time, and the man who worked constantly did not know what to do with himself. His many friends helped pass the time. Justice Douglas sent him a set of opinions from recent obscenity cases, with a note that read, "I thought you would certainly want to keep them next to your bedside." The president sent flowers and several letters. In one he wrote: "This place is not the same without you dropping in from time to time. If, however, you prefer seclusion where you are, I may just ignore orders on high and come see you. With you in the hospital and Lady Bird in the mountains, this is a mighty quiet place." A few days later, Johnson sent along a photo album of the First Family, with the inscription: "Looking at the pictures in this album reminds me of a fellow who was caught reading a telephone book. He said, 'It's a lousy plot but what a cast of characters.'"

By early May, Clifford was back at work a few hours each day. In the afternoons, he regularly took his nap in the small room off his office. He regained his strength and eventually resumed his long days as a lawyer and presidential adviser. But the view of the White House across Lafayette Park fell victim to the hepatitis. The illness had left Clifford's eyes extremely sensitive to light and he now kept the drapes drawn across the windows.

On January 12, 1967, the Washington establishment gathered at the exclusive Sulgrave Club for a party hosted by Senator Symington to celebrate the birthday of the man by then known as *the* Washington lawyer.

Two weeks earlier, Clifford had turned sixty years old and he was a legend. At the time, the District of Columbia had more than its share of attorneys. Fifteen thousand people were licensed to practice law in the nation's capital, nearly one out of every twenty lawyers in the country. Yet only a tiny handful could be called "Washington insiders," and none embodied the concept the way Clifford did. The evening's entertainment poked appropriate fun at the guest of honor.

When she had lived in Washington, Joyce Clifford Barrett had organized entertainment for various charity functions. Although by this time she was living in New York, she returned for the party and got together a group of singers to perform a series of humorous songs skewering her father. Throughout the entertainment, photographs obtained from family albums and archives at the Smithsonian Institution were flashed on a screen, showing Clifford from the age of six months through his big moments in history.

The grand finale was an altered photograph of Mount Rushmore, with Clark Clifford's august face carved into the mountain alongside the sixty-foot renditions of George Washington, Thomas Jefferson, Abraham Lincoln, and Theodore Roosevelt. Members of the audience were then informed that they would soon receive a personal phone call from Clifford himself, who would be soliciting funds to pay for the necessary renovations to the monument.

The week after the party, *Newsweek* offered a late present to Clifford that attested to his stature. Beneath the headline "Man for All Caesars," the magazine's Washington columnist and former bureau chief Kenneth Crawford wrote a lengthy article that praised his old friend Clifford as "the insider's insider — a man so knowing that Democratic presidents dating to Harry Truman have asked his advice, and yet so discreet that he keeps his spectacular office view of the White House masked behind tightly drawn curtains." Clifford was called the architect of Truman's 1948 campaign victory, portrayed as a "family lawyer" to the Kennedys, and described as one of President Johnson's closest advisers. In the best Washington fashion, the article closed by floating an intriguing trial balloon: Might Clifford be the next secretary of state?

It was the single post in government that Clifford confided in friends that he coveted. He had turned down other jobs. Truman had hinted that he could be appointed to the Supreme Court, and Kennedy had suggested naming Clifford director of the CIA. But never had he been offered secretary of state, and it was not the post in which he was destined to serve this president.

Except for the sensitivity of his eyes, Clifford had thoroughly recovered from his bout with hepatitis and, at the age of sixty, he continued to operate at the pinnacles of American power. Along with buying his advice, two of America's most influential corporations, Phillips Petroleum and Knight-Ridder publishing, had put him on their boards of directors. He was rich and strong, and he had gotten there by nourishing his own ambitions at the same time he was serving those of the nation's elected leaders.

The law firm built around this career was as unique as the man himself. It was not chance that had placed Clifford in offices less than a five-minute walk from the White House, rather than close to the federal and district courts. He rarely set foot in a courtroom, except for the occasional argument before his friend Justice Douglas and the rest of the Supreme Court. Indeed, Clifford loved to say his was "an advisory practice."

As Clifford's influence and access expanded in the Johnson years, so did the work of his law firm. Clifford needed lawyers with skills to actually try cases. Unlike the larger firms in Washington and New York, Clifford did not recruit young law school graduates. There simply was not enough margin for error. If someone did not work out in a firm with a hundred lawyers, others could carry the burden. Clifford was more selective, bringing only proven performers into his fold.

One of the firm's newer clients was El Paso Natural Gas, a major gas supplier based in Texas. For years, the company had been locked in a bitter dispute with the government over its plans to merge with Pacific Northwest Pipeline Company. Clifford's firm helped negotiate the eventual approval of the merger by the Justice Department. After the department's ruling in favor of El Paso, Clifford had sought to hire Larry L. Williams, the government lawyer who handled the case.

Initially, Clifford dispatched Carson Glass to raise the possibility with Williams. The career Justice Department litigator was intrigued with the chance to join the Clifford firm, which was at the height of its prestige. So he agreed to talk with the boss.

One evening after work in early December 1965, Williams walked several blocks from the Justice Department's massive building on Pennsylvania Avenue to Clifford's offices on Connecticut Avenue. He rode the elevator to the twelfth floor and was ushered into Clifford's cool, darkened office. Responding to Clifford's polite questions, Williams said that he had been with the Justice Department for seventeen years and that he had handled dozens of trials, both criminal and civil.

"Our firm has quite a lot of antitrust business and we could use some help," said Clifford. "How much do you make now?"

"Twenty-five thousand dollars," replied Williams.

"I will double that and, within a year, if you like us and we like you, you will become a partner," said Clifford.

The two men shook hands. By month's end, Williams moved his law books and files into one of the offices on the twelfth floor. It was not long before he recognized that this was not a traditional law firm. For one thing, it had no clients in the District of Columbia. Rather, it represented corporations scattered across the country. For another, none of the lawyers seemed to spend any time in court. Williams quickly decided that Carson Glass, who handled antitrust cases, was afraid to go into a courtroom. John Sharon and Sam McIlwain also had little courtroom experience. Three other lawyers, John Kovin, Tom Finney, and David Granger, who had recently joined the firm, struck Williams as bright and able, but none had anywhere near his level of courtroom experience. So it was natural that, when a far-reaching piece of potential antitrust litigation came into the firm, it went to Williams.

A few months after Williams joined the firm, the Supreme Court overturned the merger approved by the Justice Department, accusing the department of having "knuckled under" to El Paso in its negotiations. In response, Clifford proposed that his firm draft a bill to submit to Congress that would have the effect of negating the Supreme Court ruling, but the matter was eventually dropped.

During this period, the firm also represented J. P. Stevens Company, the nation's second-largest textile manufacturer behind Burlington. The company's reputation as a tough-minded, anti-union business was later memorialized in the movie *Norma Rae*, in which Sally Fields portrayed a Stevens worker fighting to get union safeguards. The company hardly fit with Clifford's image as a model liberal, but Stevens was a steady and lucrative client throughout the 1960s and into the 1970s as it battled the unions and various government price-fixing investigations.

Clifford also represented a number of major defense contractors doing big business with the government. Among them were General Electric, which received nearly $2 billion in defense contracts in fiscal year 1967; Radio Corporation of America, which received $268 million; Standard Oil Corporation of California, $152 million; and Du Pont, $176 million. Clifford also played a role in facilitating a merger that created a company that became the nation's largest defense contractor.

In late 1966, James S. McDonnell, the chairman and founder of the McDonnell Company in St. Louis, was approached by a group of bankers to see whether he would be interested in acquiring the troubled Douglas Aircraft Company. Since developing the DC-3 in the 1930s and making commercial airline travel profitable, Douglas Aircraft had fallen on hard times. Now the bankers were worried that the California-based company would be forced to close its doors without a merger. McDonnell, a conservative Midwesterner whose company was primarily a military-aircraft builder, grudgingly agreed to pursue the merger. But, uncomfortable with the entrepreneurial spirit of the Douglas family, he insisted that he would have the upper hand in the new company.

Once McDonnell agreed to the deal, concern focused on whether the Justice Department would invoke antitrust laws to block a deal that would create a potentially dominant aircraft company. To head off any problems, McDonnell hired Clifford's law firm, and Larry Williams and Carson Glass got on an airplane to St. Louis.

After several days of discussions with company executives and lawyers, Williams and Glass returned to Washington. Williams wrote a long memo intended to persuade his former bosses at the Justice Department that the merger would not violate antitrust laws. In addition, he argued that Douglas Aircraft was failing and the United States government, which bought some military aircraft from the company, would suffer if Douglas closed its doors.

The assistant attorney general in charge of the antitrust division at the Justice Department was no stranger to the Clifford firm. Donald Turner, a former Harvard Law School professor, had worked for Williams as a special consultant when Williams was with the government. And President Johnson had approved his nomination to the job a year earlier following a recommendation from Clifford.

Williams took the memo over to Turner and, as he looked it over, the Justice Department lawyer began to laugh. Then he searched the papers on his desk, pulled out another memo, and handed it to Wil-

Yearbook picture of Clifford at Washington University in St. Louis. He received his law degree in May 1928 and found his first job as an unpaid clerk in a prestigious St. Louis law firm (*Washington University*).

Clifford waited until his father's death to enlist in the Navy during World War II. He was stationed in San Francisco until a patron arranged his transfer to Washington as an assistant naval aide in the Truman White House (*Clark Clifford*).

Clifford (second from left, in his Navy uniform) with President Truman on the rear platform of the train en route to Westminster College in Fulton, Missouri (*U.S. Marine Corps, Courtesy Harry S. Truman Library*).

Clifford sits on the platform at Westminster College as Winston Churchill prepares to deliver his famous "Iron Curtain" speech, March 5, 1946. The address spurred Clifford's interest in foreign affairs as he rose to power in the Truman administration (*Clark Clifford*).

President Truman and Clifford on vacation in Key West, Florida. After starting in the White House as an assistant naval aide, Clifford rose to special counsel and became one of Truman's closest advisers (*U.S. Navy, Courtesy Harry S. Truman Library*).

President Truman with Clifford and other poker playing cronies aboard the presidential yacht, *Williamsburg*. Second from the right is Stuart Symington, who was one of the Cliffords' closest friends and allies in Washington (*Harry S. Truman Library*).

The three Clifford daughters (left to right, Randall, Joyce, and Margery) were photographed together in 1956 (*Clark Clifford*).

Clifford with President Kennedy at a reception in the White House Rose Garden, April 29, 1963. In addition to providing advice to Kennedy on governmental issues, Clifford handled some personal matters for the president and his wife (*John F. Kennedy Library*).

Clifford and Supreme Court Justice Abe Fortas working with President Johnson on the State of the Union address, January 12, 1966. Clifford and Fortas were two of Johnson's closest advisers even before Clifford joined the administration (*Yoichi R. Okamoto, LBJ Library Collection*).

The Clifford family posed with President Johnson and Lady Bird Johnson in the Green Room at the White House, March 1, 1968, just after Clifford was sworn in as secretary of defense. Among the hundreds of photos taken of him with dignitaries, this was one of the few Clifford displayed at his home (*Yoichi R. Okamoto, LBJ Library Collection*).

Clifford discussing Vietnam with Johnson in the White House, March 4, 1968. Clifford's doubts about the war deepened during his tenure as secretary of defense, and he played an important role in persuading the president not to escalate the fighting (*Yoichi R. Okamoto, LBJ Library Collection*).

President Johnson being greeted by Marny and Clark Clifford upon his arrival at their house, January 20, 1969. Clifford was awarded the Medal of Freedom in an impromptu ceremony in his bedroom during the party, which followed the inauguration of Richard Nixon as president (*Frank Wolfe, LBJ Library Collection*).

Clifford meets with President Carter and Zbigniew Brzezinski, his national security adviser, in the Oval Office prior to Clifford's trip to Greece and Turkey (*Jimmy Carter Library*).

With the White House in the background, Clifford walks through Lafayette Park on the way to his office in early 1980 (*Stephen Shames/Matrix*).

Clifford and former Senator Stuart Symington attending a dinner in Symington's honor at the Air and Space Museum in Washington, December 5, 1984 (*Clark Clifford*).

Actress Lynda Carter offers encouragement to Clifford moments before he and her husband, Robert Altman, testify before the House Banking Committee, September 1991 (*Pamela Price*).

Carrying his trademark fedora, Clifford leaves the House Banking Committee hearing with Marny by his side. Although the BCCI scandal cost her husband his reputation, Marny Clifford said the ordeal strengthened their marriage of more than sixty years (*Pamela Price*).

Clifford and Robert Altman are sworn in before a Senate Foreign Relations subcommittee prior to testifying about their ties to BCCI, October 25, 1991 (*AP/Wide World Photos*).

Clifford is assisted by a security guard and one of his attorneys, Carl Rauh, as he enters U.S. District Court for his arraignment on charges stemming from the secret ownership of First American Bankshares by BCCI, July 31, 1992 (*AP/Wide World Photos*).

Clifford meets First Lady Hillary Rodham Clinton at a reception in the Sculpture Garden at the White House, October 11, 1994 (*White House*).

liams. Lawyers in California representing Douglas Aircraft had written a memo warning that the merger would violate antitrust laws. Although it was protected by attorney-client privilege, Douglas Aircraft had mistakenly turned the document over to the government. It made the merger more difficult, but it was by no means an insurmountable obstacle.

Clifford did not get involved directly in negotiations over the antitrust case. In fact, Williams did not believe that Clifford was well versed in the essential elements of the nation's antitrust statutes. But Clifford's sense of the dramatic — and his flair for grandly invoking national security — added an important element to the case.

From his work on the Foreign Intelligence Advisory Board, he had gotten to know Wernher von Braun, the German scientist who was director of the American space program. At Clifford's urging, Von Braun sent a memo to the Justice Department saying that it was in the national interest for Douglas Aircraft to be saved through the merger. On April 19, 1967, without objection from the Justice Department, shareholders of Douglas Aircraft Company voted to merge with the McDonnell Company. The result was McDonnell Douglas Corporation, which immediately became the nation's fourth-largest aerospace company and went on to become the largest.

About the same time, three railroads were trying to merge: the Northern Pacific, the Great Northern, and the Burlington. An attempt many years earlier had been blocked by the government on antitrust grounds. This time, however, the railroads thought they had a better chance because the growth of trucking companies offered an alternate transporation route that cut down on the antitrust aspects. However, the Interstate Commerce Commission, which regulates transportation that crosses state lines, defeated the proposed merger by a single vote.

The railroads were shocked, and the general counsel of one of the three telephoned Clifford and asked him to represent them in an attempt to get a rehearing. Clifford accepted the case and invited Williams into his office to analyze the matter. Williams was confident that the railroads could win if they applied a second time to the ICC and emphasized that the three railroads did not compete against each other, so there would be no real loss of competition in a merger. "All we need to do is turn around one commissioner," wrote Williams in his memo to Clifford.

For some time, muckraking columnist Jack Anderson had been receiving information from the Clifford law firm. While Anderson spoke regularly with Clifford and received his share of leaks from the lawyer himself, the columnist also had a mole inside the firm itself.

This time, the mole — a lawyer in Clifford's office — provided Anderson with a copy of the railroad memo. He used it as the basis of a scathing column that accused Clifford of plotting to use his influence with the Johnson administration to win a crucial vote on the Interstate Commerce Commission. The accusation was short-lived and the commission reversed its earlier ruling by a two-vote margin. When the case was appealed to the Supreme Court, the railroads won again and the merger was permitted.

The law firm also started a major trade case in the same period. In an administrative proceeding, the Federal Trade Commission had raised allegations that General Foods, which dominated the nation's coffee market with its Maxwell House and Yuban brands, had engaged in unfair trading practices. Although General Foods came directly to Clifford with the case, he handed off the legal work to Kovin and Glass. The proceedings were to last into the 1970s, providing the firm with steady legal fees from what was known in its offices as "the coffee case."

In July 1967, the president sent Clifford back to Vietnam. He and General Maxwell D. Taylor went on a two-week swing through South Vietnam, Australia, New Zealand, Thailand, and South Korea. The mission was to assess the view of the allies on the continued American bombing of North Vietnam and the overall escalation of the war. On August 5, Clifford and Taylor returned to Washington and told reporters at Andrews Air Force Base that there was wide agreement among the allies that the pressure should be increased on the Communists. They said they had made clear to the allies that the United States was prepared to send more troops to Vietnam if necessary.

"There was unanimous agreement among all the allies that the bombing should be carried on at its present level, or possibly increased," said Clifford. He added that some allied leaders had suggested that the war be called "the War of Southeast Asia" because all of the region was at stake. The findings of these two presidential emissaries were so glowing that New York Times columnist Russell Baker mocked their assessment, dubbing it caustically "the Jim Dandy report."

After a two-hour briefing by Clifford and Taylor at the White House, Johnson relied on their assessment to announce that the United States would send 45,000 to 50,000 more troops to Vietnam in the coming months, raising the total there to 525,000. He also asked Congress for a 10 percent surtax on individual and corporate income taxes to meet the rising cost of the war.

It was partly Clifford's sense of duty to Johnson that allowed him to endorse the war so strongly in public. In private, his assessment of the trip was starkly different. One morning not long after his return from the two-week journey, Clifford was attending a breakfast when his old friend Hugh Sidey called him aside for a private conversation. Sidey asked about the particulars of the trip and Clifford said, "Hugh, they don't care about this war. Our allies aren't worried about Vietnam. They don't care about it. Why should we be there? What are we doing in Vietnam?"

The realization that Clifford was not really as hawkish about the war was shared by Richard Steadman, a Pentagon official, who had accompanied him on the trip. Steadman came to admire Clifford during their two weeks together and came away with the strong feeling that Clifford was not a supporter of the war effort.

But Clifford's personal doubts were not expressed in public. Instead, he articulated the belief that the war could be won and kept his public sentiments in line with those of President Johnson. As a result, he clashed with Robert S. McNamara, the secretary of defense.

By October 1967, the question confronting the White House was to pause or not to pause in the bombing of North Vietnam. Increasingly frustrated and depressed by the war, McNamara wrote a memorandum that called for a halt in the escalation. He advocated turning over more of the fighting to the South Vietnamese and stopping the bombing of the North by year's end. Hanoi would be forced to seek a negotiated settlement or be viewed by the world as blocking a peaceful resolution of the conflict, reasoned McNamara.

When Johnson shared McNamara's new proposal with Clifford and other advisers, Clifford argued against a halt in the bombing. It would portray the United States as weak and unwilling to continue the war, contended Clifford. The position was echoed by Fortas.

Paul Nitze, who was McNamara's deputy secretary at the Pentagon and much more conservative than Clifford, later accused Clifford and

Fortas of "pouring poison into the ear of the president" about McNamara. In Nitze's view, the two unofficial advisers doomed McNamara with their criticism of him and his memo and "sealed his imminent departure from the Pentagon."

But Clifford and Fortas were hardly alone in the advice they were giving the president to continue with the escalation. Johnson himself was not in favor of a bombing halt. Two years earlier, Johnson had halted bombing for thirty-seven days. He viewed that episode as a costly exercise that had left the impression that he was unwilling to go all-out to win the war. Further, a group of so-called "wise men" assembled by Walt Rostow, the president's national security adviser, echoed the stance of Clifford and Fortas.

Shortly after McNamara's memo, Rostow had approached Clifford with the idea of setting up a committee of outside advisers to evaluate the strategic value of the bombing campaign. They decided to convene a group of statesmen who understood the exercise of power in American foreign policy. Among those who attended the meeting in November were Averell Harriman, General Omar Bradley, Treasury Secretary Douglas Dillon, and former Ambassador to Vietnam Henry Cabot Lodge. When asked to consider not only the future of the bombing but the war itself, the group unanimously supported Clifford when he said, "If we keep up the pressure on them, gradually the will of the Viet Cong and the North Vietnamese will wear down."

By late November, Johnson had decided to get rid of McNamara. The president told Clifford that Dean Rusk might also be asked to step down as secretary of state. Earlier in 1967, Clifford had rebuffed Johnson's suggestion that he become attorney general, preferring to argue unsuccessfully that the post should go to his friend trial lawyer Edward Bennett Williams. Johnson now hinted that Clifford might have his choice of Defense or State. Clifford consulted his longtime friend Senator Stuart Symington, who advised him to accept the State Department post but to refuse the Pentagon job. "The war," warned Symington, "was so far gone he couldn't win; he could only lose."

Johnson did not raise the issue with Clifford again during December, but he seemed to be courting his adviser. On Christmas Day, the president paid a surprise visit to Clifford's house to wish him a Merry Christmas and happy birthday. The matter of Clifford joining the administration lay dormant until the new year as Johnson concentrated on preparations for his State of the Union address.

"In the past you've said your interest was foreign policy and national security," Johnson told Clifford on the night of January 18, 1968, just hours after the president had delivered the annual message to the nation. "Now I've got exactly the right place for you — secretary of defense. It will suit you and you cannot possibly have any objection to it."

Clifford did have objections. As Symington had pointed out, it seemed all he could do was lose. And, while he would have liked the prestige of being secretary of state, he really had no desire to leave his prospering law firm to try to run the Pentagon. Yet Clifford could not bring himself to turn down the plea from the president. Part of it was loyalty to Johnson. Perhaps more important, however, despite having been out of government for twenty-eight years, and despite having nourished his own ambition through his service to presidents in ways that were not always admirable, Clifford still thought of himself as a public servant. Now he would get the opportunity to serve again.

14

Counsel at War

B Y THE BEGINNING OF 1968, bands of angry demonstrators
waving Viet Cong flags were a common sight in front of the White
House. But long-haired students were not the only people concerned
about the war at the start of that pivotal year in American history. A
new Gallup poll found that 49 percent of the American people disapproved of the way in which the Johnson administration was handling
the war, which was costing the nation $2.5 billion a month and sending
thousands of young Americans to their deaths. The public's dissatisfac-
tion was beginning to resonate inside the Beltway. Senator Symington,
the nation's first secretary of the air force, had started to voice doubts in
public about the conflict. Paul Nitze, who was Defense Secretary McNamara's deputy, discussed his own deepening opposition to the war over
cocktails with Clifford at the Metropolitan Club, and the nation's press
was beginning to challenge the policy.

President Johnson announced Clifford's appointment as secretary of
defense on the afternoon of January 19. Marny Clifford was returning
home from a shopping trip when she heard the news on the radio.
"Luckily I wasn't driving," said Mrs. Clifford later. "Our Scottish chauffeur, Matthew Carolan, got very excited. Well, I did, too, frankly. Although Clark had told me about it, I didn't know the president was
going to make the announcement."

Indeed, she and her husband had discussed the job the night before,
but she had not known the appointment was coming so soon. While
the two of them had established separate lives in many ways, Marny
Clifford was apprehensive about her husband's new job. She remembered the Truman days when he had never seemed to be home. Also,
Clifford was sixty-one and she worried about the physical toll of such a
demanding job.

Different concerns swept over much of the rest of Washington when
it was learned that Clifford would replace McNamara. Clifford's hawkish
public views on the war in general and on the bombing of the North

were well known among those who opposed the conflict. They feared that the departure of McNamara, the last real doubter, would leave Johnson in the thrall of a small, hawkish circle — Dean Rusk, Walt Rostow, and now Clark Clifford.

Katharine Graham, a long-time Clifford admirer who had become publisher of the *Washington Post* five years earlier after her husband's suicide, worried that "he would just continue the policy. I thought he was a hawk." Senator Robert Kennedy, who was in upstate New York when he heard the news from an aide, remarked, "Well, at least he didn't appoint Attila the Hun." Even Clifford's old friend from the Truman years David Lilienthal said, "Clifford's appointment means that there will be no change in policy in Vietnam." Another associate from those days with a less charitable view of Clifford, Harry Vaughn, wrote sardonically to President Truman about the appointment: "The Vietnam situation should improve very shortly. . . . A man who could originate the Marshall Plan, perfect the Truman Doctrine and re-elect you in 1948 all without you realizing it should find Vietnam a pushover."

In many quarters, of course, the appointment was well received. President Johnson received congratulatory letters from many of the business leaders represented by Clifford. On Capitol Hill, where Clifford had many friends, there was nearly universal praise for him. Senator Everett Dirksen of Illinois summed up the mood among Republicans and Democrats alike when he described Clifford as a "patriot" who deserved the trust and confidence of the country.

Perhaps the most perceptive view of the appointee came from General Earle Wheeler, the chairman of the Joint Chiefs of Staff, who had debated war policy with Clifford two and a half years earlier at Camp David when Clifford's views were considerably more dovish. In a letter to General William Westmoreland, the commander of American forces in South Vietnam, Wheeler described Clifford as "very astute, very intelligent and able . . . closely in touch with congressional leaders, the business community, and the heads of the news media . . . a man of stature and achievement, one whose views must be accorded weight."

As things turned out, Clifford would surprise all of these people, but none more than the man who appointed him, Lyndon Baines Johnson. What his friends and foes alike overlooked was Clifford's essential character: above all else, he was a pragmatic man. He had never been blinded by idealism, which was both his strength and his weakness. In this case, his pragmatism would serve him and the country well, for he would train a cold, lawyer's eye on the war effort. Another element of Clifford's make-up also would have a strong influence over his conclusions about the war: he was part of the Washington establishment. As establishment opinion about the wisdom of the war began to shift, so would his. There was one other significant change: Clifford would no longer be the president's adviser; he would no longer be offering advice from the lawyerly perspective of an advocate. As secretary of defense, he would have to make his own decisions on the war.

While Clifford rejected the label, he had sounded like a true hawk since Johnson had ignored his advice in the fall of 1965. He had fallen into line behind Johnson and the president's other advisers. When he testified at his confirmation hearing on January 25 before the Senate Armed Services Committee, Clifford said he would oppose any cessation of bombing in Vietnam, because he said it had served "extremely useful purposes" in impeding the movement of Viet Cong troops and supplies into South Vietnam. His view of the Soviet Union was equally hard-line. In contrast to McNamara's suggestion that the United States should move toward "nuclear parity" with Moscow, Clifford emphatically called for establishing a clear-cut "nuclear supremacy."

Clifford's nomination was approved unanimously that same day by the committee, and the Senate confirmed him by unanimous vote five days later, on January 30. The afternoon of his confirmation Clifford found himself attending the regular Tuesday Lunch at the White House, where the president's most powerful cabinet members and advisers met and where the fare was Vietnam. As the group debated a proposal by General Wheeler to arrange a fake amphibious invasion of North Vietnam, an aide entered the room and handed a note to Walt Rostow, who slipped out. When Rostow returned, he said that American military installations and the embassy in Saigon were under heavy mortar attack. The attack turned out to be just the start of a nationwide assault by the North Vietnamese that became known as the Tet Offensive. In eight weeks of Tet, nearly 4,000 American troops were killed, five of the six major cities in South Vietnam were attacked, and the credibility of the American effort in Southeast Asia was in grave doubt in many more places.

The growing public sentiment seemed only to harden President Johnson's resolve. In February, he sent Clifford a quotation from John

Stuart Mill, the nineteenth-century English philosopher: "War is an ugly thing, but not the ugliest thing: the decayed and degraded state of moral and patriotic feeling which thinks nothing worth a war is worse."

Before Clifford could take the oath of office, business matters required his attention. The announcement and confirmation had come swiftly in those days before the intense scrutiny of presidential nominees that would mark the eighties and nineties, so Clifford needed some time to sell off his investments and sever his ties with his law firm before taking the $35,000-a-year post as secretary of defense.

By this time, Clifford had ownership interests in two dozen oil-and-gas ventures. The advice from Senator Kerr and Boots Adams had turned into investments worth millions of dollars. Clifford never saw any conflict in accepting the advice of Kerr on his investments, and he maintained that he always invested his own money and took his chances, just like anyone else. Yet, as one of his partners had inadvertently discovered, Clifford had often been given the sort of insider's deal that ensured profits.

Because the navy was the nation's largest consumer of oil, Clifford knew that he could not retain a single investment in an oil well while at the Pentagon. In negotiations with Kerr-McGee and Phillips Petroleum, he agreed to sell his interests outright for around $3 million — nearly half of his net worth in 1968, which Clifford estimated at $7 million to $8 million.

Part of that net worth came from the sale of his interest in the law firm, for which the other partners paid him $1 million. The new firm would be called Sharon, Glass, McIlwain and Finney. John Sharon, whose arrogance angered many of his partners, had insisted that his name go first, but it was the much-better-liked Finney who was chosen managing partner and who took over Clifford's big corner office.

"Tom Finney was the smartest man I ever knew," said De Vier Pierson, a prominent Washington lawyer. "He was a potent force in institutionalizing the Clifford firm. . . . He was clever, too. When Clifford left, he was the one who suggested the right name for the firm was to put Sharon's first. Finney was in last place on the letterhead, and in first place on everything that mattered."

There was no formal agreement that Clifford would return when he finished out his tenure as defense secretary, but there was a tacit understanding among the partners. "It was obvious that he was coming back," said Larry Williams. "There was no formal agreement, which would not have been right, but we knew he would be coming back. Finney was just keeping the chair warm."

The clients knew it, too. While Clifford was in the Defense Department, not a single corporation stopped paying its retainer to the firm. The point was driven home with humor in March at the press corps's annual Gridiron Club dinner, where a Clifford imposter sang: "We're parting. You go your way, I'll go mine, It's what we must do. Au revoir, Du Pont; bye-bye, G.E. But I don't mean adieu. Duty drives me to the Pentagon. But please don't learn to do without me while I'm gone."

In a similarly light vein, Clifford stepped down as president of the Alfalfa Club. Delivering the traditionally pompous, tongue-in-cheek valedictory, Clifford told the other members of Washington's political and business elite that constituted the all-male membership: "In the fifty-five-year history of the Alfalfa Club, there is one man who stands above all others. A man who, by reason of his sterling character, his mental brilliance, his unique qualities of leadership, and his unequaled success, has to be honored and loved by all. But enough about me."

Clifford's role in the Truman campaign of 1948, the ticket that had gained him entry to the inner sanctums of power in Washington for two decades, turned into a minor embarrassment shortly after his nomination as secretary of defense.

On Sunday morning, January 28, Jim Rowe was reading an article about the new defense secretary by Patrick Anderson in the *New York Times Sunday Magazine* when he came across this passage: "In 1947 Clifford's political judgment told him that Truman's only hope of re-election the next year was to go to the people with a clear-cut liberal record, and in November he submitted to Truman a remarkable, forty-three-page memorandum on political strategy."

Turning to show his wife the passage, the incredulous Rowe said, "That's my memo. He's getting credit for my memo."

This was far from the first time that Clifford had received credit for the memo actually written by Jim Rowe. Each time in the past, however, Rowe had bitten his tongue and kept silent. His feeling was that the most important thing had been to get his memo to Truman. This time, however, perhaps because of the new acclaim Clifford was receiving, he was angry and it would have consequences.

Later that week, Rowe was having lunch with Scotty Reston, the *Times* bureau chief in Washington, and he complained that the magazine had given Clifford credit for his memo. Reston followed up with an article questioning the authorship of the famous memo, touching off a series of somewhat acrimonious telephone conversations between Rowe and Clifford. Finally, near the end of February, Rowe had a change of heart. He sent Clifford a copy of his original memo so Clifford could see the similarities himself, but he also sent along a conciliatory letter.

"Really I am terribly embarrassed that I embarrassed you," he wrote. "It would be so at any time, considering how long we have known each other, but I am particularly sorry at this time when you are leaving a pleasant, influential, affluent, and happy life to take on an impossible job." Rowe continued that it was he who was guilty of "pride of authorship," and he authorized Clifford to say the two men had collaborated or even to denounce Rowe as a liar.

Clifford, wise to the ways of the press, knew the smartest thing was to let the matter die, and he did nothing to respond to the Reston piece.

In 1966 and 1967, Robert McNamara had opposed escalation of the war against hawkish pressures in government and the public. By the time Clifford became secretary of defense, public opinion had begun to shift, leaving McNamara loyalists at the Pentagon concerned about their new boss. They had hoped the replacement would be Cyrus Vance or Paul Nitze. The early mood was summed up by Phil G. Goulding, an assistant secretary of defense, when he observed: "And who had the President named to replace Robert McNamara? He had picked an intimate friend; a personal crony; a fabulously successful Washington attorney with, the newsmen wrote, fabulously successful connections. He had picked a man who, it seemed, had never really run anything except his law firm — a firm which, however successful financially, consisted of only a handful of lawyers." Goulding went on to echo most of his colleagues when he degraded Clifford's "Neanderthal views" on Vietnam.

Among the senior staff at the Pentagon, only Richard Steadman, who had gone with Clifford to Southeast Asia the previous year, offered a different view. "Don't worry about it," Steadman told his boss, Assistant Secretary of Defense Paul C. Warnke. "This guy's no hawk."

Clifford probably did not yet comprehend the scope of his new task. Not only was he taking the helm of the Department of Defense at a pivotal point in the nation's military history. He also would have to run a building where 27,000 people came to work every day and a department with an annual budget of $77 billion, 41 percent of all federal spending. Government had grown far larger and more complex in the nearly twenty years he had been away. As a result, he decided to delay his swearing-in until March 1 in order to have a chance to evaluate the job while McNamara remained onboard.

His first visit to the Pentagon was on February 8 for a meeting with McNamara, Nitze, and the assistant secretaries. As they sat around the huge oak desk that had once belonged to General John "Black Jack" Pershing, McNamara needed a haircut and the cuffs of his shirt were frayed. The contrast was sharp with Clifford, who wore one of his trademark tailored double-breasted suits, sharply pressed French cuffs, and exuded an air of elegance. He was everything that those around the table expected and dreaded, but they soon learned he was much more. Clifford was gracious and courteous and willing to admit that he was largely ignorant of many defense matters. He also was willing to ask questions, dozens of them, and many of them struck those present as the right questions.

At a dinner party in Georgetown in February, Clifford was seated next to Katharine Graham. He confided in her that, although he thought he knew something about the Pentagon from his role in uniting the armed forces under President Truman, he was learning that the job was more complex and difficult than he had imagined. Robert McNamara had run Ford Motor Company before he took over the Defense Department and Phil Goulding was right in saying Clifford had actually run little more than a boutique law firm. By and large, Clifford would leave the management of the department to Paul Nitze, whom he planned to keep on as deputy secretary, and to George Elsey, his former assistant at the White House.

Elsey had been working as the Washington lobbyist for the Pullman Company, a job he had gotten on Clifford's recommendation. The two men had talked in 1967 and early in 1968, and Elsey sensed that Clifford was not that comfortable playing the role of hawk. "He was profoundly worried and disturbed by the war in Vietnam," said Elsey. "He had expressed frustration at not being in a position to do something. When he called and said he had a spot for me, of course I was happy to go for two reasons. First was my loyalty to him. Second was my passionate conviction that we had to do anything we could to get out of Vietnam."

For his part, Nitze, the highly intellectual son of a University of Chicago Romance languages professor and a society beauty, was unhappy about having been passed over for the secretary's post. He had known Clifford since their days in the Truman administration and, while they were not close friends, Nitze had a grudging respect for Clifford. Nitze had increasingly come to view Vietnam as a costly sideshow to the superpower struggle with the Soviet Union, and he set about immediately trying to persuade Clifford of the necessity of freezing the troop level and winding down the war. Clifford was impressed enough with his deputy's reasoning to place Nitze on a task force formed to evaluate the direction of the war. In the weeks that followed, Nitze had a strong impact on his new boss.

On March 1, Chief Justice of the United States Earl Warren conducted the swearing in of Clark Clifford as secretary of defense in the East Room of the White House. Two days earlier on the same spot, President Johnson had presented the Medal of Freedom to Robert McNamara, who had been so emotional that he had been unable to respond. Now, Johnson was praising his successor and joking that the move from the "kitchen cabinet" to the real cabinet had finally made an honest man out of Clifford.

Marny Clifford stood next to her husband, holding the family Bible. Arrayed behind them were all three daughters, with their husbands and nine grandchildren. The Symingtons and other friends and associates were also part of the standing-room-only crowd. Indeed, the ceremony was delayed for an hour to give a number of senators time to finish voting and get to the White House. And the legal establishment turned out in such force that, when Liz Carpenter, Lady Bird Johnson's press secretary, remarked to a friend that she had never seen so many important Washington lawyers in one room, someone standing behind her whispered, "We all want his business."

After the public swearing in, President Johnson said, "Get all the Clifford family together. We're going to the Green Room for a photo." So Clifford and his family followed Johnson and Lady Bird into the large room not far from the more formal East Room and they all had their photograph taken with the president and his wife. When Johnson sent him a copy of the photo, Clifford had it framed and placed it on the piano at his house, one of the few mementoes of his government service that he kept on public display at the house.

The month that followed was the most extraordinary of Clifford's public service. His own memoir would compare it to tumbling down a mountain and grasping for any ledge to break the fall. In the weeks leading up to his move into the big office at the Pentagon, the doubts Clifford had expressed in 1965 had been rekindled. However, when he took office on March 1, Clifford crossed a threshold. In the words of George Elsey, Clifford "became his own man."

The first sign observed by the president came on March 4, when Clifford briefed Johnson, Vice President Hubert Humphrey, and others on the findings of the Clifford task force. The recommendations reflected Clifford's own growing uncertainty about the war. While he refused to go so far as to recommend a halt to the bombing and did not place much store in negotiations, Clifford had taken a significant step back from his previous inclination toward escalation. "We seem to be in a sinkhole," he told Johnson. "We put in more. They match us."

In an emotional debate that day, Clifford refused to endorse the military's request for more than 200,000 additional troops in the coming weeks. The question that nagged him was, will that be enough to do the job? The only sign of any support for the war from the task force was a bland endorsement of General Westmoreland's request for 22,000 new troops immediately, and even that was couched in dovish terms. "This is as far as we are willing to go," said Clifford, justifying the new troops only "out of caution and for protection." As for Westmoreland's request that Johnson call up 200,000 additional reserves, Clifford recommended that the situation be reviewed on a week-to-week basis. Within two weeks, however, Clifford's view of the war would be altered further.

During the week of March 11, two events occurred that contributed to changing Clifford's mind about the war. The first began on Monday when the Senate Foreign Relations Committee, which was headed by his friend and golf companion Senator J. William Fulbright of Arkansas, opened hearings on legislation to finance American foreign aid, including military assistance. Secretary of State Dean Rusk was the first witness and, over the course of two days of nationally televised testimony, he faced a barrage of angry criticism over the war effort from both Democratic and Republican senators. While Rusk handled the attacks with stoic calm, Clifford could see clearly that support for the war was waning on that important committee. Clifford himself had been asked to testify, but he was trying to duck the appearance by saying he had not been in office long enough to speak with authority.

On Tuesday evening, not long after Rusk finished up in the Senate, the political impact of the war was brought home. Democratic voters in New Hampshire had gone to the polls and given President Johnson's write-in campaign only a narrow victory over Senator Eugene McCarthy, who was running as the peace candidate. Although Johnson had won the primary, McCarthy's strong showing proved that his antiwar message had resonance even in the generally conservative confines of New Hampshire. The vote also got the attention of Senator Robert Kennedy.

The following day, Kennedy aide Ted Sorensen telephoned Clifford and said that the senator would like to meet with him as soon as possible. Clifford agreed and the meeting was scheduled for Thursday morning in Clifford's office at the Pentagon. Arriving with Sorensen, Kennedy got right to the point. He told Clifford that he regarded the administration's Vietnam policy as "a failure" and that he felt "compelled to take action" by his own conscience and the urging of his advisers. Unless the president could be persuaded to change his position on Vietnam, Kennedy said he would become a candidate for the presidency himself. Sorensen elaborated, suggesting that Johnson make a public statement acknowledging that the war was a failure and that he was appointing a blue-ribbon commission to recommend a new course of action in Southeast Asia.

Smiling and nodding, Clifford replied politely that the president could not possibly admit that the war was simply a mistake after eight years of escalation. Kennedy acknowledged that perhaps he was asking too much, but he pressed for a commission to reexamine the policy. He even ticked off a list of possible members, including himself. Clifford was deep into his own reevaluation of the war policy, and he did not need the help of Bobby Kennedy, whom he had never liked anyway.

Clifford reminded Kennedy that, in 1948, a revolt against Truman initiated by some Democrats had failed. This time, too, warned Clifford, Kennedy had "zero" chance of wresting the nomination away from

Johnson, and Kennedy would wind up "grievously disappointed" if he became a candidate and lost. Clifford also offered a carrot with the stick, suggesting that a number of factors, including when to start negotiations with the North Vietnamese, remained under the president's control. Nevertheless, Kennedy insisted that Johnson appoint a special commission to move toward a new policy.

That afternoon, with Abe Fortas sitting beside him, Clifford recounted his conversation with Kennedy for President Johnson. The president was furious. He felt that Kennedy, whom he often referred to as "that little shit," was trying to blackmail him. He absolutely refused to appoint a commission, particularly one with Bobby Kennedy on it. Following the session at the White House, Clifford telephoned Kennedy at Hickory Hill, the senator's home in the Virginia countryside, and relayed the news. Jack Newfield, a Kennedy aide, was standing nearby as the senator listened to Clifford and he watched Kennedy undergo an intriguing transformation. "Kennedy, who had been solemn and preoccupied all day, was acting whimsical and liberated," said Newfield. "It was now definite that he would run."

Senator Fulbright was still pushing for Clifford's testimony, and on March 15, the secretary of defense and Paul Nitze met to discuss the demand with Johnson. As an alternative to Clifford, Johnson proposed sending Nitze. The deputy responded with an extraordinary display of independence. He told Johnson that he could not defend the current policy on Vietnam before the Senate. Surprised and irritated, Johnson shot back, "Nonsense, Paul. Of course you can." Nitze was silent.

The following day, Nitze walked into Clifford's office and handed him a resignation letter. He said he could not defend the administration's policy in Southeast Asia and could therefore no longer serve at the Pentagon. When Clifford expressed shock, Nitze replied, "This is what I have been trying to tell you for the last twenty days." Refusing to accept the resignation, Clifford assured Nitze that he would not be forced to testify before the Senate Foreign Relations Committee.

Clifford's own reservations about the war kept him from going before the Senate. So he next turned to Warnke, the assistant secretary for international security affairs. A prominent lawyer with Covington and Burling before joining the Defense Department in 1966, Warnke agreed to testify. When asked by Clifford what he would say about the war, Warnke said rather obliquely that it would depend on the questions.

Fulbright, however, refused to accept the testimony of an assistant secretary. He insisted that Clifford testify. As Townsend Hoopes, another senior Pentagon official, later wrote: "Certainly, the idea of having to defend a highly dubious enterprise before informed and vehement critics, and under kleig lights for the benefit of a national television audience, was a prospect calculated to concentrate the mind wonderfully."

As Clifford looked for a way around testifying, Senator Robert Kennedy made it official. He announced his candidacy for the Democratic nomination for president. Despite Clifford's warning to Kennedy a few days earlier, he in fact considered the senator a potent threat to Johnson. Clifford remained unquestionably loyal to Johnson, but he saw no reason to fall on his sword for the president before a national television audience at a time when Johnson was vulnerable politically and, Clifford was concluding, wrong about the war. So Clifford did business the way he always had as a practicing lawyer, person to person with an old friend.

Clifford and Fulbright had often played golf together, which had given rise to a story that Clifford liked to tell on the senator from Arkansas. One day at Burning Tree, Fulbright was getting more and more exasperated by his poor play. When the ball disappeared into the rough again, he turned to his caddy and said, "You must be the worst caddy in the world." Without missing a beat, the caddy was said to reply, "Oh no. That would be too much of a coincidence."

Sitting in Fulbright's office on the Senate side of the Capitol Building, Clifford spoke honestly of his deep reservations about the war. There was a serious reappraisal under way at the White House and within the Defense Department, he said. Airing that internal debate now, before the Senate and the nation, might damage the possibility for change. Fulbright accepted his friend's assessment. Clifford would not have to testify until he was ready.

After less than a month on the job, Clifford's views on the war had undergone a dramatic change, and so had the political landscape in which the policy would be debated. The president faced Eugene McCarthy's rising candidacy and the new threat of Bobby Kennedy. A few days after his session with Fulbright, Clifford met with James Rowe to discuss the political dilemma. Rowe told Clifford that the political opposition at home threatened the president's ability to act on other issues, thereby weakening him in his bid for reelection. The admonition strengthened Clifford's resolve: the war could not be sustained politically or militarily.

The emotional turmoil was taking a toll on Clifford, as his wife had feared it would. He was working long hours under enormous stress. He barely saw Marny and the children anymore. On their birthdays that year, he gave them each the same gift — a silver ashtray embossed with the seal of the Department of Defense, which had been ordered by his secretary.

When his friend Hugh Sidey visited him in his office at the Pentagon about seven o'clock one night, he found Clifford sitting at his desk with his hands on his temples. "He looked like hell," said Sidey. "He looked haggard and drawn." As the *Time* correspondent listened, Clifford said slowly, quietly, and deliberately, "It's just not working. It's a disaster. We must find some way to get out of this war."

Now that he had changed his own views on the war, Clifford had to summon the power to change the views of the others who surrounded the president. Again and again, when his staff gathered in his office at eight-thirty every morning for their daily meeting, they heard Clifford say, "Our objective is not to prove to anyone how wrong he is. Our objective is to get them to do it our way."

He approached the challenge of turning around Lyndon Johnson on Vietnam as he did all other challenges, leaving nothing to chance. Each time Clifford was scheduled to go to the White House, he would prepare exhaustively for his presentation. As Warnke and Nitze and the others sat around his desk, they would watch and offer suggestions as Clifford, summoning the days he had studied acting, plotted his speech down to the smallest detail.

Richard Fryklund, a deputy assistant secretary for public affairs, recalled the scene this way: "He'd be leaning back in his chair looking up at the ceiling, as if the script were there, and walking himself through it as we critiqued it. He rehearsed right down to the little pleasantries. He'd say, 'At this point I'll turn to Dean Rusk and I'll wink.' And then he'd make a remark, some in-joke between two guys — 'and I'll turn back to the president and say . . .' And he would have the gestures in there."

The process also involved reaching out to others whom Clifford thought might harbor the same reservations about the war. In a reprise of the tactics employed in Harry Truman's White House, Clifford set about courting key members of the White House staff as he had once been courted by Dean Acheson and Robert Lovett.

Harry C. McPherson was drafting a major address on Vietnam that the president was to deliver at the end of March when Clifford called to solicit his "honest" thoughts on the war. Somewhat conspiratorially, Clifford confided that the time had come to "wind it down," starting with an announcement that no new substantial forces would be committed to the war. "Now you must tell me what you hear over there," Clifford instructed McPherson, "and I will keep you advised of my activities. We must be watchful for any sign that the war is to be wound up again and not down. Keep in constant touch."

Johnson remained committed to the war. On March 17, he delivered a tough speech to a farmers' group in Minneapolis. "Your President has come to ask you people, and all people of this nation, to join us in a total national effort to win the war," he said with emotion. "We will, make no mistake about it, win. . . . We are not doing enough to win it the way we are doing it now."

The speech created an uproar and reinforced in Clifford the belief that he was truly engaged in a battle for the soul of Lyndon Johnson. Without a huge change of heart by the president, all of Clifford's efforts to stop the war were doomed. So he made his own views even plainer at the Tuesday Lunch of senior advisers on March 19. When Abe Fortas provided a long explanation of the necessity of avoiding "empty peace gestures," Clifford countered by saying, "In World War II, 'prevail we will' would work because conditions were right. Now they aren't." Clifford argued that unless the current policy were scrapped, the war would only grow longer and more damaging to the country. For the first time, he proposed a "gradual approach of stop[ping] all bombing north of the twentieth parallel, if in turn the enemy would stop their artillery, rockets, and mortars from the DMZ area into South Vietnam." Johnson rejected the concept, saying it would appear that he was caving in to Kennedy's demands.

Eager to find a way of changing Johnson's mind, Clifford telephoned a few of the Wise Men who had provided the president with advice about the war over the years. These senior statesmen — Dean Acheson, George Ball, McGeorge Bundy, Douglas Dillon, Henry Cabot Lodge, Cyrus Vance, and Omar Bradley — had generally supported the war in the past. Clifford knew that Acheson had turned against the conflict. If a majority of the others had softened their positions, there might be a chance of turning around the president. First, he telephoned Acheson and Lodge, then a couple of the others. "What is your feeling now?" he asked. "Have you changed your mind about the war?" The answers were encouraging. Tet may have hardened Johnson's resolve to continue the war, but the Wise Men seemed to have been pushed in another direction by the display of North Vietnamese force and the loss of American lives.

After conducting his informal poll, Clifford suggested that the president convene another secret meeting of the Wise Men. Clifford could not be 100 percent certain that the majority would support him on Vietnam, but he saw no alternative. The most recent draft by Harry McPherson of the president's upcoming speech was tough, reflecting the hard-line stance Johnson had taken in Minneapolis.

The Wise Men began arriving quietly at the State Department on Monday, March 25. They read background papers and talked with senior officials from the State Department and Defense Department. That evening, Clifford and some other administration officials joined the elder statesmen in Secretary of State Rusk's private dining room. The meal was followed by an informal session in which the outsiders questioned Clifford, Rusk, Richard Helms of the CIA, and Deputy Attorney General Nicholas Katzenbach about the war. Clifford was succinct in spelling out what he saw as the only three options. The United States could grant Westmoreland's request for more troops, increase the bombing, and extend the ground war into Laos and Cambodia in an all-out effort to win; the country could follow the present strategy, which he called "muddling along," and provide Westmoreland with a few more troops; or there could be a bombing halt, a new strategy of using American troops only to protect South Vietnam while the Vietnamese assumed the burden of the fighting. Clifford said that, while he could live with the second option, he much preferred the third. The session was followed by formal briefings from Philip Habib of the State Department, Major General William E. DePuy, and George Carver, the CIA's chief analyst on Vietnam.

Shortly after one o'clock the following afternoon, the Wise Men arrived at the White House to meet with Johnson. McGeorge Bundy had been deputized to present their position, and his message shocked Johnson. "Mr. President," he said, "there has been a very significant shift in most of our positions since we last met. The picture in November was one of hope for reasonably steady, slow but sustained, progress, especially in the countryside, which was then emphasized to us as an area of particular importance. The picture that emerged from the discussions last night was not so hopeful, particularly in the countryside." One by one, the others had their say. Most of them echoed Bundy's concerns and urged the president to adopt a new policy toward the war. Ball and Vance went so far as to urge an immediate and complete halt to the bombing. Johnson was visibly shaken by the change of heart in most of these men.

Besides the counsel of the Wise Men, Johnson had been holding lengthy private discussions about the war with Rusk, who increasingly viewed the conflict as unsustainable. Clifford, unaware of Rusk's talks with the president and the secretary of state's own doubts, continued to view him as the main proponent of escalation.

On March 28, Clifford, Bundy, Rostow, and McPherson met with Rusk in his office to iron out the final details of the speech Johnson was to give to the nation three days later. In its eighth draft, the document was still viewed by Clifford as too focused on war instead of peace. Directing his comments primarily to Rusk, he said, "Now I make it a practice to keep in touch with friends in business and the law across the land. I ask them their views about various matters. Until a few months ago they were generally supportive of the war. They were a little disturbed about the overheating of the economy and the flight of gold, but they assumed that these things would be brought under control, and in any event they thought it was important to stop the Communists. Now all that has changed. There has been a tremendous erosion of support for the war among these men." Rusk and the others listened quietly, well aware of Clifford's ties to the business community. In reality, however, they no longer needed to be convinced.

To Clifford's surprise, Rusk did not argue with any of his suggested changes in the speech. In fact, the remainder of the conversation was spent fine-tuning the language along the lines Clifford had suggested. There was no debate over the larger policy issue; everyone had accepted that the course of the war must change.

Johnson certainly knew that Clifford now opposed the war, and he had listened intently to Rusk's arguments against it, too. If he held Clifford's change of heart against his secretary of defense, Johnson did not let on at that time. He even told Joe Califano that he intended to keep Clifford at Defense.

On March 30, when Justice Douglas held a dinner party in Clifford's honor, the president paid him the compliment of making a last-minute, unscheduled appearance. And the president asked his wife to make sure the Cliffords were invited to the White House the following evening for the historic speech on Vietnam. "He especially wanted them with us," said Mrs. Johnson.

Clark and Marny Clifford arrived at the White House shortly after eight o'clock on that Sunday evening. They were escorted to the First Family's living quarters, where they found Mrs. Johnson and a handful of aides talking quietly among themselves while the president read over his speech. The atmosphere was almost funereal as Johnson, adjusting his reading glasses, penciled in a few final changes and left for the Oval Office. The others continued to chat until a few minutes before nine, when Mrs. Johnson and Clifford walked over to the president's office. Clifford was standing just outside the doorway as the cameraman signaled "on the air" and the president began in his Texas drawl the introduction that the country had grown accustomed to: "My fellow Americans."

President Johnson then delivered the speech that marked the historic turning point in American policy on Vietnam. For the first time, he called for a de-escalation of the conflict and a curtailment of the bombing. His hope, he said, was to open the way for restraint on both sides and eventual peace talks.

"Tonight," he said, "I have ordered our aircraft and our naval vessels to make no attacks on North Vietnam, except in an area north of the demilitarized zone, where the continuing enemy build-up directly threatens allied forward positions and where the movements of their troops and supplies are clearly related to that threat."

The dramatic shift surprised the nation. But it was Johnson's final words, completed personally less than an hour before the speech, that stunned the world. "With America's sons in the fields far away, with America's future under challenge right here at home, with our hopes and the world's hopes for peace in the balance every day, I do not believe that I should devote an hour or a day of my time to any personal partisan causes or to any duties other than the awesome duties of this office — the Presidency of your country. Accordingly, I shall not seek, and will not accept, the nomination of my party for another term as your President."

Clifford was one of the few people who said he was not surprised by the president's announcement not to seek reelection. He said that Johnson had informed him of his decision before the speech. Nonetheless, Clifford was subdued and numbed when he heard Lyndon Johnson agree voluntarily to give up the one thing in life he had always seemed to want, the presidency of the United States. As the camera lights clicked off, the president's family rushed to him, hugging and kissing him. Standing beside her husband, Marny Clifford's eyes filled with tears. Clifford stood there, holding his hands behind his back, his chin up, with what Lady Bird Johnson remembered as "the oddest, most faraway expression on his face."

Within days of the speech, Clifford began calling reporters to his office at the Pentagon for briefings on how the war would be wound up. They were called background sessions because the information could not be attributed to Clifford. However, they served two important purposes for Clifford. First, they allowed him to assume the role of the primary interpreter of Johnson's speech, which gave it the most dovish spin. Second, Clifford emerged as the principal force behind the change in policy. The conventional wisdom quickly became that the president had made the critical decision to wind down the war because Clark Clifford had convinced him it was the right thing to do.

Clifford believed that he had brought Johnson over to his side, and the press gladly gave him the major share of the credit. However, Dean Rusk's shift in attitude on the war had played a critical role, too, paralleling that of Clifford. Many who participated in the Tuesday meetings and other internal debates over Vietnam felt Clifford got too much of the credit. Richard Helms, the veteran CIA official, said he attended all the decisive meetings and "never saw any evidence" that it was Clifford alone who turned around Johnson. McPherson, a loyal friend and admirer of Clifford, later wrote that "something besides Clifford's persuasiveness" changed the president's thinking. And Walt Rostow, a hawk to the end, claimed that it was Rusk who actually made the difference.

Clearly Clifford and Rusk employed different tactics in turning the president against Vietnam. Rusk, a fellow Southerner who had become very close to Johnson, preferred to speak privately with the president and win him over with the logic of his argument. Clifford tried to isolate the president by using men Johnson admired, particularly the Wise Men, to let him know that the policy in Vietnam was wrong.

Johnson did not share all of the factors that ultimately led him to his historic turn against the war. It is clear that he valued the advice he received from Clifford, that he trusted his secretary of defense and relied on him for guidance. Clifford and the president had a shared, twenty-year history that gave the secretary of defense a stature that few others had. Certainly Rusk and other influential figures inside the administration were opposed to the war by then, as was much of the country. But Clifford's opposition provided an essential catalyst for Lyndon Johnson's historic transformation.

If Johnson could forgive Clifford going dove on him, what the president could not abide was watching his secretary of defense take all the credit for such a momentous decision. Along with slighting Dean Rusk and others, Clifford seemed to usurp the role of the president himself. This Johnson saw as a sign of disloyalty, and he set about to punish Clifford. Suddenly the secretary of defense had trouble getting the president to return his telephone calls. At his eight-thirty staff meetings, Clifford complained to Paul Warnke and others. He could no longer get Johnson to sign off on anything he sent to the White House. For a time, Clifford was even cut off from important cable traffic regarding the war. The freeze treatment would pass, but Johnson's coolness would linger.

For the sixty-one-year-old Clark Clifford, his first months as secretary of defense marked a dramatic personal and professional turning point. He had turned his back on his lucrative law business and taken one of the toughest positions in government at a critical time. He had compounded the challenge in those first months by following his own convictions even though they cast him in direct confrontation with the president of the United States. His short time in the crucible of the Pentagon had seen Clifford evolve from an adviser to his own man.

And Clifford's motives in courting the press were not as self-serving as the president believed. In this instance, Clifford saw the press not only as a means for self-aggrandizement. He saw it also as a means of influencing public opinion to try to ensure that momentum inside the Johnson administration did not swing back toward escalation. These courageous steps were taken at considerable risk to his relationship with the president, and thus to his personal status in the administration and in Washington.

15

His Finest Hour

INSIDE HIS EXPANSIVE OFFICE at the Pentagon, Clifford was surrounded by clocks. Six of them related the time in the major capitals of the world. One, a ship's clock, emitted a loud tick-tock with each passing second, and never were they all quite synchronized, so the clocks would toll the passing hour discordantly. However, their message, as a visitor in the summer of 1968 observed, was the same: every hour in Vietnam cost the lives of three more American soldiers and depleted the United States Treasury by $3.5 million. Once President Johnson had committed himself on March 31, Clifford's task was to beat the clock and stop the war.

Each morning at eight-thirty, the Pentagon's senior staff would gather around Clifford's big desk. Security was tight; the conversation was restricted to those inside the room. Although the give and take would quickly turn informal, there was an order to the sessions of what Clifford called "the Eight-Thirty Group." Air Force Colonel Robert E. Pursely, Clifford's military aide, sat in the chair directly to Clifford's right. Next to him was George Elsey, his personal assistant. Then came Paul Warnke, the assistant secretary who was fast becoming a Clifford favorite. Paul Nitze, the acerbic deputy secretary, sat directly across from Clifford, and next to him was Phil Goulding, the assistant secretary for public affairs.

Often Clifford would open a meeting by describing a conversation he had had the night before. "Walt Rostow and I had a long talk last night to exchange views on where we go from here. Now I want to go over with each of you the points he made and get your reaction." What followed was usually a lively exchange of views on a variety of subjects, from NATO strategy and strategic talks with the Soviets to the Arab-Israeli war and the *Pueblo* incident. One subject, however, came to dominate the discussions: how to get out of Vietnam. The meetings lasted from an hour to two hours and at least three-quarters of each was devoted to Vietnam.

Bombing the North was not going to win the war and neither was sending twice as many American troops to fight. In fact, the group could not come up with any military scenario that would win the war in a traditional sense within a time period that would be acceptable to American public opinion, which was turning sharply against the war as the deaths rose and upheaval at home increased. Therefore, these senior officials determined, negotiations with the North Vietnamese offered the most sensible avenue for reaching a settlement.

At the eight-thirty meetings, Clifford always rehearsed what he planned to say to the press or the president on Vietnam. His custom was to draft his remarks and then share them with the group, asking for comments and suggestions. Nitze had the broadest experience in international affairs of anyone in the room and still harbored a deep resentment that he had not been given the secretary's post. A true policy professional, Nitze regarded Clifford as an amateur and frequently found his views too simplistic on such sensitive tasks as reducing troop strength or the reaction of the South Vietnamese leadership to the prospect of peace talks with the North.

"These were really very strange meetings," Nitze recalled years later. "They generally began with a draft of a speech or a letter that Clark had prepared. I generally led off by taking the view that the proposal was inherently flawed. I argued that it was no good. Pursely usually came to my defense. The next day, Clark would come back with a new draft which purported to represent 'the truth.' The same flaws were usually there in my estimation, only he presented them better. It was as though he was constantly creating a facade, which eventually became the reality. He could not distinguish between the two."

Despite his critical view of Clifford, Nitze provided essential support in the secretary's efforts to persuade the president to enter into negotiations with the North Vietnamese. The two men shared the same aim: a negotiated settlement to the war.

"There was no dissent," recalled Elsey. "As a group, we were all committed to getting us out of Vietnam. Clark Clifford dominated the discussions, but we all looked up to Nitze, too."

Having agreed to give up his presidency over Vietnam, Johnson was reluctant to take the next step and enter negotiations to end the war. He feared being seen as caving in to the Viet Cong, leaving a legacy as the first American president to lose a war. The president could not even choose a location for the proposed peace talks. One day in early April 1968, Clifford took Harry McPherson aside and told the White House aide, "Old boy, we've got more work to do. We must keep up the momentum. We must convince our friend that he should end this argument over a site. People are hungry for peace. They want us to get on with the talks."

McPherson returned to his office at the White House and dictated a memo to the president urging him to move forward on the peace talks and listing several European cities that he and Clifford had identified as possible sites for the negotiations. The morning after he received the memo, Johnson had telephoned McPherson at home in a rage. None of the cities was acceptable, shouted the president. If the North Vietnamese wanted to talk peace, they could talk peace in San Diego, said Johnson. McPherson was so angry that he shouted back at Johnson, calling him such rough names that McPherson's wife ran downstairs in dismay because she thought he was being too harsh with the plumber. When Johnson hung up, McPherson called Clifford to warn him.

Clifford took his campaign public, arguing in speeches and sessions with reporters that the only sane way out of the tragedy in Southeast Asia was through negotiations. It was a perilous course, for even as he moved toward a position not yet taken by Johnson, Clifford had to take care not to destroy his own influence by contradicting or opposing the president in public.

The problem was not only in the White House. The North Vietnamese also were dragging their feet over choosing a site for the peace talks. When the United States eventually offered several European capitals in mid-April, the North was silent. All the time, they were taking advantage of the bombing pause that Johnson had instituted with his speech on March 31 and moving troops and weapons down toward the South. Finally, on May 3, the North Vietnamese sent a message that they were willing to talk and would meet with the Americans and the South Vietnamese in Paris.

At eight-thirty the following morning, Clifford and several other senior advisers met with Johnson at the White House to receive the welcome news. A short time later, Johnson held a press conference to announce that peace talks would begin in Paris within a week. To represent him, the president selected Averell Harriman and Cyrus Vance, both experienced diplomats.

Harriman shared Clifford's belief that a negotiated settlement was the only way out of Vietnam, but Saigon was stalling on starting the talks. Throughout the summer, Clifford responded by arguing that the South Vietnamese were not true allies and the United States must move ahead with the talks on its own if necessary. An equally committed group, led by Dean Rusk, Walt Rostow, and Ambassador to Vietnam Ellsworth Bunker, contended that the United States was obligated to stand by the South Vietnamese. They marshaled their arguments to combat what they came to call "Cliffordisms." President Johnson was unable to resolve the new dilemma, so the administration remained deeply divided and the talks in Paris languished.

Faced with the threat of renewed Viet Cong aggression against the South, Johnson authorized the resumption of bombing in May even as the peace talks proceeded. On June 5, the president received a personal message from Aleksei Kosygin, chairman of the Council of Ministers of the Soviet Union. Le Duc Tho, a powerful leader of the North Vietnamese Communist Party, had stopped off in Moscow to meet with Kosygin on his way to Paris for the peace talks. He had indicated that the North was prepared for serious negotiations if the United States would again halt the bombing. Kosygin told Johnson that he and his Soviet colleagues thought a complete halt would contribute to a breakthrough and produce "prospects" for peace.

Johnson called for a meeting of his senior advisers to discuss the proposal on Sunday, June 9. Before the meeting, Clifford and Harriman met with Rusk in the secretary of state's office to go over the letter and its potential meaning. Clifford argued that it should be taken at face value; Johnson should take Kosygin at his word and respond favorably. Harriman, who had more experience dealing with the Soviets than anyone in America, said that he could not remember a Soviet cable being more direct. He agreed with Clifford and insisted that the president tell the Soviets that the United States would stop the bombing on the basis of Moscow's assurance that the North Vietnamese would respond by negotiating in good faith. Rusk asked a few questions, but said nothing about his own feelings.

However, when the three men got to the White House, Rusk took the lead and immediately attacked the Soviet cable. He advised Johnson to ignore it, claiming it was nothing more than Soviet posturing. Clifford had been sabotaged, his position destroyed before he got the chance to describe it. Before he had joined the doves, the defense secretary's views would have carried at least as much weight as those of Rusk. Now, however, Johnson accepted Rusk's interpretation and ordered him to prepare the president's reply to Kosygin. There would be no substantive response to the offer. The bombing would go on.

Because of his position in the cabinet, Clifford had to watch the presidential campaign of 1968 from the sidelines. After Robert Kennedy's assassination in Los Angeles on June 5 and the waning of Senator Eugene McCarthy's peace candidacy, Vice President Hubert Humphrey became the clear favorite to win the Democratic nomination. There was speculation in the press that Clifford was under consideration as Humphrey's running mate, but the job that Clifford admitted years later that he really expected to get in a Humphrey administration was the post he had long sought, secretary of state.

"Now, I had a marvelous team at Defense," Clifford recalled later. "I could have picked up that team. We had worked together like a Swiss watch all through that period — mornings, afternoons, nights, weekends. Everybody understood everybody else. We spoke out freely. We never had a leak from that little group. And I thought, what a wonderful opportunity, to be able to move that team, which I could have done, over to the State Department."

In fact, in his own memoir, Humphrey said that he intended to appoint Clifford as his secretary of state. Unfortunately for both men, they were in for the disappointment of their lives.

While the debate on Vietnam continued, Johnson had other tasks for his secretary of defense. When the president nominated Justice Abe Fortas to succeed Earl Warren as Chief Justice of the United States, he knew he was in for a brass-knuckled political contest. Johnson was a lame duck, and the Republicans clearly expected to elect the next president. Further increasing the problem, Johnson not only wanted to elevate Fortas to chief justice. He also wanted to nominate another old friend, Homer Thornberry, to the seat that would be vacated in the shuffle. Thornberry and Johnson had been friends since their teenage days in Texas. After Johnson was elected to the Senate, Thornberry had taken his seat in the House of Representatives. As vice president, Johnson had secured a federal judgeship for Thornberry, even swearing him in on the porch of Johnson's ranch house.

When Johnson brought up Thornberry's appointment in a meeting with Fortas and Clifford, the defense secretary objected. He argued that the elevation of one old friend to the top spot and appointment of another crony would set off a nasty political fight when it came to confirmation hearings for both men. He also pointed out that Johnson, as a lame duck, did not have the political power to force the Senate to confirm Fortas and Thornberry.

"You can't get it through now because the Republicans are planning on winning in November of '68," Clifford said. "One of the best things that could happen for this country would be for Abe Fortas to be chief justice, but you're never going to get it through."

Instead, Clifford argued, the president should ensure confirmation of Fortas by selecting a well-qualified Republican for the vacancy. He even went so far as to suggest Albert Jenner, a moderate Republican who headed a large Chicago law firm, Jenner and Block.

"The Senate will react well to that," argued Clifford. "They won't have anything against Abe particularly. He is liberal, but if they can get a good . . . solid Republican [also], they'd take it. They'd be delighted."

"Well, I don't intend to put some damn Republican on the court," Johnson bellowed in response.

Fortas, to his everlasting regret, agreed with Johnson, and Clifford's advice was ignored. When Warren resigned officially, the president nominated Fortas to succeed him as chief justice and Thornberry to take the vacant seat as associate justice.

Over the next months, the fight to confirm Fortas was an important and ultimately sad element of Clifford's life. It also drew him into a controversy.

Among the charges levied at Fortas by the Republicans was an allegation that he had violated his oath as a Supreme Court justice and the constitutional separation of powers by continuing to advise the president after joining the court. At one point, Republican Senator Strom Thurmond demanded that Clifford testify before the Judiciary Committee about his sessions with Johnson and Fortas, particularly the justice's role in advising Johnson on his 1966 State of the Union address. In a letter to the Democratic committee chairman, Senator James Eastland,

Clifford said Fortas had attended meetings "from time to time" at the White House, but that his advice to the president had been strictly limited to Vietnam. No issues involving the Supreme Court or any other judicial matter had been raised. The letter helped Clifford avoid testifying, but it was not enough to salvage the Fortas nomination as chief justice.

The justice's troubles were compounded by the disclosure that he had been paid in an odd fashion for conducting a seminar at the American University Law School in Washington while on the court. The fact that Fortas taught the seminar was no secret, but the assumption had been that he had been paid by the university. Now it was disclosed that the money had been collected from prominent businessmen by one of his former law partners. Even evidence that Fortas had not known the identities of the donors did not quiet the controversy. The matter was compounded by unproven allegations that Fortas had been paid as a consultant to a Florida foundation while serving on the court. Coupled with the evidence that Fortas had helped Johnson in extrajudicial ways, the disclosure of the American University deal was the final nail in the coffin for Fortas.

Republicans in the Senate threatened a filibuster to stop the elevation of Fortas to chief justice. On October 1, after the Democrats could not muster enough votes to stop the threatened filibuster, Fortas called Johnson and asked that his name be withdrawn. He would remain on the court, but not as its chief justice. Two days later, Thornberry echoed the withdrawal request. Both nominations were dead, just as Clifford had feared.

Relations may have cooled, but the president still recognized the usefulness of his defense secretary. Faced with an imminent increase in the price of steel in the summer of 1968, Johnson reached out to Clifford. When President Kennedy had used Clifford to negotiate with the steel industry in the early 1960s, Clifford was a lawyer in private practice. It was a different matter altogether to send him on such a mission when Clifford was defense secretary and his policies had a direct effect on the steel industry. Nonetheless, in August, Clifford held a series of secret meetings with steel industry executives.

On the morning of August 6, Clifford met with Roger Blough, the chairman of the board of United States Steel, in room 816 at the Carlton

Hotel in Washington. Two other companies, Bethlehem and Republic, had already announced plans to increase prices by five percent, and the two men had a lengthy exchange about those proposals and other industry issues.

"What do you think the government would go along with insofar as a price increase?" asked Blough.

"My private and personal view," replied Clifford, "is that the price increase put into effect by Bethlehem and Republic of five percent should be cut in half."

While not committing himself, Blough said that his company would very much like the Johnson administration to look into an important tax dispute between United States Steel and the federal government.

The same day, Clifford met with George Stinson, the president of National Steel Company. As they discussed the price increases by his two competitors, Stinson gave Clifford the impression that his company would probably not raise its prices by more than two and a half to three percent.

In one of two memos written later that day for Johnson describing his meetings with Blough and Stinson, Clifford said of the National Steel decision, "This would be exceedingly important because it would break the line which Bethlehem, Republic, et al., are trying to hold [and force them] to reverse this part of their price increase." Indeed, in much the same way he had helped Kennedy earlier, Clifford had assisted Johnson in averting a crisis in the steel industry.

Johnson provided little help to his vice president as Hubert Humphrey campaigned for the presidency against Richard Nixon. Proclaiming that he had a plan to bring an honorable peace in Vietnam, Nixon was widening his margin in the polls as the November 5 presidential election approached.

Inside the Johnson administration, efforts to come up with a peace settlement remained stalled. The South Vietnamese had refused to come to the peace table until Hanoi agreed to stop its aggression. Hanoi remained steadfast in its demand that American bombing be halted as a precondition for serious negotiations.

By mid-October, Clifford and other advisers had convinced Johnson to call a halt to the bombing in an attempt to initiate serious talks with the North. Johnson feared that a halt would make him appear to be helping Humphrey. Clifford argued that it would not affect the campaign, and he quoted Mark Twain, "When in doubt, do right."

The clocks in Clifford's office at the Pentagon were ticking. Time was running out on stopping the war under Johnson and, with Humphrey locked in a fierce battle with the former vice president, there was no certainty that Clifford would have another chance in another Democratic administration.

The South Vietnamese continued to oppose the talks and a bombing halt, posing a major obstacle to any peace settlement. It was during this crucial period that the Central Intelligence Agency learned that the Nixon campaign had been in contact with Bui Diem, the South Vietnamese ambassador to the United States. The contact was arranged by Anna Chennault, the Chinese-born widow of General Claire Chennault, the commander of the famed Flying Tigers during World War II. She also was head of Republican Women for Nixon. With her assistance, Diem had established a secret communications channel with John Mitchell, the lawyer who was running Nixon's campaign, and he kept Mitchell informed of Saigon's position. The CIA and other intelligence sources never determined exactly what information was passing between the South Vietnamese and Nixon's campaign. However, the White House reached the general conclusion that South Vietnamese President Nguyen Van Thieu was being encouraged to delay the talks until after the election.

"What was going on was that [they were saying] no more progress should be made in conducting the peace conferences because the South Vietnamese could get a better deal from the new Nixon administration than they could get from the Johnson administration," Clifford recalled years later. "There was plenty of information about the contact Mitchell was having with Mrs. Chennault. She even had a code name. She was called 'Little Flower.'"

This was a potential scandal of huge proportions, but it posed problems. The disclosure would show that the United States had been conducting intelligence operations aimed at the ambassador of an ally and a private citizen. On the other hand, it also would demonstrate that the Nixon campaign was encouraging President Thieu to drag his feet on the talks and prolong the war.

Johnson convened a secret meeting at the White House, inviting only Clifford, Rusk, and Rostow. Clifford argued in favor of full disclosure. At the very least, he urged the president to contact Nixon and threaten to expose the matter unless the communications stopped immediately. (In his memoir, Clifford contends that he did not argue for disclosing the material.) Rusk feared the disclosure would further weaken the American relationship with Thieu. He also argued that Thieu was likely to accept the American offer and come to the table in a few days.

The president considered the matter for two days. Then he summoned the men to the White House again and gave them his decision. The American people would not be told about the secret communications between South Vietnam and the Nixon campaign. It was too divisive for the country and for American relations with Saigon. Further, worried that a leak might embarrass his administration, Johnson swore the men to secrecy.

President Thieu refused to agree to participate in the Paris talks. Finally, at the end of October, a frustrated Johnson decided to go ahead with the bombing halt. He planned to tell the nation of his decision in a televised address at eight o'clock on the night of October 31. In a conference call shortly after six o'clock with Humphrey, Nixon, and third-party candidate George Wallace of Alabama, Johnson explained that a breakthrough had been reached with the North Vietnamese. In exchange for stopping the bombing, Hanoi had pledged to respect a demilitarized zone between the North and South and to sit down at the table with the South Vietnamese. As for Saigon, its representatives would be free to participate in the Paris peace talks.

Nearly four weeks passed before the South Vietnamese agreed to send a delegation to Paris. Clifford was nearly frantic. Richard Nixon had been narrowly elected president — defeating Hubert Humphrey by a slim margin — and Clifford and the Democrats were about to be swept out of office. Nixon had won in part by promising that he had a secret plan to end the war, but Clifford had little faith in the former vice president or his advisers. With time running out on his job at the Pentagon, he desperately wanted a real military de-escalation and the beginning of peace talks. In appearances on such shows as NBC-TV's Sunday news program *Meet the Press* and CBS-TV's *Face the Nation*, Clifford's zeal put him well in front of the president in pushing for peace talks.

"I am becoming inordinately impatient with the continued deaths of American boys in Vietnam," Clifford said on the CBS show on December 15. "I would like to get going at the Paris conference. I would like to get started on these plans to lower the level of combat. This isn't difficult to do. I would like to start getting our troops out of there. I would like to see a cease-fire."

While the aggressive campaign by his defense secretary made Johnson uncomfortable and sometimes downright angry, he never repudiated Clifford's statements, so Clifford kept on talking.

Yet another month went by before an agreement was reached on how to conduct the talks. Substantive talks were scheduled to begin on January 25, 1969 — five days after Richard Nixon replaced Lyndon Johnson in the White House.

A few days before the inauguration of Richard Milhous Nixon, Clifford realized that nothing was planned for Johnson after the ceremony. He would be leaving the White House in disappointment and simply returning to his beloved Texas Hill Country with Lady Bird. Relations between the two men had cooled significantly since Clifford began to oppose the war. However, he still held Johnson in high regard. So, taking a chapter from Dean Acheson's farewell party for President and Mrs. Truman in 1953, Clifford invited President Johnson and Lady Bird to a luncheon at his home following the inauguration ceremonies.

On Monday, January 20, 1969, after Nixon was sworn in as president, Lyndon Johnson got into a black presidential limousine with his wife, Lady Bird, and two daughters, Lynda and Luci. With a motorcycle escort, they drove to the Cliffords' house on Rockville Pike. The now-former president expected a quiet affair with some members of his administration and old friends. But as the car approached the Cliffords' home, they found the street lined with people. They cheered and waved signs that said "We'll never forget you, LBJ" and "LBJ, You were good for the USA." The crowd had spilled onto Clifford's large lawn and children had climbed trees surrounding the house for a glimpse of the former president. A woman waved a large American flag beside a tall man who had hoisted his young son onto his shoulders for a better view.

"It looked as if we had moved backwards in time to some particularly homey campaign rally," Mrs. Johnson later wrote in her diary.

As Johnson and his family walked up the front walk toward the house, they were mobbed by so many well-wishers that they lost Luci in the crowd. On the drive, smiling and waiting to greet them, stood Clark and Marny Clifford. The old friends posed together for photographers and then they went inside the sprawling house where so many happy Christmas parties had been celebrated in earlier years.

"Inside that warm and welcoming house there awaited us one of the most significant and dear parties we shall ever attend," Mrs. Johnson wrote in her diary.

Most of the Johnson cabinet was among the the sixty close friends and advisers invited to the party. Vice President Humphrey and his wife, Muriel, stood in one corner of the living room. Senators Birch Bayh, Henry Jackson, and Gale McGee were there with their wives. And so were Supreme Court Justice Abe Fortas and his wife, Carol.

Late in the afternoon, Marny Clifford went upstairs to powder her nose and she found the president and her husband talking in the master bedroom. Both men grinned at her, and Johnson said, "Please go downstairs and get Lady Bird. And will you also get Averell, Dean, Walt, and Bill White and bring them all upstairs."

She dutifully brought Mrs. Johnson, Averell Harriman, Dean Rusk, Walt Rostow, and journalist William White to the bedroom. There, in what he later described his memoir as "one of the most gratifying moments of that eventful day," Johnson explained quietly and earnestly that, earlier that morning, in his last official act as president, he had conferred the Medal of Freedom on the men who were present. As Marny Clifford's eyes filled with tears, Johnson thanked them for loyal service to him and to their country. Then Lady Bird Johnson, sensing that the moment should not turn maudlin, said, "It's time to go." She hugged the Cliffords, took her husband's arm, and they left for the airport and the long flight home to Texas.

Was Clifford's tumultuous tenure as secretary of defense a triumph or a failure? Among those who have sought to conduct the political autopsy of that period, there are many answers to the question. Some who observed him view Clifford's service as a disappointment because, in the end, he did not end the war. "Clifford really failed as defense secretary," said Ben Bradlee, who was editor of the *Washington Post* during Vietnam. "He took that job and, on sober second thought, his goal was to wind up the American involvement in Vietnam and he did not." For some, he seemed to take more credit than he deserved, much as he had been accused of doing in the Truman years. These people claim that Clifford was merely following public opinion in his opposition to the war.

CIA veteran Richard Helms, who sat in on many of the famous Tuesday luncheons at the White House, criticizes Clifford for taking too much responsibility for the president's change of heart and for disloyalty to Johnson. Helms and others give more credit to Dean Rusk, who eventually became closer to Johnson than Clifford or, for that matter, almost anyone else. The president himself certainly shared at least some of that sentiment, as Helms discovered when Richard Nixon dispatched him to LBJ's ranch in Texas to update Johnson on Vietnam a few weeks after Nixon became president.

"I flew down and sat in the garden room of the house," recalled Helms. "It was very pleasant. I went through my briefing, but I could see that I was losing my audience. He was dozing and not paying attention at all. When I finished, he was right there front and center.

" 'What do your notes of the Tuesday luncheons show with respect to the request for more troops?' asked Johnson.

" 'Mr. President, you told us that you did not want any notes taken of those meetings.'

" 'I thought you fellows disobeyed me,' he said.

" 'Well, Mr. President, I certainly didn't disobey you.'

" 'Well, what about the claims that others influenced me not to send more troops? I thought I was the one who made that decision,' said the president.

" 'Mr. President, I do not recall at any of those meetings anyone trying to persuade you one way or the other.'

"He was irritated that other people were claiming credit. He wouldn't single out Clifford, but it was evident to me that Clifford was one of them. But he and Lady Bird had too much respect for Clifford and had relied on him too much to criticize him by name."

While these views contain valid insights and a measure of truth, they do not convey the full extent of what Clark Clifford really did. That he was not alone in turning against the war is undeniable. That he was able to puff up his own role through his use of the press is true, too. More than anyone else in the Johnson administration, Clifford recognized that Vietnam was in part a war between the president and the press, and he astutely enlisted the press on his side, the side of ending the conflict.

Equally true, and more significant, however, was the fact that Clifford, when faced with an unwinnable war, was able to change his own mind when more scholarly men, such as Dean Rusk and Walt Rostow, could not move as quickly or as far from their original hawkish positions. He weighed the facts and followed his conscience, even if it put him in conflict with his political patron.

Clifford's transformation from hawk to dove had a strong impact on the president's own reasoning. True, the self-effacing Rusk had become a dove, too, but he refused to go so far as to abandon South Vietnam, and he had never been as public as his counterpart in the Defense Department. Clifford believed the South Vietnamese were corrupt and that the only solution was a complete withdrawal of American forces. No matter how much the president disliked Clifford's new position and no matter how embittered Johnson was about him in later years, he had to be reckoned with. Clifford, a trusted adviser for many years, had cracked the circle of hawkish advisers around Johnson. When it counted in a dangerous game, Clifford had been willing to risk the trust he had built with Johnson to follow his conscience.

Certainly, Clifford left the Pentagon in disappointment because he left without achieving a just peace in Vietnam. Under Nixon and Henry Kissinger, the war dragged on four more years and pushed the death toll from 35,000 to beyond 55,000. But in his ten months as secretary of defense, Clifford had risen to the difficult task, changing himself from a detached adviser and lawyer to a passionate and committed advocate of his own strong views. As George Elsey observed, Clifford became his own man. He did what he believed was the right thing for the country, and he did it with courage and distinction. Like his four years in the Truman administration, the experience divided his life forever into the then and the now. Clark McAdams Clifford had earned a permanent place in history.

Reflecting two and a half decades later on his tenure as secretary of defense, Clifford said, "It was really some year. Everything was just jammed into it. My best year. That was my best year."

Before 1968, he had been a power within Washington and corporate America. Now, through his service at the Defense Department and through the ubiquity of television, a generation of Americans opposed to the war knew his name and revered him for his stance. Clifford had grown so popular that the key foreign policy adviser of the incoming Republican administration had even sought his counsel on Vietnam.

In one of the small, private dining rooms of the venerable and discreet Metropolitan Club two blocks from the White House, Clifford and Henry Kissinger met for dinner in December 1968. In those days, Kissinger was not yet as famous or powerful as he would later become. A Harvard professor, Kissinger had been an adviser to Nelson Rockefeller a few weeks earlier when Nixon had given him a surprise appointment as his national security adviser, the key foreign policy post in the White House.

Clifford had gotten to know Kissinger during their trip to Vietnam together in 1965. Now, with their roles about to be reversed, Kissinger had invited Clifford to dinner at the Metropolitan Club to hear his thoughts on Vietnam for the new administration.

"I gave all the reasons I thought we should get out of Vietnam," recalled Clifford. "It just poured out of me. Vietnam was my life in those days. I would sleep it, eat it. I was obsessed."

Clifford talked for hours. He outlined his firm belief that the United States should clear out of Vietnam within a year. All authority should be turned over to the South Vietnamese leaders.

"But this is a defeat," said Kissinger.

"No, it is not," countered Clifford. "We are in a losing position. Richard Nixon can become a national hero if he just makes a plan and in a year gets out."

"President-elect Nixon should hear this," said Kissinger. "Would you be willing to come over there when he gets in town, sit down, and tell this same story?"

"I would give anything if I could have that chance," Clifford responded eagerly. "I have been involved personally and vitally and I would like so much to tell him."

"Well," said Kissinger, "I will set it up."

By the time the two men were finished, they had moved from the dining room to the lounge of the club. The other guests had left long before and finally, when the staff began to turn out the lights, Clifford and Kissinger departed.

Kissinger, whose rise to prominence as a professional political player has been viewed as signaling the end of the old establishment, never followed through. For reasons that he guessed had to do with Nixon's animosity toward anyone associated with Johnson, Clifford was not invited to share his views with the White House.

But the rest of the country, and indeed the world, still clamored for his opinions on the country's most wrenching problem as the body counts continued and the streets of America filled with more demonstrators. This new brand of popularity pleased Clifford, even if he felt little kinship with the bedraggled protestors parading through the streets of Washington and other American cities. It provided him with a stump from which to grow even more vocal in his opposition. This popularity implanted the seed of political ambition in Clifford, too. He would hide it so well that even his closest friends would not know, but this man who had never held elected office began to think of himself as a possible president of the United States.

16

Clifford for President?

BEFORE LEAVING the Pentagon in January 1969, Clifford had summoned his former law partners, one by one, to his office. Discussing his return to the firm was a mere formality. However, he also wanted to let them know that he would not be coming back alone. Clifford had decided that Paul Warnke, an assistant secretary of defense, was coming, too.

Had Hubert Humphrey been elected president, Clifford and Warnke both would have remained in government. Indeed, Humphrey later said that he would have appointed Clifford secretary of state had he won. But Richard Nixon was the victor and, shortly after the election, Clifford invited Warnke to his office for a personal conversation. He was characteristically straightforward.

"Would you like to come to work with me at my firm?" asked Clifford, explaining that he would be returning to his law practice soon.

Warnke had been a lawyer for sixteen years at Covington and Burling before joining the Defense Department in 1966. Since the election, his former partners and several other firms had approached him about joining them. Covington and Burling had grown too large for Warnke's tastes and, since he had developed a good working relationship with Clifford, he accepted the offer.

When Clifford brought each of his former partners to the Pentagon for lunch to let him know that he would be rejoining the firm and bringing Warnke, too, everything had gone smoothly. They chatted amiably about how well the firm had done in his absence and its prospects for the future. Then came the day when John Sharon arrived for his session.

Since Clifford's departure, Sharon had been at the top of the firm letterhead, and he and Tom Finney were earning the most money. Now Sharon had decided that he did not want to return to the old ways, with Clifford as a benevolent despot dictating the professional lives of everyone else. As they finished eating, Sharon pushed back his chair and said,

"Well, with reference to your coming back to the firm, we are going to have to talk that over."

Clifford was incredulous. "Let me have that again," he said.

"We are going to have to visit about that," replied Sharon. "You've been away from it, you see. We've been busy while you've been gone. So we ought to get together and see what the basis will be if you come back to the firm."

Clifford listened in smoldering silence, rocking back slightly in his chair as the man across from him talked about the firm that Clifford had started nearly twenty years before and brought to prosperity by sacrificing everything else in his life. Finally, he could no longer contain himself.

"John, you've lost touch with reality," he said in a voice as cold as steel. "I will come back to the firm and the relationship will be just as it was before. My being away hasn't changed that any, except in one respect. I want you to go back to the office and I want you to start packing right away. And within a week I want you to be out of there. Every file, every slip of paper, everything that involves you, I want out of there. If you aren't out within a week, then there are going to be real serious problems." The luncheon ended.

After Sharon left the Pentagon, Clifford called Finney and described the conversation to him. There was no room for debate, no question about Sharon's future with the firm. It would be up to Finney to enforce Clifford's edict. Finney agreed to call a meeting of the other partners later that same day. When Glass, McIlwain, and Finney met that evening in Clifford's former and future office, they were unanimous. The next morning, Finney broke the news to Sharon. Not only would Clifford return to the firm on his own terms and as its head. Sharon was to be gone by the time the great man walked through the door again. Within a couple of days, Sharon had packed his desk and every file that bore his name and left. Clifford moved back into the large corner office on February 1, 1969. Clifford never spoke to John Sharon again.

Sharon left no mourners, but Finney was angered by the arrival of Warnke and the immediate assumption that he was a direct competitor for the number two position, if not the chosen one already. It was Finney who had kept the firm rolling in the year of Clifford's absence, and he expected to be rewarded with a clear position as Clifford's successor. Now he faced a rival in Warnke, and indications were that the former

Defense Department official was Clifford's preferred choice. Warnke had taken Sharon's former office, a large, sunny room on the opposite end of the suite from Clifford. The firm's name had been changed to Clifford, Warnke, Glass, McIlwain, and Finney. At firm meetings, Clifford sought Warnke's views first. He also saw to it that Warnke was given some of the choicest clients, taking them from Glass and McIlwain. Finney appeared to face long odds if he were to surmount Warnke and take over the firm once Clifford retired.

In many ways, it was a reprise of the management style Clifford had imposed at the start of the firm in 1950. In the early days, he often assigned Glass and McIlwain the same legal task and then weighed the results of each man's performance. It seemed wasteful, particularly in a small firm, but it was Clifford's method for keeping them on their toes — and in competition with each other, rather than with him.

Finney did not want a repeat of that situation, and Warnke, recognizing Finney's value to the firm, wanted to make his peace with him and the others to ease his own transition into the firm. So within weeks, the two men met privately to make their own deal.

"The two of us agreed that neither of us would ever make more money than the other one or compete against each other," Warnke said later. "This gave us more clout with Clark because he wouldn't see us as fighting for ourselves."

By 1969, Clifford's reputation as an influential Washington lawyer was widely known. Before his ten months at the Pentagon, his name had been prominent in the capital and among major corporations. Now he was a national and even an international figure. The result was a boom for the law firm, bringing in more American clients and some new and exotic customers, too.

Not long after Clifford left the government, the Algerian government hired him for a retainer of $150,000 a year. The business came about in an unusual way. One of Clifford's longtime clients, El Paso Natural Gas Company, wanted to participate with the government of Algeria in a joint project to sell Algerian liquified natural gas in the United States. However, Algeria had broken diplomatic relations with the United States following the Arab-Israeli war in 1967 and most members of the Nixon administration viewed the Mediterranean country as a hotbed of radicals. El Paso Natural Gas, which needed government approval for the project and wanted government financing, too, called on Clifford to smooth the way for the deal in Washington.

At the time, Yolande Fox, the former Miss America and widow of Clifford client Matthew Fox, was dating Cherif Guellal, who had been Algeria's ambassador to Washington. When his country broke diplomatic relations, he resigned his post but remained in the country as Algeria's unofficial and discreet representative. Using Mrs. Fox as the intermediary, Clifford contacted Guellal and arranged to travel to the capital of Algiers to discuss the joint venture. They agreed that Clifford would represent El Paso Natural Gas, a longtime client, and the Algerian government.

For the first time, he found himself representing interests that were, if not hostile, at least potentially unfriendly to the United States. Clifford spent eight days in the capital, Algiers, discussing the project and general relations with officials there. He returned aglow with optimism, describing the country as an up-and-coming nation eager to develop its industry and reserves of petroleum and natural gas. Those energy reserves, he told American officials, could help the United States. Wrapping a client's interests in those of the American government was a familiar strategy of Clifford's, although his clients were usually American corporations. It was also a palliative designed as much for Clifford's view of himself as for the officials who heard it. By linking interests, even when there were no ties apparent to others, Clifford managed to convince himself that his legal business was, in at least a small way, an extension of his government service.

Clifford's representation of the Arabs, and the idea that he was capitalizing on his stint at the Defense Department along with his legendary access, once prompted his friend Edward Bennett Williams to perform an impromptu skit at Clifford's expense.

In an episode recounted in *The Man to See*, Evan Thomas's biography of Williams, the two men were on a private jet bound for Oklahoma on business for Phillips Petroleum when Williams began pretending that he was Clifford speaking to a delegation of Arabs in his office. "You understand, of course, that I can only get you access," Williams said, mimicking Clifford's deep voice. As the lawyer imitated the Arabs winking and pushing a bag of gold across the desk, Clifford interrupted and said, "Now, Ed, you know it doesn't work that way." According to Thomas, Williams just laughed.

Clifford's first task for the Algerians was an effort to win American government approval for a $1.2 billion plan to liquify natural gas and ship it to the United States in huge tanker ships. The involvement of El Paso Natural Gas opened the door for American financing. As part of his representation, Clifford met with officials at the United States Export-Import Bank to seek $500 million from the federal agency for the liquified natural gas project. Warnke and other members of the law firm also had contacted the Federal Power Commission, which was considering an application from three American companies to buy the gas. It was politically touchy, because the Algerians still had no diplomatic ties to the United States and there was opposition to doing any business with Algeria in some quarters of the government. As a result, some of the discussions veered from legal matters to political factors.

At a 1971 meeting with the Export-Import Bank, Henry Kearns, the bank's chairman and president, warned Clifford and Warnke that the decision to allow the importation of Algerian natural gas to the United States was a general policy decision that would be made by the Defense and State Departments and the White House itself. "Not everyone in Washington agrees with the use of Algerian gas," Kearns cautioned the lawyers.

Clifford summoned forth an argument he had used in many instances before and would use in the future, too. The American energy crisis, he contended, made importing Algerian gas a matter of vital interest to the United States government.

Kearns then suggested that if Clifford hoped to win government approval for the gas deal, he had better persuade the Algerians to settle claims with several large American corporations whose assets had been nationalized by Algeria in 1962. Within months, through Clifford's assistance, those claims were resolved and the path was cleared for approval of the natural gas project.

Americans who represent foreign interests in dealing with the United States government are required by law to register as foreign agents with the Justice Department. There is an exemption for lawyers when they do only legal work, but to maintain the exemption lawyers must avoid lobbying and other attempts to influence congressmen or government officials. Clifford and his firm chose not to register as foreign agents for the Algerian government, which eventually attracted the attention of the Justice Department's internal security section.

When attorneys from the section began investigating Clifford's activities on behalf of the Algerian government, they quickly discovered that the Algerians had hired other law firms, too. For instance, the Algerians paid $83,850 in legal fees to the New York firm of Shearman and Sterling for preparing a loan agreement. Another blue-chip New York firm, Milbank, Tweed, Hadley and McCloy, had been paid a substantial amount for preparing other financial documents. Those firms appeared to have done most of the detailed legal work, so what had been Clifford's role?

The Washington representation appeared to be more lobbying than legal work. In fact, Richard G. Kleindienst, an Arizona lawyer who had served briefly as one of President Nixon's attorneys general, had done the same work as Clifford for Algeria and had voluntarily registered as a foreign agent. After an investigation, the Justice Department concluded that Clifford's firm had done more than legal work. The department demanded that Clifford himself register as a foreign agent for the Algerians and disclose the full extent of his activities on their behalf. After initially resisting, Clifford agreed and the law firm registered.

Clifford's representation of Algeria had thrust the former defense secretary into a world of international influence peddling where he had never been before as a lawyer. The prestige he had gained as secretary of defense had been a prized commodity to the Algerians, and Clifford had sought to capitalize on his former post by casting the Algerian decision in terms of American interests. In key ways, this small case can be seen as a forerunner for a far more dramatic and damaging episode that would start a decade later.

Clifford's reputation also can be seen as a critical factor in another intriguing case that unfolded about the same time as the Algerian incident. This time, the firm was hired to represent an Israeli-owned company, which was bidding on a multimillion-dollar contract to build secret communications facilities for the American government in Iran and Turkey.

The secret facilities would entail state-of-the-art eavesdropping technology developed by the National Security Agency and other American intelligence operations. At one point, a company owned by the Central Intelligence Agency was to receive the contract in part to protect the technology, but the company ran into unrelated difficulties and had to bow out.

Because of the sensitive nature of the technology and the United

States government's "Buy American" regulations, the bidding was restricted to American-owned companies. This should have ruled out Clifford's client because it was owned by the Israeli Labor Party through its trade organization, Histadrut. To conceal the ownership, the Israelis had bought the charter of the defunct Reynolds Ball Point Pen Corporation and submitted its bid under the name Reynolds Construction Company. Essentially, the Israelis had set up a front company to deceive the American government, win the lucrative contract, and gain access to the technology that would be used in the communications network.

Hiring Clifford put the stamp of legitimacy on the company. Reynolds Construction won the contract and built the network. Several people knowledgeable about the transaction said that Clifford did the legal work for hiding the true ownership of the firm. Years later, Clifford said that he had no recollection of the client or ever having done any work for them. But the case foreshadowed things to come for Clifford and a young lawyer who would join his firm shortly.

With business booming, Clifford turned to Sam McIlwain in the spring of 1969 and said, "We've got to have some more help. We need a summer intern."

"I'll see what I can do," replied McIlwain.

At the time, the firm had seven partners and three associates. Calling the law school at George Washington University, McIlwain soon came up with the name of a bright, first-year student, Robert Altman. The son of two lawyers, Altman had grown up in Washington, attended the University of Wisconsin, and quickly earned a reputation at law school as a very hardworking student.

McIlwain was leery because the firm had hired a couple of law students who seemed to do little more than socialize while they were in the office and flirt with young female staffers when they were sent up to Capitol Hill on errands. But he was immediately impressed with Altman and hired him for the summer.

This young law student wasted no time. "Altman was probably the most enterprising and energetic clerk we ever had," recalled James Stovall, who had himself just joined the firm as a young associate. "He visited every attorney or associate every day to offer assistance. Ambitious? Of course, as most of your Washington attorneys are."

Although Clifford appeared to pay scant attention to the young clerk, McIlwain noticed that he was a diligent worker who never complained about taking on the most menial duties. The elder lawyer had often heard Clifford describe his early days working for Jacob Lashley in St. Louis and he could not help but see some of the young Clifford in Altman. At the end of the summer, McIlwain said he would like to have Altman back the following summer. Altman readily accepted.

The following February, however, Altman called McIlwain and said he would have to withdraw his acceptance. He had been elected editor of the law review at George Washington, which meant that he would not have time for a summer clerkship.

When Altman graduated from law school in 1971, McIlwain offered a job immediately. But Altman said he planned to spend the summer in Europe and was not sure what he wanted to do when he returned. He applied for a clerkship with Justice Douglas, but he was turned down. When he went for a job interview at Arent, Fox, Kintner, Plotkin and Kahn, a large Washington law firm, one of the partners, Albert Arent, took him aside.

"We'd love to have you," said Arent, "but I see that you clerked for Clifford and Warnke. Have they offered you a job?"

Altman said they had, and Arent told him, "Take it. They get the cream of the work."

Altman took the advice and the job, joining the firm in October 1971 as an associate. It would be some time, however, before Clifford began paying attention to this equivalent of the young man in the library.

By the early seventies, Clifford was a major opponent of the Vietnam War, blasting President Nixon and his advisers in speeches, newspaper articles, congressional testimony, and television appearances. The assault had started within his first months back in private practice.

Anguished about Nixon's unwillingness or inability to bring the war to a quick end, Clifford began work in February 1969 on a lengthy article for *Foreign Affairs*, the prestigious quarterly journal that was must reading for the foreign policy establishment. He planned to present a logical timetable for withdrawing American troops and ending the war. The well-placed article, while less than a broadside against the Nixon administration, would signal that Clifford still regarded himself as an important player on the stage of public opinion.

Paul Warnke felt Clifford was using the article to vent his continued frustration over the failure to end the war. However, some of Clifford's other friends and former colleagues from the Johnson administration believed the *Foreign Affairs* article was Clifford's attempt to position himself to become a presidential candidate in 1972.

Before the 1968 Democratic convention, Clifford had been mentioned as a possible candidate for vice president. Four years later, one of his intimates recalled, Clifford hoped the country might turn to a soldier-statesman, which was how Clifford viewed himself after his tour at the Defense Department. It was around this time that Stuart Symington floated the idea of a Clifford presidency, telling a reporter, "Clifford is the best-qualified man to be president that I have ever known."

Clifford himself later acknowledged that he had entertained the idea of running for president after leaving the Defense Department. However, he preferred to cast his ambitions in more general, rather self-deprecating terms.

"Sure," he said, "anybody who comes to Washington thinks about being president. I worked for a number of presidents. I'd seen how each of them would work and, from time to time, I'd picture myself doing it. Never with any seriousness, because I had never really been in politics. I had never run for elected office. You don't ordinarily, for the first time you run for elected office, run for president of the United States. I used to enjoy [the idea] occasionally. I am probably the only one who ever had that thought [about myself]."

Because Clifford was one of the few former Johnson administration officials who was not in some form of mild disgrace over Vietnam, his views on the war were accorded enormous importance. He also worked hard to expand the audience for his *Foreign Affairs* piece, going so far as to telephone Ben Bradlee, editor of the *Washington Post*, to see whether the newspaper might be interested in running the article, too.

Entitled "A Vietnam Reappraisal: The Personal History of One Man's View and How It Evolved," the article detailed Clifford's change from hawk to dove and offered his plan for a troop withdrawal. "A first step would be to inform the South Vietnamese government that we will withdraw about 100,000 troops before the end of this year," he wrote. "We should also make it clear that this is not an isolated action, but the beginning of a process under which all United States ground combat forces will have been withdrawn from Vietnam by the end of 1970." He went on to argue that only an acknowledged policy of disengagement would force the Saigon government to broaden its political base and assume more of the fighting.

Clifford's comments were similiar to recent statements by Harriman and Vance, who had been the Johnson administration's chief negotiators at the Paris peace talks. The article contained no criticism of President Nixon, and it was not far from the mark set by the Nixon administration itself. Just a few days before, the administration had announced plans to withdraw 25,000 servicemen that summer and more if the South Vietnamese forces proved capable of taking their place. But Clifford was appealing for a faster withdrawal and a strategy of total disengagement.

The impact of the Clifford article was felt far beyond the intellectual confines of *Foreign Affairs'* readership. The *New York Times* ran a lengthy front-page article on Clifford's views along with an excerpt from the article. The Sunday following publication, the *Washington Post* ran the entire *Foreign Affairs* piece on its editorial page. Other newpapers featured prominent stories on the article and Clifford was on the CBS-TV morning news the next day repeating his call for pulling American troops out of Vietnam.

The White House could not miss the publicity. Every morning the president's staff prepares a written summary of printed and television news for him. On the morning of June 19, the day the stories about Clifford's article appeared, his name was at the top of the news summary that Richard Nixon found waiting on his desk when he arrived in the Oval Office. Later that same day, Nixon found himself facing questions about the article at a White House news conference.

"Well, I noted Mr. Clifford's comments in the magazine *Foreign Affairs* and naturally I respect his judgment as a former secretary of defense," said Nixon. "I would point out, however, that for five years in the administration in which he was secretary of defense in the last part, we had a continued escalation of the war: we had 500,000 Americans in Vietnam; we had 35,000 killed; we had over 200,000 injured. And, in addition to that, we found that in the year, the full year, in which he was secretary of defense, our casualties were the highest of the whole five-year period and, as far as negotiations were concerned, all that had been accomplished, as I indicated earlier, was that we had agreed on the shape of the table.

"This is not to say that Mr. Clifford's present judgment is not to be considered because of the past record. It does indicate, however, that he did have a chance in this particular respect and did not move on it then. I believe that we have changed that policy. We have started to withdraw forces. We will withdraw more. . . . As far as how many will be withdrawn by the end of this year or the end of next year, I would hope that we could beat Mr. Clifford's timetable, just as I think we have done a little better than he did when he was in charge of our national defense."

Top White House aides were startled by Nixon's response about beating Clifford's timetable. Kissinger, Nixon's national security adviser, expressed concern that Nixon's remarks could undermine the Thieu government and might even wind up turning South Vietnamese troops against their American allies. H. R. Haldeman, Nixon's chief of staff, assured Kissinger that Nixon had spoken in anger over Clifford's article. "I feel he just wanted to hit back at Clifford, and overplayed his hand," Haldeman wrote in his diary that day.

The president's remarks were a clear sign that Clifford was angering the administration. A journalist later described the president's reaction as "classic Nixonism — the pious disclaimer followed by the distortion and innuendo."

Nixon seemed to be saying the same thing Clifford had said — turn the war over to the South Vietnamese and get out. But Clifford saw two critical differences, which doomed the Nixon plan.

"They felt that turning the war over to the South Vietnamese could be done successfully," Clifford said later. "I never had a hope for them. I had gotten to know the South Vietnamese leaders very well. They were totally undependable. Also, I had reached my own private conclusion. They did not want the war to end. That is a caustic remark to make, but they would know that the North Vietnamese would be in control. They would not be anything. So they did not want the war to end. I sensed that right away. Kissinger and Nixon and their group should have sensed it, too.

"There is another factor there," he said. "Kissinger and Nixon said we must stay the course there in order to preserve our reputation in the world. I thought that was one hundred percent wrong. We didn't have to do that. The fact is, I went through a period, attending meetings of defense ministers, where they would say, 'Mr. Clifford, why is the United States in Vietnam?' They couldn't believe we were there. It made absolutely no sense at all."

In the months that followed Nixon's impetuous statement, it became clear that the country would not meet the one-year timetable. In fact, Nixon expanded the war by bombing Cambodia. So Clifford's statements about Nixon grew harsher. As a respected corporate lawyer and former defense secretary, Clifford could not be dismissed as a radical or kook, but he became a marked man among the Nixon people.

At Kissinger's insistence, the Federal Bureau of Investigation had instituted seventeen wiretaps in late 1969. The ostensible reason was to prevent leaks of national security information, but the information that flowed to the White House from the FBI was of a decidedly more political nature. One of those whose phone was tapped was Morton Halperin, who had been on Clifford's staff at the Pentagon before moving to the National Security Council at the White House under Kissinger for a short time.

After leaving the White House, Halperin had helped Clifford as he prepared an article opposing the war for *Life* magazine. The tap picked up conversations about the article between Halperin and another former Pentagon staffer, Leslie Gelb. The FBI dutifully passed on the information to Nixon in early 1970, prompting Jeb Magruder, a White House assistant, to write a memo to Haldeman and another senior Nixon aide, John D. Ehrlichman, which said: "J. Edgar Hoover's memorandum to the President regarding the potential problem that is developing with Clark Clifford has been checked out thoroughly. He is going to write an article for *Life*. We are in a position to counteract this article in any number of ways."

One of the ways was a blistering speech written by White House speechwriter Patrick Buchanan. He worked all night on May 20 to draft a speech attacking Clifford and other leading opponents of the war. Vice President Spiro Agnew was to deliver it to a Republican gathering in Texas a few days later, but the day before the speech, Nixon had Haldeman call off Agnew. The president liked the speech, but he felt the timing was not right.

Agnew finally delivered the speech on June 20 at a Republican fundraising dinner in Cleveland. He castigated three Democratic senators — J. William Fulbright of Arkansas, Edward M. Kennedy of Massachusetts, and George McGovern of South Dakota — as well as Clifford, Harriman, and Vance for advocating an American defeat in Vietnam.

"Mr. Clifford's current writings seem to emanate from a deep desire to convince his friends he was an early convert and not some late-blooming opportunist who clambered aboard a rolling bandwagon of doves when the flak really started to fly," charged Agnew. A bit later in the speech, Agnew added, "Such things as consciences and bloodbaths now seem to have lost their relevance for Mr. Clifford, weighed against the applause of his new audience in the pages of *Life* magazine."

Another Nixon speechwriter, William Safire, met Clifford one evening in 1971 at the Georgetown home of Polly Wisner, the widow of a former CIA official, who assembled lively and politically mixed dinner parties. Nixon had just delivered a Safire-written speech on Vietnam, and Clifford, who had written a speech or two himself, offered what Safire felt was the left-handed compliment of praising the "artfulness" of the speech. Safire responded by expressing admiration for the manner in which Clifford presented "an essentially specious case" with great skill. The exchange touched off a friendly but energetic debate among the two men and other guests.

When Safire described the encounter the following day to Haldeman, he found it was like waving a red flag in front of a bull. The chief of staff launched a passionate attack on Clifford, calling him a Nixon-hater who had helped mire the United States in Vietnam and now had the gall to argue that the only way out was surrender. He told the young speechwriter that he should avoid socializing with the likes of Clifford.

Eventually, the administration's distaste for Clifford led to more than simple words. In 1972, Nixon ordered Haldeman to have a friendly official at the Internal Revenue Service obtain Clifford's tax files and begin a full audit of his finances in a search for ammunition to silence the outspoken lawyer. When the audit request was disclosed at the Senate Watergate hearings in 1973, Clifford said that he had never seen any evidence of the tax investigation. "They can plow through those returns by the hour and they won't find a dollar," he said. "My instruction twenty-three years ago when I left the Truman administration was: 'If there is a serious question about an item, pay it.' I have followed that policy ever since."

The Senate hearings stemming from the bungled 1972 break-in at Democratic national headquarters in Washington also revealed that Clifford and Paul Warnke had earned spots on Nixon's "enemies list." However, Clifford's name had been misspelled as "Gifford."

Clifford had taken great delight in Nixon's plight from the earliest days of the disclosure of the break-in and White House involvement in the subsequent cover-up by *Washington Post* reporters Bob Woodward and Carl Bernstein. In those first weeks, the *Post* was often alone in its pursuit of the story, and the White House regularly and vigorously attacked the newspaper.

Early one morning in early January 1973, when the newspaper had a particularly harsh story about Nixon, *Post* editor Ben Bradlee's telephone rang at home.

"Mr. Bradlee, I want to tell you something," said the familiar voice. "I want to tell you this. This morning I got up and put on my robe and walked to the door and opened the door. It was a beautiful day and I picked up my newspaper and looked at it and I looked up and said, 'Thank God for the *Washington Post.*' "

With that comment, the caller hung up, leaving Bradlee thinking, "If Clark Clifford is calling me up, we are going to win."

Later that day, Clifford wrote a glowing letter to Katharine Graham, the newpaper's publisher. "As the usual year end awards are being given out, I want you to know that I wish to bestow the newspaper Congressional Medal of Honor on the Washington Post," wrote Clifford. "You have the support and commendation of decent people all over the country."

What Clifford had no way of knowing on that day when he praised the newspaper's aggressive coverage of Watergate was that it held the seeds of his own torment. Washington was forever changed by the aftermath of that bungled burglary. The harsh spotlight shined on Nixon and his administration would not be turned off once the crooks were thrown from office. From that day forward, every politician and government official in the city would be fair game for a suspicious and sometimes cynical press corps. Eventually, the intensity of such scrutiny would extend to those who tried to influence government, men such as Clark Clifford.

Watergate also provoked a bizarre incident at the White House in the fall of 1973. In the famous "Saturday Night Massacre," Elliot Richardson resigned as attorney general rather than fire Archibald Cox, the special prosecutor who was investigating Watergate. Cox, of course, was fired anyway, but at great cost to Nixon's public image. In an effort to weather the building storm, Melvin Laird, who had been Nixon's first secretary of defense, was recalled to the White House as a special assistant. At a meeting of presidential advisers in the Oval Office to discuss a new special prosecutor, Laird said, "Mr. President, your real problem here is credibility, and I think you ought to seriously consider Clark Clifford."

Leaping from his chair, Richard Nixon exclaimed, "Mel, are you out of your fucking mind?"

17

A Precursor to BCCI

CLIFFORD'S CLASHES with the Nixon administration enhanced his fame and, despite the antagonism from the White House, did nothing to detract from his financial condition. "The Nixon years were for making money," he once confided.

A story circulated about Clifford in those days that was probably apocryphal but still said a great deal about his position as a fixture in the Washington legal and political community. It went like this: the general counsel of a major corporation called Clifford to ask what the company should do about a certain piece of tax legislation in Congress. "Nothing," Clifford responded a few days later, sending a bill for $20,000. The general counsel wrote back demanding a complete explanation for the size of the fee. "Because I said so," responded Clifford in a letter, which contained a bill for another $5,000.

The law firm did not seem to lose any business because of Clifford's prominent opposition to the war, although most of the firm's leading clients were corporations run by conservative Republicans. Clifford rarely discussed politics with his clients unless they involved the politics of the client's particular case. Business was business, and business was good in the Nixon years. However, Clifford's friend and fellow Johnson confidant Abe Fortas did not fare as well under the harsh scrutiny of the Republican administration.

The Republicans in the White House were eager to reconfigure the Supreme Court in a more conservative image, and Fortas was an inviting target.

Back in the fall of 1968, when Fortas was under consideration for chief justice, William Lambert, a reporter with *Life*, had pursued information that the justice had been a paid consultant to a foundation owned by Florida businessman and stock manipulator Louis Wolfson. Lambert had been unable to come up with enough information for a story then, but in April 1969 he noticed that Fortas had recused himself from the Supreme Court's decision not to hear an appeal by Wolfson and a business partner, who had been convicted in 1967 of violating securities laws.

This time, Lambert got help from a source in government, most likely someone at the Internal Revenue Service. He assembled the details of the story and was able to get confirming information from the Nixon Justice Department. Will Wilson, the assistant attorney general in charge of the criminal division, met with Lambert and later acknowledged, "In all candor, we wanted Fortas off the court."

Lambert's story hit the newsstands on May 9, 1969. He revealed that Fortas had received a check for $20,000 from Wolfson's foundation in January 1966, a time in which Wolfson was struggling to avoid indictment for stock manipulation. Although Fortas returned the check eleven months later, Lambert still found that the payment raised serious ethical questions.

The disclosure created a frenzy among Washington reporters, who staked out Fortas's house and dug for new details. On May 13, Fortas summoned Clifford to his chambers, where Justice Douglas was already deep in conversation with his beleaguered colleague. Over two days of meetings, Douglas steadfastly argued that Fortas should refuse to resign. Repeatedly, Douglas pointed out that he had weathered similar attacks on his relationship with the Parvin Foundation, a tax-exempt organization that had paid Douglas an annual fee of $12,000. Douglas had been able to protect himself by arguing that no one associated with the Parvin Foundation had ever had business before the court.

Fortas saw some hope in his colleague's argument. After all, he maintained, he had done nothing wrong. He had not interfered in any matters involving Wolfson and had recused himself when the case came before the court.

But, as Douglas later remembered those crucial meetings, Clifford countered that the attacks on Fortas would be unrelenting, fueled in no small part by the unpopularity of former President Johnson and Nixon's fervor to appoint a new justice. Fortas had no choice but to resign, said Clifford. At the end of two days of difficult debate, Fortas accepted Clifford's advice. He sent his resignation letter to Nixon late on the afternoon of May 14.

In later years, Fortas told Douglas and others that he wished he had fought the charges and remained on the bench. As Fortas changed his mind over time, Clifford tried to alter his own position on the matter. In his memoir, Clifford wrote that he had actually urged Fortas to stand and fight, a recollection that contradicted the version provided by Douglas, who was dead by the time Clifford's book was published in 1991.

Clifford's recounting of his position appears to be little more than convenient revisionism. But another observation in his book about the justice's downfall was eerily prescient when it came to Clifford's own life. "What had driven a man of such exceptional intelligence to bring himself down through such dubious financial arrangements?" Clifford wrote of Fortas. "I would ask myself this question many times in the years that followed."

Clifford had a second observation about the lessons of the Fortas affair, as he explained to an interviewer at the time. "Practicing law in Washington is like a combat soldier walking through a minefield," he said. "One mistake and you've had it."

Clifford was walking through some minefields himself in those days. Before joining the Defense Department, he had been a member of the board of directors of the National Bank of Washington. Seventy-five percent of the bank was owned by the United Mine Workers, which gave one of the most notoriously corrupt unions in the country control of the institution. When he returned to private practice, Clifford had rejoined the bank board. Among his fellow directors was A. W. "Tony" Boyle, the president of the union.

Since the middle sixties, Boyle had been under attack by dissident union members under the leadership of Joseph A. Yablonski. In December 1969, Yablonski and his family were murdered by gunmen who broke into their house, and suspicion centered on Boyle. With Boyle under scrutiny for the murder, investigators also began to focus on the union's relationship with the National Bank of Washington. Among the discoveries was that the union bosses had been milking their own members' pension fund by keeping up to $70 million in noninterest-bearing accounts at the bank. The money that should have gone for interest was being converted to profits for the bank, which wound up bankrolling limousines, lavish salaries, and other abuses for Boyle and his confederates.

In November 1970, *Washington Monthly*, a feisty liberal magazine, published a lengthy and damning article focusing on the bank board's blind acquiescence in the union's abuse of the bank at the expense of its pensioners. The article, entitled "Moral Blindness on the Distinguished Bank Board," made it clear that anyone on the board, particularly a lawyer of Clark Clifford's standing, had had a fiduciary responsibility to the miners' pension fund. Instead, the magazine charged, Clifford and other liberals had fronted for a scheme to bilk the pensioners to pay for limousines and inflated salaries for corrupt union executives.

Washington Monthly had a small but influential readership in the liberal community, so Clifford could not let the article pass. The day it ran he telephoned Charles Peters, the magazine's editor, and indulged in the sort of flattery that had worked so many times before.

"Mr. Peters," he said gravely, "I want you to know that I read your magazine from cover to cover every issue. I want you to know how deeply I am concerned about the matters you have raised. And you can be sure I will examine them most carefully."

Peters, a great admirer of Clifford's from the earliest days of the Truman administration, believed him. He kept waiting for Clifford to step forward and condemn the manner in which the bank had been run and repudiate Boyle. It never happened. Peters recalled that he was struck that the mainstream press never picked up on Clifford's role as a director of the bank and his refusal to step down when the abuses were disclosed. "It was totally left alone because of the tremendous power of Clifford's name," Peters said later. "How could the *Washington Monthly* be right to question this Washington monument? The press figured we must have gotten it wrong, so they never picked up the story."

A year later Clifford resigned quietly from the board. He said his action had nothing to do with a recent decision by a federal court judge finding the bank and its majority stockholder, the United Mine Workers, liable for $11.5 million in damages for conspiracy and mismanagement of the union pension fund. Instead, Clifford said the demands of his law practice and his expected involvement in the 1972 presidential campaign would make him too busy to fulfill his duties as a director of the National Bank of Washington.

Clifford would not be a candidate for president in 1972. That was a dream that had died an uneventful death during his time away from the heady atmosphere of the Pentagon and the White House. Instead, Clifford aligned himself with Senator Edmund Muskie, the Maine Democrat, who had been Humphrey's 1968 running mate and was the front-runner for the party's presidential nomination. Clifford quickly emerged as Muskie's chief foreign policy adviser, giving the candidate instant credibility on foreign policy and adding a new twist to Clifford's continued criticism of Nixon's war policy. Along with a forum for his antiwar sentiments, Clifford undoubtedly saw his role in the Muskie campaign as an opportunity to fulfill his ambition to become secretary of state.

At one point early in 1972, Muskie's top strategists were sitting in Clifford's office discussing the senator's plans for a trip to Moscow. Nixon had taken a tough line with the Soviets on nuclear arms control, slowing talks aimed at developing a treaty to control the spread of nuclear arms. Muskie could not decide whether to criticize the slow pace of the talks or remain silent. The criticism would make him a hero to Democrats, but he also might be seen as meddling in the negotiations for political gain.

"Senator Muskie," interrupted Clifford, "I once tried a case in St. Louis where I put a witness on the stand and I was deciding whether or not to ask him a certain question. I went ahead and, oh boy, I wished I hadn't. He gave the wrong answer and it was very painful to my client. After the trial was over, a much older colleague of mine told me, 'Young man, I have a rule that may help you in the future. Never kick a turd on a hot day.' "

With that down-home aphorism, the debate ended in laughter and Muskie remained silent on the arms talks.

It turned out that Clifford had backed the wrong candidate. When Senator George McGovern won the Democratic nomination in August, Clifford telephoned him immediately and invited him over to his law office so that he could give him a contribution. "I think he wanted to get a feeling of what kind of a candidate I was going to be," McGovern said later.

During the meeting, McGovern mentioned his campaign theme, "Come Home America," a phrase from a Martin Luther King Jr. speech. He asked Clifford what he thought of it.

"Well, I don't know what it means," said Clifford.

McGovern was puzzled. Clifford had not grasped the essential message of his upcoming campaign, ending the Vietnam War, bringing home the troops, and reuniting the country. Nonetheless, Clifford gave McGovern a $25,000 contribution and promised an equal amount later in the campaign. However, as McGovern slipped in the polls, so did

Clifford's pledge of more money. In the end, McGovern was defeated resoundingly by President Nixon.

The Democratic loss at the polls was followed by two other, more personal losses for Clifford. On December 26, 1972, former President Harry Truman died. He was buried two days later in the courtyard of the Truman presidential library in his hometown of Independence, Missouri. With space in the library auditorium limited, only 250 people were invited. Among them were Averell Harriman, Judge Sam Rosenman, and Clark Clifford. It was the simple affair requested by a plain man. There was no eulogy or hymns. The only person who spoke was a Baptist minister, who read a prayer. Then the former president's body was taken to the courtyard gravesite.

As he sat in the auditorium that day, Clifford reflected on the man who had launched his career and felt a deep sense of satisfaction for what Harry Truman had accomplished. Truman, with only a high school education, had gone from Independence to the White House. He had served ably. In Clifford's mind, Truman had saved the free world. Then he had retired with dignity and grace. "Here was a life wonderfully well lived," Clifford thought to himself. "Here was a man who made the most that anybody could make of his life. I'm sorry he is gone, but it was a great life, well lived."

A month later, Clifford found himself attending the funeral of another former president whom he had served. His thoughts at the services for former President Lyndon Johnson at the end of January contrasted sharply with those he had at Truman's service.

Even at his death, Johnson remained disillusioned with his old friend over the favorable treatment Clifford had received in the press and the criticism that Johnson had suffered. Several times since he left the White House, Johnson had complained to interviewers and others that Clifford had gotten too much credit. But as Clifford sat at Johnson's funeral, he remembered LBJ with great affection and admiration.

"Here was a man who, except for the machinations of fate, would have been unquestionably one of our most illustrious presidents," Clifford said later as he described his thoughts on that day. "His Great Society program was magnificent. He had lived with these poor people, blacks and Hispanics. And he did something wonderful for them. What an unfortunate stroke of fate that Vietnam came into his life. Most people don't remember his Great Society program. They remember an unfortunate war and they blame it to a great extent on President Johnson."

It did not occur to Clifford to reflect on the ways in which fate might alter history's perception of him in those days when he watched two more old colleagues buried. He was still riding high, energetic, and busy. Indeed, Clifford's popularity and prosperity meant that the firm could be selective in choosing clients.

A few weeks before Truman's death, Clifford received a call from a friend that led to one of his most unusual visits with a prospective client. The friend said Robert Vesco needed some legal advice and gave Clifford a number where he could get in touch with Vesco. Clifford walked down the hall to Warnke's office and asked what his partner knew about Vesco. Warnke did not know much either, but he said he would find out.

Vesco had fled the United States earlier in 1972 after being accused of looting an investment fund of $250 million. At the time, he was the most infamous white-collar criminal in the world, evading American law enforcement by escaping to Nicaragua, Costa Rica, Cuba, and the Bahamas. The same year, Vesco had contributed $200,000 to Nixon's reelection campaign.

The primary complaint against him in the United States was the accusation by the Securities and Exchange Commission that he had bilked investors and moved $250 million to foreign banks. Vesco had hired several law firms in an attempt to stop the SEC action. Now he wanted to hire Clifford to lobby Democrats in Congress.

Clifford and Warnke agreed to talk to Vesco, and on the morning of December 2 the two lawyers boarded the fugitive's private Boeing 707 jet at Dulles International Airport. The jet had a fully equipped galley, a dining room, couches, and an office for Vesco, complete with mahogany desk and a conference room. There also were a small gym, an airborne sauna, and, behind a beaded curtain, a discotheque.

As Clifford and Warnke settled into their comfortable chairs, a hostess in a Playboy bunny costume offered them a drink. They declined. About three hours later, the plane landed at Nassau International Airport and the two lawyers, sweating in their business suits as they passed through the one-story, un-air-conditioned terminal, found themselves greeted by a smiling man who looked vaguely familiar.

"Hi," said the man with a wave. "I'm Donald Nixon. I guess you know my brother."

They were driven to Vesco's house on Brace Bridge Road, where they were introduced to Vesco and several other lawyers who represented him. Over lunch, Vesco outlined his problems for them, starting with the SEC and ending with the $200,000 contribution to the Nixon campaign. He already had plenty of Republican lawyers to deal with the administration, he explained. What he wanted from Clifford and Warnke was their help in lobbying Democrats in Congress for some sort of action to get the SEC off his back.

Excusing themselves from the table, the two Washington lawyers walked out into the bright sun and discussed the case. Neither man was interested in it. It would involve a messy job of direct lobbying, something that they wanted to avoid. Returning to the house, Clifford explained to Vesco that he felt the financier already had enough lawyers. He said that he and Warnke could see no discernible legal problem for which he needed their services, so they were politely declining the case.

Clifford also turned down another notorious financier in the seventies. Adnan Khashoggi had made a fortune brokering sales of American aircraft and other defense goods to the kingdom of Saudi Arabia, where he had ties to the royal family. In some quarters, the high-living Khashoggi was described as the richest man in the world. When a Senate subcommittee and the SEC began examining whether Khashoggi's huge commissions were actually bribes, he tried to hire Clifford.

An intermediary first raised the subject with Sam McIlwain, and then Khashoggi himself telephoned Warnke. Khashoggi could not imagine that anyone would turn down the fat fees he could pay, and he even told reporters that he had retained Clark Clifford to represent him. However, Clifford agreed with Warnke that the firm should not take on the wealthy middleman because the case involved the Defense Department.

The Vesco and Khashoggi incidents illustrate that there were certain kinds of clients Clifford would not represent. His friend, trial lawyer Edward Bennett Williams, loved to test his courtroom skills in defense of mobsters and other assorted criminals, and his victories on their behalf were celebrated. Clifford practiced a different kind of law, and lending his prestige and influence to two high-profile wheeler-dealers like Vesco and Khashoggi was outside the bounds of good taste. Particularly in these days when business was rolling in and the law firm's finances were flush.

When Clifford turned sixty-five at the end of 1971, his partners had expected him to begin easing off at work. They felt reasonably sure that he would slowly start to withdraw from the firm and finally begin to enjoy his wealth, which was well in excess of $10 million. Some even thought he would begin to spend more time with his wife.

Marny Clifford continued to spend her summers at the house on Nantucket and much of the winter away on cruises. She always traveled without her husband, who said he could not stand to be confined on a ship and had no interest in sight-seeing. But there were signs that Marny Clifford was not as happy as others may have thought with her solitary travels.

In the midst of a three-month cruise to Africa, she wrote to a friend of her "ghastly homesickness." She closed the letter by writing: "My dearest love to my sweet family and friends. Lovingly Mrs. Livingston. Wonder how my husband is? Must ask Mr. Stanley."

The Clifford marriage was unusual by some standards. They spent a great deal of time apart. Where Clifford could strike even his children as distant and formal, his wife was outwardly warm and loving, with a hearty laugh. She kept the household running and organized their social life, maintaining the friendships for which her husband had little time. Once the children had grown and moved out, she pursued her own interests in interior decorating and cooking, publishing a collection of recipes from famous Washington hostesses.

Reflecting on her mother's relationship with her father years later, Joyce, a psychologist with keen insights into family life, offered a benign assessment. "They had a political life in which the wife is a great champion of her husband, very protective of the man. This was the model of public life when I was growing up in the forties and early fifties. She would become concerned if he were unfairly attacked. She was steady and supportive. She was a very wise counsel. But my mother was always her own person. She created and cultivated a great circle of friends. And she loved Nantucket and the cruises. Dad, well, Dad just wasn't the vacationing type. He was devoted to his work. That was always what was on deck and on tap with him."

Even at retirement age, Clifford remained devoted to his work. He had no intention of reducing his workload, much less retire. As he passed the next birthday and the next, he showed no sign of slacking off. He was still in the office every weekday shortly after nine in the morning and remained at his desk until seven or so at night. Saturdays he showed up to take care of the paperwork and other chores that had accumulated during the week.

Many of the men whom Clifford had served with in government had written their memoirs and then retired. Clifford had discussed the idea of writing a book with several people, but he confided that he feared that writing his autobiography or cooperating in an authorized biography would be viewed as the capstone of a career that he was not yet ready to abandon.

One of those with whom Clifford had these discussions was Harry McPherson, who had gone on from the Johnson White House to become a respected and prominent attorney in Washington. McPherson was extremely fond of Clifford, so one day he brought around a journalist, Michael Janeway, to discuss the idea of writing Clifford's memoirs.

Janeway was the son of the well-known economist Eliot Janeway. Then on the staff of the *Atlantic Monthly*, the son was a great fan of Clifford's. He particularly admired his role during the Vietnam War. Janeway and Clifford met in the lawyer's office to talk about a possible book. Clifford could not decide whether to have an autobiography, with Janeway as his ghost writer, or to permit the journalist access to his files and lengthy interviews for a biography. On one point, however, he was certain: the book would have real commercial value.

After a few meetings, Janeway, who later became dean of the Medill School of Journalism at Northwestern University, wrote to Clifford saying that the most credible book would be a biography, with Janeway granted complete access and total editorial freedom. Clifford wrote back saying that he was not ready for either a biography or an autobiography.

The troubles of the Republicans invigorated Clifford. First, Vice President Agnew resigned to avoid prosecution for taking kickbacks. Then, on August 9, 1974, President Nixon resigned the presidency to avoid impeachment for his role in attempting to cover up the break-in at Democratic headquarters at the Watergate apartment complex in Washington. The elevation of House Minority Leader Gerald Ford to the presidency seemed to open the door for a Democratic challenge. When it came, Clifford hoped to be back in the thick of the political battle. On that count, he was to be disappointed.

Watergate transformed the nation. The ripples of distrust washed over all levels of politics and politicians as the public soured on incumbents and swept them from office. In Suffolk County, outside New York

City, a new slate of county supervisors was elected. One of them was a political neophyte named Joyce Clifford Barrett. She had ridden Watergate to her first public office and, not long afterward, she paid a visit to her father.

"Now, you've been at this many years," she said. "What is your advice for me?"

Clifford had always been closest to Joyce among his three daughters. She had been the daughter with the brains, the Vassar graduate who seemed to be making a success of her life. A few years earlier, she had made her first try for public office by running for the New York State Assembly. She lost, but Hugh Carey, the Democrat who was elected governor of New York that year, praised her when he met her father not long after the election. "Would you be Joyce Clifford Barrett's father?" asked Carey with a smile. Now, with his favorite child on the cusp of a political career, her father thought for a long time before proffering his advice.

Finally he looked up with a smile, steepled his fingers in the trademark gesture that had preceded sharing his wisdom with presidents and tycoons, and said gravely, "Watch the money. In public life, there are a lot of people who come at you and they want you to do things and there is a quid pro quo. So be awfully careful what you accept and who you do business with. There will always be a string attached."

The statement was emblematic of the times. The thesis of politics in America had changed. Watergate had become a symbol and a metaphor for the abuse of government, and it was fashionable to suspect anyone associated with government. For Clifford, this was a change that would have a highly personal impact more than a decade later. The rules of government had altered, and Clifford, although cognizant of the changes, would find himself unwilling or unable to adapt to them.

Averell and Pamela Harriman lived in a beautiful home on N Street in Washington's exclusive Georgetown section, just five blocks from the home of *Washington Post* publisher Katharine Graham. When the aged Harriman had married the much younger Pamela in 1971, she had completely renovated the home, adding such extravagances as a $30,000 four-poster bed and removable glass panels for the sunporch that overlooked the terraced garden.

In February 1976, Clifford sat in the Harrimans' drawing room with the elder statesman and his energetic wife, lawyer Edward Bennett Williams, and a handful of others. The ripples of Watergate were present there, too, as they watched the early television returns projecting that the New Hampshire Democratic primary was being won by Jimmy Carter, the obscure governor of Georgia. The Democrats would regain the White House in 1976, but it was behind the candidacy of a Southern peanut farmer swept from near-obscurity by appealing to the country's anti-Washington mood following Vietnam and Watergate. During his campaign, Carter would draw the loudest applause when he pointed out that he was not a lawyer and he was not from Washington. Indeed, Carter beat President Gerald Ford without consulting anyone in Harriman's drawing room that night or any other members of the Democratic establishment in Washington. Further, the outsider theme that brought Carter to the White House meant that he and his aides had no intention of relying on Washington insiders.

The Carter presidency marked a critical turning point for Clifford. A Democrat was back in the White House, but Clifford was not. Carter would never call Clifford to his side for the sort of important advice his Democratic predecessors had deemed indispensable. There would be White House visits, and some tasks to perform at the request of the president. A diplomatic mission to India. Others to Turkey, Greece, and Cyprus. A ritual participation in ceremonies at Camp David to mark the Israel-Egypt peace accords. As he had been with the previous three Democrats who sat in the Oval Office, Clifford was always available. This time, he was rarely called. And it left Clifford puzzled and disappointed.

"Jimmy Carter, as he is called, is to me the great enigma," Clifford said not long after Carter was out of office. "I'll never solve it, at least in my own mind. He was attractive. He was intelligent, exceedingly articulate. He was honest. He was industrious. Yet in totality, his administration turned out to be a failure. Up he comes from a rural area of Georgia with a tight little group that had been with him ever since he was governor, and they moved in to take over the most difficult and complex job in the world. One would know right off hand that they were not equal to it. His major mistake was his refusal to call in to his administration experienced people who could have been enormously helpful. He should have called in a number of men who had served in the Kennedy and Johnson administrations, young men in their early fifties, who would have come at the drop of a hat. He did not choose to do it. He could have gotten together a little group of very senior men with whom he might have spent an evening every other week. He wouldn't even have to have them for dinner. Just have them come in in the evening and sit around and talk to them about his problems. Now, those suggestions were made. He refused to do it. And as a result, mistakes accumulated."

What Clifford was saying, of course, was that Carter brought his group and excluded Clifford's group, the Wise Men who had guided the nation through the postwar era, Vietnam, and the cold war. Perhaps more than any other lasting effect on Washington, Carter's ascension to power represented the rise of a new generation of leaders in the city's power structure. The process had begun with Kissinger, the academic-turned-professional adviser, but the demise of the establishment was completed by Carter, who disdained Georgetown society and its network of power as foreign to the America he knew.

Times were changing in Washington. For the first time since the city's founding, there were more private sector workers than government workers. And a rapidly growing number of those private sector employees were lobbyists, lawyers, and consultants intent on influencing government, as well as the service industries that thrived on them — restaurants, bars, and hotels. More than five hundred businesses and one thousand trade associations maintained offices in Washington to monitor and influence legislation and regulations that might affect their interests. There were forty thousand lawyers in the city, more than double the total just ten years earlier. New movements, such as the civil rights battle and Ralph Nader's consumer revolution, had spawned a new level of grassroots activists who also demanded a place at the table in Washington. The term "mass lobbying" was born in the late seventies.

Instead of such powerful figures as Kerr and Johnson crafting legislative strategy in Congress, hundreds of well-financed special interest groups were pulling and tugging policy in every direction. "The Power Game," as Hedrick Smith called it in his book of the same name, had changed dramatically.

Clifford never thought of himself as outdated. He remained a proud man, vibrant and healthy, intelligent and capable of prodigious amounts of work. On his seventieth birthday, *Post* publisher Katharine Graham captured his still-burning ambition in a glowing telegram: "You are a model to us all. You have served your country in more ways than it knows. You have been able to reap some rich rewards for work you enjoy doing and excel in. You and your much beloved Marny have been the heads of a dazzling family. Most important of all you have had and have given others a hell of a good time along the way. I know that this birthday is an important one. It marks an important mid-career milestone in all the above."

Clifford was not ready for the rocking chair, but there was uncertainty at his law firm and within Clifford himself over what the future held. These qualms grew in February 1977 when Carter nominated Warnke to be director of the Arms Control and Disarmament Agency, which was responsible for the strategic arms talks with the Russians. Warnke's departure from the firm coincided with the loss of Tom Finney, who had contracted Lou Gehrig's disease in 1976 and, by 1977, could no longer work.

Suddenly, the firm appeared to be in serious trouble. Clifford's strategy of staying small while other firms grew tremendously in the seventies had allowed him to maintain virtually complete control and made him and his partners wealthy. By the middle seventies, the partners were earning $300,000 to $400,000 each and Clifford was taking home up to three times as much. But the small size had kept out fresh blood and new leadership. With Warnke gone, Finney dying, and Glass and McIlwain nearing retirement, there was no one to lead the firm and bring in new business except the aging Clifford. More and more, Clifford seemed to be turning to Bob Altman, still a young associate, for advice and assistance.

In 1977, a group of the lawyers got together secretly and agreed to sound out other firms on the possibility of merging with the Clifford firm. There were quiet talks with senior partners at larger firms, including Hogan and Hartson, who shared the same building on Connecticut Avenue, as well as Covington and Burling and Baker and McKenzie.

At one point, John Kovin approached John Douglas, a respected partner at Covington and Burling. Would Douglas consider coming over to the Clifford firm as the designated successor to Clifford? asked Kovin. Unfortunately for Kovin, Douglas mentioned the approach to Clifford, thinking he must have known about it since Clifford's consent would be essential to any such offer. But Clifford had been kept in the dark. After politely thanking Douglas, he immediately summoned Kovin to his office and delivered a tongue lashing to the law partner who had once mowed his lawn.

"I have no intention of allowing anyone else to decide the future of the firm," he told Kovin sharply. "Further, John, I have no intention of leaving the law practice to which I have devoted my life."

Most important, said Clifford, he resented Kovin or anyone else going behind his back about matters regarding the law firm. He had been in control for nearly three decades and he deeply resented any covert actions by his partners.

The anger was genuine. He was not about to relinquish control much less merge with another firm. And the sharp exchange with Kovin, which the younger lawyer described to others in the firm, served to squelch all attempts to remake the firm.

Nonetheless, Clifford himself was worried about the loss of Warnke and Finney. He was a wealthy man who could have retired in comfort, but Clifford was determined to maintain the prosperity and prominence of the law firm that bore his name. He was too proud to watch all that he had worked to build become absorbed into the anonymity of one of the mega-firms. Nor would he stand by while his firm slipped from the top tier. If there was no one in the firm of real stature to assist him right now, he would do it himself, pretty much as he always had.

Against this backdrop of transformation in Washington's hierarchy and turmoil in his law firm, the aging lawyer returned from a round of golf on the Saturday of Labor Day weekend in 1977 to find a message that promised him a chance to get back under the big top. Bert Lance had called while Clifford was out. The president's budget director, who was in trouble up to his ears after less than a year in one of the administration's most sensitive posts, wanted to talk with him immediately. Clifford could imagine the door to the White House opening, envision himself counseling Lance and the president on how to deal with the first real crisis of Carter's presidency. What Clark Clifford had no way of predicting was the tragedy that would be spawned by that particular telephone call.

18

A Fateful Introduction

THROUGHOUT THE SUMMER of 1977, T. Bertram Lance, the onetime Georgia banker and full-time good ol' boy who had been brought to Washington by Carter as director of the Office of Management and Budget, had been besieged by the press and Congress. The attention focused on his banking activities before Carter appointed him to one of the most important posts in the federal government.

Lance had become president of the National Bank of Georgia after buying a controlling interest in the Atlanta institution. Now it turned out that his stock purchases had been financed by two large New York banks, Manufacturers Hanover Trust Company and Chemical Bank. After receiving the loans, Lance had arranged for his bank to open correspondent banking accounts with the New York institutions. Adding to the affable Lance's troubles, *New York Times* columnist William Safire suggested that he had received a third loan, for $3.4 million, from the First National Bank of Chicago because of his closeness to Carter, not his creditworthiness.

The Senate Governmental Affairs Committee had cleared Lance of any wrongdoing in July 1977, but the allegations kept piling up. In mid-August, the Office of the Comptroller of the Currency, which regulates national banks, issued a report criticizing Lance's banking practices, although it found nothing illegal in his conduct. Pressure for his resignation mounted. Abraham Ribicoff, the Connecticut Democrat who was chairman of the committee, and Charles Percy of Illinois, the senior Republican on the committee, both urged Carter to fire his budget director to avoid a protracted Senate fight.

Clifford had met Bert Lance briefly before, but did not know him well. When he returned Lance's call that Saturday evening, the lawyer readily agreed to meet with Lance early the following afternoon at the Old Executive Office Building next to the White House.

After passing through the security checkpoint inside the building and being escorted to Lance's office, Clifford found a man near the end of his rope. While the president had supported him in public, Lance confided that privately Carter and his senior advisers wanted him to resign. In fact, he and his wife, La Belle, were supposed to meet with Carter on Labor Day after the president returned from a weekend at Camp David. In his deep drawl, Lance told Clifford that he fully expected the president to ask for his resignation. Lance, a large and friendly man, told Clifford that he truly believed he had done nothing wrong and that he wanted to stay and fight.

Clifford could see that this was not exactly the situation he had envisioned. Instead of working with Lance on behalf of the president, there was a chance he would come into conflict with the man in the Oval Office, or at least with the Carter advisers who were trying to jettison Lance.

If he were to become the budget director's lawyer, cautioned Clifford, he would be obligated to put Lance's interests ahead of those of the president if they diverged. While the alliances were still uncertain, one element of the strategy was clear to Clifford. Lance should not resign.

"If you resign, no one will ever pay any attention to your defense," said Clifford. "If I am to represent you, I want to fight for your chance to defend yourself against each and every charge that has been made against you. If you defend yourself while director of OMB, you will have national attention."

Carter's helicopter touched down on the White House lawn at 2:44 on Labor Day afternoon. By three o'clock, Clifford was meeting with the president and his top assistant, Hamilton Jordan, and Jody Powell, his press secretary, in Carter's small, private office just off the Oval Office. The meeting lasted ten minutes. Clifford informed the president that Lance wanted to stay and fight, that he wanted the opportunity to defend himself before the Senate and the American public. Carter asked a few questions, then turned to Jordan and said, "This is the right course of action." Clifford thanked the president and left.

A few minutes later, Lance and his wife were escorted into the same office. Carter told his good friend the budget director that he would have the chance to defend himself, but Lance left filled with doubt about his future.

The decision to allow Lance to remain created uneasiness at the White House. There was genuine fear that Lance's troubles would spread to Carter less than nine months after the president took office as a reformer and outsider. The concern was rooted in the fact that Lance's bank had been the biggest single lender to the Carter family's peanut warehouse business in 1976. There was concern that that debt, which had reached $4.7 million, could be characterized as the de facto financing of Carter's presidential campaign, which would have been illegal. Reporters were beginning to probe the sensitive area.

Just before Labor Day weekend, Robert Zelnick, an ABC-TV investigative producer, had telephoned a White House staffer to check out a tip that the Lance allegations "touch the president." Further, a former federal prosecutor in Atlanta was claiming that Carter administration officials had concealed information on Lance from the Senate committee during his confirmation hearings.

Now, with Clifford in his corner, Lance was not going quietly. The budget director was scheduled to testify before the Senate committee on September 8, but on the Tuesday after Labor Day Clifford paid a visit to Ribicoff and Percy in Ribicoff's office. He convinced them to grant a one-week delay so that he could help prepare Lance for the testimony.

Clifford had set things in motion, but to carry out the details he turned not to Sam McIlwain, who assisted him on most congressional matters, but to Bob Altman. Since joining the firm in 1971, Altman had worked hard and impressed his colleagues as a bright, energetic lawyer. A year earlier, he had been made a partner. During his tenure, Clifford had given the young man some specific assignments and he executed them well. So when he came back from his meeting with Ribicoff and Percy, Clifford dropped by Altman's small office.

"Drop everything," said Clifford. "I want you to devote full time to Bert Lance."

The Lance defense team was based in the beige-carpeted conference room adjoining Clifford's office. There, Altman met every morning at seven o'clock with Lance to prepare for his testimony. The two men would spend the day, and long into the night, going over every detail of the charges against the budget director and scrutinizing every avenue of response and rebuttal. Clifford occasionally stopped by to consult and offer advice, and he helped craft the basic strategy. The plan was to counterattack, to go after the senators, to raise doubts about their fairness in handling the allegations against Lance. It was a tried-and-true technique of trial attorneys, one that Clifford had employed many times back in St. Louis. Clifford later explained the strategy by comparing it to a criminal case. "The idea is to get the trial directed toward trying someone else," he said. "Turn the case into a trial of the main prosecution witness. Not that I had ever heard of anyone applying this technique to the Senate."

The plan was kept under wraps. When the White House called for updates, Clifford would tell them that they were still at work. Finally, the night before Lance was to testify, Clifford permitted Hamilton Jordan to come to the conference room for a preview. Arriving in Bermuda shorts and a casual shirt, Jordan read the statement and then turned to Lance. "This is the toughest statement I have ever seen," he said in surprise. "You are attacking both the chairman and the ranking minority member. I think it goes much too far. I hope you know what you are doing."

On September 15, Bert Lance, flanked by Clifford and Altman, walked into the Senate committee room to tell his story in a nationally televised hearing. In the minutes before he spoke, the room was buzzing with expectation. Senators, journalists, and spectators alike bustled around, whispering to each other, craning for a peek at Lance's prepared testimony. To heighten the surprise and make sure that everyone listened to Lance, Clifford and Altman had refused to provide advance copies of the text. The power of Clifford's presence in the room that day was recalled later by Jack Nelson, who was covering the hearing for the *Los Angeles Times*. Annoyed by the lack of decorum, Clifford, who was standing beside Lance, surveyed the room with a look of mild consternation on his face. Then he simply raised a finger into the air. The cavernous chamber fell silent.

In a two-hour statement, Lance lashed out at the committee for ignoring his rights and treating him unfairly. The impressive performance won him applause at the end, and the senators spent the first half hour of the question period apologizing to the budget director. At a point where the questioning about some of Lance's transactions got tough, Clifford interjected calmly that Lance had determined that "the simplest thing to do was pay off the note and he paid it off."

Following the hearing, Lance returned to Clifford's office with his two lawyers. As Clifford sat behind his desk, he folded his hands and proclaimed, "Bert, I'm so proud of you. That was the best performance I've seen since Sarah Bernhardt graced the stage." When Lance said,

"Thank you, Mr. Clifford," his lawyer bestowed yet another accolade. Smiling, he said, "Bert, you can call me Clark."

Washington Star columnist Mary McGrory described the session as "a stunning reversal." Hedrick Smith of the *New York Times* said, "For the moment, he managed not only to push Senator Percy into regretful apologies about news leaks and misinterpretations, but also to win predictions from some members of the Senate committee that there would be a 'backlash of sympathy.'" Edward Bennett Williams praised Clifford, calling the job he had done "the greatest demonstration of superiority of free enterprise over government that I'd ever seen." Tommy the Cork Corcoran telephoned Clifford and told him, "I haven't seen anything like that since I saw Houdini get out of a safe underwater." Calls, letters, and telegrams flooded the White House: 2,012 supported Lance, 245 were against him.

The reprieve was short-lived. Three days after Lance's appearance, Robert Byrd of West Virginia, the Senate majority leader, told Carter that Lance would still have to resign to avoid a nasty, protracted battle. On the afternoon of September 19, a Monday, Carter told Lance that it would be best if he resigned. The details were worked out over the following two days, with Clifford talking frequently with Carter on the telephone as he and Altman helped Lance write his resignation letter. At a press conference on September 21, it was announced that the president had accepted Lance's resignation "with sorrow and regret."

After he returned to Georgia, Lance faced a series of legal investigations and a federal indictment. Clifford and Altman worked as advisers to his defense team, with Altman flying to Atlanta weekly for a period. Eventually all of the charges against Lance were either dismissed or rejected by a jury.

In some quarters of the capital, Clifford's representation of Lance before the Senate committee had been interpreted as a favor to the president. Carter, many old Washington hands presumed, had finally begun to play the game by their rules. For years, some journalists mistakenly reported that it was Carter himself who had summoned Clifford to the case.

Correcting the record at the time would have served the interests of neither Lance nor Clifford. The budget director wanted to cling as tightly as possible to Carter as he fought the charges against him in Congress and later in court. And there was no reason for Clifford to counter the mistaken notion that he had performed a service for yet another Democratic president. The truth was that Clifford had taken a case that put him into some small conflict with the president, that he had taken it at the request of Lance, not Carter, and that the budget director had been charged a handsome fee for his services.

"My Atlanta lawyer had been representing me and we talked about what was going on in Washington," recalled Lance later. "He said, 'I can't do anything in Washington. You really need somebody up there.' So we talked about a few names, and I decided to call Mr. Clifford. It was never my recollection that President Carter called him. I called Mr. Clifford that weekend."

Both Clifford and Lance disputed accounts at the time that the work had been done for free. Clifford said that he charged Lance "a reasonable fee." And Lance said he certainly remembered paying, explaining, "I paid him big time. If it was pro bono, I want to know where the refund window is."

Despite the fact that Clifford had only postponed his departure from Washington, Lance remained grateful to him. The budget director had gained the opportunity to tell his side of the story to the American people, and he believed he left with his reputation intact. Lance felt a great debt to the lawyer, and he was determined to find a way to repay him beyond his legal fee. When he did, Lance would set in motion a series of events with an outcome that no one could have predicted.

Three weeks after Lance resigned, Clifford suffered a heart attack. His wife had been out of town visiting one of their daughters and Clifford was sitting at home alone on a Saturday night. Suddenly he felt a sharp pain in his chest. He telephoned his physician and then drove himself to Georgetown University Hospital, where the pain was diagnosed as a heart attack.

With the exception of his bout with hepatitis, Clifford's health had always been good. He had avoided cancer, which had claimed his father, mother, and sister, and remained strong and active. Those deaths had left Clifford with an almost phobic hatred of hospitals and, within days of his admission after the heart attack, he insisted on being allowed to return to his home. However, he was ordered by his physician to restrict his work schedule for several months.

While he continued to go into the office almost every day, he usually left by noon and spent the remainder of the day relaxing at home. Marny Clifford remained at her husband's side during those weeks of recovery, and he was visited regularly by daughters Joyce and Randall, along with his grandchildren. Margery, by this time living in California and long estranged from her family, was unable to make the trip home to see her father.

The heart attack underscored the concerns of the other partners over the future of the law firm and its undisputed head, who was approaching seventy-one. For nearly thirty years, Clifford had resisted expanding the firm or hiring anyone who approached him as an equal. Columnist Jack Anderson, a close observer of the Washington scene and Clifford, said, "He was the sun and the other lawyers were satellites."

Although Sam McIlwain and Carson Glass had been there from the start, neither had enough influence to count with Clifford when it came to key decisions. By this time, Tom Finney was gone from the firm and he would die in 1978. Paul Warnke was absent, too, serving as chief arms control negotiator in the Carter administration. While neither Finney nor Warnke had been Clifford's equal within the firm, both had exercised some influence over his decisions. Now that small measure of checks and balances was gone. Into this vacuum stepped Bob Altman.

The Lance case had marked the beginning of the closest working relationship of Clifford's legal career. On the surface, it mirrored Clifford's role as a protégé of Jacob Lashly back in St. Louis. In this case, however, the bonds between the two men would grow much deeper. In Altman, Clifford would discover something rare — another person with a willingness to work as hard as Clifford and a determination to succeed that matched Clifford's own single-mindedness. None of the other lawyers who worked with Clifford had exhibited the traits that earned Altman a place at Clifford's right hand. Over the objections and jealousies of the more senior partners, Clifford came to rely more and more on the bright young lawyer who seemed so eager to please and willing to devote himself to his job. At the age of thirty-one, Altman was anointed crown prince, first among those who toiled in the shadow of Clark Clifford.

"He rose substantially in my estimation," Clifford said later. "The relationship went far beyond a young lawyer working for an older lawyer. I would take pleasure in imparting to him all that I had learned in my years of practice."

Indeed, their relationship would become something akin to father and son. Altman began to dress like his mentor, wearing dark-colored, double-breasted suits, and he affected some of the older man's gestures, such as steepling his fingers when he spoke. Clifford would serve as Altman's best man at his marriage to actress Lynda Carter of "Wonder Woman" fame, and the couple would name their first child after the elder lawyer.

Yet Altman lacked the stature and experience of Finney or Warnke, let alone Clifford himself. The other lawyers in the firm still mocked their situation, referring to the law firm as "Snow White and the Seven Dwarfs." But the situation was no joking matter. Another prominent Washington lawyer, who was close to Clifford in those years, described its true significance this way: "There was no mechanism at his firm to make him stop and consider whether to accept a case. It was very much a one-man firm and there was no committee to review sensitive matters for potential dangers, conflicts, or bad appearances."

Early in his administration, President Carter had assigned minor tasks to some of Washington's establishment figures. Clifford, for example, had served as his special envoy to try to deal with insoluble conflicts between the Greeks and Turks in the eastern Mediterranean and had taken on some smaller tasks. But Carter rebuffed all efforts to seek serious advice from Clifford and those like him. Robert Strauss, the Texas lawyer who became Carter's chief political troubleshooter and later envoy to the Middle East, once urged Carter and his chief outside adviser, Atlanta businessman Charles Kirbo, to listen to Clifford and others. Kirbo responded, "I think those people are just unhappy because they couldn't get a job."

Carter continued, as he had from almost the beginning of his term, to decline in the polls. Oddly, he seemed to have even less use for the lawyer who had tried to salvage his budget director's good name and, by extension, the reputation of the president.

John White, a politically savvy Texan, had been serving as deputy secretary of the Agriculture Department when Carter chose him to be chairman of the Democratic National Committee in late 1977. One of the first things White did was call on Clifford. The two men had a friendly meeting in the lawyer's office. A few days later, White mentioned to Carter that he had consulted Clifford on some political matters and relayed some of Clifford's advice. The president looked at him closely, raised his pale blue eyes, and said sarcastically, "And what else did the Wise Man say?" White never mentioned Clifford's name again to the president.

For his part, Clifford bemoaned Carter's decision to ignore him and the remainder of the Washington establishment. "He was very distressed that Carter didn't consult him, that his advice wasn't wanted," recalled Hugh Sidey of *Time*. "He once told me, 'This is a very unwise move by President Carter. He hasn't asked any advice of people who have been through this before.' Of course, it was really his own case he was making." Another time, Clifford complained, "The Georgians want to do it their own way. They don't want any gray eminences around."

Clifford, always possessed by an actor's awareness of image and presence, even found fault with Carter's speaking voice. "A speech coach can train a person's speaking voice the way a very fine singing instructor can train a person's singing," Clifford, whose voice was such a vital part of his persona, explained to an interviewer. "But you can't tell a president about that. You can't sit down with a president and say, 'Mr. President, your voice is very unfortunate.' "

But Clifford did not air his reservations publicly, and certainly not with the president himself. Rather, he sometimes wrote Carter the kind of glowing notes he had showered on Truman and Johnson. For instance, in a letter following Carter's talk before the annual Washington press corps dinner in May 1977, Clifford gushed, "Your appearance before the White House Correspondents dinner Saturday night was a spectacular success. Your humor was delightful and your delivery superb."

Later, when the president had to hold a press conference to defend his brother Billy's dealings with the outlaw government of Libya, Clifford wrote him a letter praising the session. "Your press conference with reference to your brother was not only the best press conference you have had, but it was the best conference any president has had," declared Clifford.

If Jimmy Carter and his Georgia White House felt they could run Washington without Clark Clifford, there were plenty of others who were still eager for his advice. One was Richard Helms, the veteran CIA officer, who had gotten to know Clifford during the Kennedy and Johnson years.

Helms has been described as the quintessential CIA man. For thirty years, he held key positions in the agency, including six years as director. In 1973, Richard Nixon had appointed Helms ambassador to Iran. During his tenure there, he became the target of two investigations by the Senate, beginning with the Watergate Committee and ending with the Senate Select Committee on Intelligence. Numerous times he was required to return to Washington from Tehran to testify before the committees. On many of those occasions, he had met with Clifford to get a sense of the seriousness of the inquiries and how he should respond.

In 1976, before leaving his post as ambassador, Helms learned from two Democratic friends in Washington that he was under investigation by the Justice Department for lying to the Senate Foreign Relations Committee in 1973 about CIA involvement in the Chilean elections of 1970. In his testimony, Helms had denied that the CIA had assisted the multinational company ITT in a failed attempt to stop the election of leftist Salvador Allende. By 1977, after he had left Tehran, the investigation was serious enough that Helms thought he needed a criminal lawyer. What occurred in the following months was a classic lesson in the way Washington lawyers operate behind closed doors.

First, Helms met with Clifford, who he expected would have easy access to the Carter Justice Department. But Clifford rarely took on criminal matters, so he suggested that Helms turn to Edward Bennett Williams, the city's most renowned criminal lawyer. Helms and Williams knew each other. In fact, Williams also had provided advice to Helms earlier in the seventies. When he telephoned Williams this time, the ebullient lawyer was filled with reassurance. "Stop worrying about all this," Williams urged Helms. "This is ridiculous. If they indict you, I will represent you."

As witnesses were called before the federal grand jury in Washington, the defense team formed a pretty clear picture of the evidence being assembled by the government. Indeed, one of the witnesses, Senator Stuart Symington, had provided a copy of his testimony before he testified to Greg Craig, a young associate working with Williams. Williams soon learned that the Justice Department was preparing an eight-count indictment charging that Helms had perjured himself.

Donning his hat as former chairman of the president's Foreign Intelligence Advisory Board, Clifford went to the Justice Department and pleaded the case for not charging the former CIA chief. This was vintage Clifford. He did not formally represent Helms and technically should not have been permitted to lobby on his behalf. But Clifford knew the effect of the national security argument he had used so persuasively so many times before. This time he argued that American intelligence interests abroad, and the stature of the agency at home, would be damaged by public disclosure of CIA secrets if charges were brought against the former director of central intelligence.

Most of the defense manuevering, however, was carried out by Williams, and some of it involved the time-honored Washington tradition of leaking to the press. "It's going to be like a Shakespeare play, Bobby," he told Bob Woodward of the *Washington Post* at a cocktail party that summer. "Dead bodies all over the stage. If Helms tells what he knows, the government won't be able to function. We won't be able to have an embassy in any South American capital. It'll raze the presidency, the judiciary, and the intelligence establishment if it comes out." There was no way to tell how much of the claim was exaggeration. Williams himself had no way of knowing, because Helms had never told him more than he needed to know. As Helms's biographer Thomas Powers wrote, the former intelligence chief's defense strategy was that of "a man wrapped in the flag, with a derringer peeping out between the folds."

In September and early October 1977, a series of meetings occurred between Ed Williams and senior officials at the Justice Department, including Attorney General Griffin Bell and his deputy, Benjamin Civiletti. In the end, Bell offered a deal: Helms could plead guilty to two misdemeanor charges of "misleading" the Senate committee, not the felony counts of perjury. Williams countered that Helms be allowed to plead nolo contendere, or no contest, instead of guilty and that he be spared a prison sentence. The sentence would be decided by the judge, but the Justice Department agreed not to recommend prison time.

Helms was reluctant to accept any deal that involved an admission of wrongdoing. He felt strongly that he had been honor bound not to betray the CIA in his testimony. To help persuade his client to accept the deal, Williams set up a meeting in Clifford's office.

"Well," said Clifford, drawing out the word as he seemed to ponder Helms's fate anew, "you know in the law so many of these decisions are forty-nine to fifty-one. I don't see this as that close. The only thing for you to do is to go forward with this process."

He went on to discuss the unsavory prospects presented by a trial. CIA officials would be forced to testify in public. A mostly black jury from the District of Columbia could not be expected to be sympathetic to a career intelligence agent. And any trial would be not only expensive and exhausting, but uncertain as to the outcome. Helms agreed and pleaded no contest to failing to testify fully and completely before Congress. He was fined $2,000 and given a suspended sentence of two years.

In the spring of 1978, a few months after the Helms case was settled, Clifford was invited to be the lead-off witness at hearings being conducted by the Senate Select Committee on Intelligence on the reorganization of the nation's intelligence agencies. Congress was in a mood to revise and restrain the CIA and its cousins, but Clifford took a position that was clearly out of step with the prevailing mood but quite in keeping with the worldview he had formed in the crucible of the Truman administration. Congress, he proposed, should abandon the idea of outlawing assassinations by American intelligence operatives or restricting other controversial covert activities. Clifford, the man who had helped draft the cynically obfuscatory language that created and empowered the CIA thirty years earlier, whose lawyer's eye had seen fit not to advertise the necessity of assassinations, then argued that the prohibitions were not really needed anyway.

"Of course, the United States will not engage in such activities, but is it necessary, whatever the historical record, to enshrine that principle in legislation?" asked Clifford. "It offends my regard for my country and it doesn't do any good."

Corporate America provided the bread and butter of Clifford's law practice, and the Firestone Tire and Rubber Company case was more typical of the matters that he handled in the Carter years.

On June 15, 1974, Louis and Cornelia Neal were driving with their daughter outside Las Vegas, Nevada. Suddenly one of the radial tires on their Ford Thunderbird blew out, sending the car out of control. Louis and Cornelia Neal were killed and their daughter was crippled. It was not an isolated incident. Others were suffering similar fates — in Venice, Florida; Loris, South Carolina; and Death Valley, California. Selana Lee Clement, a seven-year-old girl from Myrtle Beach, South Carolina, had her right leg amputated after a car accident blamed in part on a defective radial tire. Throughout the mid-seventies, Firestone 500 radial tires were blowing out across the country, contributing to thousands of accidents and at least thirty-four fatalities.

The Center for Auto Safety, a Washington clearinghouse founded by Ralph Nader, discovered the pattern in 1976 and opened an investigation. In 1977, the center forwarded its data to the National Highway Traffic Safety Administration, the federal agency that sets standards for cars, trucks, and tires. After evaluating the Nader claims and investigating on its own, the agency sent out questionnaires to 87,153 owners of all makes of steel-belted radial tires. The results showed that owners of Firestone tires were far more likely to have multiple tire failures than owners of other brands. The lowest percentage of complaints was 1.1 percent for Michelin; the highest was 46.4 percent for Firestone.

Firestone went to court and argued that the results of the survey should not be made public, but before a decision was made the findings were released by Nader's center. Firestone customers nationwide demanded that the highway safety agency take action against the company. The first step came in July 1978 when the Safety Administration announced an "initial determination" that the tires had a safety defect. With approximately eighteen million tires on the road, the company was facing a financial and public relations disaster unless it could stop the process short of a recall order.

Up to this point, the company had been represented by the Jones, Day, Reavis and Pogue law firm, which is based in Cleveland. The day the government issued its initial determination, Harvey Firestone, the scion of the nation's second-largest tire manufacturer, sought a different kind of help. He telephoned Clark Clifford.

Firestone had known Clifford since the tire tycoon was appointed to President Truman's internal security committee in the late forties. Now he said he wanted a settlement that would keep the tire case out of the courts and stop the federal government from ordering a recall. Clifford said he would see what he could do.

In the hierarchy of Washington, the administrator of the National Highway Traffic Safety Administration ranks fairly low, somewhere above a deputy assistant secretary at the Defense Department but far below an assistant attorney general or presidential assistant. So there was nothing unusual in Clifford's mind when he sought to raise the issue directly with Joan Claybrook, the administrator of the highway safety agency, who would decide whether to take the next step and issue a recall order. It was her response that surprised him.

"Miss Claybrook, I am Clark Clifford," said the smooth voice on the phone. "I am a Washington lawyer. I have been hired by Harvey Firestone to represent the company in the matter of the radial tires."

Clifford asked if he might visit with Claybrook to discuss the matter. The agency's relations with Firestone had been strained even in the best of times. The government still had a lawsuit pending against the company for its failure to turn over internal test results and other documents related to the 500 series tires.

With Clifford's call, Claybrook realized that the tire case had taken a sharp turn out of the regulatory domain and into the realm of politics. No matter what she said to Clifford, she assumed he could go over her head to someone at the White House. Further, she said later, "It was a very inappropriate thing for him to contact me. It was not appropriate to contact the decision maker. He should have gone to the general counsel's office." So she turned him down.

"I believe that I'm the wrong person for you to talk to, Mr. Clifford," she replied.

If he was flustered that Claybrook was going by the book, Clifford did not let on. Rather, he asked politely, "Who is the right person?" And he was directed to the lawyers in the agency's general counsel's office who were handling the case.

Claybrook grew frustrated in the intervening weeks as Clifford and lawyers from his office as well as from the Jones, Day firm met regularly with the agency's staff. When she tried to persuade the Justice Department to file a suit demanding that the company agree to a settlement, the department's lawyers refused to take the case. Claybrook never learned why the department had turned down a case in which the safety of thousands of drivers was at stake.

In the end, it was Clifford who dictated the key element of the settlement. "The company can only afford to pay a settlement of $300 million," he said at one of the final negotiating sessions. "That figure is the top, no matter how many tires are recalled." Finally, with no hope of a better settlement, Claybrook ordered the recall of approximately thirteen million Firestone tires at a cost to the company of about $300 million. In addition, Firestone paid a civil fine of $50,000 for selling a defective product.

American corporations were not the only ones seeking to enlist Clifford's influence in Washington. By the time of the Firestone settlement,

Clifford was deeply involved in representing the principals of a foreign bank in their efforts to acquire a bank in Washington. It was not Clifford's first foreign client. Nor was it his first experience in banking. But it was destined to be his most important client.

Bert Lance had brought the business to Clifford and, although few had ever heard of it before, the lawyer was intrigued by the people associated with the Bank of Credit and Commerce International. Known as BCCI, the bank had been created in 1972 by a Pakistani banker named Agha Hasan Abedi. He had persuaded the Bank of America, at the time the world's largest bank, to invest $2.5 million in his new venture, which would market itself to the rulers of the oil-rich Arab nations surrounding the Persian Gulf. Abedi had developed ties with many prominent Arabs, particularly in Abu Dhabi, during his days as a banker in Pakistan.

From those Middle Eastern beginnings, BCCI had grown rapidly. Its legal headquarters were now in Luxembourg, where there was little regulation of financial institutions, and its operating center was in London. Most of its staff was Pakistani. Its customers were mainly wealthy Arabs and the large number of Pakistani expatriates who lived and worked outside their country. Abedi, however, envisioned a far greater institution, and he was eager to begin operating in the United States. His first attempts had been rebuffed by New York State regulators in 1976. John Heimann, the state banking superintendent, had refused to allow BCCI to buy two small banks because BCCI had no central regulator to oversee and vouch for its financial condition. So Abedi decided to find another way.

In October 1977, the Pakistani banker was introduced to Bert Lance. It was just after Lance's resignation as budget director, but Abedi knew that Lance remained close to Jimmy Carter. Abedi hired Lance as a consultant to find an American bank for BCCI to buy. First, however, Abedi arranged for Ghaith Pharaon, a wealthy Saudi Arabian businessman and BCCI client, to buy Lance's own stock in the National Bank of Georgia. With money provided secretly by BCCI, Pharaon paid $2.4 million for the stock. The payment amounted to $20 a share, twice the price at which it had been selling a few weeks earlier. BCCI also loaned Lance about $3.4 million so that he could repay the debt to First National Bank of Chicago that had been questioned by William Safire.

Lance did his part. He came up with an acquisition target, Financial General Bankshares of Washington. The company was appealing because it operated twelve subsidiary banks in Maryland, New York, Tennessee, and Virginia along with branches in the District of Columbia. In these days before interstate banking, Financial General was one of the few financial institutions in the country with offices in both New York and Washington. It was perfectly placed for someone intent on making a big impact in the United States.

With the help of Jackson Stephens, a millionaire investment banker from Little Rock, Arkansas, and former Naval Academy classmate of Jimmy Carter, Lance began acquiring stock in Financial General on behalf of four Arab clients of BCCI. By the end of January 1978, BCCI's clients had quietly bought roughly twenty percent of the bank's stock. Lance and Stephens controlled another eight percent.

Financial General did not want to be taken over. On February 8, its board of directors issued a press release claiming that a foreign bank was seeking control of the company. The release did not name BCCI, but word soon leaked to the press. Confronted by the *New York Times*, BCCI officials denied any involvement in efforts to buy Financial General. Dildar Rizvi, a BCCI official, said he had spoken with Abedi, "who also denied any connection with efforts to purchase Financial General stock." The board of Financial General was not satisfied, and on February 13 the bank filed a lawsuit accusing Lance, Abedi, BCCI, Stephens, and the Arab investors of violating American securities laws by failing to disclose that they had been operating as a group to acquire control of Financial General. Lawyers for the board also met with the Securities and Exchange Commission, which enforces securities law, and persuaded the agency to open an inquiry.

Back in December, Lance had taken Abedi to visit Clifford at the lawyer's office. According to Clifford's later recollection, the conversation at the first meeting revolved around Abedi's vision for BCCI as a world banking power and Middle Eastern politics. Clifford had been impressed with Abedi. He was suave and polite, spoke perfect English, and exhibited the courtly manners that marked Clifford's own demeanor.

Now, faced with the lawsuit in February, Lance telephoned Clifford and asked if the lawyer would meet with them again. Clifford said fine, he would be glad to see them. According to Clifford's account, it was at this meeting that he learned for the first time that BCCI and the other investors were attempting to take over Financial General. He said that he agreed to defend them in the lawsuit and represent them in the investigation by the SEC. He also introduced Abedi to Bob Altman, who would be assisting him on the case. As he often did on complex matters, Clifford brought in a larger firm. This time it was Wachtell, Lipton, Rosen and Katz, a New York firm that specialized in takeover law.

Lance had a different recollection of the chronology of Clifford's involvement with BCCI, one that offers a scenario far more damaging to the august lawyer's role in the case. According to Lance's version, Clifford had investigated the bank briefly at his request in October 1977, when Lance was first approached by Abedi. He also said that he discussed the possibility of Clifford representing Abedi and BCCI at that time.

The contradiction is important. If Clifford is correct, the structure of the attempted takeover was already in place and the investors assembled before he and Altman became involved. Thus, it would have been easier for Abedi to deceive the two lawyers by portraying himself merely as a financial adviser to the Arab investors. Had Clifford been involved in the earlier stages, it was more likely that he would have known the Arab investors were potentially front men for a takeover actually financed and controlled by Abedi and BCCI.

There is evidence to support Lance, or at least to conclude that Clifford and Altman were hired before the Financial General lawsuit in February. For instance, an article in the *Washington Post* on December 18, 1977, described Lance as a consultant to Middle Eastern financial interests looking for investments in American banks and quoted Altman as his attorney. On January 30, 1978, Abdus Sami, a BCCI official in the United States, sent a memo to Abedi outlining the intentional strategy by BCCI, Lance, and others to disguise the bank's role in the takeover of Financial General. Sami said the strategy and goal had been explained to Clifford and that the lawyer had "blessed the acquisition." Last, on May 24, 1978, Clifford sent a legal bill to BCCI that dated his services not from mid-February, but from January 1978. While Lance's version and the documentary evidence may not be conclusive, they raise questions about Clifford's own chronology during this important period.

As for the SEC, the agency filed a civil lawsuit in federal court in Washington on March 17. The suit accused Lance, Abedi, BCCI, Stephens, and the four Arab investors of violating securities laws in acquiring stock in Financial General. The Arabs were Kamal Adham, who had resigned the previous year as chief of Saudi Arabian intelligence; Faisal-al Fulaij, a prominent Kuwaiti businessman and associate of the sheik-dom's royal family; Sheik Sultan bin Zayed Sultan al-Nahayan, crown prince of Abu Dhabi and brother of Sheik Zayed, the country's ruler; and Abdullah Darwaish, the financial adviser to the royal family of Abu Dhabi, who was representing one of Sheik Zayed's sons.

Even before the suit was filed, Clifford's team had worked out a settlement agreement with the SEC on terms that seemed highly favorable to Lance and the others. Without admitting or denying their guilt, the defendants consented not to violate securities laws again. They also pledged to make restitution to shareholders who had lost money as a result of the takeover effort. However, the group was not forbidden to make another run at Financial General. They only had to promise to seek approval from federal bank regulators before taking control of the company — and to keep BCCI out of any future effort, except as an investment adviser.

For Bert Lance, the settlement marked the end of his attempt to return to Washington as part owner of a major bank. The publicity associated with the SEC agreement and his own continuing troubles with federal authorities elsewhere had rendered him ineffective from Abedi's point of view.

However, Lance had brought a new player into the game, and Abedi was an old hand at renting the prestige and influence of former government officials. A few weeks after the SEC agreement, Abedi returned to meet again with Clifford and Altman. This time, he brought other BCCI officials, but not Lance. The subject was the same, taking over Financial General.

As Abedi described his desire to buy Financial General, with its multistate franchise, Altman interrupted. "But Mr. Abedi," he asked, "are you aware that BCCI will have problems getting into the United States as a bank?" Abedi acknowledged the difficulty, but he stressed that BCCI wanted to make a major acquisition in the United States, rather than start small by opening a handful of its own branches. He explained that the Arab investors who were trying to buy Financial General were friends of his. "As far as the shareholders are concerned, there is no difference between me and them," he said. "You could take it that I have authorization to act on their behalf."

Like the dispute over the initial involvement of Clifford and Altman, this would later turn out to be a crucial point. Were the investors operating as front men on behalf of BCCI in the takeover of Financial General? Or had they merely authorized Abedi to represent their interests in dealing with Clifford? For the time being, the distinction seemed to make little difference.

To the BCCI participants in the meeting, Clifford did not seem to share Altman's reservations. Speaking with his perennial authority, he explained that he had checked with the State Department and knew that Abedi was well known and well regarded in the Persian Gulf. Clifford described Financial General as "an excellent property" and said he could see great advantage in its acquisition by Arab investors. As he had done with other clients, Clifford cast the acquisition in patriotic terms. The fact that the buyers were wealthy Arabs, he pointed out, was a way of returning some of the billions of dollars that Americans were paying to the Mideast for oil.

Later, Clifford would say that he had gone so far as to contact an official at the State Department and determined that foreign acquisition of Financial General would violate no American policy. When pressed to recall the name of the person he had spoken to, Clifford would be unable to do so. But it would not have been unusual for any one of several offices at the State Department to render such a decision. And, as would later be discovered, the truth about BCCI itself was shrouded beneath layers of front companies and official secrecy.

What cannot be disputed is that when Clifford agreed to lead the effort to buy Financial General, he took a step onto a path that would lead him into one of the longest takeover fights in American banking history, provide him with an entirely new career as he entered his middle seventies, and end with him struggling to salvage the reputation he had crafted so carefully for more than half a century.

Clifford's representation of BCCI and the Arab investors marked another turning point in his career. For years, he had thrived because clients knew he had access to friends in high places. But Abedi and the other politically savvy bankers at BCCI had seen something else: Clark Clifford himself had become a stamp of approval in Washington. Paying his fees guaranteed a measure of respectability and prestige independent of Clifford's ability to influence government officials. His word alone had become a prized commodity.

19

The Deception Begins

TWO OBSTACLES stood in the way of the Arab investors' victory. First was the Financial General board, which opposed selling the institution and was pursuing its lawsuit aggressively. Second was the Federal Reserve, which, as the regulator of bank holding companies, would have to approve new ownership. Overcoming both would require more than adroit legal work. It would take a substantial dose of Clifford's prestige and powers of persuasion.

To fight the takeover, the bank board had hired Skadden, Arps, Slate, Meagher and Flom, a tough New York law firm. Operating on the theory that a good offense is the best defense, the lawyers attacked the prospective acquirers. The Arab investors, they contended, were merely front men for BCCI, which itself was unfit to own an American bank. They uncovered some evidence supporting the theory. For instance, they found that Fulaij had paid for his original Financial General stock with $3.5 million borrowed from a BCCI affiliate that he headed in Kuwait. They also discovered that BCCI had loaned an equal amount to Lance during the initial takeover attempt without so much as a signature on a loan document.

When the lawyers questioned Abedi under oath in London, he initially tried to distance himself from the takeover. However, at one point he acknowledged that he had approved the initial stock purchases. Later he tried to amend the damaging statement, saying that he was acting on instructions from an individual client.

The ambiguous relationship between BCCI, Abedi, and the investors seemed to deepen in the summer of 1978. Ostensibly to serve as the acquisition vehicle for the investors, BCCI set up a holding company in the Netherlands Antilles called Credit and Commerce American Holdings, commonly referred to by its initials, CCAH.

As for BCCI itself, the lawyers for Financial General discovered that concerns about its financial practices and overall soundness had been raised as recently as 1977 by auditors at the Bank of America. Among other things, the auditors concluded that BCCI was growing too fast and without sufficient capital to cover potential losses and remain solvent. In addition, they found that BCCI had loaned millions of dollars to people affiliated with the bank and to members of Arab royal families without sufficient collateral and sometimes without even a loan document. Bank of America had responded to the discoveries by beginning the quiet withdrawal from its partnership with BCCI. Clifford and Altman, however, were aware of the problems. Nonetheless, they continued to represent the Mideast investors.

By that time, there were other warning signals that BCCI was not what it appeared to be. As a result of its rapid growth and lax controls, the Bank of England had refused to allow the bank to engage in full banking services and blocked its attempt to expand further. However, the British regulators did not try to discover what was going on inside the bank itself. Not that the task would have been easy. BCCI, headquartered in Luxembourg, had moved some of its operations to the Cayman Islands, another haven of laissez-faire regulation.

During this period, Clifford occasionally flew to London to discuss strategy with Abedi and Kamal Adham, the former Saudi intelligence chief who described himself as the head of the investor group. Clifford was no stranger to dealing with rich clients, but after one of his trips he confided to Sam McIlwain that he was stunned at the wealth of Adham and the other Arab investors. A question had arisen about a $90 million bond necessary as part of the offering package. Rather than pay a fee to a bank to provide the bond, Adham said the investors would simply put up cash.

Often the conversations with Abedi and Adham strayed to Mideast politics. At the time, President Carter was struggling to mediate a peace agreement between Israel and Egypt and monitor the troubling rise of Islamic fundamentalists threatening the stability of Iran, a key American ally in the Persian Gulf region.

It was after one of those London visits that, on November 29, 1978, Clifford sent a memo on Mideast politics to Zbigniew Brzezinski, the president's national security adviser. Clifford had strongly recommended to Carter more than a year earlier that he not bring Brzezinski into the government. Clifford, who had known Brzezinski briefly in the Johnson administration, did not think him up to the task of serving as national security adviser. But sending the memo to Brzezinski illustrates one of the central factors that allowed Clark Clifford to survive for so long in Washington's ever-changing political world: when it came to dealing with government, he played ball with those who held the bat, not those he wished held it. In much the same way he had been willing to offer advice on Vietnam to Nixon, Clifford was now offering his expertise in foreign affairs to a man he did not necessarily respect and who was part of an administration that seemed to have little use for Clifford himself.

The substance of the memo itself, however, appears to have reflected the interests of Abedi and his political patrons in Pakistan more than Clifford's own observations and insights. Clifford did not disclose the sources of his information, saying only that he had recently returned from meetings in London with "men who are exceptionally well informed regarding the Persian Gulf region." The men, he explained, were alarmed about the threat to American interests by Islamic fundamentalists who were challenging the power of the Shah of Iran and stirring up trouble elsewhere in the region. Most of the document, however, discussed the importance of Pakistan to the United States. President Carter should invite General Mohammed Zia-ul-Haq, the military leader who had seized control of Pakistan, to the United States. Along with symbolizing the country's significance, Clifford said, Carter should use the opportunity to argue against the execution of Zulfikar Ali Bhutto, the deposed president.

Unmentioned was that Clifford's advice was based largely on conversations with Abedi and other Pakistani bankers who still had close ties to their homeland and the disgraced Bhutto regime. In fact, one reason for Bhutto's downfall the previous year was the allegation that Abedi had delivered $2 million to $3 million in cash to the president for his reelection campaign. It was widely assumed, though never proven, that the money had come from Sheik Zayed of Abu Dhabi. A week after receiving the memo, Brzezinski replied with a two-sentence letter assuring Clifford that "we are hard at work on the range of issues that you raise."

Clifford did not stop with the memo. A few months later, he telephoned Secretary of State Cyrus Vance, who was President Carter's chief Middle East negotiator. Although Vance and the administration were focusing on a peace settlement between Egypt and Israel, the deteriorating situation in Iran was causing alarm. Western governments were concerned that the Ayatollah Khomeini and his fundamentalist supporters were planning to overthrow the Shah and replace him with an extremely radical regime. Clifford, however, offered some encouragement after a meeting with Iranian moderates in Paris that was arranged by Abedi. "Clifford's interlocutors indicated that Khomeini intended to set up a government drawn from moderate secular politicians, with the Islamic clergy remaining in the background as the guiding political and spiritual force of the revolution," Vance later wrote in his memoir. The assessment would turn out to be dead wrong.

Picking up and passing on political information from the Middle East was secondary to the purpose of Clifford's frequent meetings with Abedi. What the two men were most interested in doing was countering the fears of American banking regulators. Throughout late 1978 and well into 1979, the regulators focused on the same questions raised by Financial General's attorneys: Were the Arab investors merely fronts for BCCI? Did BCCI have a hidden interest in CCAH, the holding company formed by the Arab investors to acquire Financial General? Altman assured the regulators in writing that BCCI would have neither ownership in Financial General nor contracts relating to its management or investments, but it would take Clifford's reputation to close the deal.

In February 1979, the holding company sought approval from the Federal Reserve to acquire all voting stock in Financial General. The regulators rejected the application on a technicality. Financial General had a subsidiary bank in Maryland, and a Maryland law prohibited hostile takeovers of banks. As a result, the Federal Reserve refused to approve the application after a complaint from Financial General's Maryland affiliate.

Clearly the key was removing the opposition at Financial General, thus nullifying the Maryland law and enabling a new application to succeed. As part of the strategy, Clifford lined up three prominent Americans who would seek election to the Financial General board at the annual shareholders meeting on April 30, 1980. They would be proxies for the Arab investors and help neutralize some of the xenophobia and bad feelings left over from the earlier attempts.

First, Clifford persuaded his old friend Stuart Symington, who had retired from the Senate, to become the chairman of the holding company on the Arab investors' slate of candidates. In explaining why he accepted the post, Symington, who was seventy-seven, said Clifford told him the acquisition would be "a way of getting these petrodollars back." Then Clifford brought on two other candidates, Donald Notman, with whom he had served on the board of the National Bank of Washington, and Elwood Quesada, a retired army general and a real estate developer in Washington. When Notman backed out for personal reasons, Clifford took his place on the slate.

Clifford and Altman continued to lobby behind the scenes with the Financial General board and soliciting votes from other investors. The vote was a disappointment, with Financial General's management claiming a narrow victory. Altman told reporters talks would continue in an effort to settle the takeover fight. In the meantime, another of Clifford's personal relationships succeeded.

During the Johnson administration, the lawyer had gotten to know Armand Hammer, the legendary chairman and chief executive of Occidental Petroleum Corporation. He also had a brush with Hammer when Occidental Petroleum tried unsuccessfully to take over Phillips Petroleum, where Clifford sat on the board. Hammer also happened to be a member of the Financial General board. In fact, he had tried to make peace between the board and Bert Lance during the first takeover. This time around, he sought out Clifford for settlement negotiations.

The call from Hammer came while Clifford was in Miami attending a board meeting of the Knight-Ridder publishing company, which he served as a director.

"Clark, we are just expending so much time in this fight," said Hammer, who was at his headquarters in Los Angeles. "I wonder if it wouldn't be a good idea if you and I were just to sit down and talk together. See if maybe we could reach a settlement."

"Armand, I'm ready any time," replied Clifford.

"Fine," said Hammer. "Get on back and I'll let you know."

When the two men sat down in Washington a few days later, Clifford explained that his group was getting stronger. He said he fully expected his clients to wind up with the bank. Hammer acknowledged that the takeover's momentum had not seemed to stop with the shareholder vote, and he shifted the talk to a fair price for the bank. This was a matter that the two could not decide themselves, so they scheduled another meeting with other Financial General directors.

The second session lasted a full day and resulted in a tentative agreement on price and timing. On May 21, the two sides signed a letter of understanding setting forth the basic agreement. After some additional haggling over price, a formal acquisition agreement was signed on July 25. Credit and Commerce American Holdings would buy Financial General Bankshares for $130 million in cash. The bulk of the stock would be held by three of the four original BCCI shareholders — Kamal Adham, Faisal al-Fulaij, and Abdullah Darwaish. Eleven other Middle Eastern investors would take smaller shares.

With the first part of the job accomplished, the next step for Clifford was obtaining the approval of skeptical regulators at the Federal Reserve and the Office of the Comptroller of the Currency in Washington. Little did Clifford know that he would be challenged by a bureaucrat who cared little for the lawyer's reputation and influence.

On the surface, the Financial General takeover was an unusual case for Clifford. His firm did not specialize in the arcane world of acquisitions. As he often did, Clifford brought in experts from another firm who really knew the field. Viewed in the context of his career, however, the Financial General case fit perfectly into Clifford's original definition of his firm's task. When someone had a tough problem in Washington, they should call on Clifford. What he offered was not necessarily legal expertise, but an understanding of how the bureaucracy worked and, of course, his own persuasive powers and influence. In this context, the case seemed to be perfect for Clifford, as did another he took on.

In the wake of Watergate, Senate investigators probing secret corporate payments to Richard Nixon's campaign discovered that a hundred American companies, many of them members of the Fortune 500 list of the country's largest businesses, had paid bribes regularly to foreign officials and governments to get contracts. Congress responded in 1977 by passing the Foreign Corrupt Practices Act, which made such payments illegal. The crusade then was picked up by Attorney General Benjamin Civiletti, who had been elevated to the top spot at the Justice Department after the resignation of Griffin Bell in 1979.

The first major criminal prosecution by the Justice Department focused on McDonnell Douglas Corporation, the manufacturer of civilian and military aircraft. Prosecutors uncovered evidence that senior executives had paid bribes to a relative of former Pakistani president Zulfikar Ali Bhutto, who had been executed earlier in 1979, and to

Bhutto's former chief of staff. The bribes amounted to $500,000 for each aircraft bought by Pakistan's national airline.

McDonnell Douglas tried to handle the investigation through the law firm it used in St. Louis, the company's headquarters. When it appeared that the company and several executives were about to be indicted, the corporation turned to Clifford, who a decade earlier had helped engineer the merger of McDonnell and Douglas to create one of the country's largest defense companies. The St. Louis firm had been trying to negotiate a plea bargain that would avoid the indictment of any employees and allow the company to plead guilty to the lightest charge possible. Clifford's influence was expected to close the deal.

Michael Lubin, the lead attorney on the investigation from the Justice Department's fraud section, was just five years out of the University of Miami law school. When he flew to St. Louis in late August 1979 to discuss the status of the negotiations with the company's defense team, he was a bit stunned to find himself across the table from Clifford. "Here I was a kid in my twenties up against Clark Clifford," Lubin recalled.

Lubin had been uncomfortable from the start with the idea of a corporate guilty plea, since it could be interpreted as a mere slap on the wrist for a powerful company. On the other hand, if McDonnell Douglas pleaded guilty to serious charges, it would give the department a strong negotiating position with the dozens of similar prosecutions expected in the coming months. In St. Louis, Lubin assured the company lawyers that the department would be willing to drop plans to charge the executives if McDonnell Douglas entered a plea of guilty to violating the Racketeer Influenced and Corrupt Organizations Act. Known as RICO, the law was created as a novel means of attacking organized crime families. But federal prosecutors were beginning to discover its effectiveness in dealing with a broader range of organized criminal activities.

James S. McDonnell, the eighty-year-old chairman and founder of McDonnell Douglas, had stubbornly refused to accept the plea. He was adamant that his company would not be branded a racketeering enterprise like some Mafia family. However, that day in St. Louis, Lubin got the impression from Clifford that "Old Mac" might be on the verge of changing his mind and accepting the deal.

Over the next month, Lubin worked out the details of the racketeering plea. He thought he had a deal, and the defense lawyers were scheduled to deliver the company's final response at a meeting at the Justice Department on September 26. Lubin spent the morning presenting evidence to the grand jury investigating the bribes. Shortly before the meeting, Lubin got word that Clifford had called while he was with the grand jury. Old Mac was coming to the meeting, too, despite having recently broken his hip. Clifford said he had tried to talk McDonnell out of attending, in part because anything he might say could be used against the company if the deal fell through, but McDonnell had rejected the advice.

Others involved in the case said that Clifford, relying on the technique he had pioneered for lobbying Congress nearly twenty years earlier, had encouraged McDonnell to argue personally against the racketeering charge in hopes of softening up the prosecutors for a plea to lesser charges. "It was a very naive fiasco orchestrated by Clifford," said one of the lawyers involved in the case.

The prosecutors were so anxious about a face-to-face meeting with McDonnell that they insisted on reading him his Miranda rights against self incrimination when he arrived. Clifford put up a hand and assured the young lawyers that the chairman understood the warning and would address only the proposed plea agreement.

"To make a long story short," Old Mac said, "McDonnell Douglas Corporation cannot make this settlement. I couldn't live with myself if I did. This is my baby, my little jewel. I cannot live with this settlement. I say 'I' for simplicity, but our company, our people can't. We have labored forty years ... When I graduate to another phase of existence ..." His voice cracked and one of America's leading corporate titans bowed his head and wiped tears from his eyes before telling the prosecutors that, despite the attempts of his lawyers, he could not accept the agreement. "A deep inner psyche says fight all the way," he said. "If we lose, fight on appeal. That's where it stands. That's where Old Mac stands."

Left without a deal, Lubin received approval from the deputy assistant attorney general for the criminal division, Jack Keeney, to draw up a racketeering indictment to present to the grand jury. He also mailed letters to the individual executives involved notifying them that indictments had been approved.

Clifford responded by asking for an urgent meeting. He claimed the other members of the company's board of directors were prepared to overrule the chairman and accept the plea bargain. Lubin and his partner, George Mendelson, told him it was too late. Since the letters had gone out to the individuals, accepting a plea now would make it appear that the corporation had traded its plea for dropping the charges against the executives. Exasperated and frustrated, Clifford insisted on arguing his case with Philip Heymann, the assistant attorney general in charge of the criminal division, and Keeney. Granted his session, Clifford contended that the young prosecutors were overzealous in seeking a racketeering indictment. He complained that they were acting out of vengeance because the chairman had turned down the guilty plea.

This last appeal also failed. On November 9, McDonnell Douglas Corporation was indicted on racketeering charges, and four company executives also were charged in the bribery conspiracy. Among the individuals was James S. McDonnell III, the son of the chairman and a member of the corporate board.

New lawyers were added as a full-blown defense team was assembled. The individuals were represented by Edward Bennett Williams, although he left much of the work to associates, and by two other leading defense attorneys and securities law experts, Peter Fleming of New York and Seymour Glanzer of Washington. Despite the fact that his colleagues had far more experience in criminal matters, Clifford acted as the lead lawyer, "a chairman of the board," in the words of one participant. Part of the reason was that he was the company's lawyer and the company was paying all the legal bills. Part of it was that he was Clark Clifford. The role did not mean that Clifford was involved in the day-to-day casework, a task assigned to Paul Warnke, whose return to the firm earlier in the year had led to its renaming as Clifford and Warnke.

Some participants in the defense complained that Clifford's lack of familiarity with complex criminal cases was a handicap. Two of the more experienced lawyers felt Clifford viewed the case too much in terms of public perception, rather than in the stark context of what would happen in a courtroom. "He was not fitted to do it and didn't have the instincts to do it," said one of the defense lawyers.

While they were preparing a joint trial strategy and analyzing the evidence, Clifford and others were still counting on a plea bargain that would avoid convictions of any of the individuals. Often the strategy meetings were held in the conference room at Clifford and Warnke, and on occasion they were interrupted when Clifford's secretary would buzz and say the White House was on the line for him.

By early 1980, Carter and his White House advisers realized they were in political trouble with an election approaching. They had reached out grudgingly to some in the Democratic establishment for help, including Clifford. He had been invited to the signing ceremonies at Camp David for the Israeli-Egyptian peace accord, consulted on arms control talks with the Russians, and appointed chairman of a commission that advised on ambassadorial appointments. After shunning him for the first years of his term, Carter now seemed to recognize that there was value in the type of Washington experience embodied by Clifford.

One instance was particularly telling. When Carter needed a new counsel at the White House in late 1979, he turned to Lloyd Cutler, a prominent Washington attorney whose practice was in some ways modeled after Clifford's career. When Cutler asked exactly what his task would be, the president replied, "I want you to play the Clark Clifford role." Cutler took the charge seriously enough that, in drafting a letter for Carter to sign outlining his duties, he included the language about Clifford. Over the coming months, whenever there was an attempt to exclude him from an important meeting, Cutler would gain access by telling the president or Hamilton Jordan, his chief of staff, "Harry Truman would have wanted Clark Clifford at this meeting."

In the sort of turnabout that is emblematic of Washington's tightly knit power structure, Cutler arranged for Clifford to take his place as the Washington lawyer for International Business Machines in a massive antitrust case.

In no way did Clifford play the sort of role with Carter that he had with Truman, Kennedy, and Johnson. His was mostly a ceremonial presence from time to time. Yet calls from the White House were frequent enough that they spawned a running joke among the defense lawyers in the McDonnell Douglas case. "Clifford was called out of meetings so often that when one lawyer would say, 'Wonder what's keeping him?' another would respond, 'He's probably giving the president lessons on being president.' "

Near the end of January 1980, with negotiations still under way with the Justice Department, Clifford called his colleagues on the case to say that he would not be able to attend an upcoming meeting. He explained gravely that he was going out of the country on a mission for the president. When he ran into one of the lawyers later that afternoon, Clifford amplified his remarks: "Without getting into what I am going to do, if things do not go correctly, do you have your old military uniform available?" Unsure whether Clifford was serious, the lawyer said maybe he did.

The following day, Clifford was in New Delhi conferring with Indian Prime Minister Indira Gandhi as President Carter's special envoy. The topic was whether a bold confrontation or quiet negotiation was the most effective means of gaining a withdrawal of Soviet troops from Afghanistan. In addition, Clifford carried a gift; the United States had reversed itself and would sell highly sophisticated military equipment to India.

Clifford saw nothing questionable in serving as the president's special envoy at the same time he was negotiating a plea bargain with the Carter Justice Department. These were Washington rules, after all. Conflicts of interest were lost in that vast gray swirl created by the rapidly revolving door between government and the private sector.

In fact, Clifford's role as a presidential emissary did not seem to help with Heymann or Civiletti. Not until Carter had been defeated by Republican Ronald Reagan was the McDonnell Douglas matter resolved. In the end, Old Mac was vindicated. The corporation pleaded guilty to fraud and making false statements, not racketeering. The charges against the four individuals were dismissed. Rudolph Giuliani, the assistant attorney general for the criminal division and later mayor of New York City, said there had never been enough evidence to charge the individuals. By the time of the deal, Old Mac had died.

McDonnell Douglas was not the only case pending before the federal government while Clifford was flying off to India on behalf of the president. He also was pushing for approval of the application of Credit and Commerce American Holdings to buy Financial General. Like the bribery case, however, the takeover was resolved under the Reagan administration.

In November 1980, the month that Ronald Reagan routed Jimmy Carter in the presidential election, the holding company filed a second application for Federal Reserve approval to acquire Financial General. This time, there would be no opposition from the bank's board. The application also specified that the Arab investors would be passive, relying on professional bankers to run the institution and Symington and the others to oversee policy. Since the approval by the Financial General board, Clifford and Altman had been lobbying the state and federal officials to clear the way for the application.

Abedi joined them for an important meeting with John Heimann, the former New York state banking superintendent who had become comptroller of the currency, a senior federal regulatory post. Abedi stressed that this application was different from the one that Heimann had rejected four years earlier in New York. He said BCCI's only involvement was as adviser to the Arab shareholders.

In New York, where Financial General owned two banks, Clifford reassured Jewish politicians in the state legislature that the Arab investors were moderates. For example, Kamal Adham had recently been honored by President Carter for helping bring Egypt to the bargaining table with Israel at Camp David. Clifford and Altman also assured the Maryland banking commissioner that this was a friendly transaction. And the two lawyers drove to Richmond to meet with the Virginia commissioner of financial institutions.

After twenty years as a federal bank examiner, Sidney Bailey had taken the job as Virginia's top bank regulator. He prided himself on running a tight ship, and he did not like the fact that one of the state's largest banks was going to come under the control of a foreign bank outside the supervision of American regulators.

"These are honest, honorable, upright people who would be nothing more than passive investors looking for a safe haven for their money," Clifford assured Bailey. "They perceive the United States as being the best of all safe havens right now. Investing in a banking organization is the epitome of a safe haven. They have nothing more in mind than the well-being and improvement of this institution. They intend to do nothing detrimental to the institution or misuse it."

Bailey remained unconvinced. In a voice nearly as deep as Clifford's, he replied, "You can't send the sheriff after them."

Clifford was unable to persuade him that his concerns were unfounded. Coupled with the Federal Reserve's lingering concerns about BCCI's involvement, Bailey's objections were enough to lead to an unusual hearing on the application on April 23, 1981. The purpose of the hearing was for the Federal Reserve staff to gather information for its recommendation on the application to the Federal Reserve Board, which would make the final decision.

The other federal regulators already had agreed not to object. In March, the Office of the Comptroller of the Currency had written to the Federal Reserve saying it would not oppose the takeover as long as BCCI had no role in the acquisition or management of Financial General. The letter was written by Cantwell F. Muckenfuss III, deputy comptroller. At the time he wrote the letter, it was later discovered, Muckenfuss was meeting informally with Clifford and Altman to discuss the possibility of leaving the federal agency to go to work at Clifford and Warnke. He denied that the talks had any effect on his judgment about the takeover.

At the Federal Reserve hearing, the first speaker was Sidney Bailey. He listed a series of objections, centering on the inability of American regulators to monitor the investors and what he saw as holes in their personal financial statements. Bailey said he was puzzled because he saw no legitimate financial incentive for investing $130 million in Financial General. Then he offered his own theory, saying, "One obvious plausible answer to this riddle lies in the unique position of Financial General in the market. No other single financial institution is situated in both the financial and government hubs of the United States."

Clifford followed, dismissing Bailey's concerns curtly by saying he would respond to them in writing. Then, with the style and authority that had made him a Washington legend, Clifford launched a patriotic and persuasive argument on behalf of the investors and the deal itself. Thoughtful Americans, he said, knew it was in the country's interest to bring back as many of the dollars as possible being paid to Arab oil nations. Allowing this group to invest in a bank offered a grand opportunity for the country. Further, he said the investors would be passive, leaving the management of the bank up to professionals and to a board of Americans.

"Let me conclude on a personal note," he said, lowering his voice to convey a sense of intimacy as he described his meetings in recent months with Kamal Adham. "I have come to have the deepest respect for his character, for his reputation, for his honor, and for his integrity. I'm proud to be an associate of his. I look forward with real anticipation to continuing to be an associate of his. He is the kind of man with whom I like to be associated."

Just as he had sought to gift-wrap the deal itself in the flag, Clifford was lending his prestige to Adham and, by inference, the other investors. They were good enough for Clark Clifford, so they should be good enough for the Federal Reserve. The speech crystallized exactly what Agha Hasan Abedi had seen when he hired Clifford: here was someone whose good name and reputation inoculated him and his front men against serious scrutiny.

Adham also testified, describing himself as a prominent businessman and dismissing the notion that he or the others were fronts for BCCI. "I would like to assure you that each one on his own rights will not accept in any way to be a cover for somebody else."

Lloyd Bostian Jr., a Federal Reserve staff member, noted that BCCI had served as an adviser earlier in the deal. What role did they play in the present proposal? he asked.

"None," replied Clifford emphatically. "There is no function of any kind on the part of BCCI. I know of no present relationship. I know of no planned future relationship that exists, and other than that, I don't know what else there is to say, Mr. Bostian."

Years later, Sid Bailey remembered what it was like to sit in the hearing room with the likes of Clark Clifford. "I felt like a mouse in a room full of dancing elephants," he said.

On August 25, 1981, the Federal Reserve Board unanimously approved the acquisition of Financial General Bankshares by Credit and Commerce American Holdings. There was one final delay. New York state banking regulators were still concerned about BCCI's potential role. Clifford assured the investors the problem would be resolved. The bank was as good as theirs.

Clifford's role in the transaction had gone beyond the normal duties of a lawyer and beyond his self-imposed restrictions. He had abandoned his long-held custom and lobbied regulators and legislators directly, without the protective layer of middlemen. He also had taken the unusual step of putting his personal integrity on the line by assuring the Federal Reserve that BCCI would have no role in the management of the bank.

Thirty years earlier, when he was starting his practice in Washington, Clifford would not have staked his reputation on a single client this way. Even when he served on the board of Phillips Petroleum at the same time he represented the company, Clifford had relied on other partners in his firm to directly contact federal officials. His involvement in the business affairs of Phillips had been minimal.

But times had changed in Washington and at Clifford's law firm. Rules were looser in the capital. The number of lawyers who openly lobbied the Congress and the government had soared. Because Clark Clifford and others like him had made it so, lobbying was considered respectable for lawyers in Washington. As for the law firm, it remained prosperous, but there was no longer a long line of retainer clients clamoring for the services of an aging Washington institution and his lesser-known partners.

These changes in the city and the firm had not gone unnoticed by Clifford. While his square-shouldered suits and courtly manners remained unchanged, he had lost some of the essential skepticism and distance that a good lawyer must bring to his dealings with every client. He had substituted his impressions for careful scrutiny. He had taken at face value assertions that should have been challenged and investigated. He had put himself in a situation that was an obvious conflict of interest — he was supposed to protect Financial General from the influence of BCCI at the same time he would continue receiving legal fees from Abedi, the president of BCCI. He thought he could get away with all of it because he was Clark Clifford.

Shepherding the takeover to completion, however, was only the start of Clifford's work for the Arab investors and BCCI. Even before the formal approval by the Federal Reserve Board, he had taken the Concorde to London for meetings with Adham, Abedi, and Swaleh Naqvi at BCCI's lavish headquarters on Leadenhall Street in the financial district. After a day of talk about strategy and staffing for the bank, the men adjourned for dinner in the dining room of a London hotel. There, Abedi and Adham praised the work Clifford had done in the three-year battle for Financial General and toasted its pending completion. They said they had come to know and respect Clifford and he in turn had gotten to know them and the prospects for the bank. Wouldn't it make sense, they said, for Clifford to become chairman of the new bank? Of course, he would continue with his law practice. He would even continue to represent the bank and BCCI. Along with those duties, however, they envisioned a role for him setting the policy of the new bank.

Sometimes timing is everything. Clifford had recovered fully from his heart attack four years earlier and had no intention of retiring or even slowing down. Years before, he had recognized that he could never retire the way so many of his friends and contemporaries had. His work had become his life, assuming an importance that extended far beyond providing for his family, which he had done admirably, and assuring his place in history, which he had long ago secured.

"Retirement never occurred to him," Clifford's daughter Joyce said years later. "It is not a concept that he much believes in or thinks is very healthy. I'm quite certain that somewhere in his mid-life he determined that retirement was not going to be the path that he wanted."

Clifford himself made much the same point, saying, "I cannot be inactive. Sometimes that is a little irritating to Mrs. Clifford. I am easier to live with if I am busy and accomplishing something."

Abedi's was a complex decision, rooted in the vicissitudes of human nature and in Clifford's perception of himself. It was Oscar Wilde who observed that work was the refuge of those with nothing better to do. For Clifford, work was the way in which he had defined himself throughout his life. He had been tireless in pursuit of his goal of becoming the best trial lawyer in the Midwest. Since coming to Washington, he had played an important role in many of the great events of the era. Now, despite his age and all that he had accomplished, he was not content to leave the stage. He refused to relinquish the limelight for the shadows or trade the applause for the silence. Now, as the role of lawyer and presidential adviser was wearing thin with age, he was offered the chance at playing in a new drama. And the timing seemed perfect to the man who could not retire.

With a Republican in the White House, Clifford was concerned about the prospects of the law firm. Aside from the McDonnell Douglas case, there had been few big new matters coming in, and Republican control of Washington did not promise a windfall. In his own mind, Clifford feared that he was perceived as "over the hill" and no longer taken seriously as a player on the legal scene. Here was a man accustomed to being at center stage, unwilling or unable to exit as he approached his seventy-fifth birthday.

Warnke saw it from his office down the hall from Clifford. "I think that as you get to be mid-seventies, you look around and all of a sudden your clients have retired," he said. "The general counsels [of corporations] are years younger than you are, so as a result your younger partners are much more apt to get new business than you are. And Clark, I think, did not want to have nothing to do."

But it was Clifford himself, the sharp-eyed lawyer who was able to cut to the heart of the knottiest problems, who described it best when he observed, "There wasn't anything that was coming in that made me want to get up in the morning, hurry up and get at it. Also, you get to that age, you are probably not producing the business that you used to produce when you were younger. We were continuing to have good years, as far as that was concerned, but within me was some feeling that life at the time was not nearly as productive as it had been at other stages. What most people want when they get over a certain age is tranquility, peace. I didn't want that. I was looking for something that would excite me."

Also, the prospect of running a bank was tantalizing. For most of the fifty-three years since he passed the Missouri bar and began practicing law, Clifford had solved various problems for businessmen. Some of his clients had been powerful, insightful men, such as Boots Adams of Phillips Petroleum and Howard Hughes. Others had been far less skilled and intelligent. He also had served on the boards of Phillips Petroleum and Knight-Ridder. Inevitably, he had learned a great deal about how companies are run. Some of what he had seen along the way was very good, but a large number of the businesses he had represented were poorly run. Taking over a bank offered the challenge to employ what he had learned. Furthermore, he would be starting at the top, like embarking on a political career by running for president.

"Practicing law is fun, but you are always doing something for somebody else," explained Clifford later. "Here was an opportunity to do it yourself."

Within that phrase, "doing something for somebody else," lay another aspect of the appeal of being chairman of a major bank. For all those years in the law, Clifford had found himself asking favors of other people. It was the nature of the law he practiced, the art of access and influence more than legal and courtroom expertise. This job represented the chance to exercise true power, as Clifford made clear during a visit with Robert Donovan, the Truman biographer and former newsman.

"Bob, two billion dollars," Clifford said very slowly in describing both the bank's assets and the job's appeal. "Two billion dollars."

Later, Donovan said, "You want to know why Clark Clifford went into the bank? He was attracted by the power and the money. He was wealthy, but not in billions and not in power like that. Billions of dollars is power."

Sam McIlwain, who spent more than thirty years working alongside Clifford, offered a similar assessment. "I think part of his ego was involved," said McIlwain. "I'd been out to Burning Tree Country Club with him and seen Bob Fleming, who was the head of Riggs Bank, drive up in a chauffeur-driven limousine and get out and everybody would kowtow to him. Everybody wanted to be in with the banker. Same thing with Barney Colter, who was the head of the National Bank of Washington. So Clifford could visualize himself coming into Burning Tree on a Sunday morning and all the 'How are you, Mr. Clifford?' sort of thing. He was subject to flattery, too."

A prominent Washington lawyer and intimate of Clifford's also thought flattery played a role in the job's appeal, as did the absence of anyone to say no. "They dangled in front of him the opportunity to become chairman of a bank," said the lawyer. "Had I gone to him and said that someone had offered this chance to me, I would have wagered that he would have said, 'Don't touch it.' And he would have said it for all the right reasons. But there was no mechanism in his firm to make you stop. It was very much a one-man firm, and there were no committees to review it for potential dangers, conflicts or bad appearances. If Abedi had come to me with the offer, somebody would have stopped me. Acting for BCCI and for the shareholders in the bank is an obvious conflict. We have a conflicts and bad taste committee at our firm. Most firms of any size do."

Warnke was back at the firm and might have had enough sway over Clifford to convince him not to get so deeply involved with a client. But he was devoting much of his time to fighting the arms buildup by the new Reagan administration. Also, Warnke was generally perceived within the law firm as uninterested in the details of management.

There was some precedent. Clifford had served on the board of Phillips Petroleum and represented the company at the same time. But this was a step further down a road fraught with ethical conflicts in the minds of many lawyers. The primary danger in representing a client and serving on the client's board is that a lawyer will identify too greatly with the business goals at the expense of his role as an independent legal adviser. When a lawyer becomes an operating officer of a company, as

Clifford would if he accepted the chairmanship of the bank, the dangers are magnified.

"Essentially, a lawyer who becomes an officer is really giving himself advice," said Stephen Gillers, an expert on legal ethics at the New York University School of Law. "We all know the old adage that a lawyer who represents himself has a fool for a client."

Clifford saw none of this, only the opportunity to reshape and rejuvenate his career. Upon his return from London, he had enthusiastically described the offer and its prospects to his wife. "Why don't you just relax?" asked Marny Clifford, with customary honesty. She knew the answer before ever asking the question.

"He's happiest when he's busy," she said later. "And he loves new projects. The bank was a challenge to him, and he loves challenges."

For more than three decades, she had been the dutiful Washington wife, quiet and supportive, raising the children and pursuing her own interests, understanding of her husband's long absences and deferential to the important matters that consumed his days and nights. So, as she had done many times before, she wound up offering her support as her husband embarked on his new career.

In March 1982, the last domino fell. The New York State banking superintendent finally cleared the way for the acquisition of Financial General by Credit and Commerce American Holdings, ending one of the longest takeovers in banking history. Four months later, Financial General Bankshares was rechristened First American Bankshares, a name as resplendently patriotic as that of its new chairman of the board.

20

Chairman of the Board

IN THE SUMMER OF 1982, Clifford became as consumed with
building the bank as he once had been with developing his law firm.
He found himself rising earlier and hurrying through his morning ritual
so that he could get down to the bank's offices at Fifteenth and H Streets
in downtown Washington, not far from the White House. No fig-
urehead, Clifford was a working chairman. He brought on Bob Altman
as president of the holding company and had Symington and two retired
army generals, Elwood Quesada and James M. Gavin, appointed to the
board.

George McGovern, the former senator and Democratic presidential
candidate, discovered how busy Clifford had become when he ran into
him on the street one day that summer and suggested they have lunch
soon. "I just don't do that," replied Clifford earnestly. "It takes too
much time and it's too expensive. I just go down to the local deli or the
drugstore and have a sandwich and a glass of milk. I don't ever go to
fancy restaurants. Frankly, I can't afford to."

It was not that he could not afford a $50 lunch. Rather, Clifford had
no time to spare for a long luncheon. And, unlike many powerful Washington figures, he had no need to be seen dining with important people,
as *New York Times* columnist William Safire discovered. Safire's office
was half a block from Clifford's, and one day he saw the elderly lawyer
sitting alone at the lunch counter of the neighborhood drugstore. "The
ultimate power lunch," thought Safire, who never again felt bad about
having lunch by himself.

For years, the only vacation Clifford had taken was an annual, week-
long trip to Fort Lauderdale, Florida. He stayed in a house provided by
Phillips Petroleum and, joined by Stuart Symington, Senator George
Smathers, and others, played golf and cards all week. Now, the rejuve-
nated septuagenarian decided he no longer had time for even that brief
respite. There was too much to do at the bank.

Financial General had been a tortoise in an industry rarely known for its innovation. Clifford was determined to do more than simply change the name to First American. He wanted to transform the bank into the largest and most profitable financial institution in Washington. He and Altman visited all twelve of the subsidiary banks, interviewing executives and determining who stayed and who left. To the shock of the Washington establishment, the dignified lawyer would appear in television advertisements promoting First American. Even the headquarters building itself was not spared.

The top two floors of the twelve-story building, which also housed the main branch of First American Bank of Washington, had never been completed. When Clifford first surveyed them, he found concrete floors and exposed plumbing. The executive offices were in cramped, cabinet-filled quarters on lower floors. So, with Clifford designing the space as amateur architect and Marny performing the tasks of interior decorator, they set about creating offices appropriate to the new image.

"We built it together," Clifford said proudly. "It was very personal. Here we were owned by these foreign nationals, but we wanted to be an American operation. So all of the furnishings are early American. My wife is particularly good in that field."

Indeed, Marny Clifford threw herself joyously into the task. With the exception of publishing a modestly successful cookbook in 1972, she had not worked since decorating author Lillian Smith's Brooklyn apartment three decades earlier. Now she found herself scurrying to Baltimore and New York in search of furnishings for the bank. She and her husband spent an entire day searching for chandeliers in New York City to grace the board room, the executive offices, the corporate dining room.

All of the tables, desks, chairs, and sofas were early American designs, in keeping with the bank's patriotic name. Mostly they bought top-quality reproductions, but a few pieces were expensive originals. They even hired a painter to decorate one of the entry rooms with scenes out of early American history. Clifford himself designed a graceful, open staircase leading from the eleventh to the twelfth floor.

A grandfather clock was positioned against one wall of Clifford's own office, which was done in rich woods and thick carpet. Unlike the other offices, most of the furniture in the chairman's quarters had been in Marny Clifford's family for generations. There was a chair that had belonged to Daniel Webster, which Marny's father had left to her. And, in keeping with the patriotic tone, a collection of twenty-seven American presidents on horseback by Currier and Ives lined the office walls. These, too, had originally belonged to Marny's father.

"We had wonderful compliments on it, on how attractive it was," said Clifford. "People liked to come in. They were all greatly taken with it. It wasn't too expensive because we watched it with care and kept the expense down, but a great deal of personal effort and attention had gone into this. It was personal. It was exciting. Marny got caught up in it. She was very proud."

With the stage set, Clifford embarked on his career as a banker as the situation was deteriorating a few blocks away at the law firm.

While business had held steady and even prospered during the Nixon years, the Reagan revolution was no boon to Clifford's law practice. On the most concrete level, antitrust laws were essentially entombed, robbing the firm of one of its chief areas of practice. Larry Williams, whose antitrust work had earned him as much as $440,000 a year in the past, watched his practice dry up. "If there is no prosecution, there is no defense," he said. In 1983, he took early retirement. The same year, the firm was hit with three defections. Two younger partners, Richard Spradlin and James Stoval, resigned to search for greener pastures on their own, and Alfred Cortese Jr. left to join a competing firm. Carson Glass retired and moved to Texas. Sam McIlwain went into semiretirement and became "of counsel."

As Clifford watched the lawyers leaving, he kept waiting for Warnke to take up the slack in attracting business. It never happened. To Clifford, it seemed that Warnke was spending more time on arms control issues than on the business of the law firm. Indeed, Warnke emerged as one of the most outspoken and passionate critics of President Reagan's nuclear-arms policies. More than most, Clifford understood the value of a high public profile, but he had always kept at least one eye on attracting clients. Warnke did not seem to understand that part of his role and it caused a rift between the two men. "Warnke just isn't working out the way I expected," Clifford groused to one of his partners.

Since Clifford still controlled the purse strings, he was able to reward and punish as he saw fit. As a result, Altman began earning more money than Warnke. Any doubts about who would ultimately succeed Clifford and take over the firm were removed. Since he had brought him over from the Defense Department, Clifford had expected Warnke to inherit the mantle of leadership and keep the firm alive into the next century. Now, he cast the diligent Bob Altman in that role.

Alongside Clifford, Altman was the primary partner on the only account at the firm that was growing, its representation of First American and, to a much lesser extent, BCCI. With other clients dwindling, the fees received as general counsel to First American became more essential to the firm's financial well-being as the eighties went on. Eventually, the fees topped $2 million a year and kept a third of the firm's lawyers busy. Clifford and Warnke never became quite the "one-client firm" that doomed some legal practices; Phillips Petroleum and other longtime clients continued their annual retainer payments. Nonetheless, the bank loomed larger and larger on the bottom line because there was little new business coming in. "The bank became our biggest client and it is very dangerous to get hooked on a client," John Kovin said later. BCCI also was a good client, paying the firm $500,000 a year in fees.

While the law practice seemed to be slipping except for the two banks, First American was taking off. Profits began to rise by the end of 1983 and they would continue to go up. The investors did not take dividends on their stock. Instead, earnings were turned back into the bank, improving its balance sheet to permit more growth. By the mideighties, First American Bankshares became the largest financial institution in Washington, just as Clifford had envisioned.

With its financial condition improving and Clifford installed at the helm, First American fell off the radar screen of the regulators. Concern about BCCI's role in running the bank faded. The Arab investors appeared to be passive, with Clifford and his all-American crew overseeing the operation. Routine audits of First American and its banks showed no unusual relationship to BCCI. Indeed, the company appeared to be making money and operating cleanly. Behind the scenes, however, Agha Hasan Abedi was playing a role in First American Bankshares. The question was, what was it and who did he represent?

Clifford had pledged to the Federal Reserve that an experienced banker would be hired to head the new institution. When it came to hiring a chief executive officer, Abedi participated in interviews with a series of candidates. One of the candidates, Robert Stevens, a former chairman and chief executive of BankOhio, a large bank holding company in Columbus, Ohio, was concerned enough about Abedi's role that he asked Clifford whether BCCI was involved with First American. Clifford assured Stevens that Abedi was present at the sessions only in his role as adviser to the shareholders, not as chief executive of BCCI. At this stage in his life, Clifford told the banker, he was not about to let anything tarnish his reputation. "You can rely on my integrity," he told Stevens, who accepted the position as chief executive.

While Stevens was chief executive in title, Clifford and Altman dominated the banking company. However, they received plenty of advice from Abedi, holding meetings in London, Washington, or New York to discuss everything from hiring to market strategy. Abedi and other BCCI officials seemed to have the most influence over decisions involving First American's bank in New York. They played a role in most critical decisions, including hiring of management, the business strategy, and the location of the new office on the same block of Park Avenue as the American headquarters of BCCI.

For instance, a 1983 memo from a BCCI employee to Naqvi, Abedi's second in command, suggested that First American New York would operate independently from the other First American banks. "Management style and philosophy will be on the pattern of BCCI — No interference from holding company and free hand to the management," said the memo. Later that year, Bruno Richter was first interviewed by BCCI officials for the post as chief executive of the New York bank. Only after he was recommended by BCCI did Clifford and Altman approve his hiring. Later, when Clifford and Altman became dissatisfied with Richter's performance, they discussed his dismissal with Abedi. His replacement was selected only after an interview with Abedi in London.

Yet in these instances and others, the ultimate decisions were ostensibly made by Clifford and Altman. They consulted often with Abedi. They hired employees recommended by BCCI and even some who had worked for BCCI. However, the two lawyers always maintained that the final decisions were theirs. Indeed, Clifford had come to see the bank as a very personal endeavor, as he made clear when he addressed a group of First American trainees. "You are working for a quality bank, a bank you can be proud of," he told them. "You'll never read about us in a newspaper. You do your job and you'll be proud to work here."

For the most part, the employees were indeed proud to work for the bank. One of the senior officers, for instance, was so impressed to be working directly for a man of Clifford's stature that he stood up from his desk every time Clifford called him on the telephone.

So taken was Clifford by running the bank that in the spring of 1986, his familiar, reassuring face flashed across the television screens of Washington in an advertisement for First American Bank. It was followed by the jack-o-lantern grin of TV weatherman Willard Scott and then scenes of Washington life. Rick Barrow, president of the Washington advertising agency that created the spot, said Clifford was perfect for the cameo. "He's well known, he's got the face of a statesman, and after all he is the board chairman of the bank." When the crew showed up to film Clifford's portion of the ad, they found him gracious, charming, and pleased. Joked Clifford to a reporter at the time: "I'm told I'm on the air one and a half seconds. It's my shortest TV appearance to date."

While Clifford considered the bank his first obligation, he did not abandon the political scene in the eighties. In response to the election of Ronald Reagan and the loss of control of the Senate to the Republicans in 1980, Pamela Harriman, the socialite wife of Averell Harriman, created a political action committee called Democrats for the 80's. Part of its purpose was to raise funds for favored Democratic candidates. Equally important was its role as a sort of clearinghouse for ideas aimed at rejuvenating the party. The center of the organization, dubbed PamPAC, was the Harrimans' elegant home on N Street in Georgetown. There was an annual fund-raising dinner and regular affairs called "Issues Dinners," thousand-dollar-a-night events that brought together prominent Democrats and major money.

One of the charter members, naturally, was Clark Clifford. He and Averell Harriman had been acquaintances since their days together in the Truman administration, when Harriman served as ambassador to the Soviet Union and one of Truman's closest advisers. And the two men had long moved in the same circles and remained in touch.

Harriman, the heir to a vast railroad fortune, had a long career as a financier, governor of New York, secretary of commerce, and ambassador to Great Britain as well as Russia. His first marriage had ended in divorce and his second with the death of his wife. In 1971, the patrician Harriman had shocked Washington when, at the age of seventy-nine, he married Pamela Digby Churchill Hayward, who was fifty-one. The new Mrs. Harriman had been married to Winston Churchill's only son and to

Leland Hayward, the producer of *The Sound of Music*. She was viewed in some of the city's crustier circles as a gold digger, but her husband doted on her.

Clifford, too, was quite taken by Pamela Harriman and credited her with rejuvenating the spirits of her older husband. "She just devoted herself to him," Clifford recalled. "It changed his life. He began to bloom like a rose. He had people in at the house a lot. I just marveled at the wonderful job she did with Averell. He looked younger. He seemed to hear better."

Harriman's name had provided the initial credibility for the political salon run by his wife. But it was Clifford who truly put those gatherings on the national political map.

Clifford enjoyed the evenings when he could share his reminiscences and views with a new generation of Democrats. Among those new Democrats who first met Clifford at PamPAC was John Kerry, a Vietnam hero and freshman senator from Massachusetts. Little did either man know that Kerry would later play a critical role in Clifford's life.

It was at one of those dinners in September 1981 that Clifford uttered the words that put the parties and the PAC into the headlines. Felix Rohatyn, a New York investment banker, was the speaker for the night, and he blasted Reagan's economic plan. Clifford responded by calling Reagan "an amiable dunce" and predicting his policies would soon end in failure. While the session had been off the record, it had been taped for Pamela Harriman, who was out of town. Somehow a transcript of the tape ended up in the hands of James Perry, the top political writer for the *Wall Street Journal*, who repeated the "amiable dunce" phrase in a page-one story.

Clifford was mortified. At first, he denied having uttered the words. Unfortunately, the transcript made that posture difficult. "Oh Hugh," he confided to his friend Hugh Sidey of *Time*, "I do not like this. You know this was taken out of context. I have never been contemptuous of the man in that office. I have too much respect for the office."

The remark reverberated around the country, turning Harriman's salon into the hot spot for Democratic powers and Democratic wannabes. Clifford, too, found himself in some demand again. Near the end of 1983, he was the guest speaker at a breakfast for journalists presided over by Godfrey Sperling Jr. of the *Christian Science Monitor*. As he looked up from his scrambled eggs, Clifford predicted that Reagan's foreign policy was "heading us into very serious trouble. From the time Mr. Reagan came in, he has evidenced publicly a basic hostility to the Soviet Union. It is exceedingly unfortunate and dangerous." As for Reagan's economic policies, Clifford called them "absurd" and "unrealistic."

While he still winced when someone asked about the "amiable dunce" remark, Clifford had stopped denying that he said it. During an appearance on ABC-TV in 1984, when correspondent Sam Donaldson asked Clifford if he had changed his mind about Reagan since making that famous pronouncement, Clifford smiled and said, "No, no. I still feel it."

By then, Clifford was serving on an advisory committee for former Vice President Walter Mondale, the Democratic candidate for president. While his role was mostly ceremonial and many viewed him as an irrelevant symbol of the party's past, Clifford was once again being consulted. Mondale, however, was trounced by Reagan. The president carried forty-nine states and won the electoral vote by a margin of 525 to 13. Only Franklin Roosevelt's 1936 drubbing of Alf Landon was more lopsided.

Trying to put the best face on the Democrats' defeat, Clifford told *Time*: "Every time there's been a landslide, people say the party that lost is through. Well, it doesn't happen that way and it won't this time."

Clifford was not the only partner in the firm who was in the news. So was Bob Altman, although his notices were of a decidedly different nature.

In late 1982, Altman had gone to Memphis, Tennessee, on a business trip for the parent company of Maybelline, the cosmetics firm. A Maybelline executive arranged a dinner for him that night with Lynda Carter, the statuesque Hollywood starlet who had played Wonder Woman in the television series and was now the spokeswoman for the cosmetics line. Carter's first marriage had just broken up and she found the young lawyer from Washington an intriguing change from Hollywood. A year later, Altman proposed to her in Monte Carlo.

On January 29, 1984, they were married at her home in Pacific Palisades, a ritzy community outside Los Angeles. Clifford was the best man and Agha Hasan Abedi, who also attended, gave the bride a black Jaguar automobile as a wedding gift. The marriage was a blend of Hollywood and Washington. A post-wedding party at Washington's F Street

Club hosted by Congressman James Symington brought out congressmen and senators from both parties. Clifford, who always appreciated attractive people, was quite taken by the stunning Carter. "Bob's decision to marry Lynda was an important step in his life," he later said. "She's a real star. She's not only wonderful to look at, but she understands his devotion to the law and supports him in it."

Soon Altman found himself in the tabloids. The paparazzi ambushed the couple emerging from a Hollywood restaurant and the photo was splashed across the *National Enquirer*. One observer noted that Altman looked "like a deer caught in the headlights" and "she looked smashing." In a town starved for celebrity, Altman and Carter became sought-after guests and staples of the gossip columns. The *Washington Post* referred to them as "that couple seen everywhere around town." Their move into a $2.5 million, 20,000-square-foot mansion in affluent Potomac, Maryland, was chronicled by the press. So was the birth of their first son, who was named James Clifford Altman. *The American Lawyer*, a legal publication, included a profile of Altman in an article on up-and-coming lawyers. It ended with Clifford saying, "Twenty years from now I expect him not only to be the leader of this firm but to be the leader of the bar in Washington."

For the first time, Altman had moved out from behind Clifford's shadow and, on the currency of his wife's glamour, soon found himself mixing with prominent Republicans as well as Democrats. It was a measure of the times: Bob Altman had achieved status in Washington not through government service, as had Clifford and so many others, but by marrying a starlet.

By this time, the situation was sharply different at BCCI. Abedi's bank was in serious financial trouble, losing millions and millions of dollars through bad loans and bad trades in the commodities markets. Its books were being falsified to conceal the losses and support a charade of growth and prosperity.

Moreover, some reporters had heard rumors about BCCI's difficulties and were beginning to ask questions. In investigating the bank's activities, some disturbing information had come to light. Alan Frank, an investigative reporter for *Forbes* magazine, had picked up information that indicated BCCI had been involved in money laundering. Checking out the rumor, Frank called Clifford and described what he had heard.

Clifford sounded grave and startled, and he assured the reporter that he would look into the allegations. But Frank never heard back from Clifford.

It remains unclear exactly how much the Central Intelligence Agency and other branches of the American government knew at the time about BCCI's fraudulent activities and its involvement in First American. But suspicions were clearly aroused. Intelligence documents prepared in 1985 and 1986 indicated that BCCI appeared to be involved in laundering the proceeds of drug transactions in the Caribbean. In addition, the bank's dramatic and somewhat mysterious growth had attracted the attention of intelligence agents who had come across an intriguing piece of information — that BCCI secretly owned First American Bankshares of Washington.

In January 1985, the CIA prepared a one-page report on BCCI that was so sensitive it was delivered by hand to Douglas Mulholland, a former CIA official, who was then the intelligence chief at the Treasury Department. According to a later summary of the document prepared by the CIA, the intelligence report contained the startling but unconfirmed allegation that BCCI owned a bank holding company based in Washington. Mulholland, who recognized that the CIA material was "dynamite," took the report directly to Secretary of the Treasury Donald Regan, according to the summary. Mulholland also asked the intelligence agency to identify the Washington bank and learned that it was First American Bankshares.

Secretary Regan had come to Washington from a successful career as president of Merrill Lynch, the Wall Street brokerage house and investment firm. While on Wall Street, Regan had gotten to know Clifford when the lawyer represented Merrill Lynch in the early 1960s. Regan had even sought advice from Clifford when he was invited to join the administration by President Ronald Reagan.

First American Bankshares was regulated in part by the Treasury Department. If Secretary Regan was warned in January 1985 that the CIA suspected a rogue foreign bank secretly owned First American, he might well have been expected to either alert his own regulators or raise the issue with Clifford. However, Regan later said that he had no recollection of ever hearing about the CIA information. And he said that he certainly did not discuss the matter with Clifford. Mulholland supported Regan's recollection, telling a Senate hearing that he had no memory of the CIA report even mentioning BCCI's suspected ownership of a Washington bank or of discussing the document with Regan. For his part, Clifford said that he never spoke with him after Regan joined the Reagan administration. Nonetheless, the conflicting accounts raised questions about who in government knew about the suspicions concerning the true ownership of First American Bankshares.

Since the new Arab owners had taken over First American, the company's books were showing strong growth and rising profits. In late 1984, Clifford had vowed to employees that the bank would one day be one of the nation's twenty largest financial institutions. A year later, fueled largely by the real estate boom in Washington and Northern Virginia, the bank's assets had more than tripled to $7 billion from $2.2 billion in 1982.

In late 1985, First American embarked on an ambitious and ultimately controversial acquisition. Ghaith Pharaon, the Saudi businessman who had bought the National Bank of Georgia from Bert Lance in 1978, was in financial trouble. At the start of 1985, he had pledged all of his stock in National Bank of Georgia to BCCI as collateral for loans from the institution. By the fall of the year, BCCI's auditors were expressing concern about the bank's exposure to Pharaon, whose financial condition was continuing to deteriorate. In London, Abedi decided that Pharaon would have to sell his stock in the Georgia bank so that BCCI's loans could be repaid. The buyer would be First American Bankshares.

Within BCCI, the transaction was viewed as a consolidation of BCCI's interests in the United States. In conversations with Abdur Sakhia, a BCCI official, Abedi referred to the deal as a "merger." Clifford and Altman, however, have maintained that buying the bank was an arm's-length deal that enabled them to expand into a desirable region at a favorable price. What is indisputable is that BCCI played an active role in brokering the sale.

In November 1985, BCCI held a conference in Miami for its international managers. The conference was held at the exclusive Grand Bay Hotel, where Abedi stayed in a $600-a-night suite. Clifford and Altman flew down for a private meeting with Abedi, Naqvi, and two officers from the National Bank of Georgia. After the two lawyers returned to Washington, Abedi announced to the conference that the National Bank of Georgia would be sold to Credit and Commerce American Holdings, the parent company of First American. The price, which was yet to be determined, would turn out to be strikingly high.

In February 1986, an independent evaluation by Keefe, Bruyette and Woods, an investment bank, placed the value of Pharaon's stock at between $130 million and $144 million. A second analysis by First American's own treasurer placed the value at $152 million. The treasurer acknowledged, however, that the bank's location in Atlanta might command a premium payment over that value. In May, Altman wrote to Naqvi that a price in the range of $160 million to $175 million was "nearing the point at which this purchase is too expensive." Yet a week later, after meeting in London with Abedi, Altman agreed to pay $205 million.

Throughout the transaction, which was not completed until 1987, Clifford and Altman played multiple roles. They were lawyers for First American's holding company and they also were lawyers for BCCI. Simultaneously, they were making decisions on the purchase, including the final price, as the chairman and president of First American. On top of that, Clifford and Altman themselves had borrowed a substantial amount of money from BCCI.

The loans to Clifford and Altman were a gift from Abedi that far exceeded the Jaguar the BCCI president had given to Lynda Carter as a wedding gift. In July 1986, the month after Altman had agreed to the price sought by BCCI for Pharaon's bank stock, he and Clifford bought 8,168 shares of stock in Credit and Commerce American Holdings, the parent company of First American Bankshares. Since the stock did not trade on a public exchange, it was a private transaction arranged and executed by BCCI. The lawyers paid roughly $18 million, or $2,216 a share, less than half the amount paid by another investor a few days earlier. Further, and most controversially, they did not invest or risk any of their own money. BCCI loaned the two lawyers the entire $18 million and the only collateral was the stock itself. In addition, BCCI agreed to help Clifford and Altman sell the stock at any time they chose at a price negotiated between the lawyers and BCCI.

Eighteen months later, Clifford and Altman would sell 60 percent of the stock for $6,800 a share, the highest amount ever commanded by shares in the holding company. From the proceeds, they paid off the entire BCCI loan and shared a profit of $9.8 million. They also retained debt-free ownership of the remaining 40 percent of the original block of stock.

Many aspects of the transaction made the loan unusual. For one thing, Clifford and Altman did not put up any of their own money. Banks rarely make loans equal to 100 percent of collateral; they prefer to keep a safety cushion, similar to a homeowner's down payment. In addition, BCCI assumed all of the risk, leaving Clifford and Altman with nothing to lose but the stock itself. Further, the purchase and sale were to the same man, a shadowy Middle Eastern businessman named Mohammed Hammoud. Finally, the Federal Reserve had been promised in 1981 that there would be no financial relationship between BCCI and First American. While the loan to Clifford and Altman was not a direct link, putting up the stock as collateral put BCCI in a position to own a sizable share of the banking company should Clifford and Altman default on the loan payments.

Clifford defended the loan and the stock purchase. He said he had received a modest $50,000 a year as chairman, less than peers at other financial institutions. He described the transaction as justified compensation for him and Altman because of the job they had done in turning First American into a growing, profitable enterprise. He also said it was Adham and Abedi who first proposed the purchase as a means of ensuring that Clifford, who was approaching his eightieth birthday, would remain with the bank.

"We'd had four years of stellar performance," he said later. "We had taken this outfit and really turned it around, and they wanted an additional inducement for me to stay on. . . . So we said, 'Here's the chance. We're over the hump and we would like to participate.' They said, 'We'd like you to participate.' And when it came time to work out the arrangements, they were exceedingly agreeable to doing whatever was reasonably appropriate for us to do."

Clifford was wealthy enough to have financed the entire $18 million purchase himself. In consulting a tax attorney, however, Clifford said he was told it would make better sense to finance as much of the transaction as possible to reduce taxes associated with selling other securities and to minimize estate tax problems for his family if he died.

Although Clifford describes the stock purchase as a normal business transaction, the details were kept secret. In the summer of 1986, at the law firm's regular partnership meeting, Clifford said that he and Altman had been offered an opportunity to buy stock in First American's parent company. He said the offer was available only to them because they were officers of the company. Rather than a no-risk, sweetheart deal, Clifford portrayed the investment as a step he and Altman were undertaking to keep a good client happy.

"It will be quite a sacrifice on our part, but in interest of good client relations, since we have been asked, we are going to do it," one of the partners recalled Clifford saying. "The firm and the partners will be the beneficiaries because the stock purchase will keep relations good with the client."

As for the other board members and executives at First American, they were not informed at all of the deal. When former Senator Charles Mathias, a Republican from Maryland, joined the First American board after leaving the Senate in 1986, he asked Clifford about the prospect of buying stock in the company. Unfortunately, said Clifford, all stock was held by its Arab investors. None was available to directors or officers. Not until a routine audit of bank documents in 1990 did bank officials learn that Clifford and Altman had been stockholders. Even then, the details of the BCCI loan remained hidden.

Federal bank regulators, once so concerned about the possibility of financial links between First American and BCCI, would not learn of the Clifford-Altman stock transaction until even later. When those details did finally begin to emerge, they would wreck the remains of Clifford and Warnke and cast Clifford's role with both BCCI and First American in a new light.

Clifford would later try to fend off criticism of the BCCI loan by saying that he had relied on the advice of financial experts. But it is hard to understand how Clifford, with his great concern over appearances and his shrewdness as an investor, could have failed to foresee the dangers in allowing BCCI to finance the transaction.

Indeed, Clifford's reputation for propriety and financial acumen was so great that two years earlier, Averell Harriman had entrusted him and Paul Warnke with responsibility for investing $13 million in several trusts that Harriman had established for his children, grandchildren, and great-grandchildren. In addition, after Harriman died on July 26, 1986, his widow had hired Clifford and Warnke as lawyers for his $65 million estate. Over the next few years, the two men would earn more than $250,000 in legal fees for advising Mrs. Harriman in connection with the estate. But Clifford's association with the Harriman trusts and estate was destined to bring him more troubles at a time when he could not afford them.

Those problems were far off as 1986 drew to a close. Clifford seemed to be still in his prime. At a reception in his home marking his eightieth birthday, the forty guests found Clifford as lively and vibrant as a man half his age as he moved through the many public rooms of his house, smiling and nodding slightly to his guests.

Betty Beale, a long-time chronicler of Washington society for the defunct *Washington Star*, was examining the mementos of Clifford's long career in Washington in the small barroom between the living room and the kitchen that day. On the walls were photographs of Clifford with Truman, Kennedy, and Johnson as well as letters of commendation and salutation from world leaders. As Clifford passed through the room, she stopped him and asked how he managed to look so marvelous at eighty. With a twinkle, he said, "I've observed old people and there are so many things they do that I avoid doing. For example, they slump, so I stand very erect. When they get out of chairs, they get out slowly, holding onto the sides. Well, I pop up. They like to talk about their operations and their ailments, so I never do."

There was another reason for Clifford's remarkable vigor in those days. His career at First American had invigorated not only the coffers of his law firm but Clifford himself. He was eager to get to work each day, intimately involved in the details of running the bank. "What most people want when they get older is tranquility, peace," said Clifford later. "I didn't want that. I was looking for something else that would excite me. I knew there was a built-in limitation, or a possible one. You get to a point where you don't know how your health is going to be. But I did not say to myself, 'You are going to do this for ten or five years.' As long as it was going to be interesting to me, challenging to me, and as long as I was enjoying what I was doing, I was going to do it."

In his excitement, he was drawn deeper and deeper into the operations of the bank. He and Altman made key decisions on hiring and firing in all of the bank's divisions, always after consultation with Abedi or someone else from BCCI. Perhaps it was this enthusiasm for a second chance that caused Clifford to overlook the warning signs. In another day, when things were going better at the law firm, his instinct for survival might have led him to question what was going on between First American and BCCI, and his role in those transactions. Perhaps it was an elderly man's refusal to accept tranquility and peace that would rob him of both in his final years.

Still, years later, after the bank had plunged him into a nightmare of accusation and allegation that forever altered the way he would be perceived in the history books, Clifford refused to wish away the experience.

"Even with all the trouble, I am still glad I did it," he said ruefully one morning in the spring of 1994 as he sat in the comfortable living room of the house where he had spent the last forty-four years. "It kept me active. It may have added five or ten years to my life. I cannot be inactive."

21

A Life Divided

IMPECCABLY DRESSED and smiling broadly, Clifford convened a meeting on January 14, 1988, of executives from the Knight-Ridder publishing empire and the company's lawyers in the conference room at Clifford and Warnke. The topic was how to convince Attorney General Edwin Meese to reverse the findings of his own antitrust division and approve the merger of the business operations of the *Detroit Free Press* and the *Detroit News*.

The previous year had been relatively uneventful for Clifford. The deal to buy the National Bank of Georgia had closed and the Atlanta institution was brought into the First American Bankshares family. He had had a brief fling at national politics again, courtesy of Bert Lance.

The former Carter budget director had hooked up with the Reverend Jesse Jackson's short-lived 1988 presidential candidacy. In an attempt to bolster Jackson's image with the Washington establishment, Lance had persuaded a handful of Democratic notables, led by Clifford, to sign on as campaign advisers. Clifford's heart was never in the task. He scarcely knew Jackson. But no one else had asked for his help, so he praised the candidate in a few interviews and appeared at a news conference with him. Other than that, Clifford had played no real role in a campaign that ultimately went nowhere anyway.

But 1988 would mark a turning point, the start of one of those periods of rare clarity after which a life can be divided forever. On one side of the line, everything was bright and promising, a triumph of will and wisdom. Crossing over to the other side, however, meant moving into darkness and uncertainty, grasping at the accolades of a lifetime in a vain attempt to break a heartbreaking fall from grace.

The year can be defined by two significant legal matters in which the lawyer played major roles. One, the Detroit newspaper merger, was important largely as an illustration of Clifford's sustained influence in Washington. Despite the fact that he would be eighty-two that year and would grossly mishandle a critical question in court, at its conclusion he would be honored with a triumphant dinner. Clifford came out on top. The second, involving the Bank of Credit and Commerce International and First American Bankshares, would thrust Clifford over the invisible line into a maze of unimaginable events. Although critical matters would be decided in court in this case, too, the final verdict would not be rendered there. The ultimate judgment would come in the arena where Clifford had always been at his best: the court of public opinion.

Clifford had been on Knight-Ridder's board of directors since the company was formed by the merger of the Knight and Ridder newspaper chains in 1974. However, he had only recently been brought into the attempt to combine the business operations of the two Detroit newspapers. Knight-Ridder was unhappy with the results achieved by its primary outside counsel, the Washington firm of Hughes, Hubbard and Reed.

Knight-Ridder owned the *Detroit Free Press*, and the competing *Detroit News* was owned by the Gannett Company, another publishing industry giant. The two papers were locked in a bruising, money-losing war for readers and advertisers. In an attempt to cut the financial losses, the owners wanted to combine the business operations of the *Free Press* and *News* through what was called a joint operating agreement. The efficiencies — and the truce in competition — would turn red ink into black; some projections foresaw two industry giants sharing $100 million a year in profits.

While such an arrangement would violate federal antitrust laws in most industries, the federal Newspaper Preservation Act allows for joint operations in cases where one newspaper would fail without the savings inherent in such an agreement. The intent of the law was to keep alive as many newspapers as possible.

Opponents in Detroit had expressed fears that the agreement would still the independent editorial voices of the newspapers. They argued that neither paper was in bad enough shape to close and the move was motivated solely by the greed of the companies. The Justice Department's antitrust division and an administrative law judge essentially agreed and opposed the Detroit merger. The administrative law judge, Morton Needleman, was particularly tough in his conclusions, saying that both papers had tolerated substantial losses only because they expected to be rescued by a joint operating agreement. Neither paper, he said, qualified for such assistance.

Knight-Ridder had appealed the decision, putting it into the lap of Ed Meese, the attorney general. However, the company faced an uphill battle. The record before the administrative law judge appeared airtight against the agreement. The decision to hire Clifford stemmed from the feeling that new tactics were required.

Alvah Chapman Jr., the chairman of Knight-Ridder, described hiring Clifford to the *Free Press* this way: "I said, 'Clark, we have a problem. We're hung up on the technicalities of the law, and I think there are some broader issues that we need to be dealing with.' " Jack Fontaine, the general counsel of Knight-Ridder, added, "We also thought we needed a very visible, eloquent advocate who would deliver the legal message in a more evangelical style."

Clifford had agreed to devote himself full-time to the case, and he spent hours reading the material accumulated for the hearing before the administrative law judge. He decided that the battle had been fought on the wrong terms. The assumption had been that the end result would be either a joint operating agreement or the continued fierce struggle between the *Free Press* and the *News*. Forming a new strategy, he determined that it must be cast in starker terms — either the request was granted or Knight-Ridder would close the *Free Press*, leaving Detroit a one-newspaper town.

The purpose of the January 14 meeting was to devise a political strategy to get the message across to Ed Meese. Here, too, Clifford had conceived a plan. The company would seek signed letters from key political, civic, and business leaders supporting the agreement and submit them to Meese. Philip Lockavera, a former Watergate prosecutor who had been the lead lawyer on the case for Hughes, Hubbard, argued against the letter-writing campaign. He warned that the tactic could be seen as gross political interference in what should be a strictly legal decision. Lockavera had had his chance. Clifford won the day with his argument that there was no alternative.

By the end of the month, Knight-Ridder executives were mustering support from the business and civic community while Clifford and Altman were meeting with members of the Michigan congressional delegation. The lawyers had drafted a letter to Meese and several of the congressmen, including Democrat John Dingell of Detroit, one of the most powerful members of the House of Representatives and a close friend of Robert Altman's, had agreed to sign it. In all, thirty-seven letters from business and political leaders were attached to the legal brief that Clifford and Warnke filed on behalf of Knight-Ridder. In a preamble to the brief, Clifford had warned that the *Free Press* would be closed unless Meese approved the agreement.

Faced with the political pressure, Meese approved the merger in August, reversing his own department's findings and arguing that the agreement was necessary for the survival of the papers. Meese, who was under investigation himself for unrelated matters, then resigned as attorney general.

Clifford, with the power of both the company's lawyer and a member of its board, argued that the merger should be carried out immediately, before the opponents could take action to block Meese's decision. Before the agreement could be implemented, a reporter for the *Detroit News* sought help from Ralph Nader's Public Citizen, a watchdog group in Washington that monitors corporate behavior in America. After a hurried weekend of reading on the case, Bill Schultz and David Vladeck, two lawyers at the organization, filed papers in United States District Court in Washington seeking a temporary restraining order to stop the merger. As one of his arguments, Schultz suggested that Clifford had improperly lobbied Ed Meese.

On September 8, Clifford made a rare appearance in federal court in Washington. Other lawyers on the case could probably have argued the merits of the matter better, but Clifford had an ulterior motive. He wanted to defend his honor. He denied that he had had any improper contact with Meese before the attorney general's decision. Indeed, he said, his involvement in the case stemmed from his conviction of the merits of the joint operating agreement, not from his ability to influence decision makers. Based on Clifford's defense, the judge refused to allow Schultz and Vladeck to question Meese under oath about his contacts with Clifford or any of the congressmen enlisted to support the merger. Later, the attorney general provided a sworn statement in which he said there were "no substantive" discussions with Clifford, although the two men had met privately in Meese's office in June. The topic of that discussion was never disclosed.

In addressing the merits of the case in court, Clifford's style was more emotional than legalistic. However, at every point he hammered home his theme: if Knight-Ridder does not get this joint operating agreement, the *Free Press* will be closed.

Schultz was not surprised when the judge, George Revercomb, up-held Meese's decision. Revercomb had seemed awed by Clifford's presence. In fact, Schultz had already prepared the papers to file his appeal with the United States Circuit Court of Appeals in Washington. In that forum, Clifford's emotional arguments would fall on deaf ears. The judges would want to discuss the legal underpinnings, opening a trap-door into which Clifford would stumble.

The day after Clifford argued the Knight-Ridder case in Washington, a BCCI banker named Amjad Awan was having a drink in the bar of the Grand Bay Hotel, one of his favorite haunts in Miami's Coconut Grove section. His companion was Bob Mazur, and Awan knew him as a shady businessman who laundered money for Colombian drug dealers. The topic of discussion was Clark Clifford and Bob Altman, and Awan was angry at the two lawyers.

Senator John Kerry, the Massachusetts Democrat, was chairman of a subcommittee of the Foreign Relations Committee. While examining the financial activities of General Manuel Noriega, Kerry's investigators had discovered that BCCI was helping the Panamanian strongman move funds out of his country. For several months, the inquiry had proceeded quietly. Now, however, Kerry's investigators wanted Awan, who handled the Noriega account, to testify before the subcommittee.

In the bar, Awan groused that BCCI had ordered him moved to Paris at the suggestion of Altman so that he would be unavailable to testify. For his part, Altman later would say he merely wanted Awan moved for his own safety because he was concerned about possible retaliation by Noriega. Mazur replied that he thought the bank's Washington lawyers had neutralized the Senate inquiry.

"Well, our attorneys are, they're heavyweights," said Awan. "I mean Clark Clifford is sort of the Godfather of the Democratic Party. He's been in the White House since the time of Truman. He was Truman's legal counsel. He's like eighty years old, but he's still all there. That's a very heavyweight firm."

But Awan was suspicious of Clifford. He thought that he and Altman were maneuvering to remove BCCI from its role in First American Bankshares. "We own a bank based in Washington," he confided in Mazur. "It's called First American Bank. The holding company is in Washington and there are five banks actually. First American of New

York. First American of Washington, D.C. First American of Virginia, Maryland, Tennessee, and Georgia. There are six banks. Six large banks. Bought out by BCCI about eight years ago. BCCI was acting as adviser to them, but the truth of the matter is that the bank belongs to BCCI. Those guys are just nominee shareholders."

Mazur did not respond to Awan's news about First American and BCCI. His concern was laundering drug money through BCCI's offices in Miami, where Awan worked, and Tampa. The allegation would remain secret for a while longer.

Later that month, Clifford made his first appearance in Senator Kerry's office. The two men sat in armchairs and discussed the inquiry into BCCI. So far, the bank had refused to turn over all of the internal documents about Noriega sought by the subcommittee. Now, Clifford was at his most reassuring.

"I want you to understand," he told Kerry. "We are prepared to cooperate. We want to be helpful."

His hands folded in the classic Clifford steeple, the lawyer assured Kerry that he knew of no documents regarding Noriega that were under the control of BCCI, apart from a small number already provided to the subcommittee in response to a subpoena. Kerry, only a freshman senator, wanted to believe Clifford. He did not want to buck this man and all that he symbolized in the Democratic Party. After all, Kerry had his own ambitions and he was only beginning to make his mark in the Senate. So far, however, the bank had not been cooperating.

To Clifford, John Kerry was the kind of flash-in-the-pan, handsome young politician that he had seen come and go by the dozen. The Senate inquiry was little more than a nuisance that was handled primarily by Altman while Clifford devoted himself to the Knight-Ridder case. That began to change on the afternoon of October 8, a Saturday.

Amjad Awan and several other BCCI employees had been invited to a resort outside Tampa for a reception honoring Bob Mazur and his bride, who were to be married the following day. As the afternoon slipped into evening, Awan and the other men at the party piled into limousines to go downtown for a bachelor party. As they emerged from the cars, however, they were arrested, handcuffed, and taken to jail.

Mazur was an undercover agent of the United States Customs Service. For nearly two years, he had posed as a money launderer for the Colombian drug cartels, meeting with BCCI officers around the world and discovering what appeared to be massive corruption at the bank. In all, eleven BCCI employees were charged along with the bank itself and two Colombians. At the time, BCCI was the seventh-largest privately held bank in the world, with offices in seventy-three countries and assets of $20 billion.

On the Monday following the arrests, Clifford and Altman went to work in Washington assembling a team to defend the bank and the individual employees. Clifford and Altman would not formally enter the case, although they would coordinate aspects of the defense and hire some of the top defense lawyers in Washington and Miami. Eventually, legal bills in the case would top $20 million.

The indictment prompted a brief flurry of press interest, but soon the headlines faded. Even the first dose of publicity, however, had spooked some of the partners at Clifford and Warnke. The firm had handled criminal cases for its corporate clients in the past, but those had been more genteel white-collar matters. This one smelled bad, of Columbian drug lords, cocaine, and dirty money. Paul Warnke listened to some of the others who were worried about how the firm's involvement would look to the big corporations whose retainers were the lifeblood of Clifford and Warnke. Business already was off. This would only make things worse. In December, Warnke agreed with them, and he was certain that Clifford would agree, too. After all, no one had ever been more determined to control and shape his public image than Clark Clifford. Warnke just had to make the potential dangers clear to Clifford.

"We should drop BCCI as a client," Warnke said when he finally approached Clifford late one afternoon. "It isn't the kind of work we do nor the kind of client we should be associated with."

Clifford was seated at his desk, the tips of his fingers pressed gently together in a characteristic steeple. He spoke slowly and deliberately. "I have never left a client in distress," he said gravely. "You must be there when they need you. It's a lawyer's job."

"Everybody is entitled to a lawyer, but I don't think it has to be us in this case," Warnke replied. "It's not the right image for us."

Clifford would not hear of abandoning the bank or its employees, despite the distastefulness of the allegations. Warnke and some other partners in the firm might be unhappy, but there was nothing they could do. Clifford had never run his firm as a democracy. For nearly forty years, every issue of significance was decided by one man, and that man was determined to defend BCCI.

Other matters were weighing on Clifford. In early October, the week before the BCCI indictments, he had been sitting in a federal courtroom in Alexandria, Virginia. This time, Clifford was the client, represented by lawyers from another firm in a lawsuit filed by a retired Radio City Music Hall Rockette against First American Bankshares and its directors.

The woman, Doris Sandberg, claimed that she did not get a fair price when minority shareholders in First American Bank of Virginia were required to sell their stock to the parent company a year earlier for $42 a share. Her lawyers were from the powerful Washington firm of Hogan and Hartson, led by Joseph M. Hassett, one of the firm's most brilliant litigators. After a week-long trial, the jury decided the stock was worth $60 a share, resulting in a $13 million judgment on behalf of the minority shareholders against First American, Clifford, Altman, and other directors. Adding insult to injury, the judge concluded that it was Clifford who had set the $42 price, with the other directors serving as nothing but a rubber stamp. Indeed, under questioning in the case, Clifford said he arrived at the price after he "conducted a proceeding in my mind."

Eventually the judgment was reduced to $1.3 million, which was covered by the company's insurance. However, for the few who noticed at the time, the episode had highlighted a more important issue. Had Clifford and Altman placed themselves in a conflict of interest by simultaneously representing the banking company and serving as its top executives? "Clifford had a belief that he could represent all interests in a given situation and that all interests would be served by whatever decision he made," observed Hassett.

There were troubles of a more personal nature, too. In August, Clifford's friend and longtime rival Edward Bennett Williams had died, and a final terribly sad encounter with him remained emblazoned on Clifford's memory.

Robert Strauss, who had become a leading lawyer and lobbyist, telephoned Clifford in May. He said he had not seen Williams in a long time and he had heard that he did not have long to live. Strauss proposed that he and Clifford get together for lunch with their old friend. Clifford agreed readily, arranging for the three men to have luncheon in his private dining room at First American.

Williams was thin and sallow, a ghost of the robust lawyer who had lived so high. He did not touch the food served by the white-coated waiter. When he had to go to the lavatory, Clifford stood quickly and helped him to the door. When Clifford sat back down at the table, tears welled up in his eyes and he began to sob, his whole body heaving.

"Clark, you can't do this," urged Strauss in hushed tones. "Ed will be back in a minute and he can't see you like this."

Clifford stopped crying, dipped his napkin in water to clear his face, and willed himself through the remainder of the lunch.

Now, as the year was coming to a close, Clifford had lost another even dearer friend. Stuart Symington died in December, within days of Clifford's eighty-second birthday. At a memorial service for Symington at the National Cathedral on January 10, 1989, Clifford sat near the podium waiting to deliver his eulogy. He looked out over the high-ceilinged cathedral at the senators, lawyers, and other luminaries who had come to remember Symington. When it was his turn, Clifford rose slowly and walked with great dignity to the podium.

"Stuart Symington was my best friend" began the opening to a vintage performance by Clifford. The speech was a Clifford classic, moving and concise, elegant without being maudlin, and delivered in a voice as clear and deep as it had been calling out tennis scores half a century earlier in St. Louis. And, although Clifford was not a religious man, he knew the power of the Bible and he closed by saying: "I know that Our Lord felt kindly toward Stuart Symington, and if during his lifetime Our Lord had had a chance to speak with him, I think he might well have spoken in the words He used in 12 Matthew, Verse 18, when He said: 'Here is my servant, whom I have chosen, the one I love and with whom I am pleased. I will send my spirit upon you and he will announce my judgment to the nations. He will persist until he causes justice to triumph and on him all people will put their hope.' "

The deaths of Williams and Symington had been preceded by so many others, by Kennedy, Johnson, Truman, Bill Douglas, Bob Kerr, Averell Harriman. Clifford was left to contemplate what he had come to see as the worst part of growing old — the sense of isolation and loneliness. Soon enough, Clifford would have to fight another battle, too.

But there were still times when Clifford was drawn back into the political fray, although they were less and less frequent. One came in the spring of 1989 when he was asked to lend a hand in the defense of House Speaker Jim Wright. The Texas Democrat was under scrutiny for a series of ethical lapses and potential misconduct, including a financial arrangement relating to a book he had published and his intercession with bank regulators on behalf of some savings and loan owners from Texas. After a critical February 1989 report by the House Ethics Committee, pressure had been building for the speaker to resign.

In seeking advice on what to do, Wright talked with Michigan Democrat John Dingell, an old ally in the House and one of its most powerful members. Dingell and his young second wife, Debbie, were close friends of Bob Altman and Lynda Carter, and Dingell suggested that Wright seek advice from Altman and his partner Clifford. Wright, who had been in Congress since 1955, could have called Clifford himself, but the fact that one of Washington's most powerful men sought assistance first through Altman was testimony to the younger lawyer's rising position in the city. During the weeks in which Clifford and Altman provided free advice to Wright, it was Altman who continuously took the lead, attending most of the meetings and arguing most vocally.

In April, the Ethics Committee was pressuring Wright to turn over information about his personal finances related to the book he had published, and he was resisting. There was talk of cutting a deal in which the speaker could turn over certain material in exchange for receiving only a reprimand from the committee.

"Don't turn over anything," argued Altman during a meeting in the speaker's office in the Capitol, which was not attended by Clifford. "Mr. Clifford believes you've got to fight this all the way."

"That may be great legal advice, but it is piss poor political advice," replied Tony Coelho, the California congressman who was the second-ranking Democrat in the House. "If you stonewall the committee, you are going to get kicked out of the House. You have got to turn over some stuff and cut a deal."

Clifford did believe that Wright should put up a fight. While the elder lawyer was not certain the speaker would win, he felt strongly that he should tell his side of the story in public. The position was a source of tension with the speaker's staff and other congressmen who, like Coelho, did not want to challenge the committee. They believed that the only way to avoid a forced resignation was to throw himself on the mercy of his colleagues. Altman only aggravated the tension by continuously referring to his partner as "Mr. Clifford" while referring to the speaker as "Jim."

By the end of May, Wright had become convinced that he could not remain in Congress. The charges were accumulating and only his resignation would stop the investigation. On the morning of May 31, he drove into Washington from his home in Virginia with a young aide, Mark Johnson. He had made up his mind to quit, but he was still second-guessing the decision.

"Clark says I should fight," Wright confided.

"What are you going to do?" asked Johnson.

Wright paused for a long time. "I think I'll have some remarks on the floor later this afternoon," he replied. After spending the morning alone in his office, Wright went onto the floor of the House of Representatives and delivered a stirring and emotional resignation speech. In the end, he had been unable to withstand the relentless pressure on him.

Much as he had revised the story of his advice to Abe Fortas about whether to resign from the Supreme Court in 1969, Clifford did not want to reveal that his advice had been rejected by Wright. When he was interviewed by Terry Carter, a reporter for the *National Law Journal*, in the wake of the speaker's resignation, Clifford said that it had become clear to him that Wright had to step down, leaving the inference that yet another powerful Washington figure had followed his wise advice.

Reflecting on Wright's plight much later, Clifford thought to himself, "How much rougher and more personal the game has gotten since I arrived in Washington in 1945."

What had changed in those forty-four years was that Clifford and others like him were no longer able to function with total self-confidence about their judgment and their right to power. The civil rights movement, Vietnam, Watergate, feminism, and other events and factors had destroyed the quiet certainty of those glory days. The nation had grown suspicious of power, particularly Washington power. Equally important in Clifford's case, the press corps had grown cynical about the motives of those in power. Instead of being taken at face value on the basis of his illustrious career, Clifford's background would make him a bull's-eye for reporters who had become distrustful of anyone with power and influence. Clifford was about to find out how much rougher and more personal life had become in Washington.

*   *   *

By the fall of 1989, Clifford was in an unusual alliance with the Justice Department on the Detroit newspaper case. Ed Meese's decision in favor of the joint operating agreement had put the newspapers and the Justice Department on the same side as they argued that the attorney general had the authority to decide the case without inteference by the courts.

The lawyer in charge of the case for the government was Douglas Letter, an excellent young attorney in the civil division. He had grown up in a staunchly Democratic household in Northern Virginia, so meeting Clifford was an honor and a pleasure. Letter was struck not only by the elder lawyer's politeness to him, but by the fact that he was spearheading the defense.

"Usually when I deal with a big-time partner at a big firm, I feel his mind is elsewhere until he has to focus on this case," recalled Letter. "Then he may make some general remarks and turn it over to a junior partner or associate. Clark Clifford was quite the opposite. He did almost all the talking at the meetings. It seemed clear to me that Clifford was one of the main guys doing the strategy for this case. He was running things from the newspapers' side. This guy was really in command of his faculties. It was his case."

When it came time to argue the case before the Court of Appeals in late October, Letter assumed that he would make the first remarks. After all, he had far more experience in appeals cases and the government traditionally went first to set the tone. Letter found that Clifford had a different plan. "It was absolutely clear to me that Clifford had decided he was going to go first," said the government lawyer. "All of this was said in the most courtly way, but he was going to go first. He just wouldn't entertain the idea that it might be me. Frankly, had he shown me less competence or treated me poorly, I could have told the court we had reached an impasse and the judges would have to decide who went first, but I couldn't do that. In the end, it was fortunate that he did go first."

On October 29, Clifford rose without notes and began to address the three-judge panel. Before he got far into his remarks, however, Judge Ruth Bader Ginsburg, who would one day join the Supreme Court, interrupted and urged Clifford to get to his argument. A few minutes later, Judge Laurence Silberman interrupted, too. What relevance did Clifford assign to the Chevron case? asked Silberman.

Chevron had established that the courts should not interfere with decisions made by government agencies. It was a critical precedent supporting Meese's authority to make the final decision on the joint operating agreement. Every lawyer at both tables knew about Chevron, except the one standing in front of the judges, who tried a bluff.

"I know you are familiar with it," replied Clifford. "We have been familiar with it. I'm not in position to say that I think it has any important impact upon this particular instance."

Letter was stunned. Their entire argument was buttressed by Chevron. When Clifford sat down a few minutes later and the Justice Department lawyer stepped forward, he knew he had to rectify the gross error.

"I hope, Mr. Letter, you realize there was a $64 question that Judge Ginsburg and I put to Mr. Clifford, the answer to which I think, if his answer is correct, you probably lose," said Silberman.

"Your honor," replied Letter, "I think it's a $64,000 question and . . ."

"Maybe $64 million," interjected Silberman.

Letter then went on to say that Chevron was directly on point, that it supported the position of the newspapers and the Justice Department that ultimate authority for the decision rested with the attorney general, not the courts. In late January 1989, the appeals court ruled two-to-one in favor of the newspapers, citing the Chevron precedent as a key factor. Again, the lawyers from Public Citizen obtained a stay to stop the merger.

The full Court of Appeals upheld the validity of Meese's decision. Another delay was obtained. Finally, the Supreme Court took up the case. Clifford did not appear before the court. This time, the Justice Department handled the oral presentation. On November 3, 1989, the court announced its decision — the justices were deadlocked, four to four. The tie meant that the decision of the Court of Appeals in favor of the merger was upheld and it could finally go forward.

The ninth member of the court, Justice Byron White, declined to participate in the case. As was his custom, he gave no reason for excusing himself. Bill Schultz pondered why White had bowed out. Perhaps it was because he had played professional football in Detroit. Perhaps it was the result of a chance question he had asked a Knight-Ridder executive months before at a cocktail party about the status of the merger. Perhaps it was because he and Clifford had known each other for more than a quarter century. Whatever the reason, Knight-Ridder had won, and Clifford was a hero.

The sounds of laughter and clinking glasses could be heard in the Anderson Room of the Metropolitan Club in Washington on the last day of January 1990. Knight-Ridder was hosting a dinner in honor of Clark Clifford to pay homage to his role in winning approval of the joint operating agreement.

There was no better place in all of Washington to honor Clifford. The Metropolitan Club represented tradition and power. Even in the face of the changing political and social scene, membership was still coveted. Behind the scarlet draperies and the eighteen-foot windows, inside the kelly green cardroom and the library with its fifteen thousand volumes, members could imagine that they still controlled the destiny of the nation and even the world.

Clifford himself had captured the appeal a few years earlier when he described the club to a *New York Times* reporter. "The Metropolitan Club has remained an island of stability and respector of precedence in the disturbing sea that washes around it," said Clifford, who always spoke with care when he knew he was being quoted. "So much has changed in the country. But it is still a great heaven for men here — men who come and are in government for a period of time, others who come and stay and make this home, men who were born here and live here. Washington is a unique spot. Administrations come and go, top personnel changes — there is a need for a place that offers stability and the same kind of atmosphere that was offered one hundred years ago. It is a distinction in Washington to be a member of the Metropolitan."

The menu that January night in 1990 was extravagant — poached filet of sole with Chassagne-Montrachet 1983, roast tenderloin of beef with Chateau Beychevelle 1979 — and so was the praise. Alvah Chapman and other company executives rose to honor the old man, whose photograph was on the night's printed program along with a replica of the Supreme Court's one-page decision.

Clifford was a gracious guest. As he rose to deliver his thank-you speech, he reflected on his life. "I have been working on my memoirs," he told the audience. "They have been for me the occasion to think deeply about my youth and my time with my father."

Clifford, who the previous month had celebrated his eighty-third birthday, spoke of the lamplighter who came down his street in St. Louis so long ago. In his skilled, melodious voice, he described the kindness of his father and the work ethic instilled in him by a railroad clerk whose own ambitions had gone unfulfilled. He spoke of his years as a young trial lawyer in St. Louis, and the heady days of the Truman administration. He touched on his association with John Kennedy and his tenure as secretary of defense under Lyndon Johnson.

Doug Letter was normally unimpressed by high-rolling executives and hot-shot private attorneys. But he was spellbound by Clifford's oratory. "It lasted forty-five minutes or so," he said later. "It struck me that PBS should record these long interviews with Clifford because he was such a fascinating person and had such a range of American history at his control." Warmed by the fine French wines and awed by the reveries of a master storyteller, Letter could not wait to get home so he could recount the great man's speech to his wife.

This was not Clark Clifford's last hurrah. But his life had begun its turn from one of triumph toward tragedy. Events set in motion a decade before were gaining momentum and they were about to transform this great man from venerable to vulnerable. His life would be divided, and the glories recounted with such grace on a chilly night inside the Metropolitan Club would be tarnished forever.

22

Under Siege

TWO WEEKS BEFORE he was honored by Knight-Ridder, Clifford had basked in another triumph. After months of tedious negotiations, on January 15, 1990, the Bank of Credit and Commerce International and one of its subsidiaries had pleaded guilty to laundering drug money. The plea entered in federal court in Tampa was a stunning victory for BCCI's lawyers, who had been led by Lawrence Barcella, a former federal prosecutor hired by Clifford and Altman. The bank would pay a $14.8 million fine, but it would be spared a lengthy public trial. In addition, the federal government agreed not to prosecute BCCI for any other criminal violations under scrutiny in the ongoing investigation.

By this time, Agha Hasan Abedi was barely involved in BCCI's affairs. A heart attack the previous year had left him incapacitated, and Swaleh Naqvi was running the bank. Naqvi was effusive in his praise of Clifford in the wake of the plea bargain, writing the lawyer: "On behalf of BCC and on my own behalf kindly accept our gratitude in guiding us in the most traumatic experience. We were guided by your wisdom, experience, realisms and purity of your relationship with BCC."

The expectation, at Clifford and Warnke as well as at BCCI headquarters in London, was that the plea bargain would take the pressure off the bank. Even inside the institution, few people knew the true financial condition of BCCI. The bank had been reporting steadily growing earnings since the early eighties, but the numbers were a hoax. Since the mid-eighties, when a rogue employee lost hundreds of millions of dollars speculating in the commodities markets, BCCI had been deep in the red, awash in bad loans to Arab insiders and other favored customers.

There were darker secrets, too. Along with laundering money in the Customs Service undercover operation, BCCI had helped General Noriega funnel millions of dollars out of Panama and served as banker to the Palestinian terrorist Abu Nidal. The Central Intelligence Agency had used BCCI to pay for covert operations around the world. Indeed, the agency was so thoroughly knowledgeable about its nature that Robert Gates, deputy director of the CIA at the time, privately referred to BCCI in 1988 as "the Bank of Crooks and Criminals."

The true portrait of BCCI had remained hidden behind a facade of profitability and honesty erected with the assistance of political leaders around the world. Former British Prime Minister James Callaghan had been a paid adviser to BCCI. Former President Jimmy Carter had formed a partnership with BCCI's Abedi to build hospitals and other projects in the Third World. And in Washington, Clark Clifford had been the bank's lawyer and perhaps more.

One more secret was buried within the bank. Amjad Awan had mentioned it casually to the undercover agent the month before the Tampa indictment. Since then, however, no one in law enforcement or bank regulation had investigated his claim that BCCI owned First American Bankshares.

Unfortunately for the bank and, ultimately, for Clifford, the plea agreement did not end the scrutiny. Senator Kerry criticized the plea bargain, arguing that BCCI was a corporate institution that should be barred from doing business in the United States.

Kerry was becoming a problem. Clifford and Altman began a series of maneuvers intended to both co-opt and discredit the persistent Massachusetts senator. In a direct approach, Clifford telephoned Frances Zwenig, Kerry's administrative assistant, to ask her if the senator would sign a letter praising Clifford's stewardship of First American Bankshares. Zwenig told Clifford that she did not think such a letter was appropriate, but she thought to herself, "Who am I to be telling Clark Clifford what's appropriate?"

A week later, Clifford called to renew his request. Zwenig recalled the conversation, saying, "He was very polite. It was subtle. But it was intimidation. I didn't realize it at the time, but he was trying to compromise John Kerry. He didn't miss a trick."

Indeed, had the letter been written, Clifford could have used it to deflect any attention that might come to him from the BCCI publicity. More important, the letter could have served to undercut any further investigation by Kerry into Clifford's role as a possible link between BCCI and First American.

At the same time, Clifford, Altman, and other members of Clifford and Warnke contributed $1,000 each to Kerry's reelection campaign.

On a more public front, Kerry was attacked by Senator Orrin Hatch, the Republican from Utah, who was a close friend of Bob Altman. Using a script drafted by Altman and other lawyers for BCCI, Hatch went on the Senate floor on February 22 to denounce Kerry's criticism of the BCCI plea bargain and argue that BCCI was a "good corporate citizen."

In late March, Clifford had the rare privilege of addressing a joint session of Congress. The occasion was the centennial of the birth of President Eisenhower. In recalling Eisenhower's triumphs, Clifford praised the late president's courage in supporting Israel. His remarks angered some of the Arabs involved with First American, who felt the comments about Israel were inappropriate for the head of a large, Arab-owned bank.

But the real problems were emerging elsewhere. BCCI finally had attracted the attention of the press. In May 1990, *Regardie's* magazine, a sometimes-muckraking publication in Washington, published a story by investigative reporter Larry Gurwin suggesting that First American had ownership links to BCCI. Part of the evidence was Amjad Awan's claims to the undercover agent, which had been disclosed in a document filed in connection with Awan's forthcoming trial. The same month, the *Wall Street Journal* ran a front-page article calling BCCI a "rogue bank."

When the First American board met on May 24, the directors discussed the allegations in the articles. Former Senator Mathias was particularly concerned about the implications. However, Clifford offered his reassurance that the articles were unfounded. There were no ties between the two institutions, he told the directors.

The allegations surfaced at a touchy time for First American. The bank had loaned millions of dollars to Washington-area real estate developers in the booming eighties. Now the recession had put the brakes on the boom and forced many major developers into bankruptcy. In addition, the purchase of the National Bank of Georgia had turned out to be a cash drain on the parent company. As a result, Clifford had talked briefly with NCNB Corporation, the North Carolina banking giant, about purchasing the company. When those talks fell through in the fall, Clifford and Altman had to seek $125 million in new capital from the bank's shareholders.

Throughout this period, Senator Kerry's inquiry also was proceeding, although his investigators were making slow progress in the face of a stonewall from BCCI and its lawyers. However, an offshoot of Kerry's investigation was also going forward and it would eventually bear surprising fruit.

In its early stages, the Kerry investigation was run by Jack Blum, a Washington lawyer who had moved in and out of government over the years investigating white-collar crimes and other complex financial scandals. Blum had become convinced that the federal prosecutors in the BCCI case were not pursuing the full scope of corruption at the bank.

In the spring of 1989, after he left the Senate payroll, Blum had gone to New York and met with District Attorney Robert Morgenthau and a top deputy, John Moscow.

Morgenthau was almost seventy, the dean of American district attorneys and the direct successor to such legends as the racket-busting Thomas Dewey. His father had been U.S. ambassador to the Ottoman Empire and served as secretary of the treasury under President Franklin Roosevelt.

As district attorney for New York County, Morgenthau was committed to fighting the war on drugs and, before most other law enforcement officials, he had recognized that stopping the money laundering was more important in stopping the flow of drugs than busting pushers on the streets. As a result, his office had developed a sophisticated and aggressive ability to go after the moneymen behind the drug business. Just a year earlier, Morgenthau had been the lead-off witness at a series of Senate hearings on drug trafficking and money laundering organized by Blum for Senator Kerry.

Moscow, a Harvard Law School graduate and a career prosecutor, was one of Morgenthau's senior financial crimes prosecutors. Over the years, he had developed a reputation as a no-nonsense prosecutor with the demeanor of a prizefighter and the tenacity of a pit bull.

Nonetheless, when Morgenthau sent Blum to him, Moscow was dubious of the Senate investigator's description of BCCI as a massive criminal operation that the federal government would not touch. Despite his doubts, he agreed to look into the bank and its operations after Blum explained the foreign bank's apparent secret ownership of First American Bank of New York, which gave Morgenthau's office jurisdiction to investigate.

By late 1990, the district attorney's staff had examined BCCI's activities around the world, interviewed former bank employees, and formulated the outlines of a potential criminal case. Among the targets were Clark Clifford and Robert Altman.

In December, Morgenthau's office informed the Federal Reserve in Washington that evidence indicated that BCCI had loaned $854 million to First American's shareholders. The collateral for those loans was stock in the parent company of First American Bankshares. It was the first evidence that BCCI had financed the acquisition of Financial General nearly a decade before. On January 4, 1991, the Federal Reserve ordered an investigation into BCCI's alleged control of First American by using Arab shareholders as front men.

Now the floodgates were open and all hope of sweeping BCCI's troubles aside had disappeared. Events would unfold at a dizzying pace, pushed by a torrent of stories in the press and ever-more lurid tales about the nefarious activities of BCCI. And Clifford's name cropped up in almost every story as BCCI's Washington lawyer and the chairman of the bank that BCCI allegedly owned through front men. Fairly or not, every wild allegation and each accurate revelation alike stained his reputation and raised doubts about his integrity.

On February 6, 1991, the *Washington Post* published its first in-depth investigative article questioning the true ownership of First American. Struggling to contain the damage, Clifford sent a memorandum to the other directors of First American. "Recent press accounts about First American have contained inaccuracies and mistakes concerning the company, its financial standing, its shareholders, and dealings with regulatory agencies," he wrote. "We believe it is important that our directors have available accurate information about this matter, and I am therefore distributing this memorandum for that purpose."

The document disclosed the existence of Morgenthau's criminal investigation and described the Federal Reserve investigation, focusing on the fact that the Fed's inquiry involved stock pledged as collateral for loans. "To be clear, the Federal Reserve has not suggested that BCCI ever actually controlled the management of operations at First American," Clifford wrote, giving the first hint of what would emerge as his chief line of defense in the coming months.

Any hope of quelling the storm died on March 4 when the Federal Reserve formally accused BCCI of illegally acquiring control of First

American through concealed loans to the original Arab shareholders. The millions used by Kamal Adham and the others to buy the bank, the money they had claimed was their own, had been loans from BCCI. And, like the loans to Clifford and Altman in 1986, the only collateral was the stock in First American's parent company, Credit and Commerce American Holdings. Faced with its own documents, provided to the Federal Reserve by Morgenthau's office, BCCI accepted the findings and agreed to give up its stake in First American. The same day, the Bank of England opened its own investigation of BCCI.

It might be described as "death by leaks," the Washington version of Chinese water torture. Fueled by information and allegations from Morgenthau's office and assistance from congressional investigators, the *New York Times*, *Wall Street Journal*, *Los Angeles Times*, *Time*, *Newsweek*, and the major television networks joined the story. Clifford, once a master leaker himself and never given to bouts of paranoia, became obsessed with the leaks. He decided that reporters were getting most of their information from John Moscow, whose father had been a reporter for the *New York Times*. Almost daily, Clifford and Altman found their names splashed across front pages and television screens across the country as questions were raised about whether they knew BCCI controlled the bank they headed and details were published about the multiple contacts both had had with Abedi and other BCCI officials over the years.

Still, Clifford believed that the furor would pass, and he was surprised as the magnitude of criticism increased. A man of many resources, he did not take the punishment without fighting back. He and Altman had written stern letters to *Regardie's* magazine threatening legal action. When *Time* reporter Jonathan Beatty telephoned Clifford to ask questions about the latest BCCI allegations, the lawyer berated him for the magazine's coverage of BCCI and his involvement. "I don't know how your magazine could allow this kind of treatment after all I've done for *Time*," complained Clifford, citing his helping the magazine avoid a postal increase in the early seventies. But nothing could stop the stories.

Nothing seemed able to stop Senator Kerry either. In early January, Clifford had attended a party in the Dirksen Senate Office Building to celebrate Kerry's reelection. Clifford arrived by himself in the large room where drinks and food were being served, but he was quickly spotted by Kerry's office manager and escorted to the senator's side. In congratulating Kerry, Clifford said, "Of all the races in the country, I felt yours was the most important." Later, the office manager quipped to one of Kerry's investigators that Clifford "must be in real trouble."

Indeed, Clifford's law partners were deeply concerned. At the time, there were eight partners in addition to Clifford and Altman. All were worried about the impact of the scandal on the future of the firm. Yet they also wanted to believe Clifford when he assured them that he knew nothing about BCCI's loans to the other shareholders and that BCCI had had nothing to do with running First American.

Clifford continued to be surprised by the barrage of negative publicity. Decades of hard work at tending to his reputation, courting the press, and portraying himself as an honest and honorable man seemed to have been blown to bits by an onslaught of leaks and innuendo. In the middle of May, the prestigious *New Yorker* magazine, which was owned by S. I. Newhouse, a onetime Clifford client, had begun a three-part serialization of Clifford's memoirs, *Counsel to the President*. The book itself, for which Clifford had been paid $1 million, would be published in May, a certain best-seller.

Just as he sought to cap his career with this thick testament to his wisdom, Clifford faced an onslaught of press coverage that shook him deeply. "If this is the way it is handled," he said later, shaking his head in sadness, "when the charges are made, that the press practically accepts them, it means something has happened with the ancient and honorable principle that a man is presumed innocent until proven guilty."

There did seem to be a frenzy to bring down Clifford. Part surely stemmed from his stature; the higher you are, the harder you fall, particularly in Washington. When Clifford denied that he knew anything about the secret ownership of First American, reporters shook their heads in disbelief. How could a man who had built a career on providing wise advice to presidents and corporations not have known?

The worst was yet to come for Clifford.

On the morning of Sunday, May 5, 1991, Paul Warnke was still upstairs when his wife, Jean, picked up the *Washington Post* from the front step. "Jesus Christ, you won't believe this," she exclaimed. When Warnke raced downstairs, there spread across the front page was a story on the purchase of First American stock by Clifford and Altman, in all its blazing details. The story recounted the non-recourse loan from BCCI, the $9.8 million profit shared by Clifford and Altman when they sold a portion of the stock in 1988, the lack of risk for the lawyers. "The stock transactions are the first public indication that Clifford and Altman profited personally through their private dealings with BCCI," said the story by reporters Jim McGee and Sharon Walsh.

As he pondered the consequences of the story on the fragile law firm, Warnke said to his wife, "The wheels are going to come off now."

Before the disclosure about the stock profits, the partners at Clifford and Warnke had believed Clifford when he protested that he and Altman knew nothing of BCCI's involvement and when he described their purchase of bank stock as a sacrifice. There had not seemed to be any motive for either lawyer to protect BCCI. Suddenly the risk-free stock deal, with its enormous profits, supplied a motive.

On Monday morning, the partners met quietly in small groups around the office. They had hung together in the face of the previous publicity, but there was a growing sentiment that the firm could not withstand the latest disclosure. Even John Kovin, whose law school tuition had been financed on a loan from Clifford and who had never worked anywhere else, was shaken. Something had to be done, but no one was quite sure what.

"For me, it was pragmatic," remembered Warnke. "I just thought Clifford and Warnke did not have much of a future. Our clients had stayed with us. There had been very little questioning from clients. No one had asked us to explain ourselves. But a firm also depends on a certain amount of walk-in business. When a complicated case arose, one firm that would not promptly come to mind was Clifford and Warnke."

In the middle of the week, Marny Clifford defended her husband in a *Post* article, but it was difficult to find the words. "The trouble is," she told the reporter, "you'd say exactly the same thing if you were guilty. Think about it. You would." Finally, she resorted to an odd defense. "Clark is a very simple soul," she said. "He really is. I can't remember him ever, in all these years I've been married to him, wanting something. I can think of a thousand things I want; most people can. But he is very strange that way."

His partners wanted something now. They wanted out. Within days of the *Post* story, one of them, Hal Murray, had contacted a friend at Howery and Simon, a growing Washington law firm. Murray discussed joining Howery and Simon himself and he also raised the possibility of other lawyers from Clifford and Warnke defecting to the new firm. In the coming weeks, Warnke had several conversations with out-of-town law firms about transforming Clifford and Warnke into their Washington office. The name would change, but the lawyers would remain together. Warnke even proposed that Clifford remain with the new entity, although in a diminished role. There would be no room, however, for Altman.

The summer was so different from what Clifford had anticipated. Publication of his memoir was to have been the final glory of his extraordinary career, an opportunity for reviewers and readers to reflect on Clifford's role in American history and for Clifford to bask in their adulation. He would remember it instead as the worst period of his life, a time when a lifetime's accomplishments were overshadowed by questions about his integrity and honesty. Still, there were appearances to keep up.

The sun was still up and warm on the evening of May 22 when the first limousines began to pull up outside the elegant red-brick townhouse on N Street in Georgetown. Pamela Harriman, Clifford's longtime friend and political ally, was hosting a party at her home to celebrate the publication of *Counsel to the President*.

Clifford and Mrs. Harriman had remained in frequent contact since her husband's death in 1986. Part of the connection remained politics. But they also talked often because Clifford and Paul Warnke were trustees of the funds set up by the late Averell Harriman for his heirs. However, their contact on those matters was fairly limited because most of the investment decisions were left to William Rich III, a New York financial adviser who had been hired by Harriman before his death.

Clifford would later say that he devoted little time to overseeing the Harriman trusts, an observation that was not disputed. But Rich would recall a fateful scene after the stock market crash in October 1987, when Clifford visited Rich's office and expressed concern about the impact of the crash on the trusts, comparing the collapse to the 1929 crash that had touched off the depression. Indeed, as a result of Clifford's anxiety, Rich later told *Vanity Fair*, the decision was made to diversify the Harriman fortune. One of the new investments was real estate, with consequences that would prove more unfortunate for Clifford and Pamela Harriman than the stock market crash of 1987.

However, those were not the worries bedeviling Clifford on May 22 as members of the old Washington establishment responded to Mrs.

Harriman's request that they provide a show of strength for Clifford as he confronted the BCCI allegations.

Drawn by the scent of scandal surrounding the guest of honor, reporters, photographers, and television camera crews gathered near the steps in front of the house, interviewing and photographing those who arrived. Bob Altman and Lynda Carter, who was glamorous in a black-and-white dress, stopped to chat with reporters. "People are coming here in celebration of a book that has not only historical significance but is a wonderful read," said Altman. "It is written by a man who is widely loved in this town and I think it will be a lot of fun."

Arriving to celebrate the man and the book — as well as to examine the toll taken on him by the publicity — were many of Washington's most powerful people. From Capitol Hill came such Democratic luminaries as Senators Edward Kennedy, Claiborne Pell, Paul Simon, Sam Nunn, Frank Lautenberg, Chris Dodd, and Howard Metzenbaum. From the House side came Speaker Tom Foley and Representatives John Dingell, Jack Brooks, and Patricia Schroeder. The media was well represented, too, by the likes of William Safire of the *New York Times*, Albert Hunt of the *Wall Street Journal*, and his old friend Katharine Graham, chairman of the Washington Post Company.

Metzenbaum caught the mood when he told a reporter, "I've known him over the years. I have respect for him. I think that when somebody's under fire, you don't walk away."

Over the course of about three hours, more than four hundred guests passed through the party. Clifford signed more than two hundred copies of his book. Some of those confided privately as they left that the mood was somber. "A purposeful occasion," one guest muttered to a *Washington Post* reporter. But Clifford, as he left the house shortly after nine, with Mrs. Harriman holding his right hand lightly, put on his best face and declared, "I thought it was a stunning success."

There were other simpler, quieter acts of kindness. Lady Bird Johnson telephoned Clifford and his wife several times to wish them well. Jacqueline Kennedy Onassis invited him to luncheon at her apartment in New York City. There, Clifford was able to forget about his own troubles as he reminisced about John Kennedy in the presence only of the two children, John and Caroline, and the late president's widow. A few months later, Mrs. Onassis, an extremely private person who never interfered in government matters, took the unusual step of telephoning

Senator Kerry, asking him to consider Clifford's service to the country as he continued his investigation.

Despite such displays of loyalty from old associates, despite the general critical acclaim accorded his book and the fact that it reached the *New York Times* best-seller list, Clifford felt lonely and abandoned that summer. The glorious twilight he had imagined was everywhere tainted by BCCI; scarcely a book reviewer could resist at least mentioning the scandal in evaluating Clifford's career, although the author himself had relegated his stewardship of First American Bank and the ensuing BCCI affair to a single footnote.

In the midst of a highly favorable notice that praised the book's richness and scope, Roger Morris, a former official in the Johnson and Nixon administrations, wrote in the *New York Times Book Review* that Clifford had tried to "excuse his recent connection with a drug-money-laundering foreign bank" while remaining "largely mute" on the true power that he had wielded in Washington on behalf of his clients.

BCCI was destined to be more than a footnote to his autobiography; it was to rewrite his life.

In July, regulators in seven countries simultaneously closed down BCCI's offices, leaving thousands of customers without access to their money. That same month, Clifford was forced to go to New York and undergo questioning by attorneys from the district attorney's office. Along with Morgenthau's investigation, the Justice Department had also opened a criminal inquiry into the relationship between BCCI and First American.

A short time earlier, Clifford had realized that the situation was dire enough that he and Altman needed to hire criminal lawyers to represent them in dealings with the New York and federal investigators. Clifford flew to New York alone to seek advice on who to hire from Martin Lipton, a longtime friend and a prominent securities lawyer.

"I met with him and three or four of his partners," Clifford recalled. "One of them was his white-collar criminal man. I asked them for a recommendation as to who we should get to represent us. The charges had not been filed, but we could see the clouds gathering. They recommended Bob Fiske."

Robert Fiske was a former United States attorney in New York City, a lawyer with an impeccable reputation. Clifford met with Fiske and the two men hit it off. With Altman's consent, Fiske was hired to represent both of them. But it soon turned out that one lawyer would not be enough.

As the Justice Department stepped up its investigation in Washington, Clifford and Altman decided that they needed counsel there, too. The choice demonstrated the lessons that Clifford had absorbed and practiced himself over more than four decades in Washington, where connections and prestige are at least as important as legal skills.

The man they turned to was Robert Bennett, widely regarded as heir to the title of Washington's best criminal lawyer, which had once belonged to the late Ed Williams. Bennett had good contacts inside the Justice Department, where he once worked and now was perceived as a tough but fair competitor. In addition, he was known as someone who knew how to work with the press and Congress. In fact, Bennett's name had been in the headlines recently because he had been the outside counsel who led an aggressive investigation by the Senate Ethics Committee into allegations that Charles Keating, a California savings and loan owner, had illegally influenced five senators.

"He had gotten quite a good deal of good publicity," Clifford said later of Bennett. "We wanted someone with good public standing, like Fiske had in New York."

At First American, Charles Mathias had grown increasingly concerned about the effect of the publicity on the condition of the bank. As the summer wore on, deposits were streaming out of the bank. In one month alone, customers withdrew $1 billion from their accounts. He and the other directors tried to persuade Clifford and Altman to resign in hopes of ending the outflow and saving the bank. The two lawyers refused, arguing that they had done nothing wrong and resigning would be tantamount to an admission of guilt. Finally, the bank had had enough.

On August 2, Mathias wrote a letter to Clifford on behalf of the First American board of directors. "As you know, banks depend on confidence," he wrote. "The extraordinary publicity detailing the obvious historical links that you and Bob Altman have had to BCCI and the questions this has raised with respect to First American has seriously threatened the confidence of First American's customers and depositors." He closed by saying that the "withdrawal" of Clifford and Altman was "urgently required."

Ten days later, after a tension-filled meeting of the First American board at the building Clifford so loved, he and Altman announced that they were resigning from their positions as chairman and president of First American Bankshares. The project that had so energized Clifford a decade earlier was ending in disgrace. At the same time, the law firm he had counted on to carry his name beyond his death was coming apart.

Near the end of the first week of September, an upset John Kovin knocked on Clifford's door. The elder lawyer had never bothered to explain the stock transaction to his partners. He felt no need to explain himself. He simply expected their loyalty, regardless of any allegations.

"We're very disturbed about all of these developments," began Kovin as he sat down opposite his mentor. "We don't know quite what to do. Some of the partners have young families. We have been talking with other firms and among ourselves and we have several options."

He laid them out. Some of the lawyers could leave, breaking up the group. They could go en masse to another firm in Washington. Most appealing to many of them was what they had dubbed "Plan B." A Newark, New Jersey, firm was eager to hire the group to become its Washington office. Clifford could stay on "of counsel."

A decade earlier, Kovin had gone behind Clifford's back to discuss the future of the firm with outsiders and Clifford had given him a tongue lashing. Now, the elderly lawyer sat glumly and quietly. Finally, he spoke three words: "What about Bob?"

"The best we can do is suggest that he take a leave of absence until this clears up and he can find another job," replied Kovin.

Clifford nodded silently and dismissed Kovin. On Saturday morning, he telephoned Kovin at home. For the first time, Kovin raised the stock transaction and its questionable nature. "You have no right to bring that up," thundered Clifford. "That takes a lot of gall." Kovin repeated that something had to be done about the future of the firm, and he repeated that Altman did not have enough goodwill among the other partners for anyone else to go to bat for keeping him.

It was October by the time the partners, certain that Clifford would not willingly abandon Altman, left in a group to join Howery and Simon. Only Griff Lescher and Altman remained with Clifford; out of his own pocket, Clifford would pay their salaries of $400,000 a year for Altman and $120,000 for Lescher. At the final partners' meeting that month, Clifford listened stoically as the others described the clients whose business would be going with them. He said nothing as they filed out of the conference room. Then, as he had always done, he began to plan for the future.

"I could see that from that time on I wasn't going to be actively engaged in the practice of law," he remembered later. "So the idea of starting again to build up the firm had no appeal to me. I accepted it. I deeply regretted it. I was frustrated by what I considered the gross unfairness of it, but I just faced reality."

Reality was as bleak as winter rain. He had been forced to relinquish the bank. His once-proud law firm was bowed and doomed. There was nothing left to save, nothing except the commodity Clifford had brought with him to Washington so long ago. Bruised as it was, he would not give up his good name without a fight.

23

Trial and Triumph

JOHN KERRY was angry. Finally, after three years of investigation and frustration, he had Clark Clifford under oath before his Senate subcommittee, but it was not going well. In the midst of a lunch break, he huddled with his staff in his office. They were critical of Kerry's interrogation of Clifford, chiding the onetime prosecutor for not demanding answers when Clifford said he was unable to recall specific names and dates. Suddenly the senator had had enough. "He's an old man," Kerry shot back. "He couldn't remember. I'm not going to humiliate an old man."

Clifford's testimony before Kerry at the end of October 1991 was the second time he had ventured into the halls of Congress with his side of the story. He also had granted a handful of press interviews, including one to a reporter from the *New York Times*. The article described Clifford's richly paneled office, with the curtains drawn over the White House view and the presidential medallions atop stacks of paper on his desk. It contrasted the way the bitter taste of BCCI had soured the autumn of his life. But the article by Neil A. Lewis in the spring of 1991 was most memorable for Clifford's unforgettable line in describing the dilemma that faced him with regard to BCCI's secret ownership of the bank. The man widely regarded as one of Washington's wisest lawyers, who had counseled every Democrat in the White House from Truman to Carter, had either to admit that he had been fooled or acknowledge that he had lied to banking regulators. "I have a choice of either seeming stupid or venal," he told the reporter.

Clifford's maiden public effort had come the previous month in a day-long hearing before the House Banking Committee. It was a carefully orchestrated, masterful performance intended to portray Clifford and Altman in the most favorable light. The eighty-minute opening statement by Clifford was crafted with the assistance of Democratic PR whizzes Frank Mankiewicz, Jody Powell, and Howard Paster. But before he could deliver his defense, Clifford had to sit through a pounding by

Republican after Republican. After so many years of seeing their own pilloried before Congress for influence peddling and worse, the Republicans spared Clifford nothing as he sat before them.

"The Republicans were loaded for bear, and one Republican after another would just take out after me," Clifford recalled. "You are not permitted to say anything, so it's a little difficult to sit there and hear critical comments being made and you can't do anything about it. It isn't in my nature to get angry. I was making notes about how to respond."

Finally, Clifford's turn came. He delivered his response in a strong steady voice, rarely glancing at his notes. "My judgment is questionable," he told the packed hearing, spreading his hands theatrically. "I guess I should have learned it some way. I've been in this business a long time. It's been a very active life. You learn a good deal from government. I guess I should have some way sensed it. I did not. I would have given anything if I could have avoided this past year. Still, I have to face it. In the process, I'm going to work as hard as I can to preserve my good name."

It was evening before the congressmen finished with Clifford and Altman. Many had been skeptical. How could he not have known? Republicans in particular seemed to relish the harsh glare focused on this longtime stalwart of the Democratic Party. The lone voice raised in defense belonged to young Joe Kennedy, the Massachusetts Democrat and son of the late Robert Kennedy, who had praised Clifford's service to the Kennedy family and the United States. But even Congressman Kennedy secretly harbored grave doubts about Clifford's innocence, and he had reluctantly come to the lawyer's defense after a pleading telephone call from his uncle, Senator Ted Kennedy, the night before the hearing. Other Democrats seemed saddened by the spectacle. "My heart wants to believe you," said Charles Schumer, the New York Democrat. "My head says no."

Finally, after more than eight hours of testimony, Clifford walked slowly out of the hearing room. He was slightly stooped and held his gray fedora in one hand. Marny, who had sat faithfully in the row behind her husband of sixty years throughout the long day, clutched his other hand. Trailing them, and absorbing most of the television lights, were Altman and Lynda Carter.

The House appearance had been at best a draw. True, Clifford and Altman had gotten the opportunity to tell their side of the story.

However, even those inclined to believe Clifford found a sadness at the core of his defense: Clark Clifford, who built his reputation dispensing wise advice to presidents and corporate leaders, had been fooled for a decade; he never had an inkling that the Arab shareholders were not the real owners of First American. Clifford had opted for stupid over venal.

The hearing had left Clifford a bit shell-shocked. Many times over the years, he had testified before Congress or appeared alongside clients who testified. Sometimes the sessions had been hostile. This was the first time, however, that he had found himself the subject of the hostility and suspicion that crackled in the air that day.

"You really don't know what it's like until you go through it yourself," Clifford said afterward. "I'd been through it with clients. I'd been very sympathetic with them. I'd stick very close to them during their time of trial. But it was really much worse."

The depth of her husband's troubles came home to Marny Clifford in the hearing room that day, too. She had been stunned by the television lights and the harsh questioning by the congressmen. She was fascinated by the unfolding scene, and saddened by the toll she could see it taking on her husband and his reputation.

"That day was really the beginning of the whole thing for me," she said later. "Washington had really been such a benign city when we first arrived. It was nice and old and there were very nice people. As the years went by, starting with Watergate, a poison came into Washington. And that day I saw that it was getting worse."

The late October appearance before Kerry's subcommittee was something of an anticlimax. Clifford and Altman had seen no reason to give their chief congressional nemesis first crack at them, with all of the attendant press attention. The questions were sharper. Kerry's staff had spent months and months delving deeply into the BCCI morass. But they elicited little new information. On such a critical issue as his assertion that he had checked with the State Department on the background of Kamal Adham and the reputation of BCCI in the late seventies, Clifford said that he could not recall which person or what office had provided the information that reassured him that both were reputable.

As for the defense strategy, it remained the same. Had Clifford uncovered the slightest inkling that BCCI secretly owned First American, he assured Kerry, he would have been the first to blow the whistle. Alas, he said, he did not. It almost seemed that Clifford was parodying his own appearance before the Federal Reserve hearing on the takeover of Financial General more than a decade earlier when he offered his ultimate argument that he had not known. "Did [BCCI] corrupt First American?" asked Clifford indignantly. "Not in any way. Do I ask you to take my word for that? I do. My word has been important for a great many years in Washington."

Both appearances were orchestrated events, part of the plan adopted by Clifford and some of his advisers to soften his portrayal in the press and evoke sympathy with the public. Fiske and Bennett both had reservations about the testimony, fearing that he would say something that the state prosecutors in New York or their federal counterparts in Washington could use against him later. Unlike witnesses who testified before Congress only after receiving assurances that their words could not be used against them in court, Clifford had gone forward without such a deal. The very notion struck him as too close to an admission of guilt.

"There are two courts, the criminal court and the court of public opinion," said one of Clifford's advisers. "The more important one in this case was the court of public opinion."

Eventually, however, Clifford would have to answer in the other court, too.

Almost everyone who knew Clifford was confounded by the scandal besetting him. Some reveled in his fall. Margaret Truman Daniel had harbored a dislike of Clifford for more than forty years. She felt he had stolen some of her father's glory and had never forgiven him. One day she confided to an acquaintance that she was pleased to see him under investigation. She was just glad her father wasn't alive to see it. Others treated Clifford like a man just diagnosed with an infectious disease, sympathetic but distant lest it rub off on them.

One of the clearest and saddest slights occurred in the spring of 1992. As he had every year since 1946, Clifford attended the annual Gridiron Dinner sponsored by Washington's press corps. Many times he had seen himself lampooned on the stage for upstaging Harry Truman or reminding his clients to remember him while he was defense secretary. This night, however, times were different. There was no reference to Clifford's troubles in the skit, and there was no bevy of reporters or Washington luminaries eager to be seen chatting with him.

During the show's intermission, guests got up from their tables and mingled, exchanging gossip and reviewing the satirical barbs aimed at President George Bush and his administration. Jack Nelson, the bureau chief of the *Los Angeles Times*, noticed Clifford still sitting at his table, alone and staring down. Turning to John White, the former Democratic National Party chairman who had sought Clifford's advice many years before, Nelson said, "Go over and talk to him, John. He could use a friend."

There were those who remained steadfast. Harry McPherson frequently called to offer support or simply chat, as did Jack Valenti, the former Johnson aide who was head of the powerful Hollywood lobbying organization, the Motion Picture Association of America. Cyrus Vance dropped him a note of encouragement. Clayton and Polly Fritchie, friends since the Truman days, hosted a small dinner party to buck up their old friend. When Fritchie rose to give the toast, he was careful to speak only of Clifford's past accomplishments and contributions, leaving aside all mention of the present troubles. But when Clifford stood to respond, his eyes welled up with tears and he confessed, "I have been asking myself over and over again, Where did I go wrong? What mistake did I make? What clue did I overlook?"

Within the darkness, there was one warm light. Of his three daughters, Clifford had always been closest to his middle daughter, Joyce. She was the most intellectual of the daughters, eager to engage her father in political and economic discussions. Yet there had always been a distance in the relationship, the lingering sense from childhood that her father was a man apart from the rest of the family. In her forties, after a brief term as a county legislator in New York, she had enrolled in graduate school and become a clinical psychologist with a practice in Brattleboro, Vermont.

Now, as her father faced what she described as "a body blow," it was Joyce who spent long hours talking with him about his life and the vicissitudes of Washington. Gery had been estranged from the family for many years because of personal reasons. She was divorced and living in virtual seclusion in California. Randall lived not far away in Baltimore, but she, too, kept her distance from her father and his troubles in the beginning, although that changed later.

So it fell on Joyce to help her father and, for the first time, she felt as though they spoke as equals. He listened to her observations, not only about his current difficulties but about life in general. "Over the years, we had both been working on finding a relationship between us and suddenly there it was," she recalled later. "Since the trouble, he has been more subjective and reactive. We have grown far closer."

A remarkable change occurred in Clifford's marriage. He came to depend on his wife in ways that he never had during six previous decades. Always, Clifford had been the rock, the provider, the wise locus of strength in the marriage. Now, beset by troubles he had never anticipated, the aging and tarnished legend turned to his wife for solace and strength.

They spent many hours in the late afternoons and evenings remembering happier times and struggling to understand how this tragedy had engulfed their lives. Clifford never complained about the unfairness. Never did he point the finger at Bob Altman, as so many others were doing. Even when his wife railed against the poisoned atmosphere of Washington itself, Clifford found himself unable to join in her indictment of the city that had been so good to him for so many years. What he worried about the most was his lost reputation, and his wife constantly assured him that he would triumph and win back his good name.

Pushing his fingers to his temples and leaning forward in a chair, Clifford would go back over the conversations he had had with BCCI officials and the Arab shareholders. From the very beginning, he would tell Marny, he and Altman had been told that it would be difficult to get in touch with the shareholders because they were scattered throughout the Mideast. So it had seemed natural to work through Abedi and BCCI. Then he would ask his wife, "Well, should I have wondered about that? Was there some point where I should have known what was going on. People say, 'You were representing BCCI, so you must have known.' The fact is that we would be about the last people that BCCI would tell about the fact that they were engaging in corrupt banking. They knew our reputation when they came to us. I think it was one of the reasons they came to us. And we served them well. We would be the last people that they would want to know. That I can see clearly."

Whether it was the truth or more logically simply what Clifford had chosen to believe, he refused to acknowledge any suspicions that BCCI owned First American. And when he defended his stewardship of the bank to Marny and others, Clifford invariably spoke of the great growth and profitability of First American. "The Federal Reserve gave us a clean bill of health," he would say. "We ran the bank. No one else."

Troubled as she was by the attacks on her husband, Marny Clifford welcomed the opportunity to share the burdens with him. "In this adversity, we sort of clung to each other," she remembered later. "He has always depended on me in a strange way. Perhaps it is my New England, down-to-earth quality. But this was different. Most marriages go through all kinds of different things. Some bad times and some wonderful times. We have thought it was very important for our children and grandchildren that we stay together, and I'm so very glad we did, because these last few years have been something very special. I'm very grateful for these latter years. It has done something to solidify our feelings for each other."

The young man she had met on the Rhine in 1928, whose good looks reminded her of a Greek god, was now trapped in a Greek tragedy. Although his face was lined and sometimes seemed to fall into dark folds at night, she admired him more than ever. And she refused to believe that he would not emerge triumphant.

Clifford seemed to gain strength from the drive to clear his name, but the stress took a toll, too. Beginning in late 1991, he began to complain of heart problems. He visited his cardiologist, Dr. John Russo, at regular intervals, something he had steadfastly refused to do in the past. He tired more easily. For the first time in his life, at the age of eighty-five, he began to stoop slightly as he walked.

Some days it was all Clifford could do to muster the strength to meet with Robert Bennett and one of Bennett's partners on the case, Carl Rauh. As the spring turned to summer in 1992, it became evident that Clifford and Altman would be indicted on criminal charges. In New York, Robert Morgenthau was sending a string of former BCCI and First American employees before the grand jury. The only real question seemed to be whether the Justice Department also would bring charges.

Morgenthau's office and the Justice Department had been engaged in a long-running battle over the case. The New York prosecutors felt that the feds had treated the entire BCCI case lightly, even obstructed their investigation on occasion. They also complained that the feds were reluctant to go after a figure as exalted as Clifford.

For their part, the career prosecutors at the Justice Department worried that Morgenthau's chief deputy on the case, John Moscow, was overzealous in his pursuit of a prize as big as Clifford. Moscow's theory of the case hinged on a massive conspiracy in which Clifford and Altman had knowingly worked with Abedi, Naqvi, Adham, and others to conceal BCCI's ownership and control of First American.

The New York prosecutors had amassed an overwhelming amount of circumstantial evidence indicating that Clifford and Altman were aware of BCCI's ownership of First American. There were numerous examples of the two American lawyers consulting with Abedi on hiring and strategy for the bank. Altman had attended a meeting of BCCI executives at which First American was described as part of the BCCI family.

What Moscow lacked was the one document or witness to convince a jury, beyond a reasonable doubt, that Clifford and Altman had been witting participants in the scheme, not unwitting dupes. Unfortunately, Abedi was incapacitated in Pakistan, which had no extradition treaty with the United States, and Adham was equally out of reach in Egypt. As for Naqvi and most other key ex-BCCI executives, they were in the custody of Abu Dhabi, the Persian Gulf sheikdom that had been the bank's largest investor at the time of its seizure a year before. There seemed little chance of securing their testimony either.

For a time, the prosecutors in New York thought that they could turn Clifford against Altman. The younger lawyer's name was on far more documents in the case because he had executed most of the details. He also was the one who had attended several larger meetings of the BCCI banking family. During six days of questioning in early 1992, Moscow tried to get Clifford to point the finger at Altman. Every time that Moscow suggested Altman may have known more about BCCI's role at First American than he had disclosed to Clifford, the prosecutor ran into a wall. "I don't think Mr. Altman would have known that," Clifford would respond. "He would have told me if he did."

By the end of the day-long interrogations, the prosecutors could see that Clifford was exhausted. His eyes were red-rimmed and his handsome face seemed to have collapsed into wrinkles and lines. Yet he was steadfast in denying any wrongdoing by himself or Altman.

At the conclusion of one day's session, Clifford and Fiske were walking slowly down a cluttered hallway in the lower Manhattan courts building where Morgenthau's offices were located. Barbara Jones, Morgenthau's chief assistant, walked up to Michael Cherkasky, another senior prosecutor, and said, "Mike, we're not really going to indict that man, are we?"

"I don't know, Barbara," said Cherkasky, shaking his head. "I don't know."

Cherkasky was the leader of a small contingent within Morgenthau's office that opposed indicting Clifford and Altman. It was not that they believed the two men were innocent; they thought some crimes had been committed. But they were convinced that the evidence amassed would not stand up in court. Worse than indicting an eighty-five-year-old American icon, they argued, would be indicting him and losing at trial. Those concerns were shared by officials at the Justice Department in Washington, who feared that the attorney general was being pressured into indicting the two men because of the public criticism of the department by Morgenthau and the press.

"The professionals at Justice certainly didn't feel they could go as far as Morgenthau and Moscow," said a senior federal official involved in the process. "They kept saying, 'Where is he going to get the evidence to prove this conspiracy? How righteous is this case he is planning to bring? Would we be doing the same thing if this were Joe Blow?' "

At the same time, the Justice Department lawyers were sensitive to the fact that they would certainly be criticized for giving Clifford special treatment if they chose not to bring charges against him.

The case against Clifford and Altman was the biggest of Robert Morgenthau's long and distinguished career as a prosecutor. Already his investigation had brought down one of the world's most corrupt banks and collected millions of dollars in fines and penalties. Now he and John Moscow believed that, if they could convict Clifford and Altman, they could force them to disclose how the bank had influenced American government officials and congressmen.

Cherkasky, a career prosecutor who revered Morgenthau, feared that his boss was going to make a terrible mistake. The evidence was all circumstantial; none of the witnesses had been able to testify directly that Clifford and Altman knew of BCCI's ownership of First American. And Moscow, while unparalleled as an investigator, did not have the courtroom skills to match Robert Fiske or someone of his stature. Cherkasky worried that the indictments would tarnish the real accomplishment of shutting down BCCI, and he made no secret of his vehement opposition to the planned charges.

At the same time he argued against the indictment, Cherkasky received permission from Morgenthau to open negotiations with Clifford's lawyers. He wanted to arrange a plea bargain. The defense lawyers hated Moscow and they would never have entered into serious talks with him, but they felt that Cherkasky was more reasonable and the closest thing they had to an ally in the district attorney's office.

The highly secretive negotiations began in June 1992. Cherkasky held a series of meetings and telephone conversations with Bob Bennett and Carl Rauh. Bob Fiske, who was involved in a trial in Florida, was consulted by telephone on a regular basis. After several days of talks, the lawyers struck what people close to Morgenthau's office later would describe as "a tentative deal."

Cherkasky had the best relationship with Robert S. Mueller III, the assistant attorney general in charge of the criminal division at the Justice Department, so he briefed him on the plea bargain. Mueller, who had his own reservations about the strength of the case, consulted with his career prosecutors and then agreed to accept the plea bargain on behalf of the Justice Department.

As described by three people involved in the plea bargain talks, the deal was structured this way: Clark Clifford would not be charged with a crime. Instead, he would be permitted to plead no contest to technical violations of banking regulations in a civil lawsuit brought by the Federal Reserve Board. He would not have to say that he lied to regulators, but he would admit that regulations had been violated. Altman would plead guilty to two misdemeanors, minor criminal charges that would carry no jail time. He also would give up his license to practice law for five years.

Once Cherkasky secured tentative approvals from the Justice Department and the Federal Reserve, the final step for him was getting Morgenthau to sign off on the deal. A meeting was held in the district attorney's conference room, and Cherkasky explained the details to Morgenthau, Moscow, and other senior prosecutors.

"We've done an unbelievable job against BCCI," Cherkasky told them. "We've climbed to the top of the mountain. Don't take the next step and indict, because it's a long way down."

Moscow grew increasingly angry as Cherkasky went on. Finally he blurted out a single word, "Whitewash." The deal, he argued, would make it look like they had caved in to Clifford. "This guy is a fixer and an influence peddler and we have to go after him," thundered Moscow. Furthermore, he said, the deal would not give them enough leverage over Clifford or Altman to force them to provide information about congressmen and other American officials Moscow believed were linked to BCCI.

Morgenthau, who was entering the twilight of his own career, had been energized by the investigations of BCCI and Clifford. Before the investigation had arisen, he had been giving serious thought to retiring. But the case invigorated him. Even though he recognized that the evidence was circumstantial, Morgenthau was convinced that Clifford and Altman had committed serious crimes and should be punished. For the district attorney, the sweetheart stock deal just could not be explained away. He viewed it as a bribe for the silence of Clifford and Altman. After listening to Cherkasky and Moscow and his other assistants, the district attorney rendered his verdict: there would be no deal. The investigation would proceed and indictments would be brought as soon as possible.

After the meeting, a red-faced Moscow confronted Cherkasky in the hallway. "If you didn't wear glasses, I'd punch you out," shouted Moscow, who has the muscular build of a middle-weight boxer. Cherkasky, who is tall and thin, shook his head silently and walked away.

Later, Carl Rauh acknowledged that a plea bargain had been discussed, but he denied that the talks ever reached the stage of a tentative deal. "In one of the discussions, it was discussed that Clifford would be cut out and not charged in any way," he said. "We never had a tentative deal. That's horseshit. We were talking concepts. Cherkasky wanted to make a deal. We'd talk. He'd come back. But I don't think Clifford and Altman were agreeable to any specifics. Then Cherkasky came back and said no more talks."

For his part, Clifford recalled that his lawyers had engaged in some negotiations with the district attorney's office. "Yes," he said when asked about the plea talks. "I can't remember the details. I do remember that Morgenthau's first assistant, Mr. Cherkasky, was opposed to the indictment. Apparently he told that to Fiske at one time. Later there were some plea bargain conversations. I apparently was not much involved in it because under no circumstances was I going to plead to anything."

Robert Morgenthau decided to take the gamble. From Jack Blum's inconclusive tip, the district attorney's office, led by John Moscow, had brought down what was widely viewed now as the world's most corrupt bank. It was an important victory. Now, Morgenthau was willing to stake the prestige of his office on proving that Clark Clifford and Robert Altman knew that corrupt institution had secretly owned the biggest banking company in Washington.

After it became clear that Morgenthau was within days of bringing the indictment against the two lawyers, Mueller went to William Barr, the attorney general. "We think we have the evidence to support this case," said Mueller. "We're comfortable with it. It is narrower than Morgenthau's case."

On July 27, Carl Rauh and Robert Bennett made a final plea to Morgenthau and Moscow. They argued that Clifford's health was poor, that he had heart trouble and could suffer a severe attack if he was indicted. Don't charge a man at the end of his career on such flimsy evidence, they pleaded. Morgenthau rebuffed them and said the charges would be coming soon.

A few minutes after eleven o'clock on the morning of July 29, Robert Morgenthau walked into his office, followed by several staff members and representatives of the Justice Department and Federal Reserve, to face the waiting crowd of reporters. The district attorney began to read from his prepared statement: "A New York grand jury has returned two indictments, charging six individuals, including Clark M. Clifford and Robert A. Altman, for criminal conduct arising out of the operation of the Bank of Credit and Commerce International."

The two lawyers were accused of lying to federal banking regulators about BCCI's role in First American and falsifying records to conceal the secret ownership. The most stunning — and ambitious — aspect of the indictment was the allegation that Clifford and Altman had accepted more than $40 million from BCCI over ten years in the form of legal fees, sham loans, and the rigged 1986 stock deal. The stock deal, charged Morgenthau, was a secret payoff for helping BCCI unload the National Bank of Georgia.

In Washington that same day, Mueller led a group of federal prosecutors and investigators to a podium at the Justice Department and announced that a federal grand jury also had indicted Clifford, Altman, and the bank. The federal charges were narrower, accusing Clifford and Altman of directing the clandestine efforts of BCCI to acquire First

American. Nonetheless, it was a rare one-two punch from state and federal law enforcement. If convicted of the criminal charges, Clifford faced up to eight years in prison. Altman faced an even longer term because he was named in more counts by the New York prosecutors.

Finally, the Federal Reserve filed a civil lawsuit in Washington accusing the two lawyers of lying to them and seeking fines and restitution of $80 million. The Fed's complaint ran more than a hundred pages, listing example after example of BCCI's alleged influence over the affairs of First American.

Washington's Old Guard was rattled by the indictments. Few had thought the allegations would come to this, criminal charges against one of the city's most influential and revered figures. Lloyd Cutler, who in many senses had succeeded Clifford as Washington's preeminent lawyer of influence, sounded as though he were delivering a eulogy when he told the *Washington Post*, "I've always had great affection for him as a colleague, friend, and statesman." Paul Warnke was equally somber in calling the episode a tragedy and saying, "The problem is that he was involved with a culture he did not understand. He had no background in the Middle East. He didn't recognize their values are different from ours."

Neither Cutler nor Warnke, nor many others, rallied around Clifford as an innocent man. That was left to Harry McPherson, who had remained close to Clifford since their days in the Johnson administration. "I can only believe that he will fight it and beat it because he's a man of integrity as well as high intelligence," said McPherson the day after the indictments. "It's just awful that this has happened to him, but I think he will not quit. He will not go gently into this good night."

The day before the indictments were announced, Clifford had gone to New York with Altman by prearrangement. Once the charges were made public on the afternoon of July 29, the two men appeared in New York State Supreme Court. Clifford looked exhausted as he walked into the courtroom with his lawyers and made his way silently through the throng of reporters. His eyes were ringed by dark circles and his craggily handsome face seemed to have collapsed onto his skull. In a hoarse version of his famous voice, he entered his plea of not guilty. Altman also pleaded not guilty and the two men released a joint statement to the press in which they asserted their innocence and vowed to go to trial.

What happened next did shock Clifford. He was booked on the charges, his mug shot taken, and his fingerprints recorded, "like a common criminal," he would complain later. His outrage heightened when Clifford discovered that the district attorney's office had secretly obtained a court order freezing $19.2 million in cash and securities he kept in two New York brokerage accounts.

"The night before the indictments, without any warning, without notice to me or my counsel, the prosecution slips in and gets freezes against my two accounts in New York, which is practically everything my wife and I had," complained Clifford later. "We are not given any chance to demonstrate that the basis for the freeze is totally false. They are frozen."

Neither the fingerprinting nor freezing the accounts was out of the ordinary. And providing advance notice of the freeze to Clifford would have defeated the purpose of the action, which was to make sure he did not move the money out of the country and out of the reach of the government should he lose the case and be ordered to repay it. Nonetheless, Clifford felt he was entitled to some special treatment.

Freezing the accounts provided Clifford's lawyers with some rare public relations ammunition. They argued in court and in the press that the action was unfair and disrespectful, leaving Clifford without enough money to pay the man who mowed his lawn or the doctors who were keeping him alive. Mrs. Clifford, he said, had used her own money, which was not frozen, to pay a secretary at the law firm. Bennett, never shy about trying a case in the press when it fit his strategy, accused Morgenthau and his office of trying to destroy Clifford and Altman through a ruthless prosecution.

Court documents filed in conjunction with the freeze offered an intriguing window on Clifford's personal finances. He listed his annual living expenses at $180,000, which covered such services as a driver, a cook, and a maid. In addition, the papers showed that Clifford had accomplished what he set out to do so many years before: he had provided financial security for his family. According to the filing, he was giving $325,000 a year in gifts to his three adult children. He also was paying $400,000 a year to keep the law office solvent; no fees were being collected, and Altman and Griff Lescher, the only other lawyer who had remained, had to be paid, as did the clerical staff. Now, with almost everything he had accumulated out of his reach, Clifford faced the financial uncertainty he had spent a lifetime struggling to avoid.

The aspect of the New York indictment that cut the deepest for Clifford, however, was the bribery charge. It essentially was an allegation that every legal fee the law firm had collected from BCCI and First American had been a payment for the help of Clifford and Altman in fooling the regulators on the ownership of the bank.

"Oh, that was awful," Clifford said later of the bribery count. "Some of my friends who had been right with me all the way, I sensed that it had a real impact on them. I think they had been wondering all along, 'Why would Clark get himself involved this way? This is so out of character.' Then here is this great big bribe, millions of dollars. Gee, it made them think about it."

The substantive fight in those first weeks was over where the two men would first face trial, New York state court or federal court in Washington. The defense lawyers wanted to try the federal case first because the charges were narrower. If they won in Washington, they could then argue that trying the defendants for essentially the same conduct in New York would amount to double jeopardy. Further, Bennett argued that a New York trial would amount to a death sentence for Clifford. His deteriorating heart condition demanded that he be allowed a trial in a location where he could at least sleep in his own bed at night. John Moscow scoffed at the reasoning and won a decision setting the New York trial first.

On October 4, Clifford awoke at home with a sharp pain in his abdomen. Trying to reach his wife's bedroom for help, he fainted four times at his home and lost more than a quart of blood. He was rushed to Georgetown University Hospital, where his condition stabilized and he was released after two days. His lawyers submitted medical reports to the New York judge, John A. K. Bradley, trying to get him to permit the Washington trial to go first.

On January 12, 1993, Bradley ruled that Clifford should stand trial despite his frail heart. He accused Clifford of trying to use his poor health to manipulate the criminal justice system. Further, in a highly unusual action, Bradley wrote in his order that it was his impression after reading nearly ten thousand pages of grand jury testimony that "the evidence of guilt is overwhelming."

Bradley set the state trial to begin on March 30, but in the end Altman would have to stand alone. Clifford announced in early February that he would have open-heart surgery the month the trial was supposed to begin. His physician, Wesley M. Oler, said the chances were one in five that he would die on the operating table. Without the operation, however, Oler said that Clifford would certainly not survive.

When Morgenthau's office refused to relent, Clifford's doctors informed the court that he would probably not survive if he had to stay in a New York hotel for the duration of the trial. Led by Carl Rauh, Clifford's lawyers began telling everyone who would listen that trying their client would amount to a death sentence. After five doctors appointed by the courts concurred with Clifford's physicians, Clifford's case was severed. Altman would go it alone.

On March 22, Clifford underwent three and a half hours of surgery to bypass four arteries in his heart. He survived and the doctors said his prognosis was guarded but good. The fight to clear Clifford's name, however, would be waged by Bob Altman, the man many believed responsible for the mess in the first place.

Unlike Clifford, with his courtly demeanor and record of public service, Altman had no reservoir of goodwill to draw on when the scandal broke. It was far easier for the Washington establishment to assign blame to this young upstart with the celebrity wife. Conventional wisdom was that Clifford's faculties had been slipping and Altman had led him into trouble. It was a convenient fiction, designed in part as a blanket excuse for all who had played a role in exalting Clifford and in part because Altman was an easier target.

Altman was not well liked in the Washington legal community, although he was respected and certainly had his admirers. However, as one lawyer who had opposed Clifford and Altman in the Detroit newspaper case put it, "Where Clifford was all polish and charm, Altman was brusque and mean." If it was hard to believe that Clark Clifford could get himself into such a mess, many people were less surprised — and far less sympathetic — that it had happened to his flashy, brash young partner. As a result, it was easy to blame the younger lawyer for the troubles besetting the older man.

As often happens with conventional wisdom, it was wrong. For one thing, the assessment misread Clifford's own capacities throughout the eighties. His heart might be failing, but his mind had remained sharp. As

Doug Letter of the Justice Department had seen in the Knight-Ridder case three years earlier, Clifford was still running the show. Second, those who believed Altman had steered the ship aground misunderstood his relationship with the older man. When it came to matters involving the law firm, Altman was always second in command, following Clifford's orders and executing his policies. Clifford admired Altman's dedication and capacity for work, but he never ceded his authority to him. Sam McIlwain, who had first brought Altman into the law firm twenty years before, put it bluntly when he said, "Bob Altman doesn't go to the bathroom without checking with Clark first."

Clifford himself never blamed Altman for the troubles. Their relationship, founded on work, had grown into a true friendship marked by trust and loyalty. Clifford had refused to abandon Altman when the law firm collapsed, and he had refused to hand over his partner to the district attorney's office. Now, although he maintained that he would rather have been at the defense table, too, his reputation rested in the hands of his protégé and the defense lawyers.

As they emerged from a dark sedan outside the Criminal Courts Building in lower Manhattan on March 30, Altman and his wife showed strain as they walked, hand in hand, past the television cameras and still photographers. Lynda Carter, wearing a red jacket with white cuffs, recognized a reporter in the crowd and let go of her husband's hand momentarily to bestow a kiss on the cheek of the embarrassed journalist. Altman, dressed in a tailored, double-breasted blue suit, moved stoically toward the building's elevators.

The tenth-floor courtroom was a dreary, windowless box. Beside a table with two assistants stood John Moscow, rocking on his toes like a boxer. Altman's lead attorney now was Gustave Newman, a canny New Yorker whose goatee and mustache gave him a resemblance to the painter El Greco. Newman was a shrewd pick. Robert Bennett or Robert Fiske would have been the choice had the first trial been conducted in federal court in Washington. They were accustomed to the respectful tenor and tone of such sessions. But Newman, whose clients had included mobsters and murderers, knew how the criminal courts of New York operated. He was street smart and scrappy, with a roguish charm tailored to appeal to New York juries.

Behind the lawyers on the wooden benches sat Altman's three sisters and his parents. Alongside them was Lynda Carter, easily the most-watched figure in the courtroom as she whispered to her friend Blaine Trump, the socialite sister-in-law of developer Donald Trump. Reporters and spectators filled the remainder of the small room.

Judge Bradley, a squat, bespectacled man in a traditional black robe, watched quietly as the jurors were ushered in and then allowed Moscow to present his opening statement, a description of the case that the government intended to prove. He seemed uncharacteristically nervous as he promised the jury they were about to hear a simple case. Before he could go further, Newman had jumped to his feet and theatrically objected to what he called Moscow's attempt to summarize "the context for discovery." No one on the jury had the slightest idea what Newman was talking about, but it did not matter. He had landed the first blow, signaling to everyone in the courtroom that he intended to wage a spirited defense. The Altman family smiled in unison.

It was clear from the outset that Clifford was on trial as much as Altman. Moscow described the absent lawyer as "very powerful" and contended that he had employed that power to mislead bank regulators on behalf of BCCI. For another hour, he worked chronologically through the events leading up to the takeover of Financial General Bankshares, the creation of First American, the ultimate seizure of BCCI. He punctuated his oration with references to an array of elaborate charts and he rattled off dozens of names, many Arabic or Pakistani. Moscow knew this case better than anyone. The problem was that the sixteen members of his most important audience, the twelve jurors and four alternates, were bewildered. The simple case had taken more than two hours to summarize, using the entire morning.

It was a logical time to recess for lunch, but Newman rose from his chair and asked permission to begin his opening statement. In a booming voice, he ridiculed the prosecution and their case. Ten minutes into his statement, he politely asked the judge to excuse the jury for lunch. As they filed out of the room, the words echoing in their ears were those of the defense lawyer, not the prosecutor. Moscow had painted an elaborate and confusing canvas; Newman had been far more effective with a few broad strokes.

As the trial wore on, several things became clear in the courtroom. One was that Clifford, though still recuperating from his surgery, was a strong presence in both the prosecution and defense cases. The prosecution depicted him as a pawn of a giant conspiracy orchestrated by BCCI.

Newman, showing the jurors photographs of Clifford with Harry Truman, John Kennedy, Lyndon Johnson, and Jimmy Carter, portrayed him as a patriotic American who would never stoop to criminal activity.

Also, there was the mind-numbing detail of the prosecution case. Each day, Moscow and his team rolled out documents and witnesses for the bleary-eyed jurors. The burden was on the government to prove its case, but the prosecution's lack of a coherent, easily trackable trial strategy left jurors confused and inattentive. One juror fell asleep so often he was dubbed "Sleepy" by his colleagues. When he was moved next to a court bailiff, the bailiff fell asleep, too. Every time Moscow seemed to be gathering steam, Newman interrupted the proceedings and the momentum by calling for a conversation with the judge outside the presence of the jurors. The fears of some of Moscow's colleagues appeared to be coming true: the brilliant and dedicated investigator was badly outmaneuvered in the courtroom.

Even when the trial progressed with a semblance of smoothness, Moscow had difficulty building a convincing case against Altman. Newman and his assistants were most effective on cross-examination, raising questions about motive and memory. One striking example was the cross-examination of Dildar Rizvi, a former BCCI official, who was the closest person the prosecution had to a star witness. A critical part of Rizvi's testimony involved his claim that he had attended two meetings at which Clifford had been present and discussed BCCI's takeover of First American. When it was Newman's turn to question the bank official, the defense lawyer zeroed in on the list of people Rizvi had claimed were also at the meetings. One of the other supposed participants, Newman disclosed in the questioning, had sworn that he had never attended either meeting. The disclosure was intended to raise questions in the minds of the jurors about Rizvi's entire testimony.

The controversial 1986 stock transaction, which had netted Clifford and Altman $9.8 million in profits, was at the heart of the bribery charge. A former BCCI accountant testified that Altman had dictated to BCCI the price he wanted for his shares in First American, apparent evidence that BCCI controlled the entire transaction. The defense did not dispute the testimony. Instead, on cross-examination, Newman assailed the accountant's credibility by pointing out that he had received nearly $20,000 in expenses from the government over the past year while preparing for his testimony. The perception that the witness was paid overshadowed the millions of dollars in profits collected by Clifford and Altman.

Perhaps the most critical factor for the defense was Altman himself. Considered by friend and foe alike to be a very good lawyer, he immersed himself in the case. He often whispered advice in Newman's ear, and he always accompanied his lawyers to the private conferences with the judge that were held outside the jury's hearing. Each day when the trial ended, he accompanied Newman and the others back to Newman's midtown offices to prepare for the next day. Even his relationship with his glamorous wife, highlighted by frequent kisses and hand-holding during recesses, helped soften and humanize him with the jurors.

Clifford spent the summer recuperating at his Maryland home. Some days his spirits and his health flagged, but he was consistently buoyed by Altman's regular reports at the end of each day on the progress of the trial. He read a biography of his former colleague Dean Acheson and the collected poems of W. B. Yeats. Most of his time, however, was spent thinking about the trial. Often he awoke in the middle of the night, considering how he would have handled a certain matter in the trial or reviewing a long-ago conversation with a BCCI official. The man who had planned his life so carefully to ensure that he would not depend on anyone else now sat helplessly by as others decided his fate.

He told friends and family that he wanted to regain his strength in time to testify as a defense witness at the trial.

"I've got to go there and defend my reputation," he said plaintively to his daughter Joyce one morning. "This is so frustrating. There has never been a cloud against my name and now I must defend myself."

But he was too ill to travel to New York, much less participate in the rigors of a trial. So he stayed at home, visited by his children and most of his twelve grandchildren, and tried to regain his strength. Gradually, he began to recover. Between naps, he walked the perimeter of his three-acre property. Finally, after several weeks, he felt well enough to be driven to his office each morning. By noon, however, he would be back home, drained and aching.

It soon became apparent that Clifford would not need to testify. Judge Bradley dismissed two of the most important charges midway through the trial, declaring that the prosecution had not produced enough evidence to support the allegations of bribery and conspiracy.

Throwing out the bribery charges buoyed Clifford greatly and he became convinced that there would indeed be an acquittal in New York.
During the final week of the prosecution's case, Bradley took the unusual step of granting a defense motion to remove one of the jurors.
Newman had claimed that she was demonstrating body language indicating she might be biased in favor of the prosecution. Although one
juror in favor of convicting Altman could have forced a second trial, it
was really a minor victory for the defense, just another signal of the
direction in which things were going.

On July 23, after calling forty-five witnesses and introducing three
hundred exhibits into evidence, the prosecution rested its case. Moscow
had given it everything he had, but he knew that the trial had not gone
well. The witnesses from BCCI had been stained and their credibility
damaged. The judge had already thrown out two of the most substantive charges. The defense was so confident that it decided not to even
present its side of the case. All that remained were the closing arguments
and the judge's instructions to the jurors.

The day the prosecution finished its case, Clifford, in a display of self-
confidence, ventured out in public for the first time in months. He had
lunch with Richard Holbrooke, who had written his memoirs with him
and was now President Clinton's ambassador-designate to Germany. As
the two sipped soup at the Metropolitan Club, several of Clifford's old
friends dropped by to wish him well.

Clifford was sleeping in the late afternoon of August 14, a Saturday.
Marny answered the telephone and heard Altman's joyous voice.
"Marny, they've freed me," he shouted with glee. When his ecstatic
wife woke Clifford with the news, he, too, was elated. "This is wonderful news," he said. "Wonderful news."

Altman's acquittal was Clifford's vindication. The case the prosecution had presented against Altman was the same one that they would
have presented had Clifford shared the defense table. The months of
allegations and press stories, the destruction of his law practice and the
loss of the bank, the frustration as his reputation was stained, had been
summed up by a verdict of innocent.

Throughout the rest of the evening, Clifford telephoned friends to
tell them the good news. "The most wonderful thing has happened," he
told George Elsey, his loyal second in the Truman administration and at
the Defense Department. "Bob has been cleared." An ABC-TV News

camera crew interviewed the pajama-clad Clifford at his back door as he told them, "The jury considered the case and found there was no case." Daughter Joyce was called in Vermont with the news. "Oh Poppy," she exclaimed. "You've won."

Before he finally went to bed, Clifford recalled all the nights he had awakened worried about the trial and its outcome. Turning to Marny, he said, "I hope I wake up during the night." At three or four o'clock that Sunday morning, Clifford woke up. "I just lay there and glowed," he recalled.

The size of the victory grew as the prosecution came under attack from some of the twelve people who had sat through months of trial. Newspaper and wire service stories the next day quoted jurors deriding the prosecution. Clifford clipped each story, reading the comments over and over until he had almost memorized them. Barbara Conley, the forewoman, said she was "insulted" by the government's case. Another juror said of Altman, "This man was innocent from the start, from the very first witness. There was no doubt in my mind." Another offered this stinging assessment of the prosecution case: "I thought there were a lot of untruthful statements made by prosecution witnesses, especially the BCCI guys. I found it hard to find anything credible in the witnesses' statements."

The decision had not been so clear cut. At the start of deliberation, three jurors had held out for conviction. After four days of sometimes-intense debate, they had agreed to vote for acquittal. In the end, however, the system that had charged Clifford and Altman had acquitted Altman and, in every sense but the formal one, Clifford, too.

24

The Final Curtain

N O MATTER HOW SWEET, the victory could not restore the loss. Even in the warm glow of the verdict, Clifford was aware that he could never recover all that had been taken from him. Gone was First American. New management had dismissed six thousand employees and sold the bank, erasing its scandalous name. Gone was the law firm, which he had expected to live long after he was dead. Gone, too, was the reputation that Clifford had cultivated with such care and vigor for nearly half a century.

"This is vindication, but when you have been subjected to this kind of publicity over a long period of time, then I believe you don't ever get back what you had before," he said a few days after the decision. "I will continue working at it, doing the best I can to get back as much of it as I had before, but some of it has been taken away from me I believe irrevocably and I regret that very much."

Nevertheless, he set about trying to redeem his reputation. As a young boy, Clifford had been given a copy of the Rudyard Kipling poem "If" by his father. Throughout his career, he had kept the poem beneath one of the presidential medallions on his desk. The most famous lines are the opening ones, "If you can keep your head when all about you are losing theirs and blaming it on you." For Clifford, however, the ones that rang the truest now were those that softly urged him to hold his head high as he stooped to rebuild "with wornout tools" the things to which he had given his life.

In the weeks following the verdict, Clifford began to venture out more as his strength increased. In September 1993, President Bill Clinton invited him to the White House for the historic signing of the peace accord between Israel and the Palestine Liberation Organization. After the ceremony, Clifford, who had played such a vital role in the creation of Israel, was interviewed by Fox Television. For the first time in years, there was not a question about First American or BCCI.

A few days later, Richard Holbrooke, Clifford's friend and the co-author of his memoir, was confirmed by the Senate as ambassador to Germany. Clifford was invited to the swearing-in ceremony in the richly paneled reception room on the eighth floor of the State Department. Secretary of State Warren Christopher, who knew Clifford from his own days in the Carter administration, presided. At one point, Christopher paused and looked across the room at the white-haired man standing beside his wife, who was confined to a wheelchair by circulatory problems. "I'd like to recognize one of the great men of the country, Clark Clifford," said Christopher, initiating a round of sustained applause that seemed to represent the establishment's seal of approval on his vindication.

Attending the ceremony was Jack Valenti, Hollywood's powerful lobbyist, who had known Clifford since the Johnson administration. "No one is free of sin," Valenti later recalled thinking to himself. "Clark was flawed in that he probably represented a lot of people in Washington who didn't deserve his sterling reputation. He has been damaged by the cries of those who were dealing in assumption and surmise, rather than truth. But he's no longer Clark Clifford. The tragedy is that sixty years of service are marred by unfounded allegations."

Clifford did what he could to encourage the press to write about his victory. A lengthy article in the *New Yorker*, which had published excerpts from his memoir, cast Clifford as the victim of an overzealous press and disloyal law partners. It was written by historian Michael Beschloss, who said the article was suggested by Tina Brown, the editor of the magazine. Clifford himself had floated the idea of a redemptive article in conversations with Hugh Sidey of *Time* and been turned down.

In the Beschloss article, Clifford praised Altman: "I have the greatest respect for him, and the manner in which he handled his last ordeal has deepened my respect. To go through this at a younger age — in his middle forties, I think he is — going to court every day, working every night with the lawyers. He showed character and stamina, and my admiration for him increased."

As for the former partners who had broken ranks and left the firm, Clifford was not inclined to be charitable. "The parting was not friendly," he told Beschloss. "It was just cold. They could have handled it in a way as a kind of 'merger of firms' or something and taken some of the stigma out of it. But they didn't. It was: Get away from Clifford and Warnke, because it's doomed. By that time, I could see that as far as my practicing law was concerned, it was over."

The remarks were an uncharacteristic expression of bitterness. Clifford was unfair to his former partners. They had offered to take him along. It was Clifford who had been unable to either accept a diminished role or abandon Altman.

The article was part of a larger movement within the press to present both men in kinder terms in the wake of Altman's acquittal. About the time the *New Yorker* piece appeared, Altman and his wife were interviewed by a sympathetic Diane Sawyer on the ABC-TV program *Prime Time Live*. There were stories in some publications questioning how Morgenthau could have brought such a weak case. The press, which had trumpeted every accusation and leak, was changing course again on Clark Clifford.

In late December, Clifford and Altman went to the White House for a private lunch. The invitation came from Howard Paster, who had helped prepare Clifford for his congressional testimony and gone on to become the chief White House lobbyist. Although Clifford and Altman were technically still under criminal investigation by the Justice Department, no one expected them to stand trial. Paster liked and admired Clifford, and he saw nothing wrong with bringing the men into the White House. Anyway, Paster himself was leaving the administration to become the president of the huge lobbying and public relations firm Hill and Knowlton Worldwide. There, he could follow a Washington tradition and use the influence he had gained while serving at the White House on behalf of his clients.

Recalling the visit later, Paster said, "Mr. Clifford wanted to see his old office, which is now the vice president's office. He hadn't really been to the White House for years. So we walked over there after lunch in the mess and he was very pleased."

But Clifford's redemption was far from complete. Some of Paster's colleagues at the White House criticized him for inviting the lawyer to lunch. They thought it was unseemly, given all that had happened over the past three years.

＊　　　＊　　　＊

Clark Clifford's glorious career was ending with a whimper. He and his two remaining partners, Altman and Griff Lescher, were forced to move out of the grand offices on Connecticut Avenue. An executive with an industry lobbying group got Clifford's office, with the famous view of the White House that seemed to say, "I'll be right over, Mr. President." Initially, the three lawyers were squeezed into a warren of small offices on the same floor. Instead of the paneled foyer behind the doors that said "Clifford & Warnke," visitors opened a door that bore only Altman's name and found themselves confronted with a secretary's back. After a few months in that symbolically diminished space, they moved briefly to still-smaller offices in the same building. Finally, the three lawyers and their secretaries rented space in a different building. There was no view of the White House.

Clifford was adrift. Unanchored without his law practice or the bank, he sometimes felt lonely and old. The man who was strangely ageless for so many years now looked all of his years and more. He continued to arrive at the office each morning shortly after nine, stepping gingerly out of the black Lincoln Town Car as his chauffeur held the door, graciously tipping his hat to his secretary, and collecting his mail and messages. He usually stayed until noon or so before being driven home for soup and a nap.

His health was a roller coaster. Some days he felt strong and was able to stand nearly upright. Others, pain in his back related to heart medication kept him bent over. He bore the vagaries of old age without complaint. True to the sentiment he had expressed to Betty Beale on his eightieth birthday, Clifford did not discuss his medical problems with others.

Occasionally old friends dropped by the office to chat or called on the telephone. Sometimes there would be fan mail, people expressing happiness over the verdict or sending in a copy of his autobiography for an autograph.

There was no legal work. Clifford was his own client now. Most of his time was spent working on his defense in the civil suits still pending over First American and the collapse of the law firm.

The legal bills from the criminal investigations were staggering. Skadden, Arps, Slate, Meagher and Flom, where Robert Bennett and Carl Rauh were partners, had charged $5.3 million for representing Clifford and Altman. Robert Fiske's firm, Davis Polk and Wardwell, was paid

$2.65 million. Clifford had paid Davis Polk another $264,000 to secure the release of the $19 million frozen by Morgenthau's office when he was indicted. Altman's defense by Gustav Newman had cost $1.1 million. When other legal bills and expenses related to the investigations were added in, the total reached $10 million. Clifford had advanced most of the money for both men out of his pocket. Although far from impoverished, the man who had been so driven to provide financial security for himself and his family faced another emotional loss.

The bylaws of First American Bankshares stipulated that legal costs for officers and directors would be paid if the employees were not found liable or guilty. After Altman's acquittal, he and Clifford petitioned the trustees for First American for reimbursement. The bank would not pay, refusing even to acknowledge receipt of the bills. Harry Albright, the trustee who had taken over the affairs of First American, decided that the bank need not pay anything until the bank's own civil suit against the two men was resolved.

In the spring of 1994, Clifford found something new to occupy his relentless drive. He took up the study of music, buying dozens of classical records and installing a new sound system at his house. He read a book on music written by Phil Goulding, one of his former aides at the Pentagon. He marveled that Goulding had managed to learn so much about something so seemingly inconsequential to his work. He also sent away for a mail-order course on memory, intent on improving his recall for reasons that he could not really explain except to say that he wanted the mental exercise.

"You know," he said one day that spring, "I ran this law firm here for over forty years. It took all my time. I did it with considerable expense to other things I might have wanted to do. Now I want to be in a position to do a good many other things."

Yet his essential mood seemed to be of sadness and resignation as he pondered his achievements, his losses, and his future. He had not foreseen what he set in motion when he embarked on that new career in banking. What he knew now was that the consequences of his actions could not be undone. He was not bitter so much as still numbed by the attacks and the seeming enthusiasm of his attackers.

"Something has happened with the ancient and honorable principle that a man is presumed innocent until proven guilty," he said ruefully one day. "I will swear to you that it is gone. It doesn't exist in the press. But it exists in the courtroom, thank goodness."

In a symbolic step to close that chapter, lawyers for Clifford and Altman filed a motion in 1994 asking Judge Bradley in New York to order the files and records associated with the prosecution sealed. The judge complied, writing, "The arrest and prosecution shall be deemed a nullity and the accused shall be restored, in a contemplation of the law, to the status he occupied before the arrest and prosecution."

But the stain could not be erased. Nor would other trouble stay away.

Late on the evening of September 16, 1994, a Friday, the telephone rang at Clifford's home in Bethesda. Jan Hoffman, a reporter with the *New York Times*, was calling. She wanted to ask Clifford about a lawsuit filed by the heirs of W. Averell Harriman.

After simmering for years, the Harriman family feud had finally burst into public with a nasty lawsuit filed in United States District Court in Manhattan by Harriman's children and grandchildren. The heirs had been angry since 1986, when Harriman's will left half of his $65 million estate to his wife, Pamela. The remainder had gone into trusts for the other heirs. Several of the heirs depended on income from the trusts, and in 1993 they discovered that $30 million of the money had been lost in bad real estate investments. They blamed Mrs. Harriman, then United States ambassador to France, as well as Clifford and his former partner, Paul Warnke, who had been the unpaid trustees of the trust funds. Unable to settle the matter in private negotiations, the heirs filed a lawsuit accusing Mrs. Harriman, Clifford, and Warnke of being "faithless fiduciaries who betrayed a trust and squandered a family's inheritance."

That Friday night, Clifford politely told Hoffman that he had not yet seen the suit, although he was well aware of the dispute. He was reassuring and courtly, telling her, "We have conducted the affairs honestly these many years and we do not believe there is a basis for the heirs to complain about the management of the trust."

In earlier years, Clifford's comment might have granted him a polite reprieve from the unpleasantness of a family feud. After all, he and Warnke had not been paid for their work as trustees, although they had received $250,000 in legal fees representing Mrs. Harriman as executor of her husband's estate. But these were different times. His word was no longer good. Suspicions about his honesty, never quite put to rest by the Altman verdict, resurfaced. And so did the pain.

The following week, Clifford remained at the office late into the afternoon one day, responding to questions from journalists about the lawsuit. It was nearly five o'clock before he rose stiffly from his chair, tugged on his suitcoat, picked up his fedora, and emerged from his small office. Bent by fatigue and back pain, he tipped a hand to his secretary as he said good-bye.

Looking up from her computer, Clifford's secretary, Toby Godfrey, smiled at her boss and said that he looked particularly tired. Pulling himself a little straighter, Clifford summoned a grim smile and, in a pale remnant of that wonderful actor's voice, quoted from an ancient ballad about a Scottish knight:

> *A little I'm hurt, but yet not slain;*
> *I'll but lie down and bleed awhile,*
> *and then I'll rise and fight again.*

Although it was forged in adversity, Marny Clifford treasured the strengthened bond with her husband. A few days after their sixty-third wedding anniversary in October 1994, she spoke warmly of Clifford, the way he had handled his ordeal.

"We've been learning a lot about marriage as we went along," said Mrs. Clifford, white-haired, eighty-six, and in poor health herself. "It is stronger and sounder right now than it has ever been. I have the highest admiration for him. I have never seen a stronger performance in the face of this Greek tragedy that we have been through. He does not complain. He has been simply wonderful."

She paused, lost in thought, and then resumed. "He lost his reputation, his bank, his forty-year-old law office, so many things," she said. "I don't think he's lost his reputation, but he thinks he did. He has come through it. There has never been another one quite like him."

Remembering the day on the steamer along the Rhine River when the mildly impertinent, too-handsome young lawyer from St. Louis approached her, she laughed fondly and said she liked his looks better these days. "Now he has character lines and white hair."

With the exception of Margery, the trouble had been a rallying point for the family. Suddenly this man who had seemed so formidable was revealed to be vulnerable, even needy. Joyce had been his rock, spending long hours discussing the turmoil with her father. Randall, after some years apart from the family herself, was a frequent visitor, as were the twelve grandchildren and eight great-grandchildren.

For Christmas 1994, twenty-three members of the Clifford family arrived in Washington from around the country. They gathered at the rambling house on Rockville Pike to celebrate the holiday and to honor the patriarch on his eighty-eighth birthday. As he had for the past few years, Clifford joked that they had come because they expected it to be his last Christmas. For a brief time, the house beneath the towering sycamores seemed warmed by the memories of those bygone days, the era when all of Washington seemed eager for the friendship of Clark Clifford.

Could this celebrated figure, whose advice had been sought by presidents and executives alike, really have been duped by a group of foreign bankers? Or did an aging actor, unwilling to exit the stage when his performance was concluded, deceive himself? In his heart, Clifford was convinced that he was fooled by Aga Hasan Abedi and his well-heeled front men. He truly believed in his own innocence. To think otherwise would have repudiated too much.

In examining the evidence churned up by the many BCCI investigations, no conclusive piece surfaced that fit the puzzle together finally and rendered the verdict guilty beyond a reasonable doubt. In his own relentless effort to restore his name, Clifford argued with rare passion and characteristic eloquence that he was a victim — of Abedi's skilled deception, of vengeful prosecutors in New York, of a press too willing to repeat leaks as truth and innuendo as fact.

As with most things he said, there was a measure of truth. Abedi was a master manipulator who duped politicians on four continents. Almost without exception, the prosecutors and investigators saw Clifford and Altman as part of an international banking conspiracy, although they could not prove it. And the insatiable press was eager to accept the worst about a Washington monument. But it was only a measure of truth, the one that Clifford fashioned for himself out of convenient facts. As always, he saw only what he wanted to see.

William Butler Yeats wrote that discovering the central myth of a man is the key to understanding him. With Clifford, the central myth must contain not only what happened with BCCI, but how it happened, how he allowed his good name to be used in the service of deception and corruption. It is the central question about Clifford, and the answer lies in understanding not only BCCI but the man himself.

The answer will not be found solely in the details of the BCCI–First American affair, although they are clearly important. Nor can it be discerned in the black-and-white question of criminal guilt or innocence, although much has been speculated there. Uncovering Clifford's central myth can be accomplished only by placing that scandalous episode in the context of his full life. From that vantage point, and only that vantage point, can the life be judged. Unfortunately, the view from there is sadly clear.

Clifford's was a life of extraordinary sweep, serving as a metaphor for an epoch in American political history. He rose to the heights of power and influence in a city where both are exalted, and his fall rivaled those of the protagonists in Greek tragedies. Many Clifford loyalists argue that BCCI was an aberration in an otherwise distinguished career. The career was distinguished indeed, and Clifford was a good man who served his country well in many instances. But BCCI was not an isolated incident. Rather, it was the final and inevitable act in the drama that Clifford had chosen to live.

The seeds of his downfall were planted at the beginning of Clifford's career in Washington. They were sown the first time he delivered that patented speech to a client claiming to have no influence. With those astonishingly cynical words, Clark Clifford distanced himself from his own actions, absolved himself of responsibility. In doing so, he made it inevitable that the myth he built so fastidiously would lead to his undoing. Clifford played the ultimate Washington game: image replaced reality.

He had come to Washington in simpler times. He had risen to power in the Truman administration during a period in which a handful of men arranged the fate of nations, secure in the belief that they were acting in the best interest of the country. The sense of knowing what is best for the country became ingrained in Clifford. Whether it was arranging a country retreat for President and Mrs. Kennedy or a sweetheart tax deal for the Du Ponts, Clifford comfortably aligned the national interests with his clients' interests. He justified the acquisition of First American Bankshares by saying that it was a way to recycle American dollars spent on Arab oil. Never content to be merely a lawyer once he had spent time in the White House, Clifford was forever playing the role of the soldier-stateman.

It was a part he played to perfection for years. He was handsome and courtly, articulate and logical. Like all great actors, Clifford had the marvelous capacity to make his audience feel good about itself. And like all great actors, his timing was flawless. He represented the great oil companies and defense firms in the fifties and sixties when they were symbols of American power. He moved smoothly and quietly through the corridors of Congress and the White House when backroom deals were simply the way business was done. In those years, his word was good enough.

Then the times changed. Authority itself came under attack in the seventies. Vietnam sowed a cynicism toward Washington across the country, a president was driven from office for corruption, big companies were caught in foreign bribery scandals. As Walter Isaacson and Evan Thomas described in their eulogy to *The Wise Men*, the private exercise of power began to get a bad name.

This revolution in the way Americans saw Washington was lost on Clifford. His audience changed, but Clifford did not. In the same way he refused to alter the style of his broad-shouldered, double-breasted suits, he saw no reason to give up the notion that a small group of right-thinking men could exercise power and influence without offending anyone.

He might have slipped away quietly. Many others from his era did. But Clifford differed from his friends and colleagues in refusing to retire gracefully from the new world. He had become the character he played so well. He was as unable to abandon his role as he was to change the way he played the part.

For these reasons, he happily signed on as BCCI's man in Washington, oblivious to the changes in his city. In the old days, a wink and a nod to friends at the Federal Reserve would have assured the smooth acquistion of a big Washington bank. In the old days, if some rabble-rouser in Congress like John Kerry got feisty, a few words whispered in the right ear would put him in his place. And if reporters started writing too many nasty stories, there were friends in the press who could be counted on to see things his way.

If Clifford had adapted to the changed times, he might have steered clear of the traps set by the men from BCCI. He might have recognized that men like him no longer ran the city, so he might have asked the tough questions about why the men at BCCI really wanted to make him chairman of the board. If Clifford had not dominated his law firm so thoroughly, there might have been someone to ask those tough questions for him. But he was too deeply immersed in the mythical role he had fashioned for himself. He never changed. Only the times did.

Did he know that BCCI really owned First American Bankshares? For a man who so carefully crafted a reputation for probity, the answer is worse than yes. It is that he never bothered to look. But there were others who were only too willing to look for him.

Clifford was genuinely baffled and stunned by the first questions about BCCI's illegal ownership of First American. He felt his word should have been good enough. He had chosen to believe it, ignoring the suspicions that cropped up along the way. It was not only the flattery of Abedi that blinded Clifford. It was not only the chance to revive his flagging career that caused him to fail to see how he was used. He was blinded by his own myth.

Clark Clifford's story is a genuine American tragedy. His public career had been launched with great promise, and he had fulfilled much of that promise, particularly during his tenure as secretary of defense. Accolades and wealth had been showered on him. Yet by the conclusion of his life, Clifford had undergone a complete reversal. He was transformed in his own eyes, and in the eyes of the world, from a man of power and prestige into a person whose life was ruined. He had spent half a century on a journey toward his destiny, but he had arrived only at his fate.

Notes

Chapter 1: Friend of the Court

4 Just a few months earlier: Clark Clifford to William Douglas, Container 315, Douglas Papers, Library of Congress.

4 Years later, Clifford would describe Douglas: Interview with Clark Clifford, 1994.

4 So frequently was the justice a guest: Joyce Clifford to William Douglas, Container 315, Douglas Papers, Library of Congress.

4 When Douglas threatened to sue: Inteview with John Kovin, 1994.

5 Indeed, Clifford's law office: Memorandum, Container 315, Douglas Papers, Library of Congress.

5 "Summer after summer": Interview with Sam McIlwain, 1993.

5 For instance, when he was chronically missing mortgage payments: William Douglas to Clark Clifford, June 17, 1954, Container 54, Douglas Papers, Library of Congress.

5 "Your advance is deeply appreciated": Ibid.

5 "I hate to talk personal": William Douglas to Clark Clifford, Container 315, Douglas Papers, Library of Congress.

6 Years later, for instance: William Douglas to Clark Clifford, June 6, 1966, Container 315, Douglas Papers, Library of Congress.

6 To the contrary, Douglas openly praised Clifford's: Douglas, *Court Years*, p. 187.

6 One Washington lawyer, who was involved: Interview with a confidential source, 1993.

6 While today's rules would prohibit: Interview with Stephen Gillers, 1994.

6 When asked years later: Interview with Clark Clifford, 1994.

7 Late in 1966, Ronald J. Ostrow: Interview with Ronald J. Ostrow, 1993; Simon, *Independent Journey*, pp. 392–393.

7 In defending himself: Simon, *Independent Journey*, p. 393.

7 The financial relationship: Ibid., pp. 408–409.

8 In the Phillips Petroleum case: Oral arguments, *Phillips Chemical Co. v. Dumas Independent School District*, Appeal from Supreme Court of Texas, November 17–19, 1959.

9 From the start of the firm: Interview with Sam McIlwain, 1993; Lilienthal, *Journals*, vol. 2, p. 136.

9 In 1967, for instance, he earned: Goulden, *Superlawyers*, p. 103.

10 In the words of George Reedy: Interview with George Reedy, 1993.

10 *Parade* magazine called him one of the thirty most influential: *Parade*, May 7, 1972.

11 Washington defense lawyer: Interview with Seymour Glanzer, 1993.

12 When the well-known Washington lawyer-lobbyist: Interview with a confidential source, 1993.

12 Describing Clifford in the early seventies: Interview with a confidential source.

Chapter 2: A Victorian Childhood

14 As dusk fell along Laurel Avenue: *Time*, March 15, 1948.

14 Clark Clifford lived in a rented house: *Current Biography*, 1947, p. 147.

14 Frank Clifford, a railroad auditor: Ibid.

14 Georgia's mother, Anne Curtis McAdams: Interview with Clark Clifford, 1994.

15 He was an authority: Ibid. and *Current Biography*, 1947, p. 147.

15 While Frank grew up: Clifford, *Counsel to the President*, p. 28.

15 After a tour in the U.S. Cavalry: Interview with Clark Clifford, 1994.

15 On Christmas Day 1906: Clifford, *Counsel to the President*, p. 27.

16 Clark went to kindergarten: Edward A. Harris, "New Power in Truman's Palace Guard," *St. Louis Post-Dispatch*, December 21, 1947.

16 The Cliffords had reached an early accommodation: Interview with Clark Clifford, 1994.

16 Years later, his son would have this recollection: Ibid.

16 Even as an old man: Ibid.

17 By the 1930s, she had a program: *Time*, March 15, 1948.

17 Each summer, the family: Interview with Clark Clifford, 1994.

17 The original Chautauqua: Meredith Hladik, "An American Treasure," *Country Living*, May 1994.

17 Years later, his sharpest memory: Interview with Clark Clifford, 1994.

17 At home on Laurel Avenue: Ibid.

18 From the age of five: Ibid.

18 As a teenager, Clifford: Ibid.

18 Soon after the end of World War I: Ibid.

19 To his teenage son: Marjorie Williams, "The Man Who Banked on His Good Name," *Washington Post*, May 9, 1991.

19 He was a member: Tom Ottenad, "Clifford Was a Prankster," *St. Louis Post-Dispatch*, April 1, 1969.

19 Clifford was not an outstanding student: Medved, *Shadow Presidents*, p. 217.

19 It was his father who gently guided him: Interview with Clark Clifford, 1994.

20 "It is very important": Ibid.

20 Although Clifford denied responsibility: Ottenad, "Clifford Was a Prankster."

20 Although he lived at home: Interview with Clark Clifford, 1994.

21 In his final year of law school: Ibid.

21 A friend later told Frank Clifford: Ibid.

21 "Mr. Lashly, I enjoyed your course": Ibid.

Chapter 3: Best in the Midwest

23 His first summer at Holland: Terry Carter, "The Insider's Insider," *National Law Journal*, July 10, 1989.

24 Not long after Labor Day: Ibid.

24 "Well, that didn't turn out": Interview with Clark Clifford, 1994.

25 Not long after, Robert Holland was arguing: Ibid.; Carter, "The Insider's Insider."

25 He had been dating: Clifford, *Counsel to the President*, p. 36.

25 So when Louis McKeown: Medved, *Shadow Presidents*, p. 245.

26 As a twenty-first birthday present: Interview with Marny Clifford, 1994.

26 As she looked over the tall man: Ibid.

27 In the meantime: Interview with Clark Clifford, 1994.

27 The appeal of litigation: Ibid.

28 If he ever had his own firm: Carter, "The Insider's Insider."

28 In the fall of 1930: Clifford, *Counsel to the President,* pp. 36–37.

29 "We should not leave it": Interview with Clark Clifford, 1994.

29 The elder Kimball had been a partner: Interview with Marny Clifford, 1994.

29 When they arrived back: Interview with Clark Clifford, 1994.

30 At the wedding reception: Medved, *Shadow Presidents,* p. 218.

30 Back in St. Louis: Interview with Clark Clifford, 1994.

30 He joined the St. Louis Racquet Club: Goulden, *Superlawyers,* p. 74.

30 With their blond good looks: Interview with Mrs. Otto Spaeth, 1993.

31 Once, as he was leaving court: Harris, "New Power in Truman's Palace Guard."

31 The couple's primary outside interest: Medved, *Shadow Presidents,* p. 218.

31 The couple's first daughter: Interview with Marny Clifford, 1994.

31 Not long after buying the house: Ibid.

31 "She looked at me": Ibid.

31 Marny thought briefly: Ibid.

32 "His experience brought": Interview with Clark Clifford, 1994.

32 Marny began to wonder: Interview with Marny Clifford, 1994.

32 On the nights when he was home: Ibid.

32 "If you try the other system": Interview with Clark Clifford, 1994.

32 Once, when Clifford tried to explain: Ibid.

33 "She was an only child": Ibid.

33 "I soon learned": Interview with Marny Clifford, 1994.

33 Later, he explained: Interview with Clark Clifford, 1994.

33 From Clifford's point of view: Ibid.

33 As a young man on the way up: Ibid.

34 During this period: Hoopes and Brinkley, *Driven Patriot,* p. 356.

34 Symington had come to St. Louis: Interview with James Symington, 1993.

34 He was vice chairman: Interview with Al Fleischman, 1992; Allen and Shannon, *The Truman Merry-Go-Round,* p. 60.

34 James K. Vardaman Jr.: Leigh White, "Assistant President of the U.S.A.," *Saturday Evening Post,* October 4, 1947.

34 Vardaman was also active: Interview with Marny Clifford, 1994.

35 Frank Clifford had been ill: Interview with Clark Clifford, 1994.

35 Several years earlier: White, "Assistant President of the U.S.A."

36 "You don't have to do it": Goulden, *Superlawyers,* p. 76.

36 In the fall of 1943: Unpublished *Los Angeles Times* interview with Clark Clifford, 1982.

36 Marny said she would take the children: Interview with Clark Clifford, 1994.

36 On April 28, 1944: Unpublished *Los Angeles Times* interview with Clark Clifford, 1982.

37 Just before leaving: Interview with Marny Clifford, 1994.

37 He found a bunk: Clifford, *Counsel to the President,* p. 40.

37 In July 1944: White, "Assistant President of the U.S.A."

38 As Truman biographer: McCullough, *Truman,* p. 714.

38 Shortly after FDR's death: Donovan, *Conflict and Crisis,* p. 24.

Chapter 4: "Big Fella, Ain't He"

40 As vice president: Donovan, *Conflict and Crisis,* p. 6.

40 Truman had not even known: Ibid.

40 It was a typically muggy day: Aaron Latham, "Clark Clifford: Capital Manipulator," *Esquire*, March 14, 1978.
41 No one had the title: Donovan, *Conflict and Crisis*, p. 269.
41 The day after Truman and his entourage: Interview with Clark Clifford, 1994.
41 Clifford was working: Clifford, *Counsel to the President*, p. 57.
41 Marny Clifford had remained: Ibid., p. 60.
42 David Brinkley, a young journalist: Brinkley, *Washington Goes to War*, p. 281.
42 When Truman returned: David Welsh and David Horowitz, "Clark Clifford: Attorney at War," *Ramparts*, April 1968.
42 As assistant naval aide: Abramson, *Spanning the Century*, p. 448.
42 In 1945, Symington had been summoned: Hoopes and Brinkley, *Driven Patriot*, p. 56.
42 In his typical fashion: Clifford, *Counsel to the President*, p. 71.
43 By November 1945: Ibid., p. 63.
43 Among them was James V. Forrestal: Ibid., p. 64.
43 Even worse, Vardaman had angered Bess Truman: Margaret Truman, *Harry S. Truman*, p. 290.
44 In January 1946, Truman: Welsh and Horowitz, "Attorney at War."
44 Vardaman's past returned: Clifford, *Counsel to the President*, p. 65.
44 Ultimately, Vardaman's nomination: Ibid., p. 66.
44 In January 1946, Symington: Interview with James Symington, 1993.
45 They were, as described by Walter Isaacson: Isaacson and Thomas, *Wise Men*, p. 17.
46 He and the young aide: Ibid., p. 404.
46 He was rescued: Ottenad, "Clifford Was a Prankster."
46 "If you need to stay": Ibid.
47 As he sat in a blue zipper suit: Clifford, *Counsel to the President*, p. 103.
47 The strike created a domestic crisis: Donovan, *Conflict and Crisis*, pp. 214–215.
48 Finally, he declared: Anderson, *President's Men*, pp. 114–115.
48 Charlie Ross, the press secretary: Ibid., p. 114.
49 A few minutes after four: Donovan, *Conflict and Crisis*, p. 215.
49 Clifford also reaped benefits: Medved, *Shadow Presidents*, p. 220.
50 During two years in Massachusetts: Interview with Marny Clifford, 1994.
50 Often, he could be found dining: Joseph W. Alsop and Adam Platt, *"I've Seen the Best of It": Memoirs*, p. 267.
51 When it came to Clifford: Ibid.
51 While he still played tennis: Clifford Papers, Box 25, Truman Presidential Library.
51 Truman shared Marny's love of the piano: Interview with Clark Clifford, 1994.

Chapter 5: Counsel to the President

52 Clifford dates the start: Interview with Clark Clifford, 1994.
52 Truman himself had returned: Donovan, *Conflict and Crisis*, p. 403.
53 On the night of September 12: Markowitz, *Rise and Fall of the People's Century: Henry A. Wallace and American Liberalism 1941–1948*, p. 182.
53 The following night: McCullough, *Truman*, pp. 513–517.
53 As Clifford later recalled: Interview with Clark Clifford, 1994.
53 Secretary of State Byrnes demanded: Jonathan Daniels, Clifford interview, Daniels Papers, Truman Presidential Library.
53 The White House moved quickly: Markowitz, *Rise and Fall of the People's Century*, p. 182.

53 Clifford later admitted: Clark Clifford speech, Harriman Communications Center, Washington, D.C., April 1977.

53 After a damaging week: Truman, *Year of Decision: Memoirs*, vol. I, p. 560.

54 Earlier in 1946: Acheson, *Present at the Creation*, p. 121.

54 In July, responding to Kennan's warning: Ibid.

54 For assistance, he turned to George M. Elsey: Interview with George Elsey, 1993.

54 "Could you do a study": Ibid.

55 On the night of September 24, 1946: Anderson, *President's Men*, p. 121.

55 "Therefore, in order to": Krock, *Memoirs*, memorandum reproduced on p. 477.

55 According to Walter Isaacson and Evan Thomas: Isaacson and Thomas, *Wise Men*, p. 376.

55 "There is continuous Communist": Krock, *Memoirs*, p. 477.

56 "The general pattern of the Soviet system": Ibid.

56 In preparation for defense of American interests: Ibid.

56 In analyzing the report: Garry Wills, "Keeper of the Seal," *New York Review of Books*, July 18, 1991.

56 In the early hours of the following morning: Hechler, *Working with Truman*, p. 44.

57 "This was the first time": Interview with George Elsey, 1993.

57 In 1966, he provided a copy: Krock, *Memoirs*, p. 224.

57 Clifford later maintained: Oral History, Interview with Clark Clifford, Washington, D.C., 1972, p. 72, Truman Presidential Library.

57 Just two weeks before: Anderson, *President's Men*, p. 93.

58 But Clifford again advised: Ibid., p. 94.

58 In early December: Ibid.; Welsh and Horowitz, "Attorney at War."

59 Typical of the stories: Edward Nellor, "Truman's Young Counsel Hailed as Lewis's Nemesis," *New York Sun*, December 9, 1946.

59 When asked by a reporter: Anderson, *President's Men*, p. 124.

59 "Newspaper and magazine": Ferrel, ed., *Truman in the White House*, p. 165.

59 *Life* magazine published: *Life*, June 27, 1947.

60 The *Saturday Evening Post*: White, "Assistant President of the U.S.A."

60 And syndicated columnists: Anderson, *President's Men*, p. 125.

60 He gave no speeches: Ibid., p. 124.

60 "You could always get to Clark": Interview with Robert Donovan, 1992.

60 Truman brushed off the incident: Brayman, *The President Speaks Off-the-Record*, p. 433.

60 To assuage Steelman and keep peace: Donovan, *Conflict and Crisis*, p. 299.

61 George Elsey said: Interview with George Elsey, 1993.

61 *Life*, for instance, disclosed: Anderson, *President's Men*, p. 124.

61 The following day, Symington: Clifford, *Counsel to the President*, p. 81.

61 Aware of the hostility: Donovan, *Conflict and Crisis*, p. 270.

61 He made a point of having lunch: Ibid., p. 269; *Life*, June 27, 1947.

62 Clifford also remained protective: Hoopes and Brinkley, *Driven Patriot*, p. 222.

62 At a cabinet meeting: Acheson, *Present at the Creation*, p. 295.

63 Marshall, who was in Paris: Ibid.; Welsh and Horowitz, "Attorney at War."

63 Eventually Clifford interrupted: Heller, *Truman in the White House, Comments of Charles S. Murphy*, p. 124.

63 On March 12, 1947, Truman spoke: Hoopes and Brinkley, *Driven Patriot*, pp. 301–303.

64 The tone was set: McCullough, *Truman*, pp. 548–549.

64 And *Newsweek* recognized: *Newsweek*, March 24, 1947.

64 "We had a presidential campaign": Bernstein, *Loyalties*, pp. 197–200.

64 Not until safely after the miraculous 1948 election: Clark Clifford to Harry Truman, Clifford Papers, Box 45, Truman Presidential Library.
65 In a speech at Harvard University: Isaacson and Thomas, *Wise Men*, pp. 458–461.
65 But it was Clifford and Acheson: Ferrell, ed., *Truman in the White House*, p. 170.
65 "This is going to be": Interview with Clark Clifford, 1994; Clifford, *Counsel to the President*, pp. 143–145.
66 At one point, the President remarked: Clifford, *Counsel to the President*, p. 146.
66 In early 1947, a compromise: Isaacson and Thomas, *Wise Men*, p. 404.
67 "Let me make an appointment": Interview with Clark Clifford, 1994.

Chapter 6: A Dubious Authorship

69 That night in 1947: Anderson, *President's Men*, p. 73.
69 In a letter to another friend: Clark Clifford to William O. Douglas, Box 315, Douglas Papers, Library of Congress.
70 So one day, Clifford prepared: Ferrell, ed., *Truman in the White House*, p. 204.
71 Sooner than anyone else, Rowe foresaw: Rowe-Clifford Memorandum to the President, November 19, 1947, Truman Presidential Library.
71 Further, the memo coincided with a recommendation: Hechler, *Working with Truman*, p. 61.
72 Instead of forwarding the memo to Truman: Ibid., p. 63.
72 As Clifford explained it later: Clifford, *Counsel to the President*, p. 191.
73 Less than a month after delivering the political memo: Exchange of letters between James Rowe Jr. and Clark Clifford, Clifford files, Box 13, SEC file, Truman Presidential Library.
73 In one lengthy interview: Unpublished *Los Angeles Times* interview with Clark Clifford, 1982.
73 In May 1991, the *New Yorker: New Yorker*, "Annals of Government: The Vietnam Years — Part 1," first of three excerpts from *Counsel to the President*, May 6, 1991.
74 Years later, Margaret Truman: Margaret Truman, *Harry S. Truman*, p. 387.
74 In the spring of 1947: Evensen, *Truman, Palestine, and the Press*, pp. 54–55.
75 While only about four percent of the nation's voters: Rowe Memorandum, Truman Presidential Library.
75 Further, Loy Henderson: Evensen, *Truman, Palestine, and the Press*, pp. 163 and 168.
75 On a Saturday in early October: Ferrell, ed., *Truman in the White House*, p. 197.
75 At a staff meeting the following Monday: Ibid.
76 The U.S. backing was announced: Jonathan Daniels, Interview with Clark Clifford, Papers of Jonathan Daniels, Truman Presidential Library.
76 Two days after the historic vote: Ferrell, ed., *Truman in the White House*, p. 213.
76 Clifford countered: Schoenbaum, *Waging Peace and War*, p. 169.
76 On March 18, Truman met: Ibid., p. 171.
77 No sooner had Weizmann left: Daniels, Interview with Clifford.
77 The next morning: Ibid.
77 At the White House: Ibid.
77 Clifford fingered the State Department: Schoenbaum, *Waging Peace and War*, p. 171.
77 Marshall and his undersecretary: Evensen, *Truman, Palestine, and the Press*, p. 154.
78 Attempts to craft a statement: Schoenbaum, *Waging Peace and War*, pp. 172–173.
78 Loy Henderson suggested: Evensen, *Truman, Palestine, and the Press*, p. 175.
78 Through the night: Ibid., p. 154.

78 The following day: Schoenbaum, *Waging Peace and War*, p. 172.
79 By early May, with British withdrawal set: Pogue, *George C. Marshall*, p. 372.
79 The meeting had been called: Ibid.
79 In a fifteen-minute talk: Medved, *Shadow Presidents*, p. 225.
79 "Mr. President," he exploded: Pogue, *George C. Marshall*, pp. 372–373.
80 Clifford sat in silence: Medved, *Shadow Presidents*, pp. 225–226.
80 Late that afternoon: Clifford, *Counsel to the President*, p. 15.
81 On Friday morning: Ibid., p. 21.

Chapter 7: Spoils of Victory

83 On June 3, 1948: Hechler, *Working with Truman*, p. 70; McCullough, *Truman*, p. 624.
83 In response to a question: Donovan, *Conflict and Crisis*, p. 400.
84 George Elsey later pointed out: Interview with George Elsey, 1993.
85 Reflecting the wisdom: Interview with Clark Clifford, 1994.
85 At Truman's suggestion: Phillips, *Truman Presidency*, p. 220.
85 The keynote speech in Philadelphia: McCullough, *Truman*, p. 637.
85 Clifford focused on galvanizing: Hechler, *Working with Truman*, p. 86.
86 In early September: McCullough, *Truman*, p. 657.
86 "Boys, if I had the money": Interview with Abraham Feinberg, 1994.
86 Truman wanted $100,000: Ibid.
86 Wanting to muster all the talent: Hechler, *Working with Truman*, p. 86.
87 "Clifford has gone prima donna": Ferrell, ed., *Off the Record: The Private Papers of Harry S. Truman*, p. 149.
87 The campaign journey began: McCullough, *Truman*, pp. 654 and 852.
87 A speech at the national plowing contest: Ibid., p. 64.
88 In retrospect, Clifford did not want to take full credit: Interview with Clark Clifford, 1994.
88 On October 1, two weeks into the trip: Interview with Abraham Feinberg, 1994.
88 In mid-October, *Newsweek*: McCullough, *Truman*, pp. 694–695.
89 Truman headed home to Independence: Clive Howard, "The Clark Cliffords," *Redbook*, June 1949.
89 His mood did not brighten: Isaacson and Thomas, *Wise Men*, p. 462.
89 That night, Clifford had a rare dinner at home: Howard, "The Clark Cliffords."
89 To savor the victory: Ibid.
90 In a letter to Jacob Lashly: Harry S. Truman to Jacob Lashly, file 1578, official file, Truman Papers, Truman Presidential Library.
90 Too many people in the White House: Lilienthal, *Journals*, vol. 2, pp. 433–444.
90 A source of constant tension: Tyler Abell, ed., *Drew Pearson: Diaries*, p. 25.
90 It did not stop: Ferrell, ed., *Truman in the White House*, p. 300.
90 Robert Donovan, a Truman biographer: Interview with Robert Donovan, 1992.
91 Since Clifford had helped: Lilienthal, *Journals*, vol. 2, p. 433.
91 He asked Dean Acheson: Isaacson and Thomas, *Wise Men*, p. 397.
91 Stuart Symington and George Smathers: Interview with George Smathers, 1993.
92 In early January, the speechwriting team: Phillips, *Truman Presidency*, pp. 272–274.
92 About this time, George Elsey passed on to Clifford: Donovan, *Tumultuous Years*, p. 29.
92 The concept struck Clifford: Phillips, *Truman Presidency*, p. 273.
92 The responsibility for fleshing out the concept: Interview with a confidential source.
93 Paul Nitze at State: Interview with Paul Nitze, 1993.

93 Clifford objected: Clifford, *Counsel to the President*, p. 250.

93 On January 20: McCullough, *Truman*, pp. 730–731; Anderson, *President's Men*, p. 127.

93 The only problem: Ferrell, ed., *Truman in the White House*, p. 291. In his memoirs, Clifford criticized Lovett and Nitze for blocking Point Four because of "insufficient preparation and analysis." But the objections from the State Department seem at least partially justified. As Eban Ayers noted in his diary, Clifford said, "The program had not been thought through in detail."

93 In April, Truman assigned Clifford: Morgan, *Robert S. Kerr*, p. 60.

94 In an attempt to break the impasse: Ferrell, ed., *Truman in the White House*, p. 331.

94 Early in the summer of 1949: Halberstam, *Powers That Be*, pp. 160–161; Interview with Benjamin Bradlee, 1993.

95 "This great fucking liberal": Interview with Benjamin Bradlee, 1993.

95 Now, in August 1949: "The Fair Deal Brain," *Newsweek*, August 15, 1948.

95 Along with his debt: Ottenad, "Clifford Was a Prankster." In his 1991 memoirs, Clifford admitted that he was facing "growing financial pressures," but he never acknowledged that he borrowed sums of money.

96 Instead, Clifford explained: Lilienthal, *Journals*, vol. 2, p. 443.

96 "I hate to have you go,": Anderson, *President's Men*, p. 127.

96 Truman had hinted: Medved, *Shadow Presidents*, p. 229.

96 Dean Acheson had left: Carter, "The Insider's Insider."

96 Symington and other St. Louis friends: Medved, *Shadow Presidents*, p. 229.

97 Elsey, after working closely with Clifford: Interview with George Elsey, 1993.

97 Marny Clifford had come to love: Interview with Marny Clifford, 1994.

97 In its March 1948 cover story: "Presidential Advisor Clark Clifford," *Time*, March 15, 1948.

98 Clifford was rarely home for meals: Interview with Marny Clifford, 1994; Howard, "The Clark Cliffords."

98 Although the Cliffords were members: Interview with Charles W. Lowery, 1992.

98 While Marny Clifford put up a bold front: Howard, "The Clark Cliffords."

98 Too, Marny had come to discover: Interview with Marny Clifford, 1994.

99 "I was always sure of his love": Interview with Joyce Clifford Burland, 1994.

99 At one point during Truman's 1948 campaign: Ibid.; Howard, "The Clark Cliffords."

99 For the first time in his life: White, "Assistant President of the U.S.A."

99 When he did find time: Interview with Clark Clifford, 1994.

99 Later he would voice regrets: Ibid.

100 So, as Clifford said later: Ibid.

100 "Our firm has been doing well": Ibid.

101 Miller was from St. Louis: Interview with Edward T. Miller, 1995.

101 He hired the clerical help: Interview with Sam McIlwain, 1993.

101 On December 22: Hechler, *Working with Truman*, pp. 124–125.

102 The liberal *Nation*: Anderson, *President's Men*, p. 128.

102 On the credenza behind his desk: Medved, *The Shadow Presidents*, pp. 222–223.

102 In a letter accepting his resignation: Anderson, *The President's Men*, p. 128.

102 In responding that day: Clark Clifford to Harry S. Truman, Box 1078, Truman Papers, Truman Presidential Library.

102 January 31, 1950 was Clifford's last day: Box 56, Elsey Papers, Truman Presidential Library.

Chapter 8: "I Have No Influence"

104 Clients from the old days in St. Louis: Pearson and Anderson, *Case Against Congress*, p. 308; John Osborne, "Lawyers and Lobbyists," *Fortune*, February 1952.

104 Secretary of Defense Louis Johnson: Welsh and Horowitz, "Attorney at War."

105 Years later Clifford: Interview with Clark Clifford, 1994.

105 "An advisory firm": Ibid.

106 Too many times at the White House: Schriftgiesser, *The Lobbyists*, p. 109.

106 His fees and his ego were legendary: Osborne, "Lawyers and Lobbyists."

107 Years later, he would think back: Interview with Clark Clifford, 1994

108 "I've followed your career": Ibid.

109 Hughes wanted to move: Barlett and Steele, *Empire*, pp. 162–163.

109 The application, which was drawn up: Private Exchange Application, Nevada 03416, Husite Company, United States Department of Interior, Bureau of Land Management.

109 "Since this project": Memorandum to secretary of the interior from Marion Clawson, Director, Bureau of Land Management, November 26, 1952.

110 Despite the long relationship: Clifford said in an interview and in his memoir that he never met Hughes. Sam McIlwain and Paul Warnke said in separate interviews that Clifford had described to them a meeting with Hughes.

110 As his law practice increased: Interview with Clark Clifford, 1994.

110 Even more important to the immediate success: Interview with William Kerr, 1994

111 "His answer to everything was money": Bobby Baker with Larry King, *Wheeling and Dealing*, p. 87.

112 "Kerr wanted Phillips Petroleum": Interview with Clark Clifford, 1994.

112 For many years, Kerr picked Clifford up: Interview with William Kerr, 1994.

113 The society aspect of Clifford's role: Interview with Harry McPherson, 1994; Clifford, *Counsel to the President*, pp. 276–277.

113 The relationship with Kerr: Raymond P. Brandt, "Clifford Doing Very Well Indeed," *St. Louis Post-Dispatch*, March 21, 1950.

114 By 1952, Clifford had spent enough time: Interview with Clark Clifford, 1994.

114 Clifford also needed a lawyer: Interview with Sam McIlwain, 1993.

114 McIlwain was born: Ibid.

115 Clifford's relationship with George Allen: Ibid.

115 "He was our runner": Ibid.

115 "We must do everything in our power": Welsh and Horowitz, "Attorney at War."

115 As Clifford was describing this strategy: Ibid.

116 The average retainer: Interview with Sam McIlwain, 1993.

116 But the financial success was marred: Clifford, *Counsel to the President*, p. 270.

116 Clifford's first choice to replace Miller: William Douglas to Clark Clifford, Box 315, Douglas Papers, Library of Congress.

116 Next, Clifford turned to John J. McCloy: Clifford, *Counsel to the President*, p. 271.

116 He paid a visit to President Truman: Clark Clifford to Harry S. Truman, Box 307, Truman Papers, Truman Presidential Library.

117 It was a lavish affair: Interview with Marny Clifford, 1994.

117 *U.S. News and World Report*: "Parties: Washington's 2nd Industry," *U.S. News and World Report*, March 3, 1950.

117 So Clifford was glad: Medved, *Shadow Presidents*, p. 230.

117 In March 1950: Harry S. Truman to D.C. Bar Association, Box 1578, Truman Papers, Truman Presidential Library; Hechler, *Working with Truman*, p. 122.

118 "I say, pick your party": Interview with Clark Clifford, 1994.

118 In May 1950: Grantor Indices, Land Records Division, Montgomery County, Maryland.

118 And she remembered the psychic's prediction: Interview with Marny Clifford, 1994.

118 So that month the Cliffords paid $40,000: Grantor Indices, Land Records Division, Montgomery County, Maryland; Interview with Sam McIlwain, 1993.

119 Some wags dubbed him a "five percenter": Interview with Paul Nitze, 1993.

119 "Phyllis was somewhat of a friend": Ibid.

119 President Truman accorded the Cliffords: Interview with Charles W. Lowrey, 1993.

119 Two years after Gery's debut: "Society: Joyce Clifford Curtsies at Gala Supper-Dance," *Washington Times-Herald*, June 22, 1952.

119 The next day, Clifford wrote: Clark Clifford to Harry Truman, Box 307, Personal Files of Harry Truman, Truman Presidential Library.

120 "Clifford could do anything": Interview with Sam McIlwain, 1993.

121 The value of these sorts of contacts: Osborne, "Lawyers and Lobbyists."

121 While Clifford himself never broached the color TV issue: Clark Clifford to Harry Truman, File 1056, Personal Files of Harry Truman, Truman Presidential Library.

122 His list of clients: Pearson and Anderson, *Case Against Congress*, p. 308; interview with Sam McIlwain, 1993; Foreign Agents Registration Act file No. 665.

122 He succeeded in winning: Pearson and Anderson, *Case Against Congress*, p. 307.

122 For instance, in preparing a case: Memorandum, Drew Pearson Papers, Johnson Presidential Library.

122 Sometimes Clifford's access backfired: Pearson and Anderson, *Case Against Congress*, p. 309. According to Pearson and Anderson, "It was the opposition of [John] Steelman and [Matt] Connelly which caused Clifford to lose his first big case."

123 In that first year: Interview with Sam McIlwain, 1993; Interview with Clark Clifford, 1994.

123 He was able to repay the loans: Interview with Clark Clifford, 1994.

124 Clifford vowed to himself: Ibid.

124 "He told me the whole details": Lilienthal, *Journals*, vol. 2, pp. 136–137.

Chapter 9: The Smear Artists

126 The incident occurred: Abel, *The Truman Scandals*, p. 57.

126 Among them was a report: Edward F. Ryan, "Clark Clifford Shared with Firm $25,000 Fee," *Washington Post*, February 7, 1952.

127 *Time* used the occasion: McCullough, *Truman*, pp. 863–864.

127 The dispute began: Abel, *The Truman Scandals*, pp. 57–58; Welsh and Horowitz, "Attorney at War."

128 Baldridge was called to testify: Abel, *The Truman Scandals*, p. 58.

128 However, he was questioned: Ryan, "Clark Clifford Shared with Firm $25,000 Fee."

128 "The smear artists": Clark Clifford to Harry Truman, Box 307, Truman Papers, Truman Presidential Library.

128 Truman responded: Harry Truman to Clark Clifford, Box 307, Truman Papers, Truman Presidential Library.

129 Soon his primary sponsor would be retiring: Memorandum, Box 24, Clifford Papers, Truman Presidential Library.

130 However, the president wanted to choose: Martin, *Adlai Stevenson of Illinois*, pp. 519–529.

130 Briefly, Truman reconsidered: Morgan, *Robert S. Kerr*, pp. 116–117 and 272; Clifford Papers and Memos, Box 24, Clifford Papers, Truman Presidential Library.

130 Privately, Truman had decided: McCullough, *Truman*, pp. 889–891.

131 Three weeks later: Hechler, *Working with Truman*, p. 246.

131 On March 15, Clifford wrote to Truman: Clark Clifford to Harry Truman, Box 24, Clifford Papers, Truman Presidential Library.

132 Clifford then persuaded Kerr: Morgan, *Robert S. Kerr*, p. 126.

132 Clifford knew that Kerr: Clifford, *Counsel to the President*, p. 284.

132 Nonetheless, Kerr arranged for Clifford: Les Biffle to Clark Clifford, Box 24, Clifford Papers, Truman Presidential Library.

132 A band played: Pearson and Anderson, *Case Against Congress*, p. 130.

133 He wrote a letter to Harriman: Clark Clifford to Averell Harriman, Box 24, Clifford Papers, Truman Presidential Library.

133 To his own candidate: Clark Clifford to Robert Kerr, Box 24, Clifford Papers, Truman Presidential Library.

133 As usual, Clifford's highest praise: Clark Clifford to Harry Truman, Box 24, Clifford Papers, Truman Presidential Library.

133 Aside from briefing: Martin, *Adlai Stevenson of Illinois*, p. 643.

134 Within months of Eisenhower taking office: Interview with Clark Clifford, 1994; Goulden, *Superlawyers*, p. 86; Carter, "The Insider's Insider."

135 Peress was a dentist: Adams, *First Hand Report: The Story of the Eisenhower Administration*, pp. 145–146.

135 Stevens, who knew Symington: Transcript, Box 1, Clifford Papers, Truman Presidential Library.

135 "I would suggest two things": Ibid.

136 But he did advise Stevens: Ibid.

136 He accused them of conspiring: Reeves, *Life and Times of Joe McCarthy*, pp. 627–628.

136 Symington wanted to challenge McCarthy: Transcript, Box 1, Clifford Papers, Truman Presidential Library.

137 Clifford first met Johnson: Interview with Clark Clifford, 1994.

137 Clifford and Fortas became sounding boards: Murphy, *Fortas*, pp. 239–241.

137 Fortas later described the sessions: Ibid.

138 "Why don't you call him up": Clifford, *Counsel to the President*, p. 387.

138 After Johnson suffered a heart attack: Telegram from Robert Kerr to Burl Hays, Box 13, Kerr Papers, University of Oklahoma.

138 In a letter to former President Truman: Clark Clifford to Harry Truman, December 4, 1956, Truman personal file, Truman Presidential Library.

138 "If Tommy was going to steal": Kalman, *Abe Fortas*, p. 206.

139 Max Kampelman, who had recently left: Kampelman, *Entering New Worlds*, pp. 130–131.

139 "Revson looked slick": Ibid.

140 "The committee clobbered Revson": Ibid.

140 Clifford had little use for J. Edgar Hoover: Interview with Clark Clifford, 1994.

141 "It was never politic": Ibid.

141 Planning was a family task: Interviews with Clifford and members of the Clifford family, 1994; Clifford, *Counsel to the President*, pp. 278–279.

141 In her husband's word: Interview with Clark Clifford, 1994.

142 "Clark was very generous": Interview with Marny Clifford, 1994.

142 "He has no curiosity": Ibid.

143 In one memorable skit: Interview with Dick Barrett, 1993.

143 Sometimes during those years: Interview with Joyce Clifford Burland, 1994.

144 Hughes himself was uncertain: Interview with Robert Maheu, 1993.

144 In addition to Clifford, Kerr arranged: Letter from McGee secretary to Clark Clifford, Box 13, Kerr Papers, University of Oklahoma; Clark Clifford to Robert Kerr, Box 13, Kerr Papers, University of Oklahoma.

144 Years later one of his law partners: Interviews with two former Clifford law partners who spoke on condition of anonymity.

145 Clifford displayed his gratitude: Clark Clifford to Robert Kerr, Box 853, Kerr Papers, University of Oklahoma.

145 Early in his life, Fox had made a fortune: "Matthew M. Fox, an Executive in Movies and TV, Dead at 53," *New York Times*, July 7, 1963.

145 After the Dutch began: Westbrook Pegler, "Strange Dealings in U.S. for Indonesia Trade," *New York Journal*, February 1, 1949; Hope MacLeod, "Matty Fox — TV Mystery Man," *New York Post*, June 9, 1957.

145 "That is the most beautiful woman": Interview with Clark Clifford, 1994.

146 In fact, Fox was so impressed: Foreign Agents Registration Act, File No. 665.

146 Before Truman left office: Morgan, *Robert S. Kerr*, p. 112.

146 At the time, columnist Joseph Alsop: Pearson and Anderson, *Case Against Congress*, p. 310; Goulden, *Superlawyers*, pp. 85–86.

146 In the fall of 1959, Clifford argued: *Phillips Chemical Company v. Dumas Independent School District*, Case No. 361 U.S. 376, United States Supreme Court, Washington, D.C.

147 A few months later the court ruled: Ibid.

Chapter 10: The Kennedy Connection

148 On a Saturday night, December 7, 1957: Hayman, *A Woman Called Jackie*, p. 175.

148 Early on Monday morning: The incident involving Kennedy and the Pearson allegation was recounted in Clifford's autobiography, *Counsel to the President*, Hayman's *A Woman Called Jackie*, and in interviews by Theodore Sorensen and Clark Clifford. Contradictions between the versions were minor, but when they occurred the authors relied on the interview with Clifford. Also, the direct quotes attributed to Kennedy, Joseph Kennedy, and Clifford came from that interview.

150 Before going to New York: Interview with Katharine Graham.

151 "I have something to tell you": Martin, *A Hero for Our Time*, p. 137.

151 In the letter, Kennedy asked for Clifford's assistance: Interview with Clark Clifford, 1994.

151 During the next three years: Ibid.

152 In early January 1959, Symington: White, *Making of the President 1960*, p. 36.

153 The strategy of appearing to be the candidate: Interview with a confidential source.

153 "Your strength is to be everybody's second choice": Interview with James Symington, 1993.

154 "You young men had better understand": Ibid.

154 O'Brien offered public thanks: Halberstam, *Unfinished Odyssey of Robert Kennedy*, p. 76.

154 Charlie Brown, Symington's official: Interview with George McGovern, 1993.

154 When he first came to Washington: Interview with Hugh Sidey, 1994.

155 "I remember one of the first times": Ibid.

156 Unfortunately for Symington: Ibid.

156 Even long years after Kennedy's death: Interview with Clark Clifford, 1994.

156 The "troubled matters" most likely involved a claim: Martin, *Hero for Our Time*, p. 163.

156 At another point, Kennedy complained: Isaacson and Thomas, *Wise Men*, p. 551.

157 A month before the Democratic convention: Schlesinger, *A Thousand Days*, p. 45.

157 Two weeks later, Clifford was back: Interview with Clark Clifford, 1994.

157 The Democratic convention: Events surrounding the offering and withdrawal of the vice presidential nomination to Senator Symington were described by Clark Clifford and James Symington in interviews with the authors, by Martin in *Hero for Our Time*, and by Schlesinger in *A Thousand Days*.

158 "I don't see how he can refuse": Interview with James Symington, 1993.

158 Throughout the night: Martin, *Hero for Our Time*, p. 178.

158 "I must do something": Interview with Clark Clifford, 1994.

159 So while Bobby Kennedy still fought: Robert Kennedy Oral History, Kennedy Presidential Library. Bobby Kennedy recalled returning to his brother's room and the nominee telling him, "I just got a call from Clark Clifford or somebody saying 'This is disastrous. You've got to take him.' I'm going to make an announcement in five minutes."

159 The day after Kennedy won: Clark Clifford to John Kennedy, Presidential Office Files, Kennedy Presidential Library.

159 A week later, Clifford reiterated his offer: Evans and Novak, *Exercise of Power*, p. 276.

159 Writing back, Kennedy said he had asked: John Kennedy to Clark Clifford, Presidential Office Files, Kennedy Presidential Library.

159 When Clifford met Kennedy for breakfast: Latham, "Capital Manipulator"; Martin, *A Hero for Our Time*, pp. 186–187.

160 Not long after his breakfast: Interview with Robert Healey, 1993; Clifford, *Counsel to the President*, p. 320.

160 The day after the election: Martin, *Hero for Our Time*, p. 242; Goulden, *Superlawyers*, p. 92.

160 Kennedy turned first to James Landis: Interview with Donald Ritchie, 1993.

160 It was a canny appointment: Interview with Theodore Sorensen, 1993.

161 He was often at Kennedy's residence: Ibid.; interview with Paul Nitze, 1993.

161 He flew to New York: Schlesinger, *A Thousand Days*, p. 123.

161 He also accompanied Kennedy: Clifford, *Counsel to the President*, p. 335.

161 As one reporter wrote: Pearson and Anderson, *Case Against Congress*, p. 304.

161 Joseph Kennedy was insisting that Bobby: Interview with Clark Clifford, 1994; Martin, *Hero for Our Time*, p. 254.

162 On January 19, 1961: Halberstam, *The Best and the Brightest*, p. 88.

162 One of Kennedy's first questions: Reeves, *A Question of Character*, p. 259; Warren I. Cohen, "The Fall of Clark Clifford," *The Nation*, October 5, 1992.

163 Following the inauguration: Goulden, *Superlawyers*, p. 70; Clifford, *Counsel to the President*, p. 347.

163 Former *Boston Globe* newsman: Interview with Robert Healey, 1993.

164 Journalist Haynes Johnson: Johnson, *In the Absence of Power: Governing America*, p. 95.

164 Historian Alan K. Henrikson: Alan K. Henrikson, " 'A small, cozy town, global in scope': Washington D.C.," *Ekistics* 299, March/April, 1983, p. 138.

Chapter 11: Matters of Influence

165 "Clifford?" barked the voice: Interview with Clark Clifford, 1994.

166 As liberal Democratic Senator Paul Douglas: Robert C. Byrd, *The Senate*, p. 121.

166 As Kerr himself once said: Interview with William Kerr, 1994.

166 Once Douglas got onto Finance: Interview with Howard Shulman, 1993.
166 Regarded as one of the most effective and fiercest debaters: McPherson, *Political Education*, p. 42.
166 As the *Wall Street Journal* described: Robert D. Novak, "Key Senator's Death Could Hurt Chances of Tax-Cut Program," *Wall Street Journal*, January 2, 1963.
166 Clifford had remained so close: Interview with Sam McIlwain, 1993.
166 Often, Kerr and Clifford drove to work: Interview with William Kerr, 1994.
167 The Du Pont case: Zilg, *Du Pont: Behind the Nylon Curtain*, pp. 395–396; Goulden, *Superlawyers*, pp. 94–95.
167 Over the years, Congress: Barlett and Steele, *America: What Went Wrong?*, pp. 14–15.
168 "I don't give a shit": Interview with a confidential source.
168 Kerr agreed to oversee: Ibid.
168 A few days after Kerr's introductory phone call: Interview with Clark Clifford, 1994.
169 "I've been thinking": Ibid.
169 Instead, John Sharon, a partner: Deakin, *The Lobbyists*, p. 173.
170 As the lawyers talked: Interview with Clark Clifford, 1994; Zilg, *Du Pont*, p. 396.
170 On September 23, 1961, Senator Stuart Symington: *Congressional Record*, pp. 21041–21049.
171 Two days after the President signed the bill: Clark Clifford to John Kennedy, Presidential Office Files, Kennedy Presidential Library.
172 Rumors circulated: Interview with Hugh Sidey, 1994.
173 "Hugh," he said: Ibid.
173 Soon after passage of the legislation: Interview with Sam McIlwain, 1994.
174 The first crisis of the Kennedy presidency: Schlesinger, *A Thousand Days*, p. 255.
174 He asked Clifford, who had helped: Welsh and Horowitz, "Attorney at War."
174 Established in 1956 by President Eisenhower: Interview with McGeorge Bundy, 1993.
175 For his part, Clifford once remarked: Latham, "Capital Manipulator."
175 Kenneth Crawford, an elegant old-timer: Interview with Benjamin Bradlee, 1993.
175 Jack Anderson, who has written about Washington: Interview with Jack Anderson, 1993.
175 So it came about that the press dubbed Clifford "the shadow attorney general": Latham, "Capital Manipulator."
176 "Bobby ran the department": Interview with a confidential source.
176 Even Bradlee, who was extremely close to President Kennedy: Interview with Benjamin Bradlee, 1993.
176 White House visitor logs: White House visitor logs, Kennedy Presidential Library.
176 In 1962, when President Kennedy: Goulden, *Superlawyers*, p. 99.
176 Attorney General Kennedy and Clifford: Schlesinger, *Robert F. Kennedy*, p. 404; Goulden, *Superlawyers*, pp. 99–100.
177 "Can't you just see Clifford": Anderson, *President's Men*, p. 130.
177 Robert Kennedy reluctantly dropped the investigation: Schlesinger, *Robert F. Kennedy*, p. 405.
177 Ted Sorensen remembered that the President: Interview with Theodore Sorensen, 1993.
178 In a speech in early 1963: Clark Clifford Address at Washington University, Presidential Office Files, Kennedy Presidential Library.
178 After Clifford sent him a copy: Clark Clifford letters to John Kennedy and Robert Kennedy, Presidential Office Files, Kennedy Presidential Library.
178 Soon after the inauguration: Thayer, *Jacqueline Kennedy*, p. 283.
178 "I think that is an excellent": Hayman, *A Woman Called Jackie*, pp. 324–325.
179 Returning to his office that day: Ibid.

179 One example occurred when Clifford was called on: Garry Wills, "Keeper of the Seal," *New York Review of Books*, July 18, 1991; Thayer, *Jacqueline Kennedy*, p. 229.

180 Jackie Kennedy was so pleased: Clifford, *Counsel to the President*, pp. 362–363.

180 Author Truman Capote, who knew Mrs. Kennedy: Hayman, *A Woman Called Jackie*, p. 295.

180 Clifford was not as successful: Drew Pearson and Jack Anderson, "Washington Merry Go-Round," *Washington Post*, January 25, 1968.

180 On another occasion: Interview with Clark Clifford, 1994; McGinnis, *Last Brother*, pp. 322–323.

181 Clifford intoned that it would have been "better": Interview with McGeorge Bundy, 1993.

181 In the end, Edward Kennedy followed: Bradlee, *Conversations with Kennedy*, pp. 150–151.

181 In early 1961, General Electric: Mokhiber, *Corporate Crime and Violence*, pp. 213–220.

182 "Clark, we have a tough problem": Interview with Clark Clifford, 1994.

182 Senator Estes Kefauver, the populist Democrat: Interview with John Kovin, 1994.

182 The Justice Department agreed to a payment: Welsh and Horowitz, "Attorney at War."

183 "This was something": Goulden, *Superlawyers*, p. 98.

183 In the middle of 1962, Stauffer: Jack Anderson, "It Pays to Hire the Right Lawyer," *Washington Post*, February 16, 1963.

184 "The inference and conclusions": Memorandum, Presidential Office Files, Kennedy Presidential Library.

Chapter 12: The President's Adviser

185 Clark Clifford was sitting down to lunch: Manchester, *Death of a President*, p. 140.

185 In the days immediately after: Clafin, ed., *JFK Wants to Know*, p. 284.

185 A friend recalled Clifford's concern: Duncan Spencer, "The Corridors of Power," *Washington Star*, June 29, 1975.

186 On November 27, he wrote Johnson: Clark Clifford to Lyndon Johnson, Office Files, Clifford folder, Johnson Presidential Library.

186 Later that same day, Johnson invited his former adviser: Evans and Novak, *Exercise of Power*, p. 346.

186 Clifford met with the attorney general: Transcript of telephone conversation between Lyndon Johnson and Clark Clifford, December 4, 1963, Johnson Presidential Library.

187 George Christian, Johnson's press secretary: Murphy, *Fortas*, p. 125.

187 Observed Jack Valenti: Interview with Jack Valenti, 1993.

187 Mrs. Clifford, who was known for her fine eye: Lady Bird Johnson, *A White House Diary*, p. 44.

187 Gathered around the cabinet room table: Murphy, *Fortas*, p. 126.

188 Acting at Baker's suggestion: Evans and Novak, *Exercise of Power*, p. 413.

188 Fortas's law firm, Arnold: Murphy, *Fortas*, p. 134.

188 After some cajoling: Goulden, *Superlawyers*, p. 103.

189 At the suggestion of Clifford: Evans and Novak, *Exercise of Power*, pp. 413–414.

189 The attorney general never pursued the allegations: Schlesinger, *Robert F. Kennedy*, pp. 320–325.

189 On June 11, 1964: Clifford, *Counsel to the President*, p. 395.

190 With Clifford doing the writing: Witcover, *Crapshoot*, p. 179.

190 The memo argued that Goldwater would be strong in the South: Memorandum of Remarks Made to Robert Kennedy Regarding the Vice Presidential Candidacy in 1964, Appendix A, Johnson, *Vantage Point*, pp. 576–577.

191 On July 29, a Wednesday: Evans and Novak, *Exercise of Power*, p. 445.

191 Sidey learned of Kennedy's visit: Interview with Hugh Sidey, 1994.

191 "Finally on Saturday night": Ibid.

192 So, in an attempt to diffuse: Evans and Novak, *Exercise of Power*, p. 447.

192 In his memoirs, *The Vantage Point:* Johnson, *Vantage Point*, p. 99.

193 Johnson even went so far: Johnson, *Vantage Point*, pp. 576–577.

193 "That little shit Bobby": Interview with Hugh Sidey, 1994.

193 At the Democratic convention: Evans and Novak, *Exercise of Power*, p. 54.

193 Part of his advice: Bill Moyers memorandum to Lyndon Johnson, White House Central File, Clifford folder, Johnson Presidential Library.

193 On October 7, a Wednesday: White, *Making of the President 1964*, p. 386.

193 The arrest remained unpublicized: Ibid.

194 Johnson was out of town: Murphy, *Fortas*, p. 138.

194 Newbold Noyes, the editor, recalled: John D. Morris, "Johnson Friends Called on Press," *New York Times*, October 16, 1964.

194 At the *News*, editor John O'Rourke: Ibid.

194 The *Washington Post* did not even know: Ibid.

195 About eight o'clock that night: Arthur Krock, "The Jenkins Case," *New York Times*, October 18, 1964.

195 But Liz Carpenter remembered that it was Fortas: Interview with Liz Carpenter, 1993; Kalman, *Abe Fortas*, p. 226.

196 In the fifties, Clifford had loaned Douglas: William Douglas to Clark Clifford, Container 315, Douglas Papers, Library of Congress.

196 In 1966, Clifford guaranteed a $6,150 loan: William Douglas to Clark Clifford, Container 315, Douglas Papers, Library of Congress.

197 Describing the significance: Interview with Clark Clifford, 1994.

197 One of the most interesting routes: Interview with John Kovin, 1994.

198 A few months later, Finney: Interview with Sam McIlwain, 1993.

198 In the wake of the Jenkins scandal: Ibid.

198 In August 1964, Clifford and Miller: Clifford and Miller Announcement, Presidential Files, Johnson Presidential Library.

198 The narrow study contained: Interview with Sam McIlwain, 1993.

199 Several of his partners later said: The finances and salary arrangements of the Clifford firm were described in interviews by several of Clifford's former partners. Among those who permitted their names to be used were John Kovin, Sam McIlwain, Paul Warnke, and Larry Williams. Clifford also discussed some aspects of the firm's finances in interviews.

200 "Yes, he could get angry": Interview with John Kovin, 1994.

200 Since the special tax-relief legislation: Zilg, *Du Pont*, p. 348.

200 In early July, Clifford had met: Testimony of Douglas Dillon before the Committee on Finance, United States Senate, March 17, 1965.

200 President Johnson hosted a luncheon: Guest list, White House Central File, Clifford folder, Johnson Presidential Library.

200 By early fall, the lawyers at the Treasury: Zilg, *Du Pont*, p. 398.

200 Faced with almost certain defeat: Dillon testimony.

200 Years later, Clifford remembered: Interview with Clark Clifford, 1994.

201 "I do not feel that it is proper": Testimony of Robert Knight before the Committee on Finance, March 17, 1965.

201 When Clifford hung up: Ibid.

202 In early November, Clifford wrote a memorandum: Clark Clifford to Lyndon Johnson, White House Central File, Clifford folder, Johnson Presidential Library.

202 During the following two weeks: Zilg, Du Pont, p. 398.

202 In a statement: Goulden, Superlawyers, p. 96.

203 When Bertrand Harding, the deputy commissioner: Testimony of Bertrand Harding before the Committee on Finance, March 24, 1965.

203 At one point, Johnson boasted: Patrick Anderson, "The New Defense Secretary Thinks Like the President," New York Times Magazine, January 28, 1968.

203 As Johnson began 1965: Anderson, President's Men, p. 300.

204 Often, Clifford and Johnson spoke: Medved, Shadow Presidents, p. 231.

204 Instead, he would have his driver take him: Pearson and Anderson, Case Against Congress, p. 311.

204 Walt Rostow, one of Johnson's key aides: Interview with Walt Rostow, 1993.

204 Folding his hands and summoning up: Interview with Hugh Sidey, 1994.

205 In a famous picture, the two lawyers: Official White House photograph, photo archives, Johnson Presidential Library.

205 "All of us looked on Clifford": Interview with Jack Valenti, 1993.

205 He wrote a letter to Johnson: Clark Clifford to Lyndon Johnson, Office of the President files, Clifford folder, Johnson Presidential Library.

205 When Joe Califano negotiated: Clark Clifford to Lyndon Johnson, White House Central File, Clifford folder, Johnson Presidential Library.

205 And when Bill Moyers replaced George Reedy: Clark Clifford to Bill Moyers, Office of the President files, Clifford folder, Johnson Presidential Library.

205 Rusk, for example: Schoenbaum, Waging Peace and War, p. 415.

205 And, after an early meeting: Murphy, Fortas, p. 246.

206 McGeorge Bundy, the President's national security adviser: Interview with McGeorge Bundy, 1993.

Chapter 13: "An Insider's Insider"

207 The Vietnam War began to assume a prominent place: Halberstam, Best and Brightest, p. 596.

207 Zbigniew Brzezinski: Murphy, Fortas, p. 239.

207 At one point during the discussions: Halberstam, Best and Brightest, p. 596.

208 On July 25, the last session: Notes of Jack Valenti, Office of the President files, Clifford folder, Johnson Presidential Library.

208 Three days later, President Johnson: Califano, Triumph and Tragedy of Lyndon Johnson, p. 47.

209 In late October of that year: Clark Clifford to Lyndon Johnson, White House Name File, Clifford folder, Johnson Presidential Library.

209 General William Westmoreland, the commander: William C. Westmoreland, A Soldier Reports, p. 137.

209 The only glitch came when Henry Kissinger: Hersh, Price of Power, p. 47.

210 He opposed halting the bombing of the north: Halberstam, Best and Brightest, p. 624.

210 A few months after his return from Vietnam: Patrick Anderson, "His Big Job — To End the Vietnam War," Parade, August 4, 1968.

210 Marny Clifford was on an extended trip: Memorandum to Lyndon Johnson, Office of the President files, Clifford folder, Johnson Presidential Library.

210 Justice Douglas sent him a set of opinions: William Douglas to Clark Clifford, Container 315, Douglas Papers, Library of Congress.

210 In one he wrote: Lyndon Johnson to Clark Clifford, Name File, Clifford folder, Johnson Presidential Library.

210 A few days later, Johnson: Ibid.

210 On January 12, 1967: Invitation, Container 315, Douglas Papers, Library of Congress.

211 When she had lived in Washington: Interview with Joyce Clifford Burland, 1994.

211 The week after the party, Newsweek offered: Jack Valenti memorandum to Lyndon Johnson, Office of the President files, Clifford folder, Johnson Presidential Library.

212 For years the company had been locked: Anderson, "The New Defense Secretary Thinks Like the President."

212 Initially, Clifford dispatched Carson Glass: Interview with Larry Williams, 1994.

213 "Our firm has quite a lot of antitrust business": Ibid.

213 During this period, the firm also represented: Interview with Sam McIlwain, 1993; Pearson and Anderson, Case Against Congress, p. 312.

213 Clifford also represented a number of major defense contractors: Drew Pearson and Jack Anderson, "Clifford Represents Arms Firms," Washington Post, June 26, 1968.

214 In late 1966, James S. McDonnell: Lawrence E. Davies, "Holders Approve Douglas Merger," New York Times, April 20, 1967.

214 After several days of discussions: Interview with Larry Williams, 1994.

214 Donald Turner, a former Harvard Law School professor: Jack Valenti memorandum to Lyndon Johnson, White House Central File, Clifford folder, Johnson Presidential Library.

214 Williams took the memo over to Turner: Interview with Larry Williams, 1994.

215 At Clifford's urging: Ibid.

216 This time, the mole: In an interview, Jack Anderson acknowledged that someone in Clifford's office provided him with information. However, he refused to identify the person. From other sources, the authors learned the identity of the source, but chose to keep the name confidential.

216 In an administrative proceeding: Interview with John Kovin, 1994.

216 He and General Maxwell D. Taylor: Taylor, General Maxwell Taylor, p. 338.

216 "There was unanimous agreement": Russell Baker, "Observer: Let's Hear It for a Really Swell Policy," New York Times, August 8, 1967.

217 After a two-hour briefing: White House Diary, Johnson Presidential Library.

217 One morning not long after his return: Interview with Hugh Sidey, 1994.

217 The realization that Clifford was not really as hawkish: Patrick Anderson, "Clark Clifford Sounds the Alarm," New York Times Magazine, August 8, 1971.

217 By October 1967, the question: Nitze, From Hiroshima to Glasnost, p. 270.

217 Paul Nitze, who was McNamara's deputy secretary: Interview with Paul Nitze, 1993.

218 But Clifford and Fortas were hardly alone: Murphy, Fortas, p. 250.

218 Shortly after McNamara's memo: Nitze, From Hiroshima to Glasnost, p. 270.

218 When asked to consider not only the future of the bombing: Murphy, Fortas, p. 253.

218 The President told Clifford: Goulden, Superlawyers, p. 105.

218 Earlier in 1967: Thomas, Man to See, p. 226.

218 Clifford consulted his longtime friend: Goulden, Superlawyers, p. 105.

218 On Christmas Day, the President: Clark Clifford to Lyndon Johnson, White House Central File, Clifford folder, Johnson Presidential Library.

Chapter 14: Counsel at War

220 A new Gallup poll: Gallup Poll, Vietnam Roundtable, Background Sources, Johnson Presidential Library.

220 Marny Clifford was returning: Judith Martin, "She'll Keep the Home Front Quiet," *Washington Post*, January 20, 1968.

221 Katharine Graham, a long-time Clifford: Interview with Katharine Graham, 1993.

221 Even Clifford's old friend: Lilienthal, *Journals*, vol. 2, p. 8.

221 Another associate from those days: Hechler, *Working with Truman*, p. 56.

221 President Johnson received congratulatory letters: Lyndon Johnson letter to John Conor, White House Central File, Clifford folder, Johnson Presidential Library. Conor was president of Allied Chemical and Dye.

221 In a letter to General William Westmoreland: Barrett, *Uncertain Warriors*, p. 121.

222 When he testified: Nomination of Clark M. Clifford to be Secretary of Defense, Committee on Armed Services, United States Senate, January 25, 1968.

222 As the group debated: Interview with Clark Clifford, 1994.

222 In February, he sent Clifford: Lyndon Johnson memorandum, White House Central File, Clifford folder, Johnson Presidential Library.

223 By this time Clifford had ownership interests: Interview with Clark Clifford, 1994.

223 In negotiations with Kerr-McGee: Ibid.

223 Part of that net worth: Interview with Sam McIlwain, 1993.

223 "Tom Finney was the smartest": Interview with De Vier Pierson, 1993.

224 "It was obvious that he was coming back": Interview with Larry Williams, 1994.

224 The point was driven home: Brayman, *President Speaks Off-the-Record*, p. 743.

224 Delivering the traditionally pompous, tongue-in-cheek valedictory: "Alfafa Club Names McElroy," *Washington Post*, Janaury 28, 1968.

224 On Sunday morning, January 28: Interview with James H. Rowe, 1992.

225 Later that week, Rowe was having lunch: James Rowe Jr. to Clark Clifford, Box 87, Truman Presidential Library.

225 Reston followed up: James Reston, "Clifford and the Strategies of 1948 and 1968," *New York Times*, February 12, 1968.

225 Finally, near the end of February: James Rowe Jr. to Clark Clifford, Box 87, Truman Presidential Library.

225 The early mood was summed up: Goulding, *Confirm or Deny*, p. 308.

225 Among the senior staff: Interview with Paul Warnke, 1994.

226 He would also have to run a building: "Clifford for McNamara," *New York Times*, January 21, 1968.

226 His first visit to the Pentagon: Goulding, *Confirm or Deny*, p. 310.

226 At a dinner party in Georgetown in February: Interview with Katharine Graham, 1993.

226 By and large, Clifford would leave the management: Interview with Paul Nitze, 1993.

226 Elsey had been working as the Washington lobbyist: Interview with George Elsey, 1993.

227 For his part, Nitze: Interview with Paul Nitze, 1993; Isaacson and Thomas, *Wise Men*, p. 689.

227 On March 1: Clifford Papers, Johnson Presidential Library.

227 And the legal establishment turned out: Interview with Liz Carpenter, 1993.

227 After the public swearing in: Isaacson and Thomas, *Wise Men*, p. 689.

228 In the words of George Elsey: Interview with George Elsey, 1993.
228 The first sign observed: Johnson, *Vantage Point*, pp. 398–399.
228 The first began on Monday: Nitze, *From Hiroshima to Glasnost*, p. 278.
229 On Tuesday evening, not long after: Murphy, *Fortas*, p. 259.
229 The following day, Kennedy aide Ted Sorensen: Schlesinger, *Robert F. Kennedy*, p. 851.
229 Clifford reminded Kennedy: Ibid.
230 That afternoon, with Abe Fortas: Murphy, *Fortas*, p. 259.
230 Following the session at the White House: Newfield, *Robert Kennedy: A Memoir*, pp. 237–244.
230 Senator Fulbright was still pushing: Hoopes, *Limits of Intervention*, p. 199.
230 The following day, Nitze walked: Nitze, *From Hiroshima to Glasnost*, p. 277.
230 So he turned next to Warnke: Ibid., p. 279.
231 As Townsend Hoopes, another senior Pentagon official: Hoopes, *Limits of Intervention*, p. 198.
232 On their birthdays that year: Interview with Marny Clifford, 1994.
232 When his friend Hugh Sidey: Interview with Hugh Sidey, 1994.
232 Again and again, when his staff gathered: Interviews with Elsey and Nitze in 1993 and with Clifford, 1994.
232 Richard Fryklund, a deputy assistant secretary: Marjorie Williams, "Clark Clifford: The Rise of a Reputation," *Washington Post*, May 8, 1991.
233 "Now you must tell me": McPherson, *Political Education*, p. 431.
233 On March 17, he delivered: Clifford, *Counsel to the President*, p. 507.
233 So he made his own views: Murphy, *Fortas*, pp. 261–263.
234 The Wise Men began arriving: Williams, "Clark Clifford: The Rise of a Reputation."
234 Shortly after one o'clock: Johnson, *Vantage Point*, pp. 417–418.
235 Besides the counsel of the Wise Men, Johnson: Schoenbaum, *Waging Peace and War*, p. 478.
235 On March 28, Clifford, Bundy, Rostow: McPherson, *Political Education*, p. 433.
236 On March 30, when Justice Douglas held a dinner: Clark Clifford to William Douglas, Container 315, The Douglas Papers, Library of Congress.
236 And the president asked his wife: Lady Bird Johnson, *White House Diary*, p. 645.
236 Clark and Marny Clifford arrived: Ibid.
236 "Tonight," he said, "I have ordered": Johnson, *Vantage Point*, p. 435.
237 Clifford was one of the few people: Interview with Clark Clifford, 1994; McPherson, *Political Education*, p. 438.
237 As the camera lights clicked off: Lady Bird Johnson, *White House Diary*, p. 646.
237 Richard Helms, the veteran CIA official: Barrett, *Uncertain Warriors*, p. 156.
237 McPherson, a loyal friend and admirer: McPherson, *Political Education*, p. 435.
238 Suddenly the Secretary of Defense had trouble: Interview with George Elsey, 1993; interview with Clark Clifford, 1994.
238 For a time, Clifford was even cut off: Halberstam, *Best and Brightest*, p. 652.

Chapter 15: His Finest Hour

239 Inside his expansive office: Anderson, "His Big Job — To End the Vietnam War."
239 Each morning at eight-thirty: Goulding, *Confirm or Deny*, p. 320.
239 "Walt Rostow and I had a long talk": Ibid.
240 A true policy professional, Nitze: Interview with Paul Nitze, 1993.

240 "There was no dissent": Interview with George Elsey, 1993.

241 "Old boy, we've got more": McPherson, *Political Education*, p. 440.

241 At eight-thirty the following morning: Johnson, *Vantage Point*, pp. 504–505.

242 Harriman shared Clifford's belief: Abramson, *Spanning the Century*, p. 660.

242 An equally commited group: Ibid., pp. 663–665.

242 On June 5, the president: Johnson, *Vantage Point*, p. 510.

242 Johnson called a meeting: Interview with Clark Clifford, 1994; Abramson, *Spanning the Century*, pp. 663–665.

243 "Now, I had a marvelous team": Interview with Clark Clifford, 1994.

244 "You can't get it through": Clifford, *Counsel to the President*, pp. 555–556.

244 Instead, Clifford argued: Ibid.; Simon, *Advise and Consent*, pp. 280–281.

244 Among the charges leveled at Fortas: Clifford, *Counsel to the President*, pp. 556–557; Murphy, *Fortas*, pp. 290–292.

245 Faced with an imminent increase in the price: Clifford memorandum, Papers of Clark Clifford, Box 15, Johnson Presidential Library.

245 On the morning of August 6: Ibid.

246 "This would be exceedingly important": Ibid.

247 It was during this crucial period: This incident, which remains controversial, was drawn from interviews with Clark Clifford and Walt Rostow; Clifford, *Counsel to the President*, pp. 581–583; Valenti, *A Very Human President*, pp. 373–375; Christian, *President Steps Down*, p. 94.

248 Finally, at the end of October: Johnson, *Vantage Point*, pp. 525–527.

248 "I am becoming inordinately impatient": Christian, *President Steps Down*, pp. 135–137.

249 A few days before: Interview with Clark Clifford, 1994.

249 "It looked as if we had moved": Lady Bird Johnson, *White House Diary*, pp. 779–781.

250 "Please go downstairs": Interview with Marny Clifford, 1994.

250 There, in what he later described: Johnson, *Vantage Point*, p. 567.

250 "Clifford really failed": Interview with Benjamin Bradlee, 1993.

251 CIA veteran Richard Helms: Interview with Richard Helms, 1993.

252 Reflecting two and a half: Interview with Clark Clifford, 1994.

252 In one of the small, private dining rooms: Ibid.

253 "I gave all the reasons": Ibid.

Chapter 16: Clifford for President?

255 "Would you like to come to work": Interview with Paul Warnke, 1994.

255 Since Clifford's departure: Interview with Clark Clifford, 1994.

256 After Sharon left the Pentagon: Interviews with John Kovin and Sam McIlwain.

257 Finney did not want a repeat: Interview with Paul Warnke, 1994.

257 Not long after Clifford left the government: Foreign Agent Registration Act files, Department of Justice.

258 At the time, Yolande Fox: Interview with a confidential source.

258 Clifford spent eight days in the capital: Interview with Clark Clifford, 1994; Howe and Trott, *Power Peddlers*, pp. 351–352; Goulden, *Superlawyers*, p. 89.

258 In an episode: Thomas, *Man to See*, p. 260.

258 Clifford's first task for the Algerians: Memorandum of Conversation, December 14, 1971, Export-Import Bank of the United States.

259 At a 1971 meeting: Ibid.

259 Clifford and his firm chose not to register: Foreign Agent Registration Act files, Department of Justice.

260 For instance, the Algerians paid: Ibid.

260 In fact, Richard G. Kleindienst: John P. MacKenzie, "Clifford Firm Set to File as Agent," *Washington Post*, March 22, 1975.

260 After an investigation, the Justice Department: Internal Security Section files, Department of Justice.

260 This time, the firm was hired: Cockburn and Cockburn, *Dangerous Liaison*, p. 101; interview with Ari Ben Menasche, 1994.

261 Years later, Clifford said that he: Interview with Clark Clifford, 1994.

261 With business booming: Interview with Sam McIlwain, 1993. Robert Altman declined to be interviewed for this book.

261 "Altman was probably the most enterprising and energetic clerk: Interview with James Stovall, 1993.

261 Although Clifford appeared: Interview with Sam McIlwain, 1993.

262 "We'd love to have you": Harry Jaffe, "Reversal of Fortune," *Washingtonian*, June 1991.

262 Anguished about Nixon's unwillingness: Interview with Clark Clifford, 1994.

262 Paul Warnke felt Clifford was using the article: Interview with Paul Warnke, 1994.

263 However, some of Clifford's other friends: Interview with a confidential source.

263 It was around this time that Stuart Symington: Thomas Ottenad, "Clifford Treads the Corridors of Power," *St. Louis Post-Dispatch*, March 27, 1969.

263 Clifford himself later acknowledged: Interview with Clark Clifford, 1994.

263 Entitled "A Vietnam Reappraisal": Clark Clifford, "A Vietnam Reappraisal: The Personal History of One Man's View and How It Evolved," *Foreign Affairs Quarterly*, June 1969.

264 On the morning of June 19: Morning News Play, June 19, 1969, Nixon Presidential Materials Staff, National Archives.

264 "Well, I noted Mr. Clifford's comments": Transcript of Nixon press conference, Nixon Presidential Materials Staff, National Archives.

265 Kissinger, Nixon's national security adviser: Haldeman, *Diaries*, p. 65.

265 H. R. Haldeman, Nixon's chief of staff: Ibid.

265 A journalist later described: Anderson, "Clark Clifford Sounds the Alarm," *New York Times Magazine*.

265 "They felt that turning the war over": Interview with Clark Clifford, 1994.

266 At Kissinger's insistence: James M. Naughton, "Data on Politicians Traced to Wiretaps for 'Security,'" *New York Times*, June 7, 1974.

266 One of the ways was a blistering speech: Memo For H. R. Haldeman from Pat Buchanan, May 21, 1970, Nixon Presidential Materials Staff, National Archives.

266 Agnew finally delivered the speech: James M. Naughton, "Agnew Asserts 8 Leading Antiwar Critics Prescribe Defeat," *New York Times*, June 21, 1970.

267 Another Nixon speechwriter: William Safire, *Before the Fall*, p. 310.

267 In 1972, Nixon ordered Haldeman: Haldeman, *Diaries*, p. 305.

267 "They can plow through": "Clifford Denies Undergoing Tax Audit Under Nixon," *St. Louis Post-Dispatch*, July 25, 1974.

268 Early one morning in January 1973: Interview with Benjamin Bradlee, 1993.

268 Later that day, Clifford wrote a glowing letter: Clark Clifford to Katharine Graham, January 4, 1973.

268 Watergate also provoked a bizzare incident: Higgins, *Friends of Richard Nixon*, p. 230.

Chapter 17: A Precursor to BCCI

270 "The Nixon years were for making money": Unpublished interview with Barry Bearak and Richard E. Meyer, *Los Angeles Times*, 1988.

270 A story circulated: Goulden, *Superlawyers*, p. 71; other versions of this story were related to the authors by several sources.

271 On May 13, Fortas summoned: Douglas, *Court Years*, p. 359; Clifford, *Counsel to the President*, pp. 558–559.

271 In later years, Fortas: Murphy, *Fortas*, pp. 571–572.

271 In his memoir, Clifford: Clifford, *Counsel to the President*, pp. 558–559.

272 "What had driven a man": Ibid.

272 Since the middle sixties: Gay Jervey and Stuart Taylor Jr., "From Statesman to Frontman," *American Lawyer*, November 1992; Ben A. Franklin, "Role of Coal Mine Operators Association Disputed in U.M.W. Suit," *New York Times*, February 2, 1971.

273 "Mr. Peters," he said gravely: Interview with Charles Peters, 1992; the incident is also recounted in Peters, *Tilting at Windmills*, pp. 203–204.

274 "Senator Muskie," interrupted Clifford: Interview with Harry McPherson, 1993.

274 During the meeting: Interview with George McGovern, 1993.

275 As he sat in the auditorium: Interview with Clark Clifford, 1994.

275 "Here was a man": Interview with Clark Clifford, 1994.

276 Vesco had fled the United States: Herzog, *Vesco*, pp. 200–210.

276 Clifford and Warnke agreed to talk: Interview with Paul Warnke, 1994.

276 "Hi," said the man: Ibid.

277 Clifford also turned down another notorious financier: Interview with Sam McIlwain, 1993; Ronald Kessler, *Richest Man in the World*, pp. 136–152.

278 In the midst of a three-month cruise: Cruise Letter No. 1, Harry S. Truman personal files, Truman Presidential Library.

278 Reflecting on her mother's relationship: Interview with Joyce Clifford Burland, 1994.

279 One of those with whom Clifford had these discussions: Interview with Harry McPherson.

279 After a few meetings: Interview with Michael Janeway, 1993.

280 "Now, you've been at this": Interview with Joyce Clifford Burland, 1994.

280 "Would you be Joyce Clifford": Interview with Clark Clifford, 1994; interview with Joyce Clifford Burland, 1994.

280 In February 1976, Clifford sat: Thomas, *Man to See*, p. 345.

281 "Jimmy Carter, as he is called": Unpublished *Los Angeles Times* interview with Clark Clifford, 1982.

282 On his seventieth birthday: Telegram to Clark Clifford from Katharine Graham, December 14, 1976.

283 Suddenly, the firm appeared: Interviews with John Kovin, Sam McIlwain, Paul Warnke, and other former law partners.

283 At one point, John Kovin: Interview with John Kovin, 1994.

284 "I have no intention": Ibid.; Interview with Clark Clifford, 1994.

284 Against this backdrop: Interview with Bert Lance, 1994; interview with Clark Clifford, 1994.

Chapter 18: A Fateful Introduction

285 Lance had become president: Adams and Frantz, *Full Service Bank*, pp. 31–33; Latham, "Capital Manipulator."

285 After passing through the security: Interview with Bert Lance, 1994; interview with Clark Clifford, 1994.

286 "If you resign": Interview with Bert Lance, 1994; interview with Clark Clifford, 1994.

286 Carter's helicopter touched down: Carter presidential schedule and master contact list, Carter personal files, Carter Presidential Library.

286 "This is the right course": Interview with Clark Clifford, 1994.

286 The decision to allow Lance to remain: Interview with Jody Powell, 1993.

287 Just before Labor Day weekend: Memo from White House staff member Michael Cardozo to Robert Lipshultz, the president's counsel, and Jody Powell, White House press secretary, files, Carter Library; letter from Robert Zelnick, an ABC-TV producer, to Jody Powell, Carter Library.

287 "Drop everything," said Clifford: Jaffe, "Reversal of Fortune."

288 "The idea is to get the trial": Latham, "Capital Manipulator."

288 Arriving in Bermuda shorts: Ibid.

288 The power of Clifford's presence: Interview with Jack Nelson, 1992; Truell and Gurwin, False Profits, pp. 45–46.

288 "Bert, I'm so proud of you": Lance, Truth of the Matter, p. 141.

289 Edward Bennett Williams praised: Latham, "Capital Manipulator."

290 "My Atlanta lawyer": Interview with Bert Lance, 1994.

290 Both Clifford and Lance: Ibid.; interview with Clark Clifford, 1994.

290 Three weeks after Lance resigned: Interview with Clark Clifford, 1994.

291 "He was the sun": Interview with Jack Anderson, 1993.

291 "He rose substantially": Interview with Clark Clifford, 1994.

292 "There was no mechanism": Interview with a confidential source.

292 John White, a politically savvy Texan: Interview with John White, 1992.

293 "And what else did": Ibid.

293 "He was very distressed": Interview with Hugh Sidey, 1994.

293 "A speech coach can train": Unpublished Los Angeles Times interview with Clark Clifford, 1982.

293 "Your appearance before the White House Correspondents dinner": Clark Clifford file, Carter Presidential Library.

293 "Your press conference": Ibid.

293 Helms has been described: Interview with Richard Helms, 1993; Powers, Man Who Kept the Secrets.

294 First, Helms met with Clifford: Interview with Richard Helms, 1993.

294 "Stop worrying about all this": Ibid.

294 Indeed, one of the witnesses: Thomas, Man to See, p. 340.

294 Donning his hat: Pack, Edward Bennett Williams for the Defense, p. 33; interview with Richard Helms, 1993.

295 "It's going to be like a Shakespeare play": Thomas, Man to See, p. 341.

295 As Helms's biographer: Powers, Man Who Kept the Secrets, p. 299.

295 Helms was reluctant: Interview with Richard Helms, 1993.

295 "Well," said Clifford: Ibid.

296 "Of course, the United States": George Lardner Jr., "Clifford Hits Enshrinement of CIA Curbs," Washington Post, April 5, 1978.

296 On June 15, 1974, Louis and Cornelia: Mokhiber, Corporate Crime and Violence, pp. 198–203.

297 Firestone went to court: Ibid; The Safety of Firestone 500 Steel-Belted Radial Tires, House Committee on Interstate and Foreign Commerce, Subcommittee on Oversight and Investigations, August 16, 1978.

297 Firestone had known Clifford: Interview with Joan Claybrook, 1993.

297 "Miss Claybrook, I am Clark Clifford": Ibid.

298 "I believe that I'm the wrong": Ibid.

298 "In the end, it was Clifford": Ibid.

299 Known as BCCI, the bank: The history of BCCI has been recounted in Adams and Frantz, A Full Service Bank, and Truell and Gurwin, False Profits.

299 In October 1977, the Pakistani: The BCCI Affair, Senate Committee on Foreign Relations, Subcommittee on Terrorism, Narcotics and International Operations, December 1992, pp. 123–154.

299 Lance did his part: Ibid.

300 According to Clifford's later recollection: Interview with Clark Clifford, 1994.

300 Now, faced with the lawsuit: Ibid.

301 Lance had a different recollection: The BCCI Affair, Senate Committee on Foreign Relations, pp. 128–130; interview with Bert Lance, 1994.

301 On January 30, 1978, Abdus Sami: BCCI Chronology, House Committee on Banking, Finance and Urban Affairs, September 9, 1991.

301 Last, on May 24, 1978: Ibid.

301 As for the SEC: Securities and Exchange Commission v. Bank of Credit and Commerce International et al., Case No. 78-0469, United States District Court, Washington, D.C.

302 Even before the suit: Truell and Gurwin, False Profits, p. 33.

302 As Abedi described his desire: This meeting was described by Dildar Rizvi, a BCCI executive who was present, in testimony on April 27, 1993, during the trial of Robert Altman in New York State Supreme Court, New York City. Altman was acquitted of all charges.

303 To the BCCI participants: Ibid.

303 Later, Clifford would say: Testimony of Clark Clifford before the Senate Committee on Foreign Relations, Subcommittee on Terrorism, Narcotics and International Operations, October 22, 1991.

Chapter 19: The Deception Begins

304 When the lawyers questioned: Financial General Bankshares v. Lance et al., Case No. 78-734, United States District Court, Alexandria, Virginia.

304 As for BCCI itself, the lawyers: Ibid.

305 During this period, Clifford: Interviews with Sam McIlwain and Clark Clifford.

305 It was after one of those London visits: Memorandum on the Persian Gulf, Clark Clifford to Zbigniew Brzezinski, November 29, 1978, Clifford file, Carter Presidential Library.

306 Clifford did not stop with the memo: Interview with Cyrus Vance, 1994; Vance, Hard Choices, pp. 339–340.

307 First, Clifford persuaded his old friend: Bob Adams, "Symington Called 'Front' for Arab Financiers," St. Louis Post-Dispatch, February 11, 1979; interview with James Symington, 1993.

308 "Clark, we are just": Interview with Clark Clifford, 1994; Hammer's involvement was also described in Adams and Frantz, Full Service Bank, p. 58, and Truell and Gurwin, False Profits, p. 42.

309 On May 21, the two sides signed: Adams and Frantz, *Full Service Bank*, pp. 64–65.
309 The first major criminal prosecution: Stewart, *The Prosecutors*, pp. 22–23.
310 Michael Lubin, the lead attorney: Ibid., pp. 21 and 42.
310 "Here I was a kid": Ibid., p. 42.
310 James S. McDonnell, the eighty-year-old: Ibid.
311 Clifford said he had tried: Interview with Clark Clifford, 1994.
311 "It was a very naive fiasco": Interview with Seymour Glanzer, 1993.
311 "To make a long story short": Stewart, *The Prosecutors*, pp. 45–46.
311 Clifford responded by asking: Ibid., pp. 47–49.
312 Despite the fact: Interview with a confidential source.
312 The role did not mean that Clifford was involved: Interview with Paul Warnke, 1994.
312 "He was not fitted to do it": Interview with a confidential source.
313 When Cutler asked exactly what his task would be: Interview with Lloyd Cutler, 1993;
    also Williams, "Clark Clifford: The Rise of a Reputation."
313 In the sort of turnabout: Ibid.
313 "Clifford was called out": Interview with Seymour Glanzer, 1993.
313 Near the end of January: Ibid.
315 Abedi joined them: Adams and Frantz, *Full Service Bank*, p. 65.
315 "These are honest, honorable, upright people": Sidney Bailey testimony, Senate Bank-
    ing Committee, May 23, 1991.
316 The letter was written: *The BCCI Affair*, Senate Committee on Foreign Relations, Sub-
    committee on Terrorism, Narcotics and International Operations, December 1992,
    pp. 328–329.
316 At the Federal Reserve hearing: Transcript of Federal Reserve hearing, April 23, 1981.
316 "Let me conclude": Ibid.
317 Adham also testified: Ibid.
317 "None," replied Clifford: Ibid.
317 "I felt like a mouse": Sidney Bailey testimony, Senate Banking Committee, May 23, 1991.
318 After a day of talk: Interview with Clark Clifford, 1994.
319 "Retirement never occurred": Interview with Joyce Clifford Burland, 1994.
319 Clifford himself made much: Interview with Clark Clifford, 1994.
319 "I think that as you get to be mid-seventies": Interview with Paul Warnke, 1994.
320 "There wasn't anything that was coming in": Interview with Clark Clifford, 1994.
320 "Practicing law is fun": Ibid.
320 "Bob, two billion dollars": Interview with Robert Donovan, 1993.
321 Sam McIlwain, who spent more than thirty years: Interview with Sam McIlwain, 1993.
321 A prominent Washington lawyer: Interview with a confidential source.
322 "Essentially a lawyer who becomes an officer": Interview with Stephen Gillers, 1994.
322 "Why don't you just relax": Interview with Clark Clifford, 1994.
322 "He's happiest when he's busy": Interview with Marny Clifford, 1994.

Chapter 20: Chairman of the Board
323 "I just don't do that": Interview with George McGovern, 1993.
323 And, unlike many powerful Washington figures: Interview with William Safire, 1993.
324 "We built it together": Interview with Clark Clifford, 1994.
324 A grandfather clock was positioned: Interview with Marny Clifford, 1994.
325 "We had wonderful compliments": Interview with Clark Clifford, 1994.
325 "If there is no prosecution": Interview with Larry Williams, 1993.

325 "Warnke just isn't working": Interview with a confidential source.

325 Since Clifford still controlled the purse strings: Interviews with several partners in the firm.

326 "The bank became our biggest client": Interview with John Kovin, 1994.

326 One of the candidates, Robert Stevens: The incident was described by Robert Stevens in testimony on May 13, 1993, during the trial of Robert Altman in New York State Supreme Court, New York City.

327 For instance, a 1983 memo: The memo and the episode involving Bruno Richter were part of evidence and testimony by Richter on May 5, 1993, at the trial of Robert Altman in New York State Supreme Court, New York City.

327 "You are working for a quality bank": Interview with James Schwab, 1993.

328 So taken was Clifford by running: Michael Kernan, "Clifford Stars in Bank Ad," Washington Post, April 2, 1986.

328 "He's well known": Ibid.

328 While Clifford considered: Truell and Gurwin, False Profits, p. 99; Ogden, Life of the Party, pp. 388–389 and 392.

329 "She just devoted herself": Interview with Clark Clifford, 1994.

329 It was at one of those dinners: Diana McLellan, Ear on Washington, p. 64.

329 Clifford was mortified: Interview with Hugh Sidey, 1994.

330 During an appearance on ABC-TV: Donaldson, Hold On, Mr. President, p. 282.

330 In late 1982, Altman had gone: Jaffe, "Reversal of Fortune."

331 "Bob's decision to marry": Interview with Clark Clifford, 1994.

331 One observer noted: Jaffe, "Reversal of Fortune."

331 Moreover, some reporters had heard rumors: Interview with Alan Frank, 1992.

332 In January 1985, the CIA prepared a one-page report: The BCCI Affair, Senate Committee on Foreign Relations, Subcommittee on Terrorism, Narcotics and International Operations, December 1992, pp. 292–293.

332 However, Regan later said: Truell and Gurwin, False Profits, p. 382.

333 For his part, Clifford said: Interview with Clark Clifford, 1994.

333 In late 1984, Clifford had vowed: BCCI Chronology, House Committee on Banking, Finance and Urban Affairs, September 9, 1991.

333 In late 1985, First American: Summary of Charges, Board of Governors of the Federal Reserve, in the matter of BCCI, issued July 29, 1991, and in the matter of Clark Clifford, issued July 29, 1992.

333 In conversations with Abdur Sakhia: Abdur Sakhia testimony before Senate Foreign Relations Committee, Subcommittee on Narcotics, Terrorism and International Operations, October 22, 1991.

333 Clifford and Altman, however: The BCCI Affair, Senate Committee on Foreign Relations, Subcommittee on Terrorism, Narcotics and International Operations, December 1992, pp. 385–386.

334 In February 1986, an independent evaluation: Ibid., pp. 390–391.

334 Yet a week later, after meeting: Ibid., p. 391.

334 The loans to Clifford and Altman: The existence of the loans was first revealed by Jim McGee in the Washington Post on May 5, 1991. Details of the loans are provided in the Federal Reserve charges against Clifford and in The BCCI Affair published in 1992 by the Senate Subcommittee on Terrorism, Narcotics and International Operations.

335 "We'd had four years of stellar performance": Interview with Clark Clifford, 1994.

335 Although Clifford describes the stock purchase: The failure by Clifford and Altman to disclose the terms of the stock purchase to their partners was described by several former partners in the law firm; Clifford said in an interview that he kept his law partners fully informed about the transaction.

336 When former Senator Charles Mathias: Interview with a confidential source.

336 Indeed, Clifford's reputation for propriety: Details of Clifford's relationship with and work for Pamela Harriman were provided in a civil lawsuit brought on September 13, 1994, against Clifford, Mrs. Harriman, and Paul Warnke by the heirs of Averell Harriman in United States District Court in New York City, Case No. 94-6712. Additional information came from an interview with Clifford, various newspaper articles regarding the lawsuit, and *The Life of the Party* by Christopher Ogden.

337 With a twinkle, he said: Interview with Betty Beale.

337 "What most people want": Interview with Clark Clifford, 1994.

338 "Even with all the trouble": Ibid.

Chapter 21: A Life Divided

339 Impeccably dressed and smiling: Gruley, *Paper Losses*, pp. 253–257.

341 Alvah Chapman Jr., the chairman: Ibid.

342 After a hurried weekend: Interview with Bill Schultz, 1992.

343 Schultz was not surprised: Ibid.

343 "Well, our attorneys": Transcript of a taped conversation between Amjad Awan and Bob Mazur, an undercover Customs Service agent, on September 9, 1988.

343 "We own a bank based in Washington": Ibid.

344 "I want you to understand": Interview with John Kerry, 1991.

344 Amjad Awan and several other BCCI employees: Adams and Frantz, *Full Service Bank*, pp. 234–236.

345 "We should drop BCCI": Interview with Paul Warnke, 1994.

346 Indeed, under questioning: Transcript of deposition by Clark Clifford in *Sandberg et al. v. First American Bankshares*, United States District Court, Alexandria, Virginia.

346 Robert Strauss, who had become a leading lawyer: Interview with Robert Strauss, 1993; the anecdote also was recounted in Thomas, *Man to See*, pp. 491–492.

347 "Stuart Symington was my best friend": Written remarks used by Clark Clifford at Symington's memorial service.

348 During the weeks in which Clifford and Altman provided free advice: Interview with Clark Clifford, 1994; interview with Tony Coelho, 1993; interview with Mark Johnson, 1993.

348 "Don't turn over anything": Interview with Tony Coelho, 1993.

348 Clifford did believe that: Interview with Clark Clifford, 1994; Clifford, *Counsel to the President*, pp. 648–649.

349 "Clark says I should fight": Interview with Mark Johnson, 1993.

349 When he was interviewed: Carter, "The Insider's Insider."

349 Reflecting on Wright's plight: Interview with Clark Clifford, 1994.

350 "Usually when I deal with a big-time partner": Interview with Douglas Letter, 1993.

350 "It was absolutely clear to me": Ibid.

350 On October 29, Clifford rose: The courtroom scene and the various reactions to it were drawn from interviews with Douglas Letter, James Rowley, and Bill Schultz; the transcript of the hearing; and Gruley, *Paper Losses*.

351 Bill Schultz pondered why: Interview with Bill Schultz, 1992.

352 The sounds of laughter: Gruley, *Paper Losses*, pp. 393–394; interview with Douglas Letter, 1993.

352 "The Metropolitan Club has remained": Barbara Gamarekian, "Enduring Bastion of Exclusivity for 'Gentlemen,' " *New York Times*, September 10, 1983.

352 The menu that January night: Gruley, *Paper Losses*, pp. 393–394; copy of the menu.

352 "I have been working on my memoirs": Papers of Clark Clifford.

353 Doug Letter was normally unimpressed: Interview with Douglas Letter, 1993.

Chapter 22: Under Siege

354 Naqvi was effusive in his praise: Truell and Gurwin, *False Profits*, p. 278.

354 There were darker secrets: Details of BCCI's schemes and of the CIA's knowledge of its activities came primarily from two books, Adams and Frantz, *Full Service Bank*, and Truell and Gurwin, *False Profits*, as well as a Senate report, *The BCCI Affair*, Senate Committee on Foreign Relations, Subcommittee on Terrorism, Narcotics and International Operations, December 1992. Robert Gates's reference to BCCI as the "Bank of Crooks and Criminals" was from a 1991 interview with William von Raab, the former United States Customs Service commissioner.

355 In a direct approach: Interview with Frances Zwenig, 1993.

355 At the same time, Clifford, Altman: Federal Election Commission records, Washington, D.C.

356 Using a script drafted by Altman: Interviews with confidential sources; *Congressional Record*, February 22, 1990.

356 His remarks angered some: Testimony of Kayid Shawish on May 11, 1993, during the trial of Robert Altman in New York State Supreme Court, New York City.

356 When the First American board met: Interview with Charles Mathias, 1994; *The BCCI Affair*, Senate Committee on Foreign Relations, p. 489.

357 In the spring of 1989: Interviews with Jack Blum, 1991, Robert Morgenthau, 1993, and John Moscow, 1993.

357 Nonetheless, when Morgenthau sent: Interview with John Moscow, 1993.

358 In December, Morgenthau's office: Interview with John Moscow, 1993; *BCCI Chronology*, House Committee on Banking, Finance and Urban Affairs, September 9, 1991.

358 On January 4, 1991, the Federal Reserve: *BCCI Chronology*, House Committee on Banking, Finance and Urban Affairs, September 9, 1991.

358 Struggling to contain the damage: Memorandum to Members of Boards of Directors of First American Banks, February 25, 1991.

359 He decided that reporters were getting most of their information: Interview with Clark Clifford, 1994.

359 When *Time* reporter Jonathan Beatty: Interview with Jonathan Beatty, 1992.

359 In early January, Clifford had attended a party: Interview with a confidential source.

360 Indeed, Clifford's law partners: Interviews with Paul Warnke, John Kovin, and other former Clifford law partners.

360 "If this is the way": Interview with Clark Clifford, 1994.

360 On the morning of Sunday, May 5: Interview with Paul Warnke, 1994.

361 As he pondered the consequences: Ibid.

361 Before the disclosure about the stock profits: Interviews with Paul Warnke, John Kovin, and other former Clifford law partners.

361 On Monday morning, the partners: Ibid.

361 "For me, it was pragmatic": Interview with Paul Warnke, 1994.

361 In the middle of the week: Williams, "Clark Clifford: The Rise of a Reputation."

361 His partners wanted something now: Interviews with Paul Warnke, John Kovin, and other former Clifford law partners.

362 The sun was still up and warm: Roxanne Roberts, "Clifford's Upbeat Night," *Washington Post*, May 23, 1991.

362 Clifford would later say: Interview with Clark Clifford, 1994.

362 But Rich would recall: Bryan Burrough, "The Perils of Pamela," *Vanity Fair*, January 1995.

363 "People are coming here": Roberts, "Clifford's Upbeat Night."

363 Metzenbaum caught the mood: Ibid.

363 But Clifford, as he left the house: Ibid.

363 Lady Bird Johnson telephoned: Interview with Marny Clifford, 1994.

363 Jacqueline Kennedy Onassis invited: Interview with Clark Clifford, 1994.

363 A few months later, Mrs. Onassis: Interview with a confidential source.

364 In the midst of a highly favorable notice: Roger Morris, "Playing Poker, Making History," *New York Times Book Review*, May 19, 1991.

364 "I met with him": Interview with Clark Clifford, 1994.

364 Clifford met with Fiske: Ibid.

365 "He had gotten quite a good deal of good publicity": Ibid.

365 At First American, Charles Mathias: Interview with Charles Mathias, 1994.

365 On August 2, Mathias wrote: Letter from Charles Mathias to Clark Clifford, August 2, 1991.

366 "We're very disturbed": Interview with John Kovin, 1994.

366 Out of his own pocket: Interview with Robert Morgenthau, 1993; court records in the New York State case against Clifford and Altman.

367 "I could see that from that time on": Interview with Clark Clifford, 1994.

Chapter 23: Trial and Triumph

368 John Kerry was angry: Author McKean attended this meeting as a member of Kerry's staff.

368 The article described: Neil A. Lewis, "Clark Clifford, Symbol of the Permanent Government, Is Faced with a Dilemma," *New York Times*, April 5, 1991.

368 The eighty-minute opening statement: Interviews with Howard Paster and Jody Powell.

369 "The Republicans were loaded": Interview with Clark Clifford. 1994.

369 But even Congressman Kennedy: Interview with a confidential source.

370 "You really don't know": Interview with Clark Clifford, 1994.

370 "That day was really the beginning": Interview with Marny Clifford, 1994.

371 "There are two courts": Interview with a confidential source.

371 Margaret Truman Daniel had harbored a dislike: Interview with a confidential source. Mrs. Daniel, who declined to be interviewed, also expressed disdain for Clifford in a letter to the authors on March 4, 1994.

372 During the show's intermission: Interviews with Jack Nelson and John White.

372 But when Clifford stood to respond: Marie Brenner, "How They Broke the Bank," *Vanity Fair*, April 1992.

372 Now, as her father faced what she described as "a body blow": Interview with Joyce Clifford Burland, 1994.

373 A remarkable change occurred: Interview with Marny Clifford, 1994.

373 Then he would ask his wife: Ibid.

373 "The Federal Reserve gave": Interview with Clark Clifford, 1994.

374 "In this adversity, we sort of clung to each other": Interview with Marny Clifford, 1994.

374 Morgenthau's office and the Justice: Relations between Morgenthau's office and the Department of Justice were described in interviews with Robert Morgenthau, John Moscow, former Attorney General William Barr, and several attorneys from both offices who spoke on the condition that their names remain confidential. Similarly, the division within Morgenthau's office over whether to indict Clifford and Altman was described in interviews with Morgenthau, Moscow, and two confidential sources.

375 "I don't think Mr. Altman would have known that": Interview with John Moscow, 1994.

375 At the conclusion of one day's session: Interview with a confidential source.

376 "The professionals at Justice": Interview with a confidential source.

376 Cherkasky, a career prosecutor: Interviews with two confidential sources.

377 The highly secretive negotiations: The description of the prospective plea bargain and events surrounding it were drawn from interviews with Clark Clifford, Carl Rauh, and four confidential sources who participated in the negotiations. The confidential sources were New York State and federal prosecutors involved in the negotiations. Their stories did not conflict on significant details. No one denied that plea talks were conducted, although Clifford and Rauh differed from the others in that they contended the talks did not reach the point of a solid deal.

377 "We've done an unbelievable job": Interviews with two confidential sources who attended the meeting.

378 After the meeting: Interview with a confidential source who observed the confrontation.

378 Later, Carl Rauh acknowledged: Interview with Carl Rauh, 1994.

378 For his part, Clifford recalled: Interview with Clark Clifford, 1994.

379 After it became clear: Interview with a confidential source.

379 On July 27, Carl Rauh: Interview with Carl Rauh, 1994.

379 The two lawyers were accused: Indictment, The People of the State of New York against Agha Hasan Abedi, Swaleh Naqvi, Clark M. Clifford, Robert A. Altman, and Faisal Saud Al Fulaij, Case No. 6994/92.

380 Washington's Old Guard was rattled: Phil McCombs, "The Old Guard Rattled by the News," Washington Post, July 30, 1992.

380 "I can only believe": Ibid.

381 What happened next did shock: Interview with Clark Clifford, 1994.

381 "The night before the indictments". Ibid.

381 Freezing the accounts provided: Sharon Walsh, "Clifford's, Altman's Assets Frozen," Washington Post, August 11, 1992; Walsh, "Clifford, Altman Assail Treatment by Prosecutors," Washington Post, August 18, 1992; Neil A. Lewis, "A Lawyer of the Beloved and Famous," New York Times, October 16, 1992.

382 "Oh, that was awful": Interview with Clark Clifford, 1994.

382 On October 4, Clifford awoke: Interview with Clark Clifford, 1994; Discharge Summary, Georgetown University Hospital.

382 Further, in a highly unusual action: Order by Justice John A. K. Bradley, New York State Supreme Court, January 12, 1993; Sharon Walsh, "N.Y. Judge Says Clifford Should Stand Trial There," Washington Post, January 13, 1993.

383 However, as one lawyer who had opposed Clifford: Interview with a confidential source.

384 Sam McIlwain, who had first brought Altman: Interview with Sam McIlwain, 1993.
384 The tenth-floor courtroom: Descriptions of the trial atmosphere and the actual testi-
    mony and procedures come from the authors' attendance at the trial, court tran-
    scripts, and newspaper articles by Kenneth Gilpin of the *New York Times*, Peter
    Truell of the *Wall Street Journal*, Sharon Walsh of the *Washington Post*, and Rob
    Wells of the *Associated Press*.
387 Clifford spent the summer: Interview with Clark Clifford, 1994; Michael Beschloss, "Clif-
    ford Speaks," *New Yorker*, September 6, 1993.
387 Often he awoke in the middle of the night: Beschloss, "Clifford Speaks."
387 "I've got to go there": Interview with Joyce Clifford Burland, 1994.
388 The day the prosecution finished: Beschloss, "Clifford Speaks"; Clifford's appointment
    calendar.
388 "Marny, they've freed me": Beschloss, "Clifford Speaks."
388 "The most wonderful thing": Interview with George Elsey, 1993.
389 "Oh Poppy," she exclaimed: Interview with Joyce Clifford Burland, 1994.
389 Turning to Marny, he said: Beschloss, "Clifford Speaks."

Chapter 24: The Final Curtain

390 "This is vindication": Interview with Clark Clifford, 1994.
391 A few days later, Richard Holbrooke: Interview with Jack Valenti, 1993.
391 "No one is free of sin": Ibid.
391 Clifford himself had floated: Interview with Hugh Sidey, 1994.
391 In the Beschloss article: Beschloss, "Clifford Speaks."
392 In late December, Clifford: Interview with Howard Paster, 1994.
392 Recalling the visit later: Ibid.
393 The legal bills from the criminal investigations: Motion of Clark M. Clifford and Robert
    A. Altman for Allowance of Claim for Indemnification for Legal Fees and Expenses
    from First American, *United States of America v. BCCI Holdings et al.*, Case No. 91-0655,
    United States District Court, Washington, D.C., and attached exhibits.
394 The bylaws of First American: Ibid.
394 "You know," he said one day: Interview with Clark Clifford, 1994.
394 "Something has happened": Ibid.
395 Jan Hoffman, a reporter: Interview with Jan Hoffman, 1994.
395 Unable to settle the matter: *Charles C. Ames and W. Nicholas Thorndike (as trustees) v.
    Clark M. Clifford, Paul C. Warnke, Pamela Digby Churchill Harriman, William Rich III et
    al.*; Case No. 94-6712, United States District Court, New York City.
396 Pulling himself a little straighter: Interview with Toby Godfrey, 1994.
396 "We've been learning a lot": Interview with Marny Clifford, 1994.
397 William Butler Yeats: Joseph Hassett, an attorney at Hogan and Hartson and a Yeats
    scholar, first raised the issue of the central myth in connection with Clifford in a 1994
    interview.
399 As Walter Isaacson and Evan Thomas: Isaacson and Thomas, *Wise Men*, pp. 739–741.
    The decline of the Eastern Establishment, and hence Clifford in a larger sense, also
    was dissected brilliantly by Nicholas Lemann in "Masters of the Old Game," *Vanity
    Fair*, October 1994.

Bibliography

Interviews
Rudy Abramson, David Alyward, Susan Mary Alsop, Jack Anderson, Donald Barlett, Dick Barrett, Joseph Barr, William Barr, Betty Beale, Jack Blum, Benjamin Bradlee, Steve Brogan, McGeorge Bundy, Joyce Clifford Burland, Liz Carpenter, Maxine Cheshire, Pat Choate, Joan Claybrook, Clark Clifford, Marny Clifford, Richard Coburn, Tony Coelho, Greg Craig, Lloyd Cutler, Robert Donovan, George Elsey, Rowland Evans, Abraham Feinberg, Al Fleishman, Joseph Fowler, Stephen Gillers, David Ginsberg, Seymour Glanzer, Toby Godfrey, Katharine Graham, Larry Gurwin, Joseph Hassett, Robert Healy, Seymour Hersh, Richard Helms, Jan Hoffman, Michael Janeway, Mark Johnson, William Kerr, Senator John Kerry, Richard Kleindienst, John Kovin, Charles Kurrus, Bert Lance, Chiles Larson, Douglas Letter, Joel Lisker, Charles Lowery, Robert Maheu, Senator Charles Mathias, Senator George McGovern, Sam McIlwain, Harry McPherson, Morton Mintz, Russell Mokhiber, Robert Morgenthau, John Moscow, Jack Nelson, Paul Nitze, James Olson, Ronald J. Ostrow, Howard Paster, Charlie Peters, De Vier Pierson, James Rowe Jr., Byron Parham, Jody Powell, Carl Rauh, George Reedy, Walt Rostow, William Safire, Bill Schultz, Howard Shulman, Hugh Sidey, Senator George Smathers, Mrs. Otto Spaeth, Jim Schwab, Theodore Sorensen, Stanley Sporkin, James Steele, Robert Strauss, James Symington, Evan Thomas, Peter Truell, Paul Warnke, John White, Larry Williams, Jack Valenti, Cyrus Vance, William Vanden Heuval, John Zentay, and Frances Zwenig.

Selected Books
Abel, Jules. *The Truman Scandals*. Chicago: Henry Regnery, 1956.

Abell, Tyler, ed. *Drew Pearson: Diaries 1949–1959*. New York: Holt, Rinehart and Winston, 1974.

Abramson, Rudy. *Spanning the Century: The Life of Averell Harriman, 1891–1986*. New York: William Morrow, 1992.

Acheson, Dean. *Present at the Creation: My Years in the State Department*. New York: W. W. Norton, 1969.

Adams, James Ring and Douglas Frantz. *A Full Service Bank*. New York: Pocket Books, 1992.

Adams, Sherman. *First-Hand Report: The Story of the Eisenhower Administration*. New York: Harper and Brothers, 1961.

Allen, Robert S. and William V. Shannon. *The Truman Merry-Go-Round*. New York: Vanguard Press, 1950.

Alsop, Joseph W. with Adam Platt. *"I've Seen the Best of It": Memoirs*. New York: W. W. Norton, 1992.

Alsop, Stewart. *The Center*. New York: Harper and Row, 1968.

Anderson, Patrick. *The President's Men*. Garden City, NY: Doubleday, 1968.

Asbell, Bernard. *The Senate Nobody Knows*. New York: Doubleday, 1978.

Baker, Bobby, with Larry L. King. *Wheeling and Dealing: Confessions of a Capitol Hill Operator.* New York: W. W. Norton, 1978.

Ball, George W. and Douglas B. Ball. *The Passionate Attachment.* New York: W. W. Norton, 1992.

Bamford, James. *The Puzzle Palace.* Boston: Houghton Mifflin, 1982.

Barlett, Donald L. and James B. Steele. *America: What Went Wrong?* New York: Touchstone, 1994.

———. *Empire: The Life, Legend and Madness of Howard Hughes.* New York: W. W. Norton, 1979.

Barrett, David M. *Uncertain Warriors.* Topeka: University Press of Kansas, 1993.

Beatty, Jonathan, and S. C. Gwynne. *The Outlaw Bank: BCCI.* New York: Random House, 1993.

Bernstein, Carl. *Loyalties.* New York: Simon and Schuster, 1989.

Birnbaum, Jeffery H. *The Lobbyists.* New York: Times Books, 1992.

Black, Hugo L. and Elizabeth Black. *Mr. Justice and Mrs. Black: The Memoirs of Hugo L. Black and Elizabeth Black.* New York: Random House, 1986.

Bradlee, Benjamin C. *Conversations with Kennedy.* New York: W. W. Norton, 1975.

Brandon, Henry. *Special Relationships.* New York: Atheneum, 1988.

Brayman, Harold. *The President Speaks Off-the-Record.* Princeton: Dow Jones Books, 1976.

Brinkley, David. *Washington Goes to War: The Extraordinary Story of the Transformation of a City and a Nation.* New York: Alfred A. Knopf, 1988.

Broder, David. *Behind the Front Page: A Candid Look at How the News Is Made.* New York: Simon and Schuster, 1987.

Califano, Joseph A. Jr., *The Triumph and Tragedy of Lyndon Johnson.* New York: Simon and Schuster, 1991.

Carter, Rosalynn. *First Lady from Plains.* Boston: Houghton Mifflin, 1984.

Christian, George. *The President Steps Down: A Personal Memoir of the Transfer of Power.* New York: Macmillan, 1970.

Clafin, Edward B., ed. *JFK Wants to Know.* New York: William Morrow, 1991.

Clifford, Clark with Richard Holbrooke. *Counsel to the President.* New York: Random House, 1991.

Cockburn, Andrew and Leslie. *Dangerous Liaison: The Inside Story of the U.S.-Israeli Covert Relationship.* New York: HarperCollins, 1991.

Cohen, Michael J. *Truman and Israel.* Berkeley: University of California Press, 1990.

Cohodas, Nadine. *Strom Thurmond and the Politics of Southern Change.* New York: Simon and Schuster, 1993.

Davis, Deborah. *Katharine the Great: Katharine Graham and the Washington Post.* New York: Harcourt Brace Jovanovich, 1979.

Davis, Michael D. and Hunter R. Clark. *Thurgood Marshall: Warrior at the Bar, Rebel on the Bench.* New York: Birch Lane Press, 1992.

Deakin, James. *The Lobbyists.* Washington, DC: Public Affairs Press, 1966.

———. *Straight Stuff: The Reporters, The White House and The Truth.* New York: William Morrow, 1984.

Donaldson, Sam. *Hold On, Mr. President.* New York: Ballantine, 1988.

Donovan, Hedley. *Right Places, Right Times.* New York: Simon and Schuster, 1989.

Donovan, Robert J. *Conflict and Crisis: The Presidency of Harry S Truman, 1945–1948.* New York: W. W. Norton, 1977.

———. *Tumultuous Years: The Presidency of Harry S Truman, 1949–1953.* New York: W. W. Norton, 1982.

Douglas, Paul H. *In the Fullness of Time: The Memoirs of Paul H. Douglas*. New York: Harcourt Brace Jovanovich, 1971.

Douglas, William O. *The Court Years, 1939–1975: The Autobiography of William O. Douglas*. New York: Random House, 1980.

Drosnin, Michael. *Citizen Hughes*. New York: Holt, Rinehart and Winston, 1985.

Eisenhower, Milton S. *The President Is Calling*. Garden City, NY: Doubleday, 1974.

Evans, Rowland, and Robert Novak. *Lyndon B. Johnson: The Exercise of Power*. New York: New American Library, 1968.

Evensen, Bruce J. *Truman, Palestine, and the Press*. Westport, CT: Greenwood Press, 1992.

Felsenthal, Carol. *Power, Privilege, and the Post: The Katharine Graham Story*. New York: G. P. Putnam's, 1993.

Ferrell, Robert H., ed. *Off the Record: The Private Papers of Harry S. Truman*. New York: Harper and Row, 1980.

———, ed. *Truman in the White House: The Diary of Eben A. Ayers*. Columbia, MO: University of Missouri Press, 1991.

Gitenstein, Mark: *Matters of Principle*. New York: Simon and Schuster, 1992.

Goulden, Joseph C. *The Best Years, 1945–1950*. New York: Atheneum, 1976.

———. *The Superlawyers*. New York: Weybright and Talley, 1972.

Goulding, Phil G. *Confirm or Deny*. New York: Harper and Row, 1970.

Gruley, Brian. *Paper Losses*. New York: Grove Press, 1993.

Halberstam, David. *The Best and the Brightest*. New York: Random House, 1972.

———. *The Powers That Be*. New York: Alfred A. Knopf, 1979.

———. *The Unfinished Odyssey of Robert Kennedy*. New York: Random House, 1968.

Haldeman, H. R. and Stephen Ambrose. *The Diaries of H. R. Haldeman*. New York: G. P. Putnam's, 1994.

Hayman, David C. *A Woman Called Jackie*. New York: Carol Communications, 1989.

Hechler, Ken. *Working with Truman*. New York: G. P. Putnam's, 1982.

Heller, Francis H. *The Truman White House: The Administration of the Presidency 1945–1953*. Lawrence, KS: Regents Press of Kansas, 1980.

Hersh, Seymour M. *The Price of Power: Kissinger in the Nixon White House*. New York: Simon and Schuster, 1983.

———. *The Samson Option: Israel, America and the Bomb*. London: Faber and Faber, 1991.

Herzog, Arthur. *Vesco*. New York: Doubleday, 1987.

Higgins, George V. *The Friends of Richard Nixon*. Boston: Little, Brown, 1975.

Hoopes, Townsend. *The Limits of Intervention*. New York: David McKay, 1969.

Hoopes, Townsend and Douglas Brinkley. *Driven Patriot: The Life and Times of James Forrestal*. New York: Alfred A. Knopf, 1992.

Howe, Russell Warren and Sarah Hays Trott. *The Power Peddlers*. Garden City, NY: Doubleday, 1977.

Isaacson, Walter and Evan Thomas. *The Wise Men*. New York: Simon and Schuster, 1986.

Jeffreys-Jones, Rhodri. *The CIA and American Democracy*. New Haven: Yale University Press, 1989.

Johnson, Haynes. *In the Absence of Power: Governing America*. New York: Viking, 1980.

Johnson, Lady Bird. *A White House Diary*. New York: Holt, Rinehart and Winston, 1970.

Johnson, Loch K. *America's Secret Power: The CIA in a Democratic Society*. New York: Oxford University Press, 1989.

Johnson, Lyndon Baines. *The Vantage Point*. New York: Holt, Rinehart and Winston, 1971.

Kalman, Laura. *Abe Fortas*. New Haven: Yale University Press, 1990.

Kampelman, Max M. *Entering New Worlds*. New York: HarperCollins, 1991.

Kernell, Samuel and Samuel L. Popkin, eds. *Chief of Staff: Twenty-Five Years of Managing the Presidency*. Berkeley: University of California Press, 1986.

Kessler, Ronald. *The Richest Man in the World: The Story of Adnan Khashoggi*. New York: Warner Books, 1986.

Kochan, Nick and Bob Whittington. *Bankrupt: The BCCI Fraud*. London: Victor Gollancz, 1991.

Kornbluth, Jesse. *Highly Confident: The Crime and Punishment of Michael Milken*. New York: William Morrow, 1992.

Krock, Arthur. *Memoirs: Sixty Years on the Firing Line*. New York: Funk & Wagnalls, 1968.

Lance, Bert with Brad Gilbert. *The Truth of the Matter*. New York: Summit Books, 1991.

Lasky, Victor. *It Didn't Start with Watergate*. New York: Dial Press, 1977.

——— . *Jimmy Carter: The Man and the Myth*. New York: Richard Marek Publishers, 1979.

Lilienthal, David E. *The Journals of David E. Lilienthal 1945–1950*. 2 vols. New York: Harper and Row, 1964.

Manchester, William. *The Death of a President*. New York: Harper and Row, 1967.

Markowitz, Norman D. *The Rise and Fall of the People's Century: Henry A. Wallace and American Liberalism, 1941–1948*. New York: The Free Press, 1973.

Martin, John Barlow. *Adlai Stevenson of Illinois*. New York: Doubleday, 1976.

Martin, Ralph G. *A Hero for Our Time: An Intimate Story of the Kennedy Years*. New York: Macmillan, 1983.

McCullough, David. *Truman*. New York: Simon and Schuster, 1992.

McLellan, David S. and David C. Acheson. *Among Friends: Personal Letters of Dean Acheson*. New York: Dodd, Mead, 1980.

McLellan, Diana. *Ear on Washington*. New York: Arbor House, 1982.

McPherson, Harry. *A Political Education*. Boston: Little, Brown, 1972.

Medved, Michael. *The Shadow Presidents*. New York: Times Books, 1979.

Millis, Walter, ed. *The Forrestal Diaries*. New York: Viking, 1951.

Mokhiber, Russell. *Corporate Crime and Violence*. San Francisco: Sierra Club Books, 1989.

Mollenhof, Clark R. *The President Who Failed: Carter Out of Control*. New York: Macmillan, 1980.

Morgan, Ann Hodges. *Robert S. Kerr: The Senate Years*. Oklahoma City: University of Oklahoma Press, 1977.

Murphy, Bruce Allen. *Fortas: The Rise and Ruin of a Supreme Court Justice*. New York: William Morrow, 1988.

Navasky, Victor S. *Naming Names*. New York: Viking, 1980.

Newfield, Jack. *Robert Kennedy: A Memoir*. New York: Dutton, 1969.

Nitze, Paul H. *From Hiroshima to Glasnost*. New York: Grove Weidenfeld, 1989.

Ogden, Christopher. *The Life of the Party*. Boston: Little, Brown, 1994.

Oudes, Bruce, ed. *From the President: Richard Nixon's Secret Files*. New York: Harper and Row, 1989.

Pack, Robert. *Edward Bennett Williams for the Defense*. New York: Harper and Row, 1983.

Pearson, Drew and Jack Anderson. *The Case Against Congress: A Compelling Indictment of Corruption on Capitol Hill*. New York: Simon and Schuster, 1968.

Peters, Charles. *Tilting at Windmills*. Reading, MA: Addison-Wesley, 1988.

Phillips, Caleb. *The Truman Presidency*. New York: Macmillan, 1966.

Pogue, Forrest C. *George C. Marshall, Statesman 1945–1959*. New York: Viking, 1987.

Powers, Thomas. *The Man Who Kept the Secrets: Richard Helms and the CIA*. New York: Alfred A. Knopf, 1979.

Prados, John. *Keepers of the Keys: A History of the National Security Council from Truman to Bush*. New York: William Morrow, 1991.

Reeves, Thomas C. *The Life and Times of Joe McCarthy*. New York: Stein and Day, 1982.

——— . *A Question of Character: A Life of John Kennedy*. New York: The Free Press, 1991.

Reston, James. *Deadline: A Memoir*. New York: Random House, 1991.

Ritchie, Donald A. *James M. Landis: Dean of the Regulators*. Cambridge: Harvard, 1980.

Ross, Irwin. *The Loneliest Campaign*. New York: New American Library, 1968.

Safire, William. *Before the Fall: An Inside View of the Pre-Watergate White House*. Garden City, NY: Doubleday, 1975.

Salisbury, Harrison. *Without Fear or Favor: An Uncompromising Look at The New York Times*. New York: Times Books, 1980.

Schlesinger, Arthur M. Jr. *Robert Kennedy and His Times*. Boston: Houghton Mifflin, 1971.

——— . *A Thousand Days*. Boston: Houghton Mifflin, 1965.

Schriftgiesser, Karl. *The Lobbyists*. Boston: Little, Brown, 1951.

Schoenbaum, Thomas J. *Waging Peace and War: Dean Rusk in the Truman, Kennedy and Johnson Years*. New York: Simon and Schuster, 1988.

Schrag, Peter. *Test of Loyalty*. New York: Simon and Schuster, 1984.

Sidey, Hugh. *John F. Kennedy, President*. New York: Atheneum, 1963.

Simon, James F. *Independent Journey: The Life of William O. Douglas*. New York: Harper and Row, 1980.

Simon, Senator Paul. *Advise and Consent*. Washington, DC: National Press Books, 1992.

Stewart, James B. *The Partners*. New York: Simon and Schuster, 1983.

——— . *The Prosecutors*. New York: Simon and Schuster, 1987.

Sulzberger, C. L. *An Age of Mediocrity: Memoirs and Diaries 1963–1972*. New York: Macmillan, 1973.

——— . *Last of the Giants*. New York: Macmillan, 1970.

Taylor, John M. *General Maxwell Taylor: The Sword and the Pen*. New York: Doubleday, 1989.

Thayer, Mary Van Rensselaer. *Jacqueline Kennedy: The White House Years*. Boston: Little, Brown, 1971.

Thomas, Evan. *The Man to See*. New York: Simon and Schuster, 1991.

Trento, Joseph J. *Prescription for Disaster*. New York: Crown, 1987.

Trento, Susan B. *The Power House*. New York: St. Martin's Press, 1992.

Truell, Peter and Larry Gurwin. *False Profits: The Inside Story of BCCI, the World's Most Corrupt Financial Empire*. Boston: Houghton, Mifflin, 1992.

Truman, Harry S. *Years of Decision: Memoirs*. Vol. 1. Garden City, NY: Doubleday, 1956.

Truman, Margaret. *Harry S. Truman*. New York: William Morrow, 1972.

Tyler, Patrick. *Running Critical*. New York: Harper and Row, 1986.

Urofsky, Melvin I., ed. *The Douglas Letters*. Bethesda, MD: Alder and Alder, 1987.

Valenti, Jack. *A Very Human President*. New York: W. W. Norton, 1975.

Vance, Cyrus. *Hard Choices*. New York: Simon and Schuster, 1983.

Wallace, Mike and Gary Paul Gates. *Close Encounters: Mike Wallace's Own Story*. New York: William Morrow, 1984.

Westmoreland, General William C. *A Soldier's Report*. New York: Doubleday, 1976.

White, Theodore H. *America in Search of Itself*. New York: Harper and Row, 1982.

——— . *The Making of the President 1960*. New York: Atheneum, 1961.

———— . *The Making of the President 1964.* New York: Atheneum, 1965.

———— . *The Making of the President 1972.* New York: Atheneum, 1973.

Witcover, Jules. *Crapshoot: Rolling the Dice on the Vice Presidency.* New York: Crown, 1992.

Zilg, Gerald Colby. *Du Pont: Behind the Nylon Curtain.* Englewood Cliffs, NJ: Prentice-Hall, 1974.

Selected Articles

Adams, Bob. "Symington Called 'Front' for Arab Financiers." *St. Louis Post-Dispatch,* February 11, 1979.

"Alfalfa Club Names McElroy." *Washington Post,* January 28, 1968.

Anderson, Jack. "It Pays to Hire the Right Lawyer." *Washington Post,* February 16, 1963.

Anderson, Patrick. "Clark Clifford Sounds the Alarm." *New York Times Magazine,* August 8, 1971.

———— . "His Big Job — To End the Vietnam War." *Parade,* August 4, 1968.

———— . "The New Defense Secretary Thinks Like the President." *New York Times Magazine,* January 28, 1968.

Baker, Russell. "Observer: Let's Hear It for a Really Swell Policy." *New York Times,* August 8, 1967.

Beschloss, Michael. "Clifford Speaks." *New Yorker,* September 6, 1993.

Brandt, Raymond P. "Clifford Doing Very Well Indeed." *St. Louis Post-Dispatch,* March 21, 1950.

Brenner, Marie. "How They Broke the Bank." *Vanity Fair,* April 1992.

Burrough, Bryan. "The Perils of Pamela." *Vanity Fair,* January 1995.

Carter, Terry. "The Insider's Insider." *National Law Journal,* July 10, 1989.

"Clifford Denies Undergoing Tax Audit Under Nixon." *St. Louis Post-Dispatch,* July 25, 1974.

"Clifford for McNamara." *New York Times,* January 21, 1968.

Clifford, Clark. "A Vietnam Reappraisal: The Personal History of One Man's View and How It Evolved." *Foreign Affairs Quarterly,* June 1969.

Clifford, Clark with Richard Holbrooke. "Serving the President: Vietnam Years — 1," excerpt from *Counsel to the President. New Yorker,* May 6, 1991.

Cohen, Warren I. "The Fall of Clark Clifford." *The Nation,* October 5, 1992.

Davies, Lawrence E. "Holders Approve Douglas Merger." *New York Times,* April 20, 1967.

Franklin, Ben A. "Role of Coal Mine Operators Association Disputed in U.M.W. Suit." *New York Times,* February 2, 1971.

Gamarekian, Barbara. "Enduring Bastion of Exclusivity for 'Gentlemen.'" *New York Times,* September 10, 1983.

Harris, Edward A. "New Power in Truman's Palace Guard." *St. Louis Post-Dispatch,* December 21, 1947.

Henrikson, Alan. "'A small, cozy town, global in scope': Washington, D.C." *Ekistics* 299, March/April, 1983.

Hladik, Meredith. "An American Treasure." *Country Living,* May 1994.

Howard, Clive. "The Clark Cliffords." *Redbook,* June 1949.

Jaffe, Harry. "Reversal of Fortune." *Washingtonian,* June 1991.

Jervey, Gay and Stuart Taylor Jr. "From Statesman to Frontman." *American Lawyer,* November 1992.

Kernan, Michael. "Clifford Stars in Bank Ad." *Washington Post,* April 2, 1986.

Krock, Arthur. "The Jenkins Case." *New York Times,* October 18, 1964.

Lardner, George, Jr. "Clifford Hits Enshrinement of CIA Curbs." *Washington Post*, April 5, 1978.

Latham, Aaron. "Clark Clifford: Capital Manipulator." *Esquire*, March 14, 1978.

Lemann, Nicholas. "Masters of the Old Game." *Vanity Fair*, October 1994.

Lewis, Neil A. "A Lawyer of the Beloved and Famous." *New York Times*, October 16, 1992.

———. "Clark Clifford, Symbol of the Permanent Government, Is Faced with a Dilemma." *New York Times*, April 5, 1991.

MacKenzie, John P. "Clifford Firm Set to File as Agent." *Washington Post*, March 22, 1975.

MacLeod, Hope. "Matty Fox — TV Mystery Man." *New York Post*, June 9, 1957.

Martin, Judith. "She'll Keep the Home Front Quiet." *Washington Post*, January 20, 1968.

"Matthew M. Fox, an Executive in Movies and TV, Dead at 53." *New York Times*, July 7, 1963.

McCombs, Phil. "The Old Guard Rattled by the News." *Washington Post*, July 30, 1992.

Morris, John D. "Johnson Friends Called on Press." *New York Times*, October 16, 1964.

Morris, Roger. "Playing Poker, Making History." *New York Times Book Review*, May 19, 1991.

Naughton, James M. "Agnew Asserts 8 Leading Antiwar Critics Prescribe Defeat." *New York Times*, June 21, 1970.

———. "Data on Politicians Traced to Wiretaps for 'Security.'" *New York Times*, June 7, 1974.

Nellor, Edward. "Truman's Young Counsel Hailed as Lewis's Nemesis." *New York Sun*, December 9, 1946.

Novak, Robert D. "Key Senator's Death Could Hurt Chances of Tax-Cut Program." *Wall Street Journal*, January 2, 1963.

Osborne, John. "Lawyers and Lobbyists." *Fortune*, February 1952.

Ottenad, Thomas. "Clifford Treads the Corridors of Power." *St. Louis Post-Dispatch*, March 27, 1969.

———. "Clifford Was a Prankster." *St. Louis Post-Dispatch*, April 1, 1969.

"Parties: Washington's 2nd Industry." *U.S. News and World Report*, March 3, 1950.

Pearson, Drew and Jack Anderson. "Clifford Represents Arms Firms." *Washington Post*, June 26, 1968.

———. "Washington Merry-Go-Round." *Washington Post*, January 25, 1968.

Pegler, Westbrook. "Strange Dealings in U.S. for Indonesia Trade." *New York Journal*, February 1, 1949.

"Presidential Advisor Clark Clifford." *Time*, March 15, 1948.

Reston, James. "Clifford and the Strategies of 1948 and 1968." *New York Times*, February 12, 1968.

Roberts, Roxanne. "Clifford's Upbeat Night." *Washington Post*, May 23, 1991.

Ryan, Edward F. "Clark Clifford Shared with Firm $25,000 Fee." *Washington Post*, February 7, 1952.

"Society: Joyce Clifford Curtsies at Gala Supper-Dance." *Washington Times-Herald*, June 22, 1952.

Spencer, Duncan. "The Corridors of Power." *Washington Star*, June 29, 1975.

"The Fair Deal Brain." *Newsweek*, August 15, 1948.

Vardaman, James K., Jr. "Assistant President of the U.S.A." *Saturday Evening Post*, October 4, 1947.

Walsh, Sharon. "Clifford's, Altman's Assets Frozen." *Washington Post*, August 11, 1992.

———. "Clifford, Altman Assail Treatment by Prosecutors." *Washington Post*, August 18, 1992.

———— . "N.Y. Judge Says Clifford Should Stand Trial There." *Washington Post*, January 13, 1993.

Welsh, David and David Horowitz. "Clark Clifford: Attorney at War." *Ramparts*, April 1968.

Williams, Marjorie. "Clark Clifford: The Rise of a Reputation." *Washington Post*, May 8, 1991.

———— . "The Man Who Banked on His Good Name." *Washington Post*, May 9, 1991.

Wills, Garry. "Keeper of the Seal." *New York Review of Books*, July 18, 1991.

Index